AFTER SOWETO

AFTER SOWETO

An Unfinished Journey

JOHN D. BREWER

CLARENDON PRESS · OXFORD

1986

Oxford University Press, Walton Street, Oxford OX2 6DP
Oxford New York Toronto
Delhi Bombay Calcutta Madras Karachi
Petaling Jaya Singapore Hong Kong Tokyo
Nairobi Dar es Salaam Cape Town
Melbourne Auckland
and associated companies in
Beirut Berlin Ibadan Nicosia

Oxford is a trade mark of Oxford University Press

Published in the United States
by Oxford University Press, New York

© John D. Brewer 1986

British Library Cataloguing in Publication Data
Brewer, John D.
After Soweto: an unfinished journey.
1. Soweto (South Africa)—Politics and
government
I. Title
968'.221   DT944.S/
ISBN 0-19-827480-7

Library of Congress Cataloging in Publication Data
Brewer, John D.
After Soweto.
Bibliography: p.
Includes index.
1. Anti-apartheid movements—South Africa. 2. South
Africa—Politics and government—1978- . 3. South
Africa—Economic conditions—1961- . 4. Riots—
South Africa—Soweto. 5. Soweto (South Africa)
I. Title.
DT779.952.B74 1986   305.8'00968   86-18283
ISBN 0-19-827480-7

Set by Spire Print Services Ltd., Salisbury, Wilts
Printed in Great Britain
at the University Printing House, Oxford
by David Stanford
Printer to the University

*For Fatima in the hope that one day she
may see the society of which we dream,
and for Sonny who I hope has found his.*

Preface

Apologists for apartheid should heed the words Dylan Thomas wrote on the death of his father: 'do not go gentle into that good night . . . rage, rage against the dying of the light.' For this study is about a light in South Africa that refuses to be extinguished, in that it examines African opposition to apartheid since the Soweto uprising in 1976. The term 'opposition' requires explanation. It derives from the Latin *opponere*, meaning 'to place against', and implies resistance, competition, and antagonism. Edward Stanley, Earl of Derby, once remarked that the duty of Her Majesty's Opposition in the House of Commons was to oppose everything and propose nothing. Stanley's remark comments on the distinction between the negative act of opposition, that is being ranged against, and the more positive act of proposition, that is offering an alternative. Contrary to Stanley's opinion, most opposition does involve proposition. When Sir Winston Churchill quoted his father, Lord Randolph, as saying that the duty of an Opposition was to oppose, he had in mind the duty to constitute an alternative government with different policies.

This study focuses on three loosely related themes: establishing the African community's continued antagonism to apartheid since 1976; examination of the particular forms by which they have resisted it; and some evaluation of the social, political, and economic programmes offered as alternatives. Emphasis will be on the first two elements since not all opposition does involve proposition in South Africa, where the alternative of a free, non-racial, politically egalitarian society needs no justification. I freely admit my prejudice for such a society. This is a view I share with the majority of Black South Africans. This is much the same vision of the future as Nelson Mandela's: a vision in which none will be held in servitude and slavery and in which poverty, want, and insecurity shall be no more. Many readers may see this ethical commitment as a severe constraint. Moral evaluation of apartheid remains a central preoccupation of much of the literature, partly no doubt because people are attracted to the subject as a moral issue. Criticism of this moralistic approach is valid. However, the effort to be objective does not require an emotional detachment or a lack of commitment to change. Just because injustice causes moral indignation, it does not prevent the identification of injustice where it exists. Being objective requires avoidance of the delusion that moral indignation is a substitute for hard analysis. Max Weber provides support for this view. Those who would quote his insistence on a value-free science misread him. Weber did not call for an abstention from moral commitment — it would have been impossible for him as a political activist with a social conscience. Value relevance can intercede in the choice of subject to investigate; thereafter fact and value should be separated and not confused with each other.

This study remains very much a factual one. It is more than a polemical denouncement of apartheid (although by implication there is that) and more than mere disgust (although there is that as well). Rather, it undertakes to anchor African opposition to apartheid in the changed conditions of post 1976 South Africa. It seeks to locate opposition into the changed social conditions, where there has been a relaxation of the petty restrictions governing social life; in the economic conditions, which have provided some relative advancement and occupational mobility for a privileged group of Blacks; and in the political conditions, where, after 1976, a heightening of political consciousness has occurred and where relatively more effective, sponsored platforms have been defined by the state, from which have flowed new levels of political activity.

At one and the same time such a study is annoyingly narrow and widely illuminating. This enigma lies at the heart of the book's content and approach. It examines African opposition to apartheid inside South Africa since 1976. The central conclusion is that this opposition has been transformed as a result of the impact of the Soweto uprising in such a way as to sustain and strengthen it. Such a project is narrow because it does not entail a general history of South Africa during this period, nor an overall account of politics in that time. It does not explore, for example, the international dimension to modern South Africa or the challenging turmoil of its economy. All this is to say that the study does not provide a general account of the dynamics of modern South Africa: these have been made subordinate to an analysis of protest within the

African community inside South Africa. However, this broader context is discussed in the Introduction.

Such a narrow focus is, nevertheless, in itself illuminating. The analysis as a whole puts a welcome emphasis on African initiatives inside South Africa aimed at bringing about social, economic, and political change. The role played by such initiatives is lost sight of in most of the literature on South Africa since the uprising. This contrasts markedly with the number of excellent studies on early African nationalism and the African National Congress. The problem posed by internal dissent since 1976 has been underplayed as the emphasis has shifted towards the international dimension or the external liberation forces. This study attempts to correct the balance.

In writing this book I have incurred many debts to friends, colleagues, and students at the University of Natal, the University of East Anglia, and Queen's University, Belfast. My debts to them are too lengthy to list. However, two people warrant special mention. I should not despair for South Africa if the friendship I received while there from Fatima Meer and Peter Derman is an example of the kindness, warmth, generosity, and humour that resides in her Black and White communities. I am grateful to former colleagues and students in South Africa for teaching me just how complicated South Africa is and how easy it is to mask this complication by the injudicious use of conceptual categories of whatever persuasion. I especially thank Lawrence Schlemmer, Hilstan Watts, and David Ginsberg.

Some of the material here has been presented before various audiences and I am grateful for the benefit this has provided. I thank audiences at the University of Lesotho, the University of East Anglia, the University of Aarhus, Denmark, the Institute of Commonwealth Studies, London, and the Arnold Bergstraesser Institute, Freiburg.

I am very happy to acknowledge the help and assistance of many friends and colleagues who read the manuscript. Jack Spence, John Blacking, and Adrian Guelke read the manuscript in its entirety. The kindness and support of Jack Spence has been invaluable. Other colleagues and friends gave constructive comments on parts: Heribert Adam, Richard Hodder-Williams, Lawrence Schlemmer, Fatima Meer, Roseinnes Phahle, Chris Rootes,

Shula Marks, and Peter Derman; I thank also Roy Wallis for his kind support. Finally, my thanks to Grace, Bronwen, and Gwyn—last but not least.

J. D.B.
Belfast, 1986

Contents

List of Tables

List of Maps

List of Figures

Abbreviations

ANC	African National Congress
ASB	Afrikaanse Studentebond
AV	Afrikanervolkswag
AWB	Afrikaner Weerstandsbeweging
AZACTU	Azanian Confederation of Trade Unions
AZAPO	Azanian People's Organization
AZASM	Azanian Students' Movement
AZASO	Azanian Students' Organization
BAB	Bantu Administration Board
BCMA	Black Consciousness Movement of Azania
BCP	Black Community Programmes
BMWU	Black Municipal Workers' Union
BPC	Black People's Convention
CIS	Counter Information Services
COSAS	Congress of South African Students
COSATU	Congress of South African Trade Unions
CUSA	Council of Unions of South Africa
CRC	Coloured People's Representative Council
DWEP	Domestic Workers and Employers Project
EEC	European Economic Community
FAK	Federasi van Afrikaanse Kultuurverenigings
FOSATU	Federation of South African Trade Unions
GWU	General Workers' Union
HNP	Herstigte Nasionale Party
IBR	Institute of Black Research
ICU	Industrial and Commercial Workers' Union
IRA	Irish Republican Army
MWASA	Media Workers' Association of South Africa
NFC	National Forum Committee
NMC	National Manpower Commission
NRP	New Republic Party
NUM	National Union of Mineworkers

NUSAS	National Union of South African Students
OAU	Organization of African Unity
PAC	Pan African Congress
PEBCO	Port Elizabeth Black Civic Organization
PET	People's Experimental Theatre
PEP	Progressive Federal Party
PLO	Palestinian Liberation Organization
SAABTU	South African Association of Black Trade Unions
SAAWU	South African Allied Workers Union
SABC	South African Broadcasting Corporation
SABRA	South African Bureau of Racial Affairs
SABTU	South African Black Theatre Union
SACTU	South African Congress of Trade Unions
SADF	South African Defence Force
SAIC	South African Indian Congress
SAIRR	South African Institute of Race Relations
SASM	South African Students' Movement
SASO	South African Students' Organization
SATS	South African Transport Services
SCA	Soweto Civic Association
SSRC	Soweto Students' Representative Council
SWAPO	South West African People's Organization
TUACC	Trade Union Advisory Co-ordinating Council
TUCSA	Trade Union Council of South Africa
UBC	Urban Bantu Council
UDF	United Democratic Front
UN	United Nations
UNITA	Uniao Nacional para a Independencia Total de Angola
USA	United States of America
WASA	Writers Association of South Africa
WRAB	West Rand Administration Board

Introduction: Internal Dissent and its Wider Context

THE SOWETO UPRISING AND ITS EFFECTS

Asa Briggs once wrote that authors reveal much about themselves by the title they choose for their work. Undoubtedly this is true here: I believe the opposition to apartheid shown in the Soweto uprising was the start of an unfinished journey. These words are carefully chosen. Of course, neither the uprising itself, nor the opposition since, existed in a vacuum immune to other events inside or outside South Africa, nor were they unaffected by a long history of protest. The events of 1976 have their precursors, and African[1] opposition to apartheid has a long and brave history which should not be devalued.[2] The history of the ANC and related movements is one of great courage, conviction, and endurance. They have left a legacy of pride and an example of leadership for many Black South Africans. One of the central themes of Nolutshungu's account of modern South Africa is that Black protest shows a 'remarkably uniform developmental trajectory'.[3] Although it reached unprecedented heights, the 1976 uprising was in a long tradition of mass struggles in South Africa which began by asserting often fairly minimal demands and precipitately found themselves in full-scale confrontation with the state. This historical legacy was an important ingredient of the events in 1976 and of those since. Thus, in discussing the forms of resistance used after 1976, it is necessary to trace them back to earlier periods and organizations. Morover, the uprising itself should be set in the context of its immediate antecedents. It was the culmination of a number of influences from which it took its character, such as the downfall of the colonial regimes in Mozambique and Angola, and increasing worker activism.[4] Following the narrow view of causation in John Stuart Mill, it is not disputed that the events of 1976 were merely the 'effect' of preceding events which formed the 'cause' of the uprising.

The point I wish to argue is different. I use the term 'start' because whatever the 'cause', the resulting 'effect' was unique. The events of 1976 influenced a chain of subsequent events which together have altered the nature of African opposition since. While the problems Black South Africans face may be old and familiar, the circumstances within which they confront these problems are new. So too are the alliances and strategies employed to solve them. The 'revolutionary terrain' in South Africa since 1976 has changed.[5]

The localized nature of the 1960 incidents in Sharpeville, because of their failure to provoke subsequent discontent elsewhere, make the events of 1976 the first mass Black revolt. This is certainly how the events were perceived by the participants—64 per cent of African, 54 per cent of Indian, and 69 per cent of Coloured respondents in a sample of 500 saw the events as a 'rebellion, revolt and mass protest'.[6] In other words, Blacks perceived the events in political terms as a mass challenge to apartheid, and one of the lasting influences has been the politicization of Blacks in South Africa.[7] This was a feature after Sharpeville but the politicization it initiated was short-lived and quickly followed by a hiatus. In many ways Sharpeville was the culmination of a long period of unrest, not its initiation. The events of 1976 were the complete opposite: the period of unrest they initiated has yet to subside. The now banned *Weekend World* provided testimony to this influence on the first anniversary of the events: 'The African phenomenon that was June 16 amazed not only the outsiders but also the insiders because it was so big, so big it was indescribable. The people walked the way of unity. And tall. Walk tall we did. We were once the enemies of fear. Fear burst through during frustration and claustrophobia. We all smoked tear gas and swallowed bullets, we all died so that we should live in peace. We were reborn. We were new people. We are different.' Phil Mtimkulu, four months later, echoed this assessment: 'The hearts and minds of Soweto people have undergone a revolutionary change and it is difficult to see them reverting to their former ways.'[8]

The eight years from 1976 to 1984, which are covered in this study, bear out such an assessment. Symbolically 1984 was set to be a prophetic year. In South Africa it was the year which saw the introduction of the new constitution and initiated some limited power-sharing with Coloureds and Indians. It also witnessed a concerted and sophisticated political campaign by African political movements against the constitution, and saw Africans mobilize themselves and engage in bomb attacks, political violence, mass demonstrations, boycotts, and industrial strikes in order to pursue that opposition. Indeed the events in Sharpeville in August and September 1984 bear an uncanny resemblance to those of Soweto in June 1976. In both instances Africans took to the streets in massive demonstrations to voice their demand for political and civil justice, and they continued to push this demand despite the deaths of their colleagues, shot by the police. That history could so sadly repeat itself in this way is testimony to the fact that the Soweto uprising did indeed have the effect on Black politics which earlier assessments thought likely.

The wealth of diverse research which has appeared on South Africa since 1976 has commented upon the influence of the events on the country's subsequent development. Leading analysts both of a liberal and of a Marxist persuasion, whether inside or outside South Africa, have all acknowledged this influence when writing about South Africa.[9] In discussing the events, some authors link them with the Natal strikes or the collapse of the Portuguese empire in Africa, while others argue for the essentially unique contribution of the uprising. Even Hirson, who is foremost among those who link the events with industrial and colonial conflicts, admits that 1976 'surpassed any political struggle' in South Africa.[10] This influence is also referred to by the South African media, businessmen, and politicians, and occasionally also by government ministers.[11]

Differences of opinion among analysts emerge when the precise nature of the influence is clarified. Using the now popular terminology of Gramsci, some writers believe the events stimulated an 'organic crisis' which affected the economic, political, and cultural spheres of society.[12] Others believe them to have had primarily a political effect and to have 'changed the face of politics in Southern Africa' generally.[13] Lodge argued that the events were influential in initiating the present 'direct' phase of resistance to apartheid.[14] Hermann Giliomee refers to them as having led to the 'parting of the ways', by which he means the split in South African politics between those supporting a negotiated settlement on a power-sharing basis and those who opt for an imposed political order achieved by maintained coercion or bloody revolution.[15]

However great the differences may be between the different accounts of the process of change and reform in South Africa, there is much greater agreement in the view that the events of 1976 were crucial in beginning or reinforcing the slow, often hesitant, process of liberalization and reform which characterizes modern South Africa.

It is possible to summarize these analyses and to indicate the nature of the influences which the events had. The international and economic repercussions were felt almost immediately. As Price emphasizes, Soweto and its aftermath of repression demonstrated anew the pariah status of South Africa within the international community. Moreover, South Africa was more vulnerable at this time because her position was weaker than for many decades.[16] She had lost the cordon sanitaire that had previously separated the Republic from the Black-ruled countries in the north. Economically, South Africa was also more exposed than she had been earlier. The 1960s had seen the development of her economy, based upon large-scale involvement by foreign-owned multinational corporations. This meant that to the existing trade dependence of the South African economy was added the need to maintain ready access to foreign markets, both for capital and technology and as outlets for its goods. The international repercussions that followed Soweto struck at this economic vulnerability. Not only was the flow of new capital funds inadequate after 1976, but foreign firms began to repatriate an unusually large proportion of their local profit rather than reinvest them in South Africa. Together with the lack of new foreign investment, this ensured a dramatic turn-about in the country's net capital flow. The capital account swung from a net inflow of R528m. in the last half of 1976 to a R810m. outflow in 1977. This increased to a net outflow of R1,370m. in 1978.[17]

The expansion of exports is an important element in the growth of South Africa's economy, and thus political constraints on foreign trade posed a significant threat to the country's long-term economic health. The uprising showed how domestic political arrangements could threaten to interfere with the ability to export goods. Problems with short-term commercial credits, and threats by foreign governments to disinvest, combined with such problems to demonstrate to the South African government that it could not rely on apartheid as a long-term strategy for the maintenance of

White supremacy. It was in this context, Price argues, that the government began to see the necessity of reform.[18] Businessmen came to recognize that stability meant reform. The preference for stability through reform was expressed many times after 1976. Dr Jan Marais, National Party MP for Pinetown and a former Trust Bank Chairman, was explicit when he said in 1978 that South Africa needed a Black middle class. An easing of discrimination was called for by, among others, the Johannesburg Chamber of Commerce, the Association of Chambers of Commerce, the Pinetown Chamber of Commerce, the Southern and Western Transvaal Chamber of Commerce, the United Building Society, the Urban Foundation, the Tongaat Sugar and Huletts Corporation, and the Pietermaritzburg Chamber of Commerce. Although economic growth is not incompatible with apartheid,[19] the drive for economic growth and political stability is changing the nature of the controls operating on the Black population in such a way as to obscure their once obvious racial nature. The appearance of apartheid is changing.

In short, the opposition shown in 1976 and since has been legitimated by being shown to be effective. The influence of the events on the consciousness of Whites has been as important as that on Blacks. Initially Whites saw it as mere lawlessness and violence, and by comparing opinion surveys before and after, research showed that Whites lost their 'sympathy for the hopes and aspirations of Blacks'.[20] The immediate shock response was an increase in the war mentality of the state and Whites generally. The Voortrekker youth movement now has regular contact with the SADF and, *inter alia*, the youngsters are shown how to detonate a landmine, fire the Kalashnikov AK-47 assault rifle, the LMG machine gun, the R-1 rifle, and the RPG rocket launcher. An English-speaking daily newspaper congratulated itself that the weapons 'had hardly any kick-back and could be operated by a twelve year-old boy'.[21] There is a plethora of female pistol clubs and semi-official commando groups were initiated in 1979 mobilizing recruits on the theme of 'Are You Prepared', with posters showing the silhouette of a man in firing stance with gun poised. Area defence units have also been formed by the government to act as a part-time rural militia. They are intended to have a protective role in guarding White settlements and farms and a reactive role in backing up the security forces. The categories of people

eligible for conscription have also been expanded: there has been
an extension of the upper age limit to 55 years and national service
is expected soon to involve Coloureds and Indians. The greatest
change, however, came with the 1984 South African Citizenship
Draft Bill, which required all male children of immigrants who are
between the ages 15 and 25 to take out South African citizenship
in order to become eligible for conscription, or lose their permanent residence rights. This measure came into effect on
11 October 1984. It had been held up since 1978 for fear of the
effect it might have on the influx of new immigrants—a particularly sensitive issue after the decrease in immigration following the
Soweto uprising. With the recession in the Western world, the
inflow of new settlers has now reached a point where the government can contemplate such a measure. In 1982 45,600 immigrants
came to live in South Africa, representing a 41 per cent increase
over the 1978 figure. Between 1978 and 1982 there was a 69
per cent drop in the numbers leaving South Africa. One effect of
the measure is to increase the number of immigrants with South
African citizenship and who are thus eligible to vote—a point
which led many English-speaking newspapers to support the
measure.

Notwithstanding this increase in the war mentality of Whites,
there was a reasoned response to the events, for their influence on
the political thinking of the government has been tremendous. An
arch-critic of apartheid, Colin Legum, after briefly returning to
South Africa, wrote in 1981: 'changes are to be expected after a
period of twenty years . . . but to find that South Africa has
changed almost beyond recognition came as a sharp surprise . . . it
has shifted from the political axis around which it has turned for
the last 300 years.'[22] The changes of policy, particularly associated
with P. W. Botha's administration, cover the fields of sport, labour,
the constitution, land tenure, local government autonomy, and the
removal of petty apartheid restrictions. They represent an enormous change when compared to the policy pursued by Afrikaans
governments since 1948. However, evaluations of this kind
depend on their reference point: the changes are not enormous
when consideration is given to how far the liberalizations have to
proceed in order to satisfy African expectations of change. There
is a depressing disagreement between current African expectations
and the willingness of the state to reform.[23] The changes which are

discussed in the following pages, such as trade union reforms, the constitution, land tenure, and local autonomy for Africans, are shown to be double-edged. They constitute refinements in control rather than its relaxation. They clearly show that what has triumphed in South Africa is change as an idea rather than as a practice. None the less, Guelke was correct when he argued that while it is reasonable to claim that the idea of change has made more headway than change on the ground, even the limited changes that have taken place present a challenge to many of the assumptions commonly made about the nature of South African politics.[24]

Above all, it is possible with hindsight to see that the events had perhaps their greatest effect on the political behaviour of Blacks. It is this which has given the events of 1976 an aftermath which has so far lasted for a decade. Nyameko Pityana once wrote that Soweto saw the emergence 'of a new breed of Black man'.[25] There was a new-found confidence after 1976, a concomitant determination not to accept South African society as unchanging or unchangeable, and a psychological and physical preparedness to act. In the early 1970s Blacks generally were politically apathetic because they considered the power structure as impermeable. A decade later, on the basis of his opinion surveys, Schlemmer considers Africans to be more politically conscious than any other group.[26] Political self-effacement and quiescence have given way to a willingness to take risks, even a readiness to secretly help the banned ANC. Whereas Africans did not compare themselves with Whites in 1970, equality with Whites became the overriding issue by the 1980s. If faced with a choice, between 70 and 80 per cent preferred equality with Whites and lower material gain rather than continued inequality coupled with higher material gain. In a survey for the Buthelezi Commission published in 1981, more than 90 per cent spontaneously said that there would be bloodshed and revolution if no structural changes occurred within ten years. The apartheid system is no longer regarded as invincible. In the same survey only 20 per cent of Africans polled agreed with the statement that 'Mugabe could not have won against the South African army'. Anger about the system measured in repeated tests by the same analysts has steadily increased since 1976.[27]

This confident yet angry defiance is nowhere better demonstrated than in the township protests of August and September

1984 and throughout 1985, when large crowds defied bans on public demonstations in order to attend the funerals of youths killed by police. In their grief they chanted the names of Mandela, Sisulu, and Tambo and wore T-shirts bearing ANC slogans. This confidence and defiance demonstrates what effect the events of 1976 and since have had on Black protest and resistance. There is no separation, therefore, between politicized attitudes and militant action.

What is perhaps most significant is the nature of the Black political activity which the uprising helped to initiate. Opposition has permeated every level of African life in South Africa today in a way that only happened briefly during the defiance campaign. Fatima Meer, after a further visit from the Special Branch in the furore over Steve Biko's death, remarked that for Blacks generally, 'life is politics and politics is life'. This is a cliché whose origins lie in centuries of political struggle; it is none the less true for that. Yet it needs serious examination for this truth to be revealed. The word 'politics' is used in two senses when it is applied to South Africa. All this opposition is political in the sense that it is either focused on changing the loci of power and its distribution, or involves some critical judgement of its present loci and distribution. Such opposition is expressed in many facets of ordinary African life. For example, it is true of the indigenous poetry emerging from literary groups in the urban townships and in the newly formed sects who combine worship with organizing as vigilante groups because they reject state mechanisms of social control. It is true of the brave schoolchildren who boycott classes, of the workers who face imprisonment due to industrial action and of the press which suffers intimidation because of its copy. Life indeed has become politics. But it is not politics in a narrow sense, where politics pertains to the organizational pursuit of goals within a constitutional framework which defines the procedural rules whereby decisions are made through negotiation and compromise. The very reason why opposition is being directed through ordinary African life is because this narrow political expression is denied them. They are denied effective and legitimate institutional representation and are not allowed to participate in constitutional frameworks. This creates a conundrum. In the narrow sense full political expression is denied, so politics in the broader sense has taken over African life and has made opposition to apartheid more dispersed than it might otherwise have been. In considering African opposition to apartheid, therefore, the focus should be directed away from formal political channels towards ordinary daily life.

The following chapters document how this protest is manifested in Black literary writings, the Black press, through revolutionary terror tactics, outbreaks of collective action, homeland political organizations, urban political movements, and in the factory.[28] Precisely because internal protests do not exist in a vacuum but occur in a wider context of social, political, economic, and international events, the broader context will be sketched first in the remainder of this introduction.

One of the fascinations of South Africa is that it continues to be shaped by international and internal economic and political forces which originally have scant connection with the confrontation between Black and White, but which can yet influence Black protest in many diverse ways. There are many links between internal Black opposition and, for example, the South African economy, international economic and diplomatic pressure, the external liberation forces, and the government's political problems with the Afrikaans right wing. So complex are the interconnections that the state is hindered in its attempt to influence any one sector by the often unintended consequences this has on the other areas, and the process of government-led reform is limited.

MODERN SOUTH AFRICA IN RECENT RESEARCH

For no other country does the question of the direction of future change dominate as it does in the case of South Africa. Yet, as these forces interact, it is also more difficult to predict than anywhere else. According to Arthur Lovejoy's famous argument, the central terms used in a historical epoch often provide a key to an understanding of that time. Discussion of South Africa in the period since 1976 is obsessed by two key words—change and crisis. Perusal of the titles authors have given their work easily confirms this to be the case.[29] Neither term is completely accurate as a description of South Africa in this period.

The pragmatic approach to apartheid which Adam predicted in 1970 has given rise to what he and Giliomee call a 'managerial approach' by the government, in which economic growth and political stability are the key aims of government; aims to be achieved by 'change' and 'reform'.[30] Giliomee describes 'reform' as the catchword of this period.[31] There are essentially three processes which the government has in mind when it talks about reform and change.[32] There is the process of educating and training Blacks to allow them upward economic mobility. The intention is to produce a middle class which can be used as an ally of the Whites, in the belief that this Black middle class will have a vested interest in political stability and racial capitalism. This is commonly referred to as the process of *embourgeoisement* or co-option.[33] In addition there is the process of regional development aimed at alleviating the poverty of the homelands. Finally, there is the process of granting parliamentary representation to Coloureds and Indians, while creating structures to allow Africans to pursue their political demands through either homeland parliaments or local councils in the townships. Most analysts are not confident that these reforms are genuine or sufficient. There are some writers on South Africa who represent any change which does not overthrow capitalism as illusionary and inadequate, but non-Marxists are equally strong in their condemnation of the process of reform in South Africa. The term 'sham reform' has been invented to accommodate those changes which alter the appearance of apartheid without dismantling the system of White dominance.[34] As long as the dual imperatives of the maintenance of White privilege and the perpetuation of capitalism remain so vital to the South African government, very few analysts are likely to find the changes adequate. So the term 'change' requires clarification, but change, at least at the outer edges of apartheid, has occurred.

Nor is the term 'crisis' fully accurate. For anyone who walks the bustling streets of Johannesburg and Cape Town 'crisis' seems a particularly inappropriate description of the society. Nevertheless, literature on the theme abounds. Scholars cite sets of statistics and other evidence to demonstrate that the country is in the grips of a crisis, usually described as organic. The use of the term 'crisis' is, however, dependent upon what symptoms are used as the critical signs of crisis. What for one author is a symptom of crisis can for another be a sign of growth and progress. For example, Hill leaves his readers in no doubt that real change is taking place in South Africa as a result of the legislative implementation of the Wiehahn and Riekert Commission reports,[35] whereas these commissions are presented by Saul and Gelb as evidence that the ruling élite is 'running scared' as they respond in an *ad hoc* fashion to the problems generated by the organic crisis.[36]

There are many who dispute the view that 'crisis' is an appropriate description of the society. When reviewing the persistent predictions of imminent revolution in South Africa, R. W. Johnson cynically remarked that the clock seemed permanently stuck at five minutes to midnight.[37] With the moral desire most commentators have to see change occur in South Africa, we are apt to forget the resilience of the regime, as Gann and Duignan reminded us.[38] Yet whatever feelings the term 'crisis' conjures up, it cannot be disputed that the regime faces severe inter-linked problems, of which internal Black opposition is only one. It is to the nature of these problems that we now turn, for they provide the broader context within which internal African protest operates.

THE DYNAMICS OF MODERN SOUTH AFRICA

The more substantial and sustained challenge to White political domination which has occurred since 1976 has coincided with the collapse of the Afrikaner's confidence in apartheid. Defensiveness, confusion, and also perhaps what Conor Cruise O'Brien calls the 'unexpected force of guilt', have all led to a growing apprehensiveness among Afrikaners and to a sense of facing a crucial turning-point. It is for this reason that the Afrikaans historian and political scientist Hermann Giliomee termed the years since 1976 a distinct period in South Africa's history.[39] In 1979 Williem de Klerk, another *verligte* Afrikaner, wrote of the 'fear and confusion' among Afrikaners as they approached 'the politically dangerous eighties'. The 1980s have so far proved to be dangerous, and not just in politics.

It is now obvious to most Afrikaners that the consequences of apartheid have been massive rural over-population and economic underdevelopment, the destruction of environmental and human resources in the rural areas, chaotic ubanization,[40] an increase in rural poverty, and an intensification of the pattern of urban migration with all its attendant problems. Whatever the intention behind the policy of restricting Africans to the homelands, the final result will be massive urbanization. It has been estimated by the Unit for

Futures Research at the University of Stellenbosch that by the year 2000, the urbanized component of each community will be 93 per cent for Whites, 92 per cent for Asians, 86 per cent for Coloureds and 75 per cent for Africans. This implies an increase in the total urban population from 12 to 40 millions in 18 years, 34 millions of which will be African.[41] As far as employment is concerned, this means that Africans will be coming on the job market at the rate of 201,000 per year. Professor Nattrass estimated in January 1986 that 10m. new jobs were needed by the year 2000 to reduce unemployment and to cope with new entrants into the labour market. In the 15 years up to 1983, a total of 150,000 decentralized jobs were created in the rural areas: just over half of one year's requirement if Africans are to stay in the rural areas. If apartheid is to be only partially successful, jobs, social services, and infrastructures will have to double to maintain the grossly inadequate development levels which exist at present. Despite the policy of decentralization of economic resources to the rural areas, the urbanized component of the African population can still be expected to double as the rural areas prove unable to sustain their level of population, which, at 45–50 per 1,000, is among the highest in the world.[42] However much the government may resent or even deny it, the process of African urbanization is taking on a momentum of its own, with spontaneous settlements spreading on the edge of most of the major cities. As new urban forms emerge, they become part of the reality facing Blacks and the state, either promoting or constraining further economic, political, and social change.[43]

Urbanization takes peculiar forms under apartheid. Fair and Davies have recognized a process of 'constrained urbanization', with influx control holding at bay some of the forces promoting the rapid growth of cities elsewhere in the underdeveloped world.[44] As a result of influx control, South Africa is about 8 per cent less urbanized than other comparable countries. To put it another way, without influx control up to three million more Africans would have been in the cities.[45] But the pressure of urbanization means that influx control is breaking down. Even government planners project a doubling of the African urbanization rate in the years up to 2,000, which cannot occur without influx control collapsing. The existence of settlements like Crossroads within 'White' areas suggests that containment is breaking down as harsh necessity drives increasing numbers of Africans to seek an escape from rural poverty.

Some of the immediate problems facing the state were addressed by the Wiehahn and Riekert Commissions. Among other things, which are discussed in later chapters, the commissions urged the establishment of a labour bureau to perform the function of labour supply control which had hitherto been accomplished by the pass laws. The objective is to facilitate labour mobility within 'White' South Africa, while tightening up on influx from the homelands. Wilson sees this as fortifying the use of the homelands as a reserve to which the state can export unemployment and redundancy.[46] How effective this will be in halting the pressure of urban migration is difficult to judge, although one Afrikaans academic recently wrote that 'uncontrolled and chaotic urbanization by people who no longer can survive in the homelands, will be the single most important development in South Africa over the next decade'.[47] It carries with it a great potential for conflict and violence. Whites will find it difficult to resign themselves to huge Latin American-style shanty towns on the rims of the cities. Apartheid bureaucrats will insist on clearing squatter camps and some of the urban Blacks will find their living standards undercut by competitors willing to work for any wage. One of the reasons why Inkatha and the trade union movement assume so much importance in the internal political struggle is because they are the only organizations to mobilize support amongst the squatters and migrant workers who live in the shanty towns. Whether these fragile urbanites become a militant or a radical force will depend much on which one wins the battle to mobilize them. Feelings of insecurity among Whites are made worse by the fact that the African population, which is undergoing the most rapid process of urbanization and dislocation, has the least developed constitutional and political structures to cope with the socio-economic realities which this change places them in. Hence the importance of the battle between Inkatha and the trade union movement to win the support of those within the African population who suffer the most under urban dislocation.

There are other effects. To cope with this massive urban migration, in the next twenty years more housing, jobs, and services will have to be created than in the last three centuries. It is clear that this will put an enormous strain on the South African economy and its ability to respond to particular political policies. The economy is not the success story which some people assume. Nor, it must be cautioned, is it in the state of near collapse which many critics allege. Sets of statistics can be used to back either assessment. What is certain, however, is that the economy is not as strong as it was and is becoming increasingly unable to fund apartheid. The corollary is also true: it is too fragile to be able to fund the cost of dismantling apartheid. For example, the costs of dismantling apartheid in education alone are enormous. The attainment of equality in educational provision would cost a staggering R5,700m. per year by the end of the century. Despite the amount spent on African education, very little either has been, or can be, done to achieve parity with other groups. In 1980–1 per capita expenditure on education was R913 for every White schoolchild, R513 for Indians, R253 for Coloureds, and R140 for ever African schoolchild.[48] This disparity is reflected throughout the education service, manifesting itself in higher teacher–pupil ratios in African schools, and poorer teacher training. In higher education there is an even greater disparity in per capita expenditure. In 1979 the White universities spent an average of approximately R2,133 per student, African universities spent about R1,733, and the Indian university at Durban Westville spent R1,006. If the trends in expenditure are considered after the initial period of expansion of African universities, spending on African universities rose by 19 per cent from 1976 to 1979, while that on White universities rose by 48 per cent. The gaps are therefore widening. This is the magnitude of the task if apartheid in education is to be scrapped. The Education Minister for the Kwa Zulu government estimated the increases which would be required if his department was to be brought into parity with the White Natal Education Department. They amounted to a tenfold rise in teacher salaries, sixteen fold increase in services, eighteen fold increase in hostels, twenty-three fold increase in capital works and a four hundred fold rise in loans and bursaries for student teachers.[49] The economy is too fragile to fund such a policy.

The gold price should not be taken as the main barometer of the South African economy's strength. In 1980 gold exports represented 37 per cent of all exports and a high gold price gave South Africa a surplus of about R3 billion on the balance of payments current account. A drop in the gold price transformed this into a deficit of R3.7 billion in 1981. The gold price may affect how people view the prospects for growth, but it does not alter the underlying trends. The growth rate has been low over the last twenty years, at 2.3 per cent per annum. This is lower than the newly industrializing countries like Brazil, Greece, and Hong Kong.[50] From being a labour-absorbing economy it has turned into a labour-extruding economy. South Africa is drastically reducing its migrant workers from neighbouring countries and the newly independent homelands, an action which reflects the phenomenal growth of manufacturing and tertiary industry. This labour extrusion is occurring at a time when Africans in the homelands are increasingly dependent on migrant labour. Thus, South Africa is simply unable to grow fast enough to provide for its rapidly increasing African population. The Minister of Finance, Barend du Plessis, explained to businessmen in December 1985 that the growth rate for that year was 3 per cent below that which was needed to satisfy all the demands made of the economy.

This slowing down in the growth rate affects all South Africans, but particularly Black South Africans. Meth once said that the 'fiscal crisis of apartheid is manifest not in huge and growing budget deficits, but rather in the continued deprivation suffered by the voteless South African masses'.[51] One such deprivation is a high level of unemployment among Blacks generally. Saul and Gelb show that Black unemployment in the 1980s has risen more quickly than ever before.[52] In a survey in 1980 of political attitudes among males with legal residence in Kwa Mashu township near Durban, it was found that 38.75 per cent were currently unemployed and 64.6 per cent had been unemployed sometime within the previous year.[53] Although the official figure for unemployment in the three Black communities during July 1984 was only 7 per cent of the economically active population, the unofficial figure is estimated to be up to three times that—African unemployment figures are notoriously difficult to estimate.[54] Unemployment has historically been connected with Black protest and it was significant that Black unemployment rose sharply before the events of 1976.[55] It was a factor in the Sharpeville protests of 1984 when a 30 per cent rent increase was to be levied on residents who already faced high unemployment.

It tends to be South Africa's economic position which leads many Marxists to use the term crisis when referring to the country.

The problem is that South Africa is suffering from both inflation and recession.[56] Not only are the policies needed to deal with these two ills essentially contradictory but their costs also tend to be borne by different groups. Whites feel the impact of inflation to a greater extent than they do that of recession. They hold political power and consequently the present economic policy is directed more towards controlling inflation. This policy is not without costs, for the measures applied intensify the recession. They particularly increase unemployment, which is largely borne by the Black communities. During 1984–5 unemployment rose in alarming proportions, increasing by 120 per cent to the year ending June 1985. In October 1985 the government introduced a R600m. emergency plan for job creation and retraining. But in January 1986 South Africa's inflation rate still reached an all-time high of 20.7 per cent. The effects of this high inflation rate began to be felt during 1985. The unemployed were not the only casualties. Compulsory liquidations rose by 107 per cent between 1984 and 1985, insolvencies by 103 per cent, and gross domestic expenditure fell by 9 per cent. This also has effects on the rate of unemployment. As long as the inflation rates in South Africa's main competitors are down to a quarter of this figure, the economy will be ill placed to take advantage of any upswing in the world economy.

While the South African economy is temporarily fragile, demands have been made by critics in the West to destabilize South Africa further by artificially lowering the gold price still more.[57] A high gold price is usually the means by which the government staves off balance of payments problems and provides growth. Coincidentally the effects of such a policy were demonstrated when a fall in the gold price occurred through market forces in July 1984. It caused a run on the rand and a rise in bank rate to a record 22 per cent. In August 1984 the government introduced a package of emergency measures that were the most drastic in recent history, and which had the effect of pushing up the prime lending rate to 25 per cent, with additional knock-on effects in business and trade. A general sales tax on all goods stood in September 1984 at 7 per cent and in the first quarter of that year there was a sizeable deficit of R400m. on the current account of the balance of payments.[58] The deficit for the last quarter of 1983 was R977m. In the 1985 budget the general sales tax was increased to 12 per cent and a 7 per cent surcharge was levied on personal income tax. Just prior to the budget the government announced pay cuts for civil servants, government ministers and MPs. The government also froze repayments on foreign debts. But the sharp devaluation of the rand against other currencies helped exports; with imports remaining static there was a surplus on the current account in the first quarter of 1985 of R4 billion, which in May 1985 encouraged some banks to reduce their prime lending rate to 23 per cent. With this export-led surplus, 'crisis' seems too strong a word to describe the economy.

Yet the economy is only one factor in modern South Africa. The economy's performance has repercussions elsewhere, and these ripples often outlast the original stimulus. While the gold price is low and economic hardship hits Whites hard, support is given to the arguments of the government's right wing critics who claim that South Africa simply cannot afford expensive constitutional structures. In an attempt to reduce state expenditure, the government introduced a compulsory fee-paying system in White schools in 1985. *Die Vaderland* tried to explain to its readers that this was necessary in order to give Black education a larger share of the education budget so as to to redress the existing imbalance. Right wing critics may be less charitable. What adds to the chagrin of these critics is that they see these expensive efforts at reform being rejected by the Black South Africans they are intended to placate.

Beyond their effects on Whites, these economic problems have also politicized Blacks and affected Black protest. The massive rent and service charge increases in the urban townships, which followed on from the high inflation rate and the emergency measures, enhanced the campaign against the new constitution during 1984. This discontent will be discussed in a subsequent chapter. Another contributory factor to the discontent was the introduction of an equal tax system in 1984 as part of the government's attempts to deracialize the economy. Blacks now pay tax at the same rate as Whites, reducing the take-home pay of most Black workers. While any attempt at equality is to be applauded, it does mean that although Blacks pay the same tax they receive fewer benefits compared to Whites.

The economy affects Black protest in other ways. One particularly important problem which the state has to contend with is the problem of high unemployment among educated Black youths. As the state's expenditure on Black education increases at the same

time as the recession deepens, a pool of highly educated unemployed or underemployed Black youths will be created. Since 1971
there has been a 1,070 per cent increase in Standard 10 enrol-
ments for Africans. The Unit for Futures Research at the University of Stellenbosch has estimated the number of students who can
be expected to attain Standard 10 certificates by the end of the
century to be 272,417. Of these 80 per cent will be Black. Africans
will provide 68.2 per cent of the total. In 1953, the corresponding
figure for Africans was only 500; by the year 2000 it will be
185,807.[59] Traditional employment patterns cannot absorb such
numbers. Education is already a source of politicization in South
Africa and Black opposition can only be strengthened when educated Black youths add to this the experience of unemployment. A
high gold price is required to ensure the economic growth necessary to provide Blacks with work opportunities commensurate
with their education. To fail in this, Giliomee wrote, 'would mean
we are sowing the seeds of revolution'.[60] At the moment, the lurch
between boom and recession does not afford much opportunity to
avoid the politicization of Black youth.

There are yet further influences on Black protest which derive
from the economy. Many analysts have commented upon the shift
in the domestic economy from the primary industries towards
secondary industries. The influence this has had on the attitudes of
Afrikaners towards change was noted by Nolutshungu as far back
as 1970.[61] It became an important theme of Adam and Giliomee's
later analysis of Afrikanerdom.[62] This influence upon Afrikaners
will be discussed shortly, but first the influence upon Black protest
should be mentioned. After the Second World War, South Africa's
manufacturing and commercial sectors became increasingly important to national income, labour employment, and the direction of
economic policy. Agriculture and mining were once the dominant
sectors, but by 1975 manufacturing and commerce contributed
nearly half the national income, and twice as much as farming and
mining. There was some time lag before the government adapted
itself to this. It gave special consideration to farmers, with the
system of influx control being erected mainly (but not exclusively)
to serve their interests and labour needs.[63] Only by the 1970s did
the government's realization of the importance of the manufacturing sector to economic growth become translated into policies
which served their interests for a stable and permanent labour

force. In its decision to train Blacks as skilled labourers and recognize their permanency as such, the government was also influenced by a decline in the growth of the White labour force. As a result of declining fertility among Whites, a temporary sharp drop in immigration, and the extension of the period of military training, the annual expansion of the White labour force fell by 63.4 per cent between 1976 and 1979. The limited number of Whites, together with the statutory and extra-legal barriers to the training of Blacks, created a skill shortage in the 1970s which spurred inflation and retarded growth.[64] In 1977 45 per cent of a sample of businessmen thought that difficulties in acquiring adequate skilled labour were causing low productivity. By 1980 this figure had risen to 80 per cent.[65] By 1977 government figures showed vacancies for 99,000 workers in the professional, semi-professional, and technical grades. Projections indicate that by the year 1990 there will be a shortage of 758,000 skilled workers unless the positions are filled by Blacks. The labour reforms following the Wiehahn and Riekert Commissions amount to a refusal to allow White-dominated unions to prevent members of other ethnic groups from occupying jobs which the White unions cannot fill from their own ranks. Thus, whereas Whites represented approximately 18 per cent of the total labour force in 1982, future projections show that of the new entrants into the labour market between 1982 and the year 2000 only 7 per cent will be White. By the year 2000 Blacks will comprise two-thirds of all artisans and apprentices.[66]

The increasing importance of skilled Black labour has had many consequences. The wage gap between the races has closed. Average wages in real terms rose by 24 per cent for Whites in the period 1970–80, compared with an increase of 15.2 per cent for Coloureds, 36.8 per cent for Indians, and 68.5 per cent for Africans. This trend is continuing. In 1982 salaries increased for Whites by 15 per cent, which was 4 per cent below that for Africans, 3 per cent below that for Coloureds, and 8 per cent below the rate for Asians. The changes are even more startling if 1960 is taken as the base year.[67] A tremendous imbalance in wages still remains but there has been a more powerful effect on the occupational structure of Blacks, as Table 1 illustrates. Some sense of proportion needs to be kept for there are limits to the extent to which economic change can erode apartheid. In this

Table 1. *Occupation by Race Group*

Occupation Group	White		Coloured		Asian		African*	
	1960	1980	1960	1980	1960	1980	1960	1980
Professional/ Technical	137,858	371,300	13,973	51,280	5,202	22,520	48,487	177,180
Administrative/ Management	58,889	125,820	1,442	3,000	2,371	4,280	5,716	4,040
Clerical	276,452	505,220	8,965	69,940	8,197	53,000	19,276	200,640
Sales	97,535	195,620	10,415	38,300	22,938	37,220	28,894	166,200
Service	58,951	155,820	117,649	152,840	14,597	16,580	711,115	1,102,890
Agricultural	117,358	88,900	127,575	154,680	11,575	5,900	1,474,860	1,114,340
Production	375,735	434,400	214,071	387,280	43,155	103,940	1,315,760	2,143,220

* 1980 figures exclude workers in the independent homelands.
Source: South African Digest, 8 Apr. 1983, p. 9.

instance there are limits to the extent to which a Black middle class can be created in South Africa. Robert Davies used minimum and maximum estimates of the number of non-manual jobs which could be created for Blacks in circumstances of a very favourable annual growth rate of 5 per cent to argue that there is little opportunity of any dramatic improvement. Even with the new positions which could be created, no more than 8.7 per cent of the economically active African population would occupy 'supervisory' or 'mental' positions by 1990.[68] None the less, there have been other effects of this change in the occupational structure of Blacks. There has been a definite increase in Black economic power. Professor Nattrass from Natal University's Development Studies Unit has estimated that 40 per cent of total personal income was earned by Blacks in 1983 compared with 26 per cent only ten years before.[69] Until recently Blacks were almost totally devoid of economic power. Precluded from ownership of land, they were unable to acquire ownership or control of resources. Blumenfeld shows that, without resources, Blacks were unable to accumulate wealth; and being unskilled and in excess supply, they had no market power. While the ownership of resources is still largely denied to Africans, in other respects the balance of economic power has shifted.[70] The acquisition of skills has enabled an increasingly large proportion of Black workers to increase their earnings, raising not only the number of employed but also the average wage and hence the Black community's share of national income. This in turn has increased the consumption power of Black South Africans and therefore made economic prosperity partly dependent on the growth of the Black market. In 1983 it was estimated by the Bureau of Market Research that Africans alone consumed 66.6 per cent of non-durable products and 40 per cent of all national sales. In addition, rising incomes have permitted a process of wealth accumulation, as evidenced in the emergence of Black-owned investment banks and other institutions for mobilizing the savings of Blacks. Blumenfeld argues that all these developments have promoted the rise of the market power of Black South Africans.

It is not just as consumers that Blacks have economic power. They are establishing an economic power base as workers and producers. In particular Black trade unionism is beginning to provide a source of economic power in the absence of direct access to political power or to wealth and resources. Such economic power can be temporarily reversed by the political power of Whites. Unemployment among Black workers forms a serious constraint on the growth of Black bargaining power. So too does the prospect of being 'endorsed out' to the homelands. Yet, in spite of all these constraints, Blumenfeld correctly insists that a shift in economic power is taking place.[71]

It is tempting to dismiss changes such as this, but as John Rex once said, those who fall into this trap must be 'curiously blinkered if they cannot see the difference in sociological and political terms between capitalism operating under conditions of White supremacy and a non-racial capitalism'.[72] Some of the consequences which he foresaw would have wide-ranging effects on the social structure. If Blacks enter the better-paid jobs there would be class divisions of a new kind amongst Blacks and Whites, and an African bourgeoisie and aristocracy of labour would exist to a degree which has not been evident before. Moreover, poor-Whitism would exist on a scale which was never envisaged as likely.[73] One other reason why these changes should not be dismissed is because this economic power has political effects. It is comparatively easy to crush township and rural revolts, but it is more difficult to break a sustained offensive by Black trade unionists or by Black consumers. This is why these spheres have become politicized in recent years as opposition is being pursued through transport and consumer boycotts and through workplace and community strikes.

The state's hope is that Blacks will be bought off by the co-option policy. Nolutshungu feels the policy of co-option is doomed to failure, primarily because Black attitudes have become militant and politicized.[74] Indeed, there is survey evidence to suggest that those with the most militant political attitudes are precisely the upwardly mobile, economically privileged Blacks subject to the co-option policy. Schlemmer summarized this material to conclude that the political culture of militancy, pride, and an assertion of rights to share South Africa equally with Whites, is the culture of the Black educated élite.[75] The longitudinal studies conducted by the Arnold Bergstraesser Institute show this pattern to have existed since 1974 and to have been sustained since. This militancy manifested itself in attitudes towards political rights, the democractic process, tribal ties, political change, and support for political violence.[76] The support for militancy was first noticed in Mayer's pioneering research among urban Africans and has been repeated by Mayer since.[77] Also there is no division between attitudes and behaviour as the better educated and economically mobile Blacks provide the main constituency for the leading Black political organizations. In terms of political affiliations, the radical organizations, like the ANC and Black Consciousness groupings have greater support among the better educated and more affluent Blacks.[78] In her study of African politics, Gerhart states that among the 28 top executive positions in the ANC and PAC, all but four were filled by people from the 'professional élite' and 'other middle classes'. Only two people were not university trained.[79] Studies of the membership of these groups have confirmed that the same holds true of rank-and-file supporters.[80] It is almost the case that these groups, which are subject to the co-option policy, constitute what Habermas calls 'educated labour' which Rootes has shown to be one of the leading revolutionary forces in capitalist societies.[81]

The economic fragility of South Africa has international as well as internal dimensions. Since the middle 1970s there has been, according to Nolutshungu, ample evidence of a concern and of a growing conviction in the West that South Africa must be urged, pressured, and cajoled into finding alternatives to apartheid.[82] Giliomee believes that foreign pressure in the form of threats of sanctions, boycotts, and disinvestment played a significant part in the deliberations of the Wiehahn Commission and in the decision of the National Party to accept most ot the recommendations.[83] Dugard has argued that international pressure against apartheid was influential in abandoning old-style apartheid in 1959 in favour of separate development.[84] The most severe pressure is applied through the multinational corporations. In the 1970s South Africa was short of capital, with the country having to attract between 7 and 10 per cent of its capital needs from abroad in order to maintain an annual growth rate of 5 per cent. Soweto stopped the flow of capital into South Africa and speeded its movement in the other direction. It has since resumed flowing into South Africa, but the immediate post-Soweto period acts as a constant reminder of what could happen should foreign capital cease to flow again.

Many of South Africa's critics have placed great faith in the power of the international community to influence the nature and pace of change. The issue of international pressure has caused a great deal of speculation.[85] Accordingly, the West's view on what change is desirable in South Africa bears investigation. In an excellent account of the relationship between the West and South Africa, it was argued by Barber and colleagues that the West believes the best way forward is to give discreet encouragement to the relatively reformist elements within the National Party, while at a more superficial level giving what encouragement is possible to Black organizations.[86] To do otherwise is to risk a period of chaos, in view of the West's security and economic interests in South Africa. Yet, such is South Africa's pariah status internationally that even those in the West who stress the importance of South Africa as an economic and military ally hesitate to demonstrate open support for South Africa. The relationship between them remains uneasy.[87] Such are the cross-cutting links between them that the West tends to vacillate between doing nothing, taking half-hearted actions, and warning Pretoria of sanctions, but without any evident commitment to such a policy.[88]

Despite the fact that international economic sanctions are the most widely canvassed instrument for exerting external pressure on South Africa, Barber and colleagues show that they are inherently unworkable because of the economic interdependence between the West and South Africa. Sanctions are likely to have less effect than imagined for it cannot be taken for granted that economic damage will lead to political change. Moreover, they will create costs for the West in terms of lost export trade, lost minerals, and reduced military support.[89] This is one of the factors that tends to be ignored when all the attention is focused on what pressure the West can apply to South Africa. Berridge's interesting analysis of Anglo–South African diplomacy between 1950 and 1970 shows that South Africa was able to apply leverage in the West and particularly in Great Britain. The economic strength of South Africa came from its hold over the British economy. Imports from the Republic were small when judged in proportion to the total, but they included raw materials of enormous importance to British industry, energy, and defence, and for the Bank of England's financial role. Such dependence enabled Pretoria to weaken the British economy by the application of various pressures, and to threaten reprisals as well as to offer rewards for compliance. Berridge discusses the Simonstown agreements, the post-Sharpeville crisis, and the policy of the 1964 Labour government to show that South Africa had the will and the means to carry out her threats. The fact that these were on occasion carried out highlights the dilemma of British governments, for this clearly shows that they were also under great pressure from an anti-South Africa lobby.[90]

Such is the interplay of economic and international–diplomatic pressure that South Africa's ability to apply her own international pressure depends very much upon the strength of her domestic economy and the position of gold in the money markets, which also tends to be variable. As a corollary, the weaker gold and the domestic economy are, the more susceptible South Africa is to international pressure.[91] So the policy pursued by the West and South Africa towards each other has not been consistent, but is contingent upon immediate economic circumstances.

None the less, the West does have an effect inside South Africa which is both real and symbolic. In discussing what influence the West has had, Legum felt that international pressure has helped to radicalize Black attitudes and make Whites more sensitive to Black aspirations.[92] This is in part because international pressure identifies apartheid as being internationally illegitimate as well as giving moral legitimacy to Black demands. This is one of the ways international pressure has influenced Black protest and resistance. Practical support has also been forthcoming, whether in the form of voluntary codes or financial or physical support for external liberation movements. But the South African government is not a passive actor in this, and the pressure which the West can apply should not be over-emphasized. South Africa's diplomatic accord with neighbouring states in 1984 strengthened her against any international vulnerability. The accord provided some international legitimacy, increased trade, and began moves against ANC bases in the neighbouring states. The Botha government is attempting to manage its international environment in such a way as to strengthen its internal position. Again this side of the coin tends to be ignored as attention is directed on what internal policy shifts are engaged in to placate international pressure.

One of the ways it has been able to do this in the past is through South Africa's role in the regional economy, and particularly through its political and economic destabilization policies.[93] Despite anti-apartheid hostility, the value of South Africa's two-way trade with the rest of Africa has always been high.[94] In 1981 the balance of this trade was R1,400m. and imports from African countries reached R317m. By 1985 South Africa's exports to other African countries increased to R1.58 billion. It was trade at these levels which made destabilization possible.

Prediction in human affairs is precarious and often haunts the forecasters. In dismissing van den Berghe's prediction in 1965 that revolution would occur in South Africa by 1970, Adam was sufficiently impressed by the diplomatic efforts South Africa was making to predict in 1971 that more and more African countries would settle for peaceful co-existence with the Republic.[95] Thompson appears to have been rash when in 1975 he disputed Adam's prediction, for events in 1984 seem to confirm Adam's view.[96] With the 1984 accord the policy is not so much neutralization of neighbouring countries, as Price termed it,[97] or destabilization as it is more frequently described, but the generation of positive diplomatic and economic ties.[98] The Botha government signalled this in 1982 when it met with Kaunda. Comment in the Afrikaans press said that South Africa was emerging from her 'isolation'; the more liberal newspapers like *Beeld* emphasized that South Africa would emerge even further if she engaged in greater efforts to make internal changes. Botha abused the Conservative Party as being neo-Nazi and held up his meeting with Kaunda as justification for the internal policy changes which the Conservative Party were criticizing: international events were being used to control Botha's internal political environment.

This manipulation was considerably facilitated by the 1984 accord with neighbouring states and Botha's diplomatic visit to Europe. This was alleged to signify a thawing in South Africa's diplomatic isolation and was used by Botha to justify his reforms against various attacks from the Afrikaans right wing. Botha can point to the removal of ANC bases from South Africa's borders, the resumption of tourism to Maputu, and the enhancement of trade and diplomatic links. All these contributed to a growing optimism amongst most Whites. *Rapport* was even prepared to argue after Botha visited London that he should meet with the ANC so long as he did not do so under the threat of violence.[99] Republic Day celebrations in 1984 were marked by the Black campaign against the new constitution, public demonstrations and street violence. But it was also the day when the *Citizen* wrote, 'there is an air of peace, a feeling of change, that has brought the hope that we can resolve not only our internal problems but help to resolve those of the sub-continent of which we are a part . . . Republic Day 1984 is a day when reform has begun, peace has arrived and we can go forward to fulfil our destiny as a leading power in Africa'.[100] The *Citizen* obviously had Whites primarily in mind. Dr Motlana, reflecting the views of urban Blacks, was critical of the accord, feeling it did nothing to alleviate the 'real issue', which he described as 'internal relations' and the threat of violence. He expressed his continued support for the ANC and criticized Machel's statement that the ANC should now become a civil rights movement. The obvious contradiction between the *Citizen*'s response and that of Motlana is one of the reasons why international events cannot be used successfully to control internal Black politics, even if they can do so to a certain extent for White politics. The adjectives used to describe Botha upon his return from Europe in the White press, such as 'hero', 'pioneer', and 'conqueror', with Botha being likened to Jan van Riebeeck, were not the adjectives used by Africans on the streets of the townships or in the factories as they fought the police, buried their dead, and chanted ANC songs. Just how long Botha can use international events to manage internal politics is, therefore, in doubt. International events do nothing to increase the legitimacy of apartheid for Blacks. It is difficult to see them assuaging the feelings of Whites for much longer as Whites face economic recession, continued terrorist attacks, and violent mass protests by Blacks.

The threat posed by the terror tactics of the external liberation forces was one of the crucial factors lying behind the accord with neighbouring states. Terrorism in South Africa has increased in frequency and ruthlessness since 1976 and the removal of ANC bases was an important clause in the accord. In his discussion of Black politics since 1945, Tom Lodge concluded his account of exile politics by arguing that it would be wrong to fall into the temptation of belittling the exile phase of Black resistance.[101] Trivial and frustrating it may on occasions have been, but the external movements were able, after 1976, to respond creatively to the dramatically altered internal situation and in so doing to shape the behaviour of the new generation. This is tantamount to saying that the greatest effect of the external liberation movements has been felt when they fought the struggle *inside* South Africa.

The politicization of Black South Africans since 1976 has in particular led the ANC to become directly involved in the internal political struggle. By 1984 its twin strategy was the combination of the use of terror and sabotage with mass mobilization through internal political surrogates. The ANC found reliance on external politics alone to be insufficient in the rapidly escalating political struggle inside South Africa. It also realized that external pressure alone will not destroy apartheid.

Notwithstanding the hopes of the exiles in London, New York, or various African capitals, it is unrealistic to expect that apartheid will crumble by external pressure alone short of economic sanctions and massive military intervention by the West, the Soviet Union, or Black Africa. Except for the ANC's historic symbolic significance, it is difficult to understand why, when discussing how the forces of opposition are being organized in South Africa, authors such as Saul and Gelb, for example, rely solely on discussing the external movement.[102] The ANC itself has realized that the decisive battle is being fought inside South Africa. The ANC has a complex external structure which is vital to the effectiveness of its internal campaigns, yet it has become so involved in the political struggle inside South Africa that it is now difficult to classify it as an external movement. Not since 1960 has there been such a close relationship between the ANC and the internal political struggle, such that if fundamental change is ever to take place in South Africa as a result of Black pressure, it will be generated primarily by the kind of internal pressure that is now evident.

It is not just the ferocity and intensity of the political struggle within the Black communities which is characteristic of the post-1976 period. Just as fierce a struggle has emerged within the Afrikaans community, where a serious challenge to the political authority of the government has developed. The reforms introduced by the government have done little to appease Black South Africans, but they have alienated significant sections of the White right wing. With the economic recession, some Afrikaners are arguing that South Africa cannot finance political change and point to the obvious fact that the changes which have been introduced have done little to win internal Black support or international respect. The inference the right draws from this is that it is better not to bother with reform at all. The inference

English-speaking Whites draw is that further rapid reform is needed in order for it have the desired international and internal effects. The inference which the government draws is that change has to be proceeded with slowly so as to avoid alienating the right wing. To its Black citizens it points to the appearance of change, while to White South Africans it emphasizes how the pace of change will be determined by the interests of their separate group identity. For example, Williem de Klerk, one of the most vocal reformist Afrikaners, wrote that the new politics pursued by the Botha government 'is in essence a politics of compromise which looks to close co-operation but with full retention of self-determination, group rights and the full maintenance of an own sphere of life ... the border line will be drawn at self-determination—in the church, in politics, education, living space, and group facilities. These are the non-negotiable aspects which the Afrikaner will defend with force of arms.'[103] One wonders what there is left to co-operate and negotiate about; clearly the government is caught in the position of recognizing the need for reform but of having so far introduced insufficient change to win much support from Blacks, although it has done sufficient to erode some of the White support it was once guaranteed. This impasse has considerable effects on Black opposition. It gives validity to the claim that the state is not interested in real reform. There are equal consequences in White politics by giving substance to the view that the government is no longer interested in maintaining White privilege. The government's arguments in disputing either view are taken as evidence for the other, so the predicament seems permanent.

There has been a belief ever since 1971 that Afrikanerdom was relaxing apartheid. For example, Adam felt that this was a necessary result of the pragmatic approach which he discerned in Vorster.[104] Price thought it to be the effect of a new freedom to pursue survival now that the governing élite was unencumbered by the doctrinal constraints imposed by an earlier obsession with ethnic identity.[105] A similar view was proposed by van Zyl Slabbert, who referred to the decrease in the cultural exclusivism of Afrikaners.[106] Nolutshungu saw it as the consequence of the changing social and economic position of Afrikaners.[107] Although all are important, and linked with each other, the latter explanation has dominated the literature up to this point. It is easy to summarize the lines of influence which social and economic changes are said to have had upon the Afrikaner's willingness to reform.

When the National Party came to power in 1948 the gap in the per capita income of English and Afrikaans speakers was wide and to the advantage of the English. The 'poor Afrikaner' problem was one of the most important concerns of the Broederbond. At this time, although it was primarily an ethnic party, the National Party's main class base came from the farming and mining communities.[108] Residential patterns reflected this. Significant numbers of English-speakers were first attracted to South Africa by the mineral boom and settled mainly in the burgeoning small towns surrounding the rural areas. By contrast Afrikaners were essentially a rural people, constituting what Park called a 'folk culture'. Though a drift by Afrikaners to the towns was discernible by the late nineteenth century, coinciding with the emergence of a landless class of poor Afrikaners, the move was initially from the country areas to the small towns. Only subsequently has there been a move to the large urban centres. At the beginning of the century 72.2 per cent of Afrikaners lived in the rural areas. This declined by 1946 to 39.6 per cent.[109] In the decades since, the Afrikaans community has undergone rapid urbanization and industrialization. The economic advance of Afrikaners has been phenomenal.[110] The government at first used the public and semi-state apparatus to promote Afrikaner economic progress. The public corporations at the senior and middle levels are now almost exclusively staffed by Afrikaners, and the public sector's share of the economy has almost doubled. The Afrikanerization of public sector personnel was due not just to economic factors, such as the movement of English speakers to the more lucrative private sector: equally important have been the political factors which influenced the government to appoint Afrikaners to key posts in order to buttress its political control and ensure the proper administration of apartheid policies. By 1976, 60 per cent of the White labour force in the public sector was Afrikaner, comprising 35 per cent of all economically active Afrikaners.[111]

Paralleling this expansion in the public sector has been the emergence of an Afrikaner private sector, especially in investment, banking, and insurance. The phenomenal growth of manufacturing and tertiary industry, and the relative decline of agriculture and mining, have had a well-established influence on employment patterns among Afrikaners. Crucially, these structural changes have created cleavages within the once ethnically solidified Afrikaans community which have weakened ethnic mobilization. This has caused a political realignment around the interests of what Adam called the new alliance of Afrikaner technocrats, transnational businessmen, academics, and formerly excluded middle groups.[112] The more traditional interests within Afrikanerdom of agriculture and mining have lost influence to this new alliance; and the clamour for change from within the Afrikaans community is being led by this new alliance.

Survey material quite clearly shows that high education and middle-class status have a strong link with attitudes in the Afrikaans community towards change. The 24 per cent of Afrikaners whom Hanf described in his sample as being 'open to change' came exclusively from occupational groups representing various components of the new alliance—the professions, academics, businessmen, and the media. Although there were wide differences between Afrikaans and English speakers as a whole, for these groups the differences in attitude towards change were negligible. The only difference Hanf noted was in how fast to move in implementing change.[113] These findings are in accord with the view that the chief obstacle to reform is the resistance to change among farming and mining interests, the Afrikaner unions, and the lower-rung officials in the apartheid bureaucracy who administer Black affairs.[114] These are people whose material self-interest leads them to oppose land reform, the extension of trade union rights to Blacks, and administrative devolution, and to be in favour of such things as job reservation, population relocation, and artificially high wages for Whites: people who depend upon and benefit from the continued exclusion of Blacks.

From this situation arise those embarrassing instances where the government's commitment to reform is obstructed by the interpretation of policy by lower-rung officials. This is especially the case where the changes are administrative rather than legal. The relaxations of control in the areas of sport and public entertainment, and the removal of petty apartheid notices in post offices, railway stations, public parks, and so on have been achieved without a change in the law. This presents problems since the dispensations are not allowed on universal criteria but depend on the particularities of each case, leading to uncertainty and confusion. It also allows officials a degree of discretion. Thus at the same time as the government was trying to court Coloureds to persuade them to participate in the new constitutional framework, a Coloured school principal was prevented from sitting his University of South Africa examinations because White candidates objected to sharing the examination hall with him. An official in Pretoria City Council temporarily resurrected the apartheid notices in the city's parks. Three of the seventeen public parks were closed to Blacks, dividing fences were erected, and guard dog patrols were used to reinforce the decision. Pressure eventually made the council change its mind, but instances like this can be repeated many times. They are inherent to the government's policy of implementing most reforms through administrative practice rather than legislative changes.

One of the more important developments which has arisen from the growth of an Afrikaner bourgeoisie is the link with the English-speaking business sector. This has brought with it a change in economic and political thinking. Giliomee argues that the government no longer believes that the state should be used solely for the economic advancement of Afrikaners: they have fully arrived as a bourgeoisie, so there is increasing state support for Afrikaner and English capital. Afrikaners have lost their distrust of big business and the private sector.[115] This was predicted by Nolutshungu, among others, in 1971 and again in 1975.[116] As Saul and Gelb now write, this 'meeting of the minds with the multinational corporations has meant a much stronger political base for the "liberalization" of racial capitalism'.[117] This is because political and economic change has the support of big business.

One other result of these economic changes which has had equally wide-ranging political consequences, is the removal of special state protection from the White working class. Giliomee refers to White workers as having lost, with the government at the moment being indifferent to their demands.[118] The government was influenced in this by the sharp drop in immigration and a decline in the White fertility rate, which in turn produced a large absolute decrease in the White labour force. The interests of capital require a stable and contented labour force, and this had increasingly to be drawn from the ranks of the Black population. The interests of the White working class, with their artificially high wages, lost influence with the government. The changes following the Wiehahn Commission not only increase the bargaining rights of Black workers, they also substantially reduce the bargaining power of White workers. Black advance in the future may increasingly come at the expense of White workers rather than employers. Whereas White workers could previously set wages for themselves, and for Black workers too, they now have to deal with Black workers who are organized and backed by an effective trade union movement. Thus Giliomee disputes Johnstone's view, propounded in 1970, that the two goals of prosperity and White supremacy supplement one another, for to White workers the Botha government is seen as spelling bourgeois prosperity and bourgeois supremacy.[119]

Afrikaner politics are now class politics, not ethnic politics. Politics are therefore subject to class divisions within the Afrikaans community. Charney has interpreted the split within the National Party and the formation of the Conservative Party in class terms, arguing that it is the product of an Afrikaner bourgeoisie seeking new political alliances.[120] O'Meara had made a similar point in his analysis of the Information Scandal.[121] O'Meara's recent research on the Broederbond shows that class divisions within Afrikanerdom are not new, and argues that Afrikaner politics up to 1948 can only properly be understood when seen as the result of changing class alliances, rather than as an expression of national or ethnic consciousness.[122] But it is significant that O'Meara concentrates on the period up to 1948. There is a view, forwarded by Adam and van Zyl Slabbert, that after 1948 class divisions become less important because of the effectiveness of Afrikaner nationalism as a mobilizing force encouraging ethnic solidarity, such that van Zyl Slabbert shows that ethnic unity among Afrikaners was the product of the 1948 election victory, not its cause.[123] The thrust of this argument is not that class divisions have suddenly appeared among Afrikaners, but that those forces which once used to obscure class differences after 1948 have now become less effective as a result of the social and economic advance of Afrikaners. Afrikaners are no longer able to act as a unified ethnic group pursuing exclusive ethnic goals. The demand for economic growth, rather than separate development, has removed special state protection from the White working class. The central concern of governments after 1948 was to implement apartheid policies, to protect White workers, to decrease the numbers of Blacks in

'White' areas and to curb the economic mobility of Blacks through the pass laws and the colour bar in industry. With the *embourgeoisement* of Afrikaners, notions of an exclusive ethnic identity are fast losing their appeal. The call for economic growth is more attractive. Thus, the National Party, which was once a coalition of class elements within the Afrikaans community, is now ridding itself of those elements (the White working class) which cause dissonance in the party, and bringing into alliance sections of business, the English-speaking community, and some from within the Black communities.[124]

As Nolutshungu ably reminded us, one should not under-emphasize the importance of politics in favour of some economic or class determinism when discussing modern South Africa. This new class alliance has led to crucial political problems for the government which have come to have an independent effect on the nature and dynamics of modern South Africa. The extension of limited citizenship rights to Black 'urban insiders', in an attempt to provide a stable and contented labour force, has been criticized by the co-opted groups because the changes lack substance. Though intending to increase its legitimacy in this way, the actions of the state have in fact served to undermine it more fundamentally. The liberalization measures are reinforcing the changes affecting Black economic power and together they are providing 'urban insiders' with a structural and institutional base from which to lead Black opposition. This study shows that those groups which are at the forefront of Black protest are precisely those which are the object of the state's co-option policy.

It is not only Black protest which provokes political problems for the government. The defection of the Afrikaner right wing is no less a political problem which has become independent of its economic origins. The Conservative Party has achieved noticeable success in mobilizing support among those sections of the former Afrikaner ethnic movement which had been jettisoned. For a long time the increasing divergence of interests and attitudes within Afrikanerdom was institutionalized within the National Party without splitting the superficial ethnic solidarity of Afrikanerdom. It was only in 1979–80 that Schlemmer wrote in a postscript to the Arnold Bergstraesser Institute's study that the 'influence of the traditional lobbies and their support in the National Party organizations and in the parliamentary caucus is strong enough to hold the leadership to established party policies. Pragmatism is thus confined within the narrow limits set by the workings of ethnic nationalism and of the inner circle of the power élite. Great pressure will be required to transgress these limits or establish new ones.'[125] The pressure came in the form of a right wing reaction to the liberalization measures introduced since 1978–79 and the formation of the Conservative Party.

The history of party politics in parliamentary democracies shows most splits to be ephemeral. This is not the case in non-democratic societies like South Africa where greater power resides in the party caucus. This split is fundamental and represents the divergence of interest between the Afrikaner bourgeoisie and working class, between what Adam and Giliomee call the 'ideological hardliners', who favour the implementation of strict separate development, and the 'pragmatists', who desire political stability and economic growth, and who wish to this end to create a stable and contented Black work-force through a series of liberalization measures.[126] It is a conflict between an ideological and managerial approach to government, summed up less well perhaps by de Klerk's famous contrast of *verkramptes* and *verligtes* respectively. It is a clash of interest which transcends the National Party, and the split has gone much further than the defection of sixteen MPs. The National Party was only the political wing of the whole Afrikaner ethnic movement, and the split has been repeated in every one of the myriad institutions which once made up the movement: the Broederbond, the Dutch Reform Church, the Afrikaans-speaking press, Afrikaner student organizations, cultural bodies, clubs, town councils, school boards, business associations, trade unions, and even the Afrikaner scouting and first-aid organizations. In the face of this split, the National Party is in the uncomfortable position of having to defend change and justify reform against its right wing critics. Some of the government's left wing critics hope that this will lead to a greater commitment to reform among the National Party.[127] This political debate about reform among Afrikaners simultaneously stimulates expectations among Blacks.

The debate about reform has been fought in the Afrikaans-speaking press. When the *verligte* editor of *Die Transvaler*, the official party newspaper in the Transvaal, and once edited by Verwoerd, was ousted from his post because of his liberal views, the government was able through one of its commissions to restructure the Afrikaans press in the Transvaal. *Die Transvaler* was transformed into an evening paper and switched to Pretoria, servicing the conservative North Transvaal. *Beeld*, as the liberal newspaper from the Cape which supports the government in its reforms, was made the only Afrikaans morning daily in the Transvaal. The man over whom this press battle was fought was later instated as editor of the liberal Sunday newspaper *Rapport*, also from the Cape. An editorial in *Die Transvaler* presented the restructuring as a decision dictated by market considerations, but the liberal press and other conservative newspapers did not fail to comment on its political significance.

The debate is also being publicly conducted in the church. Religion is a vitally important element of the political thinking of Afrikaners and it was inevitable that theologians would become involved in the debate about reform. The Dutch Reform Churches spent decades endeavouring to provide a spurious scriptural justification for apartheid, but some ministers have publicly condemned apartheid as unChristian. Past orthodoxies do hold greater sway among the hierarchy of the church, and the referendum campaign in November 1983 demonstrated how wide the split within it was. Representatives of the three major Afrikaner churches rejected the new constitution at a meeting in Pretoria in September, referring to it as unjustifiable according to the Bible. A group of churchmen in the Transvaal circulated a pamphlet on the constitution claiming among other things that it was communist-inspired. Treurnicht seized upon this ferment and criticized Muslim participation in the constitution of a supposedly Christian country. The debate over the repeal of the Mixed Marriages and the Immorality Acts provides another example of how divided the church is. The parliamentary select committee discussing the acts recommended in August 1984 that they be scrapped. It received only five submissions suggesting their retention. The Hervormde Kerk gave one. While theologians of the larger Ned Geref Kerk interpreted the laws as deviating from the Bible's teachings on marriage, the executive body of the church asked for the retention of the laws 'on practical grounds'. It referred to 'practical grounds' because the use of scriptural grounds was made impossible by an earlier decision that racism was unscriptural and a sin. In October 1982 the General Synod announced that it was to review the famous policy statement 'Race and National Relations in the Light of Scripture', but only at the next synod in four years' time. The Prime Minister and the liberal Afrikaans press criticized this delay, but a decision was wrung from the General Synod that racism was unscriptural and a sin. They also passed an unopposed motion that there was no sin in 'racial awareness'.

Empirical evidence has emerged which shows that a major shift in the political thinking of Afrikaner students has occurred. A study undertaken by Stellenbosch's political science department in 1974, 1978, and 1981 indicates that the students strongly endorsed the policy of reform associated with P. W. Botha.[128] Stellenbosch students are ahead of other Afrikaner students in this respect. A poll in 1983 among the Afrikaans-speaking student body revealed that support for integrated universities was much higher among students at Stellenbosch, which services the metropolitan Cape, than at the University of Pretoria, in the heart of conservative rural North Transvaal. The University of Stellenbosch was once the avant-garde of the apartheid idea but the intellectual climate has now changed. The Rector of Stellenbosch has advocated full integration and *Die Matie*, the student newspaper, openly attacks apartheid. The Afrikaans student body Polstu, which demands equality between the races, began at Stellensbosch. For a long while the university was disaffiliated from the main Afrikaans student body, the Afrikaanse Studentebond, which was much more conservative. However, reflecting the new interests in Afrikanerdom, the July 1983 congress of the ASB underwent a radical shift and criticized the government's reforms for not going far enough. By the 1984 conference the right wing students had mobilized sufficient support to ensure that the conference voted upon and supported a motion stating that it was not competent to discuss political matters. The main representative of the *verligte* students, Lucius Boates, was twice defeated in elections for office.

This mollification of the relatively reformist sections within the ASB occurred at the same time as those in favour of reform within the Federasi van Afrikaanse Kultuurverenigings, the major Afrikaner cultural body, managed to oust its former conservative leadership. In 1983 it was decided that although Coloureds (sometimes described by White Afrikaners as 'Brown Afrikaners') had a leading role to play in the propagation of Afrikaans culture, they should not be admitted to FAK membership. There had been support for admittance from rank-and-file members, but the executive decided against it. Membership for Coloureds became more likely after the 1984 conference when far right wing candidates were defeated in election contests for the executive and the chairmanship of the FAK. The new chairman, Professor Gawie Cillié, spoke of the FAK's new task as being to 'set about sharing the joy of our inheritance with others'.

The Broederbond is the most important Afrikaner organization of all. O'Meara's research shows that it was the mastermind of Afrikaner capitalism and through ideological, cultural, and economic mobilization of the *Volk*, defined Afrikaner culture as bourgeois.[129] It did this in the belief that Afrikaner self-identity and solidarity was essential to the maintenance of South Africa's racial capitalism, and it played a critical role after 1948 in fostering the former in order to maintain the latter. The changes in the nature of Afrikanerdom have now persuaded it that ethnic solidarity is not necessary for economic growth and it is firmly behind the government in this view. The former conservative chairman, Professor Carel Boshoff, who is also chairman of the reactionary South African Bureau of Racial Affairs, resigned from his position in the Broederbond when, in his capacity as chairman of SABRA, he wrote a report which described the constitutional proposals as farcical. He was replaced as chairman of the Broederbond by the liberal Professor de Lange who chaired the enquiry which made far-reaching and controversial proposals for reform of the education system. Given the symbolic place of the Broederbond in Afrikaner thinking, and its very real practical role in public affairs, the decision to break with it indicates how vast are the divisions within the Afrikaans-speaking community. The *Citizen*, itself on the right of English-speaking newpapers, was not exaggerating when it described Boshoff's resignation upon political grounds as a 'remarkable change in the hegemony of the *Volk*'. Yet such is the nature of the political disputes within the Afrikaner community that even more remarkable events occurred within the year, with the formation of the rival Afrikanervolkswag in May 1984.

The more appropriate model for the AV ought to be the Ossewabrandwag rather than the Broederbond or the FAK. It may be translated literally as 'People's Guard', and although it describes itself as a cultural organization, as the early Ossewabrandwag also did, its intentions are aggressively political. Chief figures in its formation were Mossie van den Berge (a Hervormde Kerk minister), members of the paramilitary Afrikaner Weerstandsbeweging, and politicians from the HNP and the Conservative Party. Boshoff is a leading member of the new organization and among its founder members it can also claim a former Speaker of Parliament, a former Transvaal Administrator, and a former leader of Aksie Eie Toekoms (Action Our Future)—a group of conservative academics formed in 1981 and pledged to defeat the reforms of the National Party. The AV is essentially an alliance of Afrikaans-speaking reactionary, political, and paramilitary groupings camouflaged as a cultural organization. It was launched on a wave of emotional zealotry. The rhetoric, which conjured images of war, the paramilitary trappings, such as armed and uniformed bodyguards, and the *Führer*-style salute of the organization, all caused the press to liken the organization to the Nazis—the model also for the Ossewabrandwag. Botha has referred to it as neo-Nazi. But this did not prevent the South African Broadcasting Corporation from devoting a great deal of television time to covering the launch live. They relayed the ugly scenes of uniformed men saluting and brandishing arms, and calling Botha a traitor. Obviously there is some sympathy for the new organization within the hierarchy of the SABC.

It is a reflection of the divisions within the Afrikaner political élite when former pillars of the establishment like Treurnicht and Boshoff are prepared to consort with an organization whose paramilitary character is so manifest. Furthermore they lend such an organization some credibility. But this association works both ways, for Boshoff was affected by his connection with the AV: he was called upon to resign from his professorship in theology at the University of Pretoria and from his leadership of the Voortrekkers. He stuck doggedly to both for he was earlier forced to relinquish his positions in the FAK and the Broederbond.

Few Afrikaners are Broederbonders and only a minority are involved in the promotion of culture, but most are churchgoers and the majority vote. The next major battleground is likely to be in the Afrikaner churches and here the far right is well entrenched. Few Afrikaners will be unaffected by that conflict when it arises. The battle at the polls so far seems to have been won by the pragmatists with the far right parties having a limited electoral base.

South Africa's leading psephologist, Lawrence Schlemmer, calculated that in the general elections of 1970, 1974, and 1977, the National Party drew between 83 and 85 per cent of the Afrikaner vote. In the 1981 election this slumped to 63 per cent, with 33 per cent having voted for the far right parties compared with 7 per cent in 1977. Support from English speakers also declined. It was down to 28 per cent compared to 33 per cent in 1977.[130] However, the moves within the National Party toward reform since 1981 have enabled the government to rescue some of its declining support. According to a nation-wide opinion poll among Whites conducted by Mark-en Meningsopnames for the Afrikaans Sunday newspaper *Rapport* in July 1984, support for the Conservative Party was waning while the National Party gained support in both language groups and particularly among English-speakers. Two years previously, 15 per cent of all White voters said they supported the Conservative Party, against 43 per cent for the National Party. The 1984 poll indicated an overall support for the Conservative Pary of 9.8 per cent and 56 per cent for the National Party. Currently the Conservative Party argues that it intends to create a White South African nation, of which the Afrikaners will be the core. This ascendency for Afrikaners ensures the Conservative Party little English-speaking support. As an amalgam of many far rightist groups, the party only succeeded in drawing to itself one such group from within the English-speaking community, the largely unknown South Africa First Campaign under its president Brendan Wilmer. Currently the main support for the Conservative Party comes from within the Afrikaans-speaking community, but even within this community its electoral base is narrow. By-election results and the results of the referendum on the constitution show that the party has a very real but limited base in agricultural seats in the *platteland*, in mining districts, and in other predominantly White working-class seats. Average figures in opinion polls obscure the base which the Conservative Party has among those sections of the Afrikaner community who have been dropped from special government protection as a result of the liberalization measures in the economy.

In the referendum held on 2 November 1983, the White electorate gave its approval to the constitutional reforms proposed by the government. Altogether there was a poll of 75.6 per cent, with 66.3 per cent voting in favour of the proposals. But those in favour constituted only 50.13 per cent of all those who were entitled to

Table 2. *Voting Intentions Among Whites (1984)*

	English-speakers (%)	Afrikaans-speakers (%)
National Party	35.2	69.1
PFP	39.3	2.6
Conservative Party	0.7	15.7
HNP	1.1	2.3
New Republic Party	10.4	1.4
No vote	13.3	8.9

vote, which puts a different complexion on the results. Overall 700,000 voters rejected the constitution, while another 628,602 did not vote. The 'yes' vote received strong majorities in fourteen of the fifteen referendum voting regions and lost by only a small margin in the Pietersburg region of North Transvaal. Map 1 indicates the geographical spread of support in favour of the new constitution. Support was less strong in the agricultural and mining regions. Although part of the 'no' vote reflected the rejection of the proposals by some of the English-speaking community for not going far enough.

Right wing votes in a number of provincial and parliamentary by-elections confirm the support which the Conservative Party possesses among those Afrikaners most affected by the loss of special government protection. In May 1983 Treurnicht retained his seat at Waterberg, polling 47 per cent of the vote, with the National Party achieving 32 per cent and the HNP 21 per cent. Although this represented the only victory for the party, the four by-elections taking place in the rural *platteland* during May 1983 showed that it represented a sizeable constituency, for the National Party garnered 21,578 votes while the combined right wing opposition polled 196 votes more. After these results Professor Willem Kleynhans claimed that the Conservative Party had emerged as a powerful force, and Schlemmer estimated that if a general election were to be held at that time, a combined right wing assault would see the rightist parties able to win between nineteen and thirty-four seats from the National Party, nine of which were fairly safe for the right wing candidates.[131] Since then the Conservative Party has made further strides in by-elections. They gained the Soutpansberg seat after Fannie Botha was forced

Introduction

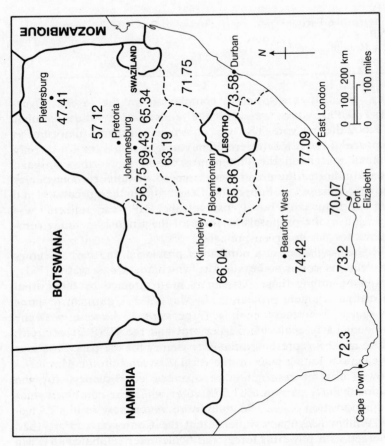

MAP 1. Support for the constitution in the referendum by polling area

to resign under allegations of corruption. The National Party had a 6,000 majority in this *platteland* constituency in 1981. The provincial contest in the same seat also saw the victory of the Conservative Party candidate. The National Party managed to retain the Middelburg provincial seat in the *platteland*, but the combined right wing vote exceeded the winner by 428 votes. In the Potgietersrus provincial by-election in the *platteland*, the Conservative Party won by 1,034 votes. This particular contest also marked the beginnings of an electoral pact between the HNP and Conservative Party. After a lengthy period of negotiations and a number of earlier decisions against a pact, the contest in Potgietersrus showed how beneficial a pact could be to the far right parties. On 8 August 1984 the two parties formally agreed to an electoral alliance under which they will not stand against each other. The by-elections which occurred in December 1984, partly as a result of Koornhof's move to the President's Council with the trimming of the Department of Co-operation and Development, saw the National Party win with reduced majorities in all eight contests. In Primrose, in a straight fight with the Conservative Party, the majority was reduced from 4,399 in 1981 to 748. The right wing vote strengthened by 22.55 per cent. In May 1985, the provincial by-election in Harrismith resulted in a win for the National Party of 247 votes over the Conservative Party.

Significantly most of these by-elections occurred in rural areas where the Conservative Party is strong. In urban Randburg during February 1984, the National Party was able to win control of the town council from the PFP, and in the Rosettenville provincial seat in Johannesburg the National Party won easily over the Conservative Party with a majority of 1,798. The corollary of this poll is that the Conservative Party's first venture to an urban seat saw it muster 2,405 votes. In the by-elections in December 1984 which occurred in the Cape, the right wing advance was only 7.5 per cent. Indeed, the Primrose result must be compared with the 1982 by-election results in Germiston. They are neighbouring urban working class constituencies, and in 1982 the National Party obtained 43 per cent of the vote compared with 53 per cent in 1984. The parliamentary and provincial by-elections which took place in Port Elizabeth in May 1985 saw the National Party candidates win with majorities comparable to 1981. In the October 1985 by-elections the HNP took Sasolburg from the

National Party, and another four seats were won by the National Party with greatly reduced majorities. The one exception was the predominantly English-speaking constituency of Port Natal. This result seemed to confirm an opinion poll conducted by *Rapport* in July 1985, which indicated that P. W. Botha's support was increasing among English-speakers but declining among Afrikaans-speakers. A problem for the government in this political crisis is that the deep *platteland* still has an unequal influence on parliamentary politics. To counter the liberal English-speaking vote, located predominantly in the urban areas, and to reflect the National Party's former power bloc in the rural *platteland*, the party maximized the number of rural seats (by having a minimum number of voters in each) and minimized the number of urban seats (by having a maximum number of voters in each). South African electoral laws provide for a discrepancy of up to 30 per cent in the number of votes between urban and rural seats and the rural vote is loaded since it favours the farming and mining interests who once provided the main constituency within the National Party. Now that the ideological divisions within Afrikanerdom have altered this, it is likely that in the next delimitation of constituencies this process will be reversed to reflect the new constellation of interests within Afrikanerdom generally.

Thus, with the township disturbances in 1984–5 and the campaign of opposition towards the constitution from Blacks and right wing Afrikaners, the government was besieged from all sides. On the day the new constitution came into effect and Prime Minister Botha became acting Executive President, awaiting the formation of an electoral college to make this official, *Beeld* showed mixed emotions as it expressed disappointment at the unrest and gave a warning that further change needed to be got underway rapidly. 'What a shame it is that the day on which South Africa embarks upon its new dispensation, the day that we all hope will be recorded in our country's history as a historic day, was characterized by unrest and a bomb explosion . . . it serves as an illustration of the dilemma in which our country still finds itself, and as a reminder of how far we still are in reality from a complete solution for all our people.'[132] The Executive President is being pulled in conflicting directions as his government tries to satisfy those pressures pushing for change while respecting the powerful material and psychological interests which the right wing in South Africa represent. This dilemma has consequences for Black protest and resistance. The power of the right reduces the pace of reform, as Hill's study ably demonstrated,[133] which increases the gulf between the appearance of reform and its reality and so increases Black frustration. It has caused the state to over-react in its response to the township disturbances, leaving over a thousand people dead during 1984 and 1985 in violence related to the unrest. Since 1976 the toll is near three thousand. For the seven and a half months in which the state of emergency was in force in 1985 to quell township disturbances, the death rate was an average of over 100 per month. This tough response is felt by the government to be necessary to show to the right that it has not gone soft on Black opposition. Editorials in a number of liberal Afrikaans newspapers criticized the severity of the government's response, although not papers like *Die Transvaler* and *Die Afrikaner*. As in 1976 this over-reaction only intensifies the anger of Black South Africans, so that funerals of fellow protesters, for example, become highly charged political events, often leading to more funerals, and so the cycle continues. It is in this sort of atmosphere that internal Black opposition adds one further element to the matrix of economic, political, and international problems which face the state in modern South Africa.

THE LIMITS TO REFORM FROM ABOVE

Two points are worth emphasizing about the dynamics of modern South Africa. The greatest problems which this matrix presents are being experienced inside South Africa. While they may have external ramifications, the major battles are internal ones. What goes on outside South Africa can reinforce, or hinder what takes place within but cannot alone greatly affect internal conditions unless economic sanctions or direct military intervention are undertaken. Secondly, the complexity of the inter-connected problems faced by the state works against the process of government-led reform.

During the formative years of separate development, analysts of South Africa were obsessed with the monolithic character and ideological zeal of the state and with outlining all the reasons why a violent revolution was almost inevitable. These views were strongly challenged in the 1970s. Merle Lipton argued that 'authoritarian reform' was occurring in South Africa, and Adam developed the thesis that the state was flexibly responding to new circumstances by adopting whatever means were most conducive to the preservation of White domination.[134] Heribert Adam painted a scene showing that the regime had a remarkable talent for controlling the process of change. While Adam never argued, as some of his critics have claimed, that there was no stumbling block to the state's ability to manage the process of reform, he did underestimate the limits to the process of authoritarian reform. It is entirely unrealistic to suggest that the only changes which can be expected to occur in the future are those approved by the state. Rex lists other crucial variables such as South Africa's role in the world economy, the activities of the external liberation movements, and the internal breakdown in law and order.[135] More recent research by Adam seems to agree with the view that there are forces which will prove difficult for the state to control and manage.[136] Much of the literature in recent years dismisses the claim that it is possible for South Africa to move away from the present system through reform from above. Nolutshungu believes that the state cannot manipulate class divisions so that they supersede racial divisions. In this way the state will not be able to shed its racialist nature.[137] In short, any reform from above will be unable to disguise the nature of apartheid and appease Black South Africans. Giliomee identifies other reasons why he considers authoritarian reform to be unworkable and, again, the emphasis is upon the inability of this process to meet the demands of Black South Africans.[138] The state, he argues, simply misperceives the needs of its Black citizens. The strong inclination is particularly to see urban Blacks as concerned with the improvement of their material position, and while they may not be prepared in the long run to trade this off against meaningful political rights they will be appeased by it for a considerable period. The English-speaking community is considered as a living example of a group whose material prosperity appears to be an adequate compensation for its lack of political power.[139] The parallel with Zimbabwe is striking here. Whites in Zimbabwe believed Blacks were more interested in economic advancement, but in the end political demands were stronger. Mildly reformist policies in social and economic matters will do little to quell the

African demand for political representation at the centre of power. In this regard the moderate support among Whites for the new constitution is a two-edged sword. It can be seen as Whites endorsing some devolution of power, but also as Whites accepting a policy which Africans entirely reject. This misperception of the needs of Black South Africans, and Africans especially, is conjoined by the state's underestimation of the capacity of Africans to inflict damage on the state.

As great as internal Black pressure is and will remain, it is not the only factor which presents obstacles to the government's successful management of the process of change. To the factors listed by Rex should be added such things as continued international and diplomatic isolation, despite the tactical accord with neighbouring states, and such internal problems as the power struggle with the Afrikaans right wing. Above all, there are simply too many links between elements of the matrix of problems facing the state for it to be able to control and dictate the nature and pace of change; there is far too much potential for authoritarian reform to get out of control as unintended and unforeseen consequences follow in one area from the government's attempt to meet the challenge presented by other areas.

There are many examples showing that these unintended consequences have already occurred and it is possible to imagine more. Some examples have been cited previously. The government is already aware that one of the unintended consequences of the policy of restricting Africans to the homelands is chaotic and uncoordinated urbanization as influx control breaks down under the economic necessity to move, even illegally, to the city. It was once estimated that a rural dweller would be 465 per cent better off by working illegally in the urban areas for six months and paying the penalty rather than waiting for a pass to pursue work legally.[140] The shanty towns, squatter camps and random shacks which surround most of the large industrial areas have great potential as bases for political opposition. This is certainly the fear of a number of White liberals, who argue that the fragile urbanites who cluster in the shanty towns will be a more revolutionary force than the settled and permanent 'urban insiders'.[141] Although such a view can be disputed,[142] there is still potential for much unrest among the new urbanites.

The government must also be aware that its attempt to confer industrial democracy upon Blacks has only exacerbated the demand for political democracy. Black trade unions who lack Black political representation have simply turned the factory floor into a political arena. The granting to Coloureds and Indians of a form of limited political representation in Parliament which excludes Africans has increased the pressure from Africans for parliamentary representation, and seen even the moderate Inkatha movement query its own peaceful and pluralist approach toward the state. Additionally, the constitution has increased political polarization not only between Africans and the other Black communities but also inside the Coloured and Indian communities. Quite fierce, aggressive, and unpredictable political struggles are taking place within the Coloured and Indian communities and all are ultimately linked to the original attempt to confer industrial democracy without political democracy. One effect of the constitutional proposals was to unite the various forces in the Black communities which opposed the constitutional reforms. This unity was reflected in the formation of the United Democratic Front and its strong links with most sections of the trade union movement; and while polarization between supporters and opponents of the constitution within and between the Black communities has increased as a result of the reform, it has forced the opposition forces who oppose the reform to unite in their campaign against it. This unity has had tremendous unforeseen political consequences in the fight against apartheid.

Engaging in sham reform has not dampened the opposition of the majority of Black South Africans, yet proceeding with expensive and costly reforms does hamper the recovery of the economy. The reduction in state expenditure is a vital part of the recovery and some South African newspapers urged, for example, that the opening of the new parliaments should not be an expensive and glorious affair. This itself will do little to swell the state's coffers, but the Conservative Party has gone one stage further and argued that the state cannot afford to fund political change at all. Any slowing down in the pace of change, whether from economic recession or right wing influence, will only intensify the dissatisfaction of the majority of Blacks, yet continuing with reform brings its own costs. Encouraging Black advancement affects the privileges of Whites, the security of their employment and the size of their wage packet. The revival of White trade unionism has been one unintended consequence of Black advancement. It also affects, for example, the education of Whites. The government was forced in 1985 to introduce a system of compulsory fees in White schools; the economy can no longer finance the expansion of Black education without pruning the budget for White education. Black advancement also affects the residential exclusivity of White cities. The repeal of the Mixed Marriages Act and the Immorality Act in 1985 has ramifications for the Group Areas Act: it is impossible to allow people to marry if they cannot live together. The pressure for the repeal of the Group Areas Act has intensified following the repeal of the acts. Empirical research has shown that Whites generally are not in favour of social integration,[143] yet it is the corollary of conjugal integration. Should social integration be allowed, no matter how qualified, this will add to the pressure from Blacks for political integration.

At the moment the state is attempting to control the pace and nature of change by proceeding with Black advancement without granting political citizenship to Africans. One manifestation of this advancement is the expansion of Black education. However, the growth of an educated Black élite without the commensurate economic and occupational opportunities creates a pool of highly educated Black unemployed or underemployed youths. Educational advancement may only result in politicization of Black South Africans. Already the growth of anger and militancy among Blacks has led to greater support being publicly expressed for the ANC and there is, as a consequence, greater sympathy for the use of political violence.[144] The increased frequency and ruthlessness of political violence is something the state, and Whites generally, are having to adjust to. As Northern Ireland shows, this is both a financial drain and an emotional one.

Black economic advancement is a consequence of the drive for economic growth which is itself intended to satisfy the material aspirations of all South Africans. This consequence of economic growth has led some Whites to challenge the very need for economic growth. The Conservative Party has criticized the government, saying it over-emphasizes the economic needs of people at the expense of the emotional, cultural, spiritual, and identity needs of the separate groups within society: a willingness to be poorer but purer. One unintended consequence of the drive for economic growth has therefore been to reinforce the political gulf within the Afrikaner community and add to the challenge to the state's political authority. Any move to placate the right as a result of this challenge not only affects the left: it will have international effects also. Clamping down heavily on internal Black protest, as the state did in 1984 and 1985, whether to ease the transition of its policies or to appease right wing claims that the state is going soft on Black opposition, can lead to international disapproval. The EEC, for example, made public its condemnation of the detention of UDF activists and any goodwill Botha created on his European tour might well have been dispelled. Blacks are able to manipulate the support of the West, as six UDF members did by seeking and being granted refuge in the British consulate in Durban. This manipulation has effects both inside and outside South Africa. Internationally, for example, it adds pressure on the neighbouring states to renege on the accord.

Perhaps the greatest unintended consequence of authoritarian reform has been the provision for Black opposition of a new terrain with a new set of problems, issues, and circumstances. Rather than leading to the diminution of Black protest, the response of Black South Africans to this new terrain has strengthened Black protest. This is one of the important limits to the reform-from-above process, for it questions the government's ability to control and manage the process of change. Internal Black protest is, therefore, one of the key elements of modern South Africa.

STUDIES OF INTERNAL BLACK PROTEST SINCE 1976

Though internal Black opposition is an element, and some might say the most important element, of the complex matrix of problems which faces modern South Africa, surprisingly it is the one which has received least attention in the academic literature. There is a growing literature on the West's relationship with South Africa in the post-1976 period[145] and there are fewer, though none the less important, analyses of South Africa's economy,[146] but the number of studies on Black initiatives for change inside South Africa since 1976 is slight in comparison. This is surprising because many studies of the Soweto uprising predicted that it would have lasting effects on subsequent Black opposition.[147] Yet what studies of Black protest there are have been abstract, limited in their range, or too brief. Sam Nolutshungu's account is a theoretical exegesis which provides no empirical data on what is happening in the townships, schools, or factories.[148] Inkatha has provoked the greatest amount of literature. Southall's work on the organization is an excellent account of its role in current Black politics[149] and other writers have published work on Inkatha which reflects it importance,[150] yet Inkatha remains a peripheral organization to the extent that it is isolated from the radical Black organizations and has little support among the militant and politicized urban Black population. A broader frame is needed so that Inkatha's position can be set within the wider opposition struggle since 1976. The same criticism applies to those analyses of the Black trade union movement which have appeared, for concentrating on one element of the liberation struggle gives too limited a range.[151] A broader range is well provided by Tom Lodge, whose account of Black politics since 1945 is encompassing in its scope. Unfortunately the period since 1976 is only briefly treated in what the author admits is little more than a postscript.[152] The analysis also ignores the more spontaneous acts of resistance such as school boycotts, the community battles over rent, housing, and transport, and, most crucial of all, it does not touch upon the explosion of industrial unrest.

The study presented here attempts to provide a fuller account of African protest since 1976 covering most of the forms of resistance employed in this period. Lodge ends his postscript by saying that even 'this superficial analysis [indicates] . . . that a qualitative transformation has taken place in African political life . . . The complex combination of social forces present in Black resistance have succeeded in igniting a conflagration which no amount of repression or incorporation will succeed in extinguishing'.[153] The nature of this transformation is left unexplained. By providing an empirical account of African opposition between 1976 and 1984, this study sets out to demonstrate the validity of Lodge's closing assessment and to explain why African opposition has changed since 1976 in a direction which sustains and strengthens it.

The following chapters document how this antagonism and resistance is manifested in Black literary writings and the Black press, through revolutionary terror tactics, outbreaks of spontaneous collective protest, homeland political organizations, and urban political movements, and in the workplace. The study considers the pursuance of opposition through spontaneous and unorganized collective action such as occurs frequently in Black schools, and through such organizations as the ANC, the trade union movement, Inkatha, and Black Consciousness groupings. In the process, it also identifies the constraints operating on African opposition. There are essentially two aims behind this project. The first is to systematically outline and discuss the various forms of resistance used since 1976. This is presented in a narrative fashion and these chapters can be read independently as separate case studies in forms of resistance. The second aim is to build this description into an analysis, showing the post-1976 period to have fundamentally changed African opposition in such a way as to strengthen it. This analytical discussion is presented in the Conclusion.

The new conditions facing African opposition are the reasons why I use the term 'unfinished' in the title of this study. The aim is only to chart the 'journey' which this opposition has taken between 1976 and 1984. Precisely because the journey is unfinished, opposition will continue and may eclipse much of what is said here. Conversely, however, the outcome of this study is a better understanding of this future. It provides an analysis of some of the variables which determine the outcome of the journey—the nature of African opposition, the dilemmas facing it, the self-imposed constraints, and the nature and extent of those constraints emanating from the state. Common sense indicates that the eventual end of the journey will depend on much more than these variables. If one were concerned with the journey's end or with predicting estimated time of arrival, factors such as international economic and diplomatic pressure and the crisis of will in Afrikanerdom would have to be considered alongside internal African pressure. This study has a more limited brief, which is one of its limitations. There are others.

The arguments that follow are inherently descriptive. That is, they seek to locate the features of African opposition in the historical, social, economic, and political context existing for Africans after the uprising. Philosophers of social science teach that no description is theory-neutral. This descriptive account is infused with analytical and theoretical insight, but it does not apply one theoretical model to South African society, either Marxist or liberal-pluralist. In this sense it is open to the charge of eclecticism. The application of a theoretical model is often done in physical isolation from the society to which it is applied. The descriptive brief of this study required an extensive period of fieldwork in South Africa, and the three years spent there allow more complete immersion than would otherwise have been possible. This first-hand experience itself contains limitations: the study does not concern itself with opposition outside South Africa and ignores the liberation forces in exile and international economic and diplomatic pressure.

A final constraint on this study is the almost exclusive concentration on the African community. The term 'Black' is a racially inclusive one used to refer to Coloureds, Asians, and Africans and when the more preferable term 'Black' is used it relates to all three communities. I am concerned primarily with the African community, and in concentrating on it attention is focused on the largest of the Black communities and the one most politically and economically disadvantaged. In dealing with the African community focus is also directed onto the one that is the most politically active. It is wrong to assume that the dynamics of opposition are the same in all three Black communities, although much of what is said about African opposition will also apply to the Asian and Coloured communities.

Notes

1. I use the term 'Black' to include Indian, African, and Coloured South Africans. Where I use the term 'African' I am restricting what is said to this community alone.
2. The list of published works on this is voluminous. Some of the best are G. Gerhart, *Black Power in South Africa*, Berkeley, University of California Press, 1979; E. Feit, *African Opposition in South Africa*, Standford, Hoover Institute Press, 1967; T. Karis and G. Carter, *From Protest to Challenge*, 4 vols., Stanford, Hoover Institute Press, 1972–77; E. Roux, *Time Longer than Rope*, Madison, University of Wisconsin Press, 1966. One of the most recent volumes is T. Lodge, *Black Politics in South Africa Since 1945*, London, Longman, 1983.
3. S. Nolutshungu, *Changing South Africa*, Manchester, Manchester University Press, 1982, p. 206.
4. See B. Hirson, *Year of Fire, Year of Ash*, London, Zed Press, 1979, for a discussion of these influences. Also T. Lodge, *op. cit.*, pp. 325–6.
5. J. Saul and S. Gelb, *The Crisis in South Africa: Class Defence, Class*

Revolution, London, Monthly Review Press, 1981. One other book which earlier predicted that new revolutionary conditions were emerging in South Africa was B. Davidson, J. Slovo and A. Wilkinson, *Southern Africa: The New Politics of Revolution*, Harmondsworth, Penguin, 1976.

6. Institute of Black Research, *Soweto: A People's Response*, IBR, 1976, p. 20–1.

7. One of the ways I wanted to test this politicization was by its influence on the Africanization of first Christian names in the African communities of Johannesburg and Durban. Looking at the degree of Africanization before and after the uprising would have provided some small insight into the effects of the events on the consciousness of parents. Africanization was expected to vary with the age of the father, sex of the child, first Christian name of the father, and geographical location. The registration of new birth forms, lodged with the Department of the Interior, gave all these variables. My request to consult the forms was passed on to the Department of Co-operation and Development. Eventually Andries Treurnicht refused assistance.

8. The issues of 5 June and 7 October 1977 respectively.

9. Among others see J. Rex, *Apartheid and Social Research*, Paris, UNESCO Press, 1981, p. 14; R. Price, 'Apartheid and White Supremacy: The Meaning of Government-Led Reform in the South African Context', in R. Price and G. Rosberg, *The Apartheid Regime*, Berkeley, Institute of International Studies, 1980, pp. 310–11; A. Mafeje, 'Soweto and its Aftermath', *Review of African Political Economy*, 11, 1978, p. 17; R. First, 'After Soweto: A Response', ibid., p. 94; B. Hirson, 'Books of the 1976 Revolt', ibid., p. 101; A. Callinicos and J. Rogers, *Southern Africa After Soweto*, London, Pluto, 1977, p. 9; H. Giliomee, *The Parting of the Ways*, Cape Town, David Philip, 1983, p. xi; S. Nolutshungu, *Changing South Africa*, p. 77; J. Saul and S. Gelb, *The Crisis in South Africa*, pp. 1–20.

10. B. Hirson, 'Books of the 1976 Revolt', p. 101.

11. See S. P. Botha in the special issue on politics and trade unionism in the *South African Journal of Labour Relations*, 7, 1, 1983.

12. See J. Saul and S. Gelb, op. cit., and H. Wolpe, 'Apartheid's Deepening Crisis', *Marxism Today*, January 1983.

13. A. Callinicos and J. Rogers, *Southern Africa After Soweto*.

14. T. Lodge, op. cit., p. xiii.

15. H. Giliomee, *The Parting of the Ways*, pp. xi, 165.

16. R. Price, 'Apartheid and White Supremacy', p. 313.

17. Ibid., pp. 313–15.

18. Ibid., p. 316.
19. The best summary of the debate on economic growth and its influence on change is provided by L. Schlemmer and E. Webster, *Change, Reform and Economic Growth*, Johannesburg, Ravan Press, 1978.
20. Institute of Black Research, p. 20.
21. *Daily News*, 13 March 1980.
22. *Observer*, 25 April 1981.
23. I have discussed these changes elsewhere and shown this contradiction: 'The Concept of Political Change and the Language of Change in South Africa', *Africa Quarterly*, 21. 1, 1981; 'Racial Politics and Nationalism: The Case of South Africa', *Sociology*, 16. 3, 1982.
24. A. Guelke, 'Change in South African Politics?', *Political Studies*, 31, 1983, p. 485.
25. 'The Black Consciousness Movement and Social Research', in J. Rex, op. cit., p. 180.
26. See L. Schlemmer and D. Welsh, 'South Africa's Constitutional and Political Prospects', *Optima*, 30.4, 1982; L. Schlemmer, 'Conflict in South Africa: Build-Up to Revolution or Impasse?', European Consortium for Political Research, Freiburg, W. Germany, 20–5 March 1983.
27. See L. Schlemmer, ibid., pp. 15–16.
28. I ignore that opposition manifested through the church and religious sects, although the role of Bishop Tutu and the South African Council of Churches is briefly mentioned in Chapter 4. For a discussion of the politicization of religion in South Africa, see J. Blacking, 'Political and Musical Freedom in the Music of some Black South African Churches', in L. Holy and M. Stuchlik, *The Structure of Folk Models*, London, Academic Press, 1981; M. West, *Bishops and Prophets in a Black City*, Cape Town, David Philip, 1975.
29. For example, there is S. Nolutshungu's *Changing South Africa*; C. Hill, *Change in South Africa: Blind Alleys or New Directions*, London, Rex Collings, 1983; R. W. Johnson, *How Long Will South Africa Survive?*, London, Macmillan, 1977; H. Adam and H. Giliomee, *Ethnic Power Mobilized: Can South Africa Change?*, New Haven, Yale University Press, 1979; F. Parker, *South Africa: Lost Opportunities*, Aldershot, Gower, 1984; J. Saul and S. Gelb, *The Crisis in South Africa*; H. Wolpe, 'Apartheid's Deepening Crisis'; H. Giliomee, 'Crisis and Co-Option in South Africa', European Consortium for Political Research, Freiburg, 20–5 March 1983. Review articles reflect this. There is A. Guelke's 'Change in South African Politics?'; R. Hodder-Williams, 'Well, Will South Africa Survive?', *African Affairs*, 80, 1981; V. Belfiglio, 'How Will Majority Rule

Come About in Azania/South Africa?', *Journal of Modern African Studies*, 21.3, 1983.

30. See H. Adam and H. Giliomee, *Ethnic Power Mobilized*, and H. Giliomee, *The Parting of the Ways*, pp. 34–43.
31. H. Giliomee, *The Parting of the Ways*.
32. Ibid., p. 136.
33. For a critique of co-option see among others, H. Giliomee, 'Crisis and Co-Option in South Africa'; S. Nolutshungu, *Changing South Africa;* S. Greenberg, *Race and State in Capitalist Development*, New Haven, Yale University Press, 1980.
34. For example see F. van Zyl Slabbert, 'Sham Reform and Conflict Regulation in a Divided Society: South Africa—A Case Study', European Consortium for Political Research, Freiburg, 20–6 March 1983. Also see J. Seidman, *Face-Lift Apartheid*, London, 1980, for an equivalent term.
35. C. Hill, *Change in South Africa*.
36. *The Crisis in South Africa*, pp. 63 ff.
37. R. W. Johnson, op. cit., p. 288.
38. *Why South Africa Will Survive: A Historical Analysis*, London, Croom Helm, 1980.
39. H. Giliomee, *The Parting of the Ways*, p. x.
40. The term 'chaotic' needs to be clarified. Urbanization is chaotic to the extent that it is an unintended consequence of an intentional influx control and separate development policy. In as much as it is unintended, urbanization remains uncoordinated and unplanned.
41. Quoted by F. van Zyl Slabbert, op. cit., pp. 14–17.
42. S. Cilliers and C. Groenewald, *Urban Growth in South Africa 1936–2000*, Stellenbosch, University of Stellenbosch, 1982.
43. For an analysis of new urban forms see D. Smith, *Living Under Apartheid*, London, Allen and Unwin, 1982.
44. 'Constrained Urbanization: White South Africa and Black Africa Compared', in B. Berry, *Urbanization and Counter-Urbanization*, Beverley Hills, Sage, 1976. Also see Fair and Schmidt, 'Constrained Urbanization: A Case Study', *South African Geography Journal*, 56.2, 1974.
45. Estimated by H. Giliomee, 'Crisis and Co-Option in South Africa', p. 6.
46. F. Wilson, 'The Economics of Rising Expectations', *Race Relations News*, August 1979. Also see in this respect C. Murray, 'Ethnic Nationalism and Structural Unemployment: Refugees in the Orange Free State', *The Societies of Southern Africa in the Nineteenth and Twentieth Centuries*, 12, Institute of Commonwealth Studies, University of London; D. Goldblatt, 'The Dumping Ground', *Observer*, 8 February 1982.

47. H. Giliomee, 'Crisis and Co-Option in South Africa', p. 6.
48. Quoted by L. Schlemmer, 'Education and Change in South Africa', paper for the conference on education and consociational conflict management in plural societies, Metzeral, 25–6 March 1983, p. 6.
49. O. Dhlomo, 'View from the Homelands', *Energos*, 8, 1983.
50. *Financial Times*, 20 September 1982. Also see A. Callinicos and J. Rogers, op. cit., p. 69.
51. C. Meth, 'Recession–The Limits of Fiscal Policy', *Indicator: Economic Monitor*, 1.1, 1983, p. 15.
52. J. Saul and S. Gelb, op. cit., p. 11.
53. J. Brewer, 'The Membership of Inkatha in Kwa Mashu', *African Affairs*, 84, 1985, p. 122.
54. David Webster estimated in 1982 that unemployment was 24 per cent of the labour force. Quoted in the SAIRR, *Survey of Race Relations 1982*, Johannesburg, SAIRR, 1983, p. 73. This also quotes Jim Keenan as claiming that unemployment in 1982 was 3m., whereas the Current Population Survey data put African unemployment at only 480,000 and total unemployment at 510,000. Even this conservative figure represented an increase in total unemployment of 105 per cent from 1981.
55. Noted by T. Lodge, op. cit., pp. 326–8; L. Schlemmer, 'Urban Violence in South Africa', *New Society*, 37, September 1976; B. Hirson, *Year of Fire, Year of Ash*.
56. See J. Nattrass, 'The Proposed Constitutional Change and the Economy', *Indicator: Economic Monitor*, 1.1, 1983, p. 5.
57. See D. Piachaud, 'Attack Gold and Smash Apartheid', *Guardian*, 8 August 1984.
58. Quoted in the *South African Digest*, 4 May 1984, p. 16.
59. Quoted by L. Schlemmer, 'Education and Change in South Africa', p. 12, and H. Gilomee, 'Crisis and Co-Option in South Africa', p. 8.
60. H. Giliomee, *The Parting of the Ways*, p. 33.
61. S. Nolutshungu, 'Issues of the Afrikaner "Enlightenment"', *African Affairs*, 70, 1971, p. 23.
62. H. Adam and H. Giliomee, *Ethnic Power Mobilized*, Chapter 7.
63. See H. Wolpe, 'The "White Working Class" in South Africa', *Economy and Society*, 5.2, 1976; H. Giliomee, *The Parting of the Ways*, pp. 48–50. See also M. Lipton, *Capitalism and Apartheid*, London, Temple Smith and Gower, 1985.
64. McGrath claimed that although skill shortage is alluded to in the financial and popular press and by government spokesmen, it is merely conventional wisdom. In reality, he contends, there is little shortage: it is being used as a convenient smokescreen behind the cover of which the state can create a Black *petite bourgeoisie*. See 'Shortages of Skilled Labour Power and Capital Restructuring in

South Africa', mimeo., University of Natal, 1980, p. 22.

65. Quoted by H. Giliomee, *The Parting of the Ways*, p. 50.
66. Ibid., p. 149.
67. Thus, between 1960 and 1980 the real personal income of Whites in South Africa rose by 155.2 per cent, that of Coloureds by 246.6 per cent, that of Asians by 332.5 per cent, and that of Africans by 220.8 per cent. *South African Digest*, 13 July 1984, p. 2.
68. R. C. Davies, 'Capital Restructuring and the Modification of the Racial Division of Labour in South Africa', *Journal of Southern African Studies*, 5.2, 1979.
69. 'Social Change and the South African Economy', *Indicator*, Feb. 1983.
70. 'Economic Relations and Political Leverage', in J. Barber, J. Blumenfeld, and C. Hill, *The West and South Africa*, London, Routledge and Kegan Paul, 1982, pp. 86–7. Also see F. Wilson, 'The Political Implications for Blacks of Economic Changes Now Taking Place in Southern Africa', in C. Thompson and J. Butler, *Change in Contemporary South Africa*, Berkeley, University of California Press, 1975; F. Wilson, 'Current Labour Issues in South Africa', in R. Price and G. Rosberg, *The Apartheid Regime*.
71. Ibid., p. 87.
72. 'Structural and Cultural Factors in a Liberated South Africa', in J. Rex, *Apartheid and Social Research*, p. 194. Also see H. Adam, 'Racist Capitalism versus Capitalist Non-Racialism in South Africa', *Ethnic and Racial Studies*, 7.2, 1984.
73. Ibid., p. 194.
74. S. Nolutshungu, *Changing South Africa*, Part 2.
75. 'Conflict in South Africa: Build Up to Revolution or Impasse?', pp. 14 ff. and 'Education and Change in South Africa', p. 6.
76. T. Hanf *et al.*, *South Africa: The Prospects of Peaceful Change*, London, Rex Collings, 1981, pp. 238, 330, 332–4, 336–8, 346–9.
77. *Townsmen or Tribesmen*, London, Oxford University Press, 1963; id., 'Class, Status and Ethnicity as Perceived by Johannesburg Africans', in L. Thompson and J. Butler, op. cit.; id., 'Good and Bad Whites', paper for the conference on South Africa in the comparative study of class, race and nationalism, New York, September 1982.
78. T. Hanf, op. cit., p. 357.
79. G. Gerhart, *Black Power in South Africa*, p. 319. See also P. Walshe, *The Rise of African Nationalism in South Africa*, Berkeley, University of California Press, 1971, pp. 44–8.
80. See L. Schlemmer, 'Black Consciousness: Pride and Dignity or

Militancy and Racism', *South African Journal of Sociology*, 20, 1979; J. Blacking, 'The Power of Ideas in Social Change: The Growth of the Africanist Idea in South Africa', in D. Riches, *Queen's University Papers in Social Anthropology*, Belfast, Queen's University, 1978.

81. C. Rootes, 'Student Radicalism: Politics of Moral Protest and Legitimation Problems of the Modern Capitalist State', *Theory and Society*, 9, 1980. For an application of Habermas' work on 'educated labour' to protest in South Africa, see J. Brewer, 'Black Protest in South Africa's Crisis, *African Affairs*, 85, 1986.

82. S. Nolutshungu, *Changing South Africa*, pp. 98–9.

83. H. Giliomee, *The Parting of the Ways*, p. 51.

84. J. R. Dugard, *Independent Homelands—Failure of a Fiction*, Johannesburg, SAIRR, 1979, pp. 3–4.

85. Among the literature which discusses the relationship between the West and South Africa, see J. Barber, J. Blumenfeld, and C. Hill, op. cit.; J. Barber, *The Uneasy Relationship: Britain and South Africa*, London, Heinemann, 1983; F. Clifford Vaughan, *International Pressures and Political Change in South Africa*, Cape Town, Oxford University Press, 1978; and earlier classics like J. Spence, *The Strategic Significance of Southern Africa*, London, Royal United Services Institution, 1970; J. Spence, *Republic under Pressure: A Study of South African Foreign Policy*, London, Oxford University Press, 1965; G. Berridge, *Economic Power in Anglo-South African Diplomacy*, London, Macmillan, 1981. Also see R. Price, 'Pretoria's Southern Africa Strategy', *African Affairs*, 83, 1984.

86. J. Barber, J. Blumenfeld, and C. Hill, *The West and South Africa*, p. 3.

87. This gives the title to J. Barber's new work, *The Uneasy Relationship: Britain and South Africa*.

88. J. Barber, J. Blumenfeld, and C. Hill, op. cit., p. 35.

89. Ibid., p. 6.

90. G. Berridge, *Economic Power and Anglo-South African Diplomacy*.

91. See R. W. Johnson, *How Long Will South Africa Survive?*; id., 'Has South Africa Still a Future?', *New Society*, 8, April 1982, pp. 63–4; D. Piachaud, 'Attack Gold and Smash Apartheid', *Guardian*, 8 August 1984.

92. 'South Africa in the Contemporary World', in G. Price and R. Rosberg. op. cit., p. 295.

93. Destabilization has become a telling phrase used by S. Jenkins in a long survey in *The Economist*, 21 June 1980. Also see R. Price, 'Pretoria's Southern Africa Strategy'; S. Jenkins, 'Destabilization in Southern Africa', *The Economist*, 16 July 1983.

94. S. Nolutshungu, *South Africa in Africa*, Manchester, Manchester University Press, 1975.

95. H. Adam, *Modernizing Racial Domination*, Berkeley, University of California Press, 1971, p.121. See also H. Adam, 'Internal Constellations and Potentials for Change', In L. Thompson and J. Butler, op. cit.

96. J. Thompson, 'White Over Black in South Africa: What of the Future?', in L. Thompsom and J. Butler, op. cit., p. 400.

97. R. Price, 'Pretoria's Southern Africa Strategy'.

98. Jenkins now argues that, with the accord, Pretoria's destabilization policy is at an end for the time being. See 'Regional Stability in Southern Africa', *Optima*, 3.2, 1984.

99. See the issue of 3 June 1984.

100. 31 May 1984.

101. Op. cit., p. 317.

102. Op. cit., pp. 134 ff.

103. Quoted in the *South African Digest*, 19 November 1982, p. 9.

104. H. Adam, *Modernizing Racial Domination*.

105. R. Price, 'Apartheid and White Supremacy: The Meaning of Government-Led Reform in the South African Context', in R. Price and G. Rosberg, op. cit., p. 330.

106. 'Afrikaner Nationalism, White Politics and Political Change in South Africa', in L. Thompson and J. Butler, op. cit., pp. 3–12.

107. 'Issues of the Afrikaner "Enlightenment"' op. cit., p. 23. See also *Changing South Africa*, op. cit., pp. 75 ff. Such a view is particularly associated with the work of H. Adam and H. Giliomee. For modern restatements of this view see H. Adam, 'Ethnic Politics, Violence and Crisis Management: A Comparative Exploration', European Consortium for Political Research, Freiburg, 20–5 March 1983; id., 'Racist Capitalism Versus Capitalist Non-Racialism in South Africa'; id., 'Minority Monopoly in Transition: Recent Policy Shifts of the South African State', *Journal of Modern African Studies*, 18.4, 1980; H. Giliomee, *The Parting of the Ways*, p. xii, xvi, 48–50, 52–61.

108. H. Adam and H. Giliomee, op. cit., p. 161; D. O'Meara, 'White Trade Unionism, Political Power and Afrikaner Nationalism', *South African Labour Bulletin*, I.10, 1975; D. O'Meara, *Volkscapitalisme: Class, Capital and Ideology in the Development of Afrikaner Nationalism 1934–48*, Cambridge, Cambridge University Press, 1983.

109. G. Waters, 'South Africa's Urban Transformation: A Study in the Sociology of Urbanization', paper for the Association of Sociologists in Southern Africa, Maseru, 26–8 June 1979; D. Welsh, 'The

Growth of Cities', in M. Wilson and L. Thompson, *The Oxford History of South Africa*, Vol. 2, London, Oxford University Press, 1971. See also id., 'The Political Economy of Afrikaner Nationalism', in A. Leftwich, *South Africa: Economic Growth and Political Change*, London, Allison and Busby, 1974; S. Cilliers and C. Groenewald, *Urban Growth in South Africa 1936–2000*.

110. See H. Adam and H. Giliomee, op. cit., pp. 145–76; D. Welsh, 'The Political Economy of Afrikaner Nationalism'.

111. H. Adam and H. Giliomee, op. cit., p. 165.

112. H. Adam, 'Ethnic Politics, Violence and Crisis Management: A Comparative Exploration', p. 11.

113. T. Hanf op. cit., pp. 130, 156, 214–15, 222–3, 226–9.

114. H. Adam and H. Giliomee, op. cit., pp. 186, 192–3, 221–5.

115. H. Giliomee, *The Parting of the Ways*, pp. 15–16.

116. S. Nolutshungu, 'Issues of the Afrikaner "Enlightenment"', op. cit., p. 25, and 'The Impact of External Opposition on South African Politics', in Thompson and J. Butler, op. cit., p. 403. For his current views see *Changing South Africa*, p. 75.

117. J. Saul and S. Gelb, *The Crisis in South Africa*, p. 34.

118. H. Giliomee, *The Parting of the Ways*, p. 17–18.

119. Ibid. Johnstone's original article was 'White Prosperity and White Supremacy', *African Affairs*, 69, 1970. See also his *Race, Class and Gold*, London, Routledge and Kegan Paul, 1976. This is also a view criticized by M. Lipton, op. cit.

120. 'Class Conflict and the National Party Split', *Journal of Southern African Studies*, 10.2, 1984.

121. 'Muldergate and the Politics of Afrikaner Nationalism', *Work in Progess*, Johannesburg, 1982.

122. *Volkscapitalisme*.

123. 'Afrikaner Nationalism, White Politics and Political Change in South Africa', in L. Thompson and J. Butler, op. cit.

124. See H. Giliomee, *The Parting of the Ways*, p. 52.

125. T. Hanf, *South Africa: The Prospects of Peaceful Change*, p. 429.

126. H. Adam and H. Giliomee, op. cit., p. 219. See also H. Giliomee, *The Parting of the Ways*, pp. 34–42; Hanf, op. cit., p. 428.

127. L. Schlemmer, 'Political Change in South Africa', paper delivered at Queen's University, Belfast, 26 October 1983.

128. Quoted in H. Giliomee, *The Parting of the Ways*, p. 163.

129. *Volkscapitalisme*.

130. Quoted by H. Giliomee, *The Parting of the Ways*, p. 113.

131. L. Schlemmer, 'May By-Election Results', *Indicator: Political Monitor*, 1.1, 1983, p. 32.

132. 4 September 1984. Within two days Botha was elected State Presi-

dent unopposed. The electoral college was dominated by National Party nominees—50 to the Coloureds' 25 and Indians' 13 representatives.

133. C. Hill, *Change in South Africa*.
134. M. Lipton, 'South Africa: Authoritarian Reform?' *The World Today*, 30, 1974; H. Adam, *Modernizing Racial Domination*.
135. 'Introduction', in J. Rex, *Apartheid and Social Research* p. 22.
136. See 'Minority Monopoly in Transition' and 'Ethnic Politics, Violence and Crisis Management: A Comparative Exploration'.
137. S. Nolutshungu, *Changing South Africa*, especially Part 2.
138. H. Giliomee, *The Parting of the Ways*, pp. 147–57.
139. Ibid., p.149.
140. Professor Jan Lange, University of South Africa, quoted in D. Goldblatt, 'The Dumping Ground', *Observer*, 8 February 1982.
141. This was the view expressed at the Freiburg conference in March 1983 by Giliomee, 'Crisis and Co-Option in South Africa', F. van Zyl Slabbert, 'Sham Reform and Conflict Regulation in a Divided Society: South Africa—A Case Study', and L. Schlemmer, 'Conflict in South Africa: Build Up to Revolution or Impasse?'. Some of the papers from the conference are to be published in T. Hanf, *Deeply Divided Societies: Violence and Conflict Management in South Africa, Northern Ireland, Israel and Lebanon*, Munich and Mainz, Kaiser and Grunewald, 1986.
142. See J. Brewer, 'Black Protest in South Africa's Crisis', op. cit.
143. This was even the case for those Afrikaners who were most disposed to political change among Hanf's sample; See T. Hanf, *South Africa*, pp. 226–9. A study based on the attitudes of 3,391 South Africans from all racial groups conducted by G. Scholtz and J. Oliver for the Human Sciences Research Council in South Africa unearthed interesting data. The study, published in August 1984, showed that 50.1 per cent of all respondents expected South Africa to be totally integrated in 'the far future'. But this expectation seems not to be welcome among Whites, for, to give examples, only 26 per cent of Whites were prepared at that time to accept mixed seating in a sporting arena; more than 60 per cent favoured retaining the Immorality and Mixed Marriages Acts; 77 per cent of Afrikaners were in favour of the Group Areas Act; 64 per cent of English speakers preferred separate voters' rolls. See *South African Digest*, 24 August 1984, p. 5, 21. These findings emerged at a time when a parliamentary select committee recommended the repeal of the Immorality and Mixed Marriages Acts. *Die Vaderland* posed the obvious question of whether the government should proceed with its process of reform of the laws, but it warned against this 'under-

standable doubt', pointing to the fact that: 'anybody under 50 has virtually no knowledge of White survival without these laws. Through the years we have been so indoctrinated with the idea that White survival and retention of identity are impossible without these laws that it is hard to think of alternatives ... the government should continue with reforms in respect of these acts' (21 August 1984). The laws were repealed in 1985.

144. See particularly, L. Schlemmer, 'Conflict in South Africa: Build Up to Revolution or Impasse?', pp. 20–2. While there is an expectation that political violence will arise in the future if change is not introduced, the attitudinal support for political violence should not be over-emphasized. See Chapter 2 below, also J. Brewer and J. Smyth, 'A Comparison of Political Violence and Conflict Management in South Africa and Northern Ireland', European Consortium for Political Research, Freiburg, 20–5 Mar. 1983, reprinted in T. Hanf, *Deeply Divided Societies*.

145. In addition to the work referred to in note 85 above, see C. Legum, *The Western Crisis Over South Africa*, New York, Africana, 1979; D. G. Anglin *et al.*, *Conflict and Change in Southern Africa*, Washington, University Press of America, 1978; S. Amin, 'The Future of South Africa', *Journal of Southern African Affairs*, 2.3, 1977; P. Barker, 'South Africa's Strategic Vulnerabilities', *African Studies Review*, 20.2, 1977; A. Hero and J. Barratt, *The American People and South Africa*, Cape Town, David Philip, 1982.

146. A. Callinicos and J. Rogers, *Southern Africa After Soweto*; J. Saul and S. Gelb, *The Crisis in South Africa*; H. Wolpe, 'Apartheid's Deepening Crisis', *Marxism Today*; J. Seidman, *Face-Lift Apartheid*, London, 1980; R. Davies, 'Capital Restructuring and the Modification of the Racial Division of Labour', *Journal of Southern African Studies*, 5.2, 1979; D. Posel, 'State Ideology and Legitimation: The Contemporary South African Case', paper presented at the conference on South Africa and the comparative study of class, race, and nationalism, New York, Sept. 1982. From the other tradition of South African historiography, see H. Giliomee, 'Crisis and Co-Option in South Africa'; J. Nattrass, *The South African Economy: Its Growth and Change*, Cape Town, Oxford University Press, 1981; Centre for Applied Social Sciences, *Indicator: Economic Monitor*, University of Natal.

147. Noted by F. Molteno, 'The Uprising of 16 June', *Social Dynamics*, 5.1, 1979, p. 76, and 'South Africa 1976: A View from Within the Liberation Movement', ibid., 5.2, 1979. This view is perhaps best expressed by B. Davidson, J. Slovo, and A. Wilkinson, who argued that the whole period following 1976 would see a new politics of

revolution. See *Southern Africa: The New Politics of Revolution*.

148. *Changing South Africa*.

149. 'Buthelezi, Inkatha and the Politics of Compromise', *African Affairs*, 80, 1981, and 'Consociationalism in South Africa: The Buthelezi Commission and Beyond', *Journal of Modern African Studies*, 21, 1983.

150. L. Schlemmer, 'The Stirring Giant: Observations on the Inkatha and Other Black Political Movements in South Africa', in R. Price and G. Rosberg, op. cit.; J. Kane-Berman, 'Inkatha: The Paradox of South African Politics', *Optima*, 30, 1982; J. Brewer, 'The Modern Janus: Inkatha's Role in Black Liberation', Institute of Commonwealth Studies, *The Societies of Southern Africa in the Nineteenth and Twentieth Centuries*, 12, 1981; id., 'The Membership of Inkatha in Kwa Mashu', *African Affairs*.

151. See, for example B. du Toit, *Ukubamba Amadolo*, London, Onyx Press, 1978; D. du Toit, *Capital and Labour in South Africa: Class Struggle in the 1970s*, London, Routledge and Kegan Paul, 1981, Part 3. Also see various issues of the *South African Labour Bulletin*.

152. *Black Politics in South Africa Since 1945*, p. 321.

153. Ibid., p. 356.

1

Soweto and Collective Action

The growing literature on the events of 1976 contains disputes over the causes of the events and of the precise role played by the key forces in African opposition such as the ANC, worker militancy, and Black Consciousness organizations.[1] It is the intention of this chapter to describe the events of 1976 and similar events since. With hindsight it has been possible to locate these events and link them with others in a long history of Black resistance, and to delineate the influence of various organizations and tendencies within Black protest. Such attempts can miss the special quality which characterized the events of 1976. Their outbreak at the time took most people by surprise, for they were spontaneous, leaderless, and unexpected, circumventing the usual channels of protest and resistance. The terms 'collective behaviour' or 'collective action' have been used to describe this kind of spontaneous, direct mass protest. There is a tradition in social science called the theory of collective behaviour, which sees collective action in a pejorative sense as non-rational panics, crazes, delusions, and fads;[2] hence the resemblance between what they call collective behaviour and deviant behaviour. The theory of collective behaviour has been criticized on many accounts and these will not be repeated here. The view of collective action as abnormal and non-rational is its most important limitation.[3] Others see collective action in more positive terms as unorganized group action which is transitory but intense.[4] The term 'unorganized' is not meant in the sense of being rule-less or norm-less behaviour, but in the sense of being spontaneous and separated from formal structures. Nor is it irrational: it can contain important rational elements both in its choice as a strategy in political opposition and in the calculation of its political effects. The position taken here follows this more positive usage.

THE EVENTS OF 1976

Incidents of mass collective action do not conform to one theoretical explanation or to one descriptive stage-by-stage process because of their spontaneity, the different purposes involved, and the absence of formal structures. These are of little general use, but the diversity of the events involved in any incident of collective action does require some mechanism to organize the mass of disparate data. This is essentially done as a means to aid description of the events. Four elements can be used to help understand the incidents occurring in 1976 and after:

1. *Structural conduciveness.* This simply means that a society or a particular state of affairs holds the possibility for a given action to occur. By this is meant more than the potential for mass action being greater in densely populated areas like Soweto. It implies that South Africa had internal contradictions conducive to the collective action.

2. *Shared social image.* The internal contradictions of a society are in a dialectic relationship with the members of that society who live with them. Change is not merely a response to structural factors but often depends on how these factors are perceived. A particular set of social conditions are interpreted and this cognition comes to influence the perception of further social conditions. Therefore 'conducive' is a relative term. The interpretations of the actors themselves on what is conducive have to be taken into account. Soweto students shared a social image that apartheid was unjust which resonated with the structural conduciveness of South Africa's racially divided society.

3. *Precipitating factors.* These are invariably emotionally charged. However, they only serve to symbolize, in a more dramatic way, the structural conduciveness of society to the collective action. They do not themselves manufacture this conduciveness. In Soweto the Afrikaans language issue and the provocative role of the police on 16 June were precipitating factors.

4. *Mobilization.* This is often a function of communication between members of a social group and the persuasion that collective action is possible and desirable. Emergent leadership becomes important here, urging the masses to further concrete action. The Soweto Students' Representative Council served this role to a limited extent.

These processes will focus our descriptive analysis.[5]

Excellent chronologies of the events exist.[6] The story they tell is of a localized protest by Soweto students against the decree that they be taught half their subjects in Afrikaans, which developed into an incident of collective action that drew in the whole Black community and challenged the entire system of exploitation and oppression. The incidents in Soweto continued from 16 to 19 June and spread very quickly. By 25 June the major incidents throughout the country were over, leaving isolated sporadic outbreaks. The Minister of Police announced a death toll of 176, although a *Sunday Times* reporter estimated 376, and John Kane-Berman reached a figure of 499.[7] The leadership shown in Soweto by senior students was codified by 2 August to form the SSRC.[8] On 4 August a march into Johannesburg resulted in further deaths after police action, and this precipitated a reinvigoration of the collective action. Stay-aways were urged, asking parents and workers to boycott work. Three successful stay-aways followed, and also some clashes with hostel workers. On 1 September the major incidents in Cape Town began. By November the final call for a stay-away was unheeded, and the incidents thereafter became isolated and sporadic. Nearly one million students, workers, and parents in over two hundred Black communities had participated,[9] and the momentum had been sustained over a period of at least four months.

Structural conductiveness

It is necessary to distinguish between long-term and immediate factors. Many studies discuss the long-term factors, setting the events in a tradition of popular struggles against colonial rule in Southern Africa generally. It is not the intention to discuss these influences here, for this chapter is not an attempt to explain the causes of the uprising, only to describe its course and effects. Attention will be concentrated on some of the immediate factors which explain their particular outbreak in the townships and the specific participation of students.

Overlying these events was systematic structural exploitation. The seeds of this lie in the nature of the urban townships as the most immediate symbol of African subjugation and exploitation. Urban townships are simply dormitories for African labour with no infrastructure to fulfill their people's needs. They exist only to provide a labour pool. Technically the inhabitants live in 'White group areas' (except for townships in homelands bordering on cities in 'White areas') and the inhabitants outnumbered Whites there by four to one in 1974.[10] As demands for labour increase, the problems of these dormitories increase. Soweto, for example, built officially to house 600,000, contained 1.6m. in 1980. There were a staggering 12,500 people per square kilometre compared with only 1,400 in neighbouring White Johannesburg. By the end of the century the population density will have soared to 24,000 per square kilometre, and the pressure on housing parallels this. In 1979 there was a shortage of 33,000 houses, with only four hundred being built a year. Houses have inadequate facilities which compound the problem of overcrowding. Consistent with the poverty of their inhabitants (in 1976 43 per cent of Soweto's population were below the poverty datum line), many houses lack modern amenities like electricity, bathrooms, hot, and in some cases cold, running water. Some houses even lack ceilings to act as insulation. At the time of the 1976 disturbances urban Africans lacked the incentive for improvement which is fostered by private ownership. Following the uprising they were allowed leasehold rights on a ninety-nine year lease, although in 1985 the government acknowledged that urban Africans should have freehold rights, which it intended to introduce in 1986.[11]

Social and recreational facilities in townships are sparse. Trade is strictly limited to a number of sites owned by Whites. Industry does not exist except on the most primitive level of home-based industry. Petrol stations can be found but car repair facilities are not permitted. In fact, as a city Soweto is in a state of collapse. A group of government architects discovered that only a twelve-hour supply of water can be held in Soweto's reservoirs yet consumption increases by 17 per cent annually. This self-indictment was made worse when they also revealed that the sewage system cannot cope, thus restricting further housing development, and overflows in storms; the electricity supply is overloaded and no additional houses can be added to the 20,000 with electricity; the roads are untarred, dangerous to traffic, and inadequate to encourage the free flow of vehicles.[12] To be added to these discomforts is the insecurity inhabitants have from high African unemployment, with its consequent failure to meet township costs, resulting in a loss of residential rights and *de facto* deportation to the homeland. There is also the constant fear of police harassment through 'pass laws' and influx control.

Especially conducive for student participation in the collective action was the nature of Black education.[13] Education in South Africa has been relatively neglected, largely because the attention of critics has been directed to the more immediately arresting features of apartheid.[14] Yet education does not exist in a vacuum from its political, social, and economic context; the educational system for Blacks directly reflects a racially divided society. One of the reasons why the educational aspirations which Black parents have for their children are so high, is because their own lack of education is one of the most manifest and obvious factors associated with their own lack of privilege and status in a segregated society. Research for the Buthelezi Commission showed that 'equal education' was the most favoured resource which Black respondents felt would 'improve their life chances'.[15] It was considered more important than increases in wages, and far above the right to vote or the release of imprisoned leaders. Yet Hanf has demonstrated that the major significance of education in South Africa lies in its negative role as a focus of conflict.[16] Many of the most bitter conflicts throughout the world have centred on the issues of either access to or quality of education for the different groups in divided societies. Education in South Africa has been politicized. It is seen as a very salient issue and hence a focus of protest and even for militant mobilization. This applies particularly to those involved in the educational process who perceive the effects of the separation and under-funding of Black education. This explains the pattern over recent years of Black pupil and student unrest which points to more or less complete political alienation. It is for this reason that Brooks and Brickhill place the main emphasis of their analysis of the causes of the uprising on the education system itself.[17]

There are other reasons why the mass demonstrations were generally limited to teenagers and young adults. Mid-1976 was a time of rising unemployment, particularly for African youth. The impact of this on young people's views and expectations was probably aggravated by the fact that the rise in unemployment came after a period of economic prosperity in which Black opportunities and wages improved. Whereas the fall of the Portuguese empire in Africa, and other factors like the introduction of new homeland citizenship legislation and the increase in worker mili-

Table 3. *Black Education 1975–1976*

	African	Coloured	Indian	Whites
Teacher–pupil ratio	1 : 32	1 : 30	1 : 22	1 : 20
No. of matriculated teachers (%)	13.1	24.9	66.1	64.9
Teachers with degrees (%)	2.4	4.0	18.5	32.1
Government expenditure per pupil (R)	41.50	140.0	190.0	644.0

tancy, affected all Blacks, the primary factor which affected young Black youths was the education system itself. This certainly heightened tensions. The comparatively low expenditure on the education of Black South Africans has resulted in over-crowded and ill-equipped schools, high teacher–pupil ratios and very often poorer-qualified teachers. 'Bantu education', as it was then known, was in a state of crisis (see Table 3).

The situation has not improved much since 1976. Teacher–pupil ratios in 1983 were: White, 1 : 18.2; Asian, 1 : 23.6; Coloured, 1 : 26.7; African 1 : 42.7. In 1981 the average figure for all the homelands was 1 : 43.5. The government defends this situation in a number of ways.[18] The most fallacious is by arguing that Whites pay the taxes, which ignores the contribution Blacks make through indirect taxation, labour, and low wages. It makes great play of the fact that it spends more on Black education than any other government in Africa. However, the reference group by which Blacks judge themselves is the White group in South Africa, not the group the government is using in this argument. Total spending on African education is impressively outstripping the growth of White educational spending by 25 per cent.

By way of comparison with expenditure after the uprising, expenditure on African education in the 'White' areas in 1983–4 was R561m., while that in all the homelands was R607m. To put

Table 4. *African Education: Total Expenditure (Rm.)*

Year	1972–3	1973–4	1974–5	1975–6	1976–7
Expenditure	77.3	97.3	138.34	166.17	176.7

Table 5. *Per Capita Expenditure by Race for Selected Years (R)*

Race	1972–3	1973–4	1974–5	1975–6	1976–7	1981–2	1982–3
African*	22.5	28.5	39.5	41.5	48.5	165.23	192.34
White	343.0	387.0	605.0	644.0	654.0	1,221.0	1,385.0
Differential (%)	93.45	92.64	93.48	93.66	92.59	86.46	86.11

*Excludes 'independent' homelands.

this in perspective, Table 5 shows the leeway to be made up.[19]

The increases in expenditure on African education are impressive. The Department of Education and Training, which deals with African education, had a 1,603 per cent increase in its budget between 1972 and 1983. More pupils are being taught than ever before and since 1976 the number of African high schools has increased by 560 per cent.[20] In February 1984 the Department of Education and Training announced its intention to spend R18.25m. on classrooms in Soweto alone. But the gap to be made up is enormous and Black education generally remains considerably underfunded compared to White education.

These facts have bequeathed to African education, and Black education generally, many problems. Some are administrative, with African education being the responsibility of the homeland government in rural areas and the central government in urban townships. Shortage of space is chronic. At the beginning of the 1978 academic year, 3,000 African schoolchildren in Durban were unable to enrol in schools due to overcrowding. The same situation was repeated the following year. In Soweto at the beginning of 1979, there were on average sixty-five children per classroom and thousands were still turned away. The shortage of teachers compounds the shortage of space and, to the detriment of education standards, classes are platooned or merged in an attempt to cope. Double sessions (the same teacher for two classes per day) and the platoon system (two teachers for two classes but in the same room) affect a large number of African children. Between 1980 and 1982 1,086,462 African schoolchildren were involved in double sessions, and 214,049 in the platoon system.

This situation has a number of consequences which build upon one another to have ramifications for collective action in South Africa. Supply and demand are far out of equation and the consequence is that those who decide who may enter school have enormous informal power. In the Kwa Zulu homeland this has led to a measure of corruption. Allegations made in the press and vindicated by Oscar Dhlomo, Kwa Zulu Minister of Education, reported that some principals and members of school councils in rural areas accepted bribes from pupils desperate to be admitted to school. Similarly, children born in areas where there are no secondary schools are resorting to bribes in order to complete their schooling in other areas. Certain principals were buying books wholesale and selling them to their pupils at highly inflated retail prices and insisting they purchase the book before being allowed to enrol.[21] The authorities in some areas resort to an equally illegitimate mechanism to equate demand and supply, by delaying marking year-end examination results and insisting that pupils are not allowed to proceed to the following year without them. This is known to have happened in Natal for the 1979 and 1980 academic years, and is suspected to have occurred for a longer time in other areas where overcrowding is more intense.[22] This gives the lie to any claim of universal education for Africans. A year before the Soweto uprising, the Minister of Bantu Education, as he was then known, revealed that a quarter of the African school-going population failed to receive any education.[23]

The cumulative result is that it takes longer for Africans to complete their education. In 1975, the median age of African schoolchildren in Form V, the last year at school, was 19.31 compared with 17.43 for Whites.[24] As a direct consequence of its education system for subordinate racial groups, the government is producing a student body more mature in age, experience, and emotion than is normal. This is also a result of beginning African schooling at seven years of age, a year later than for Whites. Africans can be in early middle age before they have completed a decade in employment, and the 'young generation' takes on a different meaning from the one it bears in Western societies, where from an early age the young are financially able to constitute themselves as a distinct market and where their secondary education is completed in their middle teens. The social category of 'youth' for Africans in South Africa has extended barriers at the top end.[25]

The implications of this are profound. Any collective action appealing to the younger, more militant generation can call upon a larger social category than normal and any school-based protest involves those relatively more mature and experienced than is usual.[26] In an attempt to alleviate the consequences of this, the Department of Education and Training gazetted a new regulation in 1981 laying down age limits of sixteen years for African pupils in Standard 5, eighteen years in Standard 8 and twenty years in Standard 10. The social conditions affecting the lives of many pupils result in many having to skip a year or two to work in order to support their families and to raise enough money to return to school. Consequently, it is difficult for many African pupils to matriculate. COSAS feared that the regulation would be used to bar students on political grounds. It is difficult to know how many students have been barred, but in 1982 COSAS estimated that 980 students had been refused admittance on age grounds in the Port Elizabeth area alone. In 1983, the Department of Education and Training announced that only 63 students had been refused admission on age grounds in Soweto during the year. However, at the beginning of the year the department sent a directive to schools that pupils over the age of twenty-one and who had failed matriculation would not be allowed to repeat. The same strictures applied to Junior Certificate students over the age of eighteen. This directive affected thousands of students who had failed their examinations at the end of 1982, and was one of the factors behind the student unrest in 1983. This attempt to depoliticize education failed miserably, as we shall see below.

These are some of the factors that were conducive to the Soweto uprising. The government did not hold them as the cause: to have done so would be having to recognize the rot in the social order it upheld. Only weeks before, Manie Mulder, Chairman of the West Rand Administration Board remarked that the people of Soweto were 'perfectly happy'.[27] Lack of foresight by administrators was one of the condemnations the Cillié Commission made. The Commission's report recognized 'certain injustices' due to influx control and the Group Areas Act, which were 'secondary causes'. But after four years of deliberation, the primary cause it found was intimidation by agitators urging participants to mindless acts of violence and arson. In other words, the incident was presented as a purely transitory, unpredictable, essentially non-rational, and apolitical occurrence unconnected with the activities of the state. This is a theme which recurs many times, and the Cillié Commission only adumbrated interpretations at the time. Rather than education itself, the Regional Director of African Education in Northern Transvaal, F. J. Wiese, laid the blame with obstreperous African teachers: 'Most of them are lazy and are not capable of teaching the syllabus . . . The problem is that the standard of teaching is low and the onus lies on the teachers.'[28] In a BBC interview, reported in the *Rand Daily Mail*, the Minister of Police reassured listeners that the fundamental insecurity of Africans was not the cause. Elsewhere he confirmed that agitators were responsible, and identified them with the Black Power Movement.[29]

This type of interpretation inpugns the motives of participants.

It is elaborated by Robert Hitchcock in *Flashpoint South Africa*, where the theory of collective behaviour is utilized to portray the events as riotous crowd behaviour.[30] Like the psychological writers on the crowd such as Le Bon, Tarde, and Sighele, Hitchcock directs attention away from societal conditions to the participants, who are characterized as either misguided, politically subversive, criminal, or destructive. This bias excludes the possibility that 'riots' can be political or purposeful. To some extent, however, Hitchcock is forced to concede a minimum of political content when he attributes the riots to communist agitators—half suggesting that Africans themselves are incapable of initiating rational resistance.

Shared social image

Whatever structural factors were involved, they were given their effect by the shared image of the participants. In fact, participants were making a serious political challenge. A sample of Africans in Durban saw the incident as a rational demonstration, a calculated means to an end. Only 14 per cent expected the government to be 'unmoved' and merely 3 per cent saw it as an 'irrational act of barbarism'.[31] As for the participants themselves, the seriousness of their political challenge is evident in their shared social image that apartheid was, and is, unjust. One sees the operation of this image, for example, in the choice of targets. The destruction—for destruction there was—was not mindless and indiscriminate. Logic was applied in the selection of targets that symbolized apartheid—either in the sense of the political withdrawal of parents, such as the shebeens, or as agents of oppression, like the buildings, offices, and vehicles of the Bantu Administration Boards and the Urban Bantu Councils, police vehicles, post offices, magistrate courts, the houses of Black policemen, and, of course, schools. The first recognized leader of the SSRC, Tsietsi Mashinini, provided testimony to this. The participants had had enough not only of oppression in schools 'but in the system of the country, the way laws are made by a White minority'.[32] This rational shared image is also seen working in the positive contribution participants made to improving their local communities. They undertook a campaign against drinking which resulted in a marked drop in the crime rate, and initiated primitive urban renewal schemes like cleaning up the litter in Soweto. Grocery parcels were distributed to some needy families and help was offered to others who could not meet their rent.[33]

Students had a shared social image which challenged the wider context within which education in South Africa exists. Further evidence of this is shown by the demands that emerged from participants in the course of events, and by the SSRC's attempt to draw in workers and parents. The stay-away call for 13–15 September objected to wage cuts. However despite extending beyond education, the demands remained unspecific and generalized. In reality there was little to mobilize workers on. The success of the first three boycotts was therefore all the more remarkable. Workers were mobilized as a racial category, not on either class or economic issues, but as 'Black Mums and Dads'. On urging a fourth stay-away from 1–5 November, the SSRC called upon the government to resign, to release detainees, and to free Blacks from the 'shackles of the oppressor'. A leaflet issued with the fourth boycott addressed itself to 'Black fathers and mothers, brothers and sisters', and urged solidarity with those who died. The dead were portrayed as fallen 'Black sons and daughters' in the 'Black struggle', not as colleagues in a proletarian class struggle. Fisher has shown how workers did not identify with Black Consciousness[34] and this is one of the reasons why worker support was always variable and dwindled towards November. Mobilizing in terms of a contrived Black ethnicity met with little sustained success. Webster offers further reasons: for example, employers took the stand that participating in the stay-aways would jeopardize workers' employment. Coinciding with Black unemployment, this tougher attitude made workers reluctant to continue their participation, although not to lend sympathy. Some workers had already been dismissed and in particular, migrant workers feared deportation to the rural areas.[35] It is significant that on 1 November when the Cape Town and Johannesburg stay-aways failed, there was almost 100 per cent boycott of examinations in the Transvaal and Cape Province. The precise relationship between workers and students in the liberation struggle has since become a source of debate among Marxists.[36] In this way it is possible to draw a parallel between the students of 1976 in South Africa, and the campus protests in Europe and America during the 1960s. What began as a focus on educational problems widened to social, economic, political, and community issues. Nevertheless, history did not repeat itself. The students of 1968 rejected the material acquisitive goals which were their parents' vicarious fulfilment. The opposite occurred in South Africa eight years later. Here students shared a social image whch made them fight to remove racial blocks to their unequal participation in, and enjoyment of, the material benefits of society.

Precipitating factors

With startling clarity, the epitaph on the gravestone of one of Soweto's dead illustrates the importance of initial triggers: 'The blood, the tears of a Black man. It will make the struggle vivid.' The Afrikaans language issue was insufficient on its own to act as this precipitation. The Cillié Commission and the South African Institute of Race Relations document the discontent on this issue which spread from as early as February. Sporadic incidents of collective protest had erupted but every time the police persuaded students either to return to school or to disperse peacefully. The morning of 16 June was different for two reasons. The size of the protest had grown from a few hundred to ten thousand. This huge march converged on Soweto's Orlando West Junior Secondary School, where the strikes had first started, and was met by a handful of police. The major precipitating factor was the provocative action the massively-outnumbered police took—leaving a young African dead and thousands smarting from tear gas. The children retaliated and the participants swelled in number to 30,000 within a few hours. Had the police not opened fire the students might have dispersed after their meeting. Hector Peterson's death transformed the situation. On the 4 August when a similar march occurred and deaths resulted, it precipitated an escalation of the collective protest; when the students marched into Johannesburg on 23 September there was no tear gas and no shooting and the students remained orderly.

The chronology of events on the morning of 16 June tends to be confusing, receiving different accounts. Many of the eyewitnesses said the conflict began when the police seized placards and tried to stop the march. The students taunted them and the police responded with tear gas. Some reports told of stones being thrown and the shooting then beginning, while others said the police opened fire before stones were thrown. This is a debate of little importance: it is only important if the actions of that day are seen as the cause of the conflict. In reality, the students and police were in a conflict not of their own making originating long before whatever events took place. Something entirely different could have ignited the spark, for its causes lay outside the immediate participants and events. The Cillié Commission, on the other hand, accepted the police views of events—that agitators were responsible for provoking the crowd, stones were thrown, warning shots were fired, and, fearing for their lives, the police fired on those inciting the crowd. Caveats exist in this interpretation. A senior police officer at the time admitted no warning shots were fired.[37] While the police claimed the first death was of an African who had been taunting them, pathologists' evidence showed he was shot in the back, obviously not in an aggressive stance facing the firer. If he was killed by a bullet meant for another, it seems to indicate that the firer taking aim did not do so with care or deliberation. School principals complained the police were firing indiscriminately. On 19 June *The Star* published an astonishing photograph of a fleeing person about to be shot in the back. In one sense this debate also matters little: what was important for future events was that this is how Africans defined the situation.[38] Whatever the true picture, participants perceived the police firing in panic and, in fact, pathologists' evidence and press reports vindicate this view.[39] This is in sharp contrast to the police evidence believed by the Cillié Commission. Credulously, its report ran: 'After considering all the evidence, the Commission cannot accept that the police used firearms when everything was still quiet and calm.'[40] This judgement should not be seen merely in terms of the political interest of the Commission that made it. Only fifteen Blacks under the age of eighteen were among the 503 people who testified. By far the largest group of witnesses were policemen.

The attitudes of the police therefore bear consideration. Brigadier Visser, Divisional Commander of Police in Soweto spoke of the incident: 'Naturally', he said, 'force had to be met with force.' Implicit in this is the view that students were intimidated into making a forceful protest they would not otherwise have made: 'suddenly this erupted among a minority who took control and the community was scared either to oppose them or stop them.'[41] This restates the conventional view of participants held by the government. They were a senseless, suggestible mob; and a mob is by nature uncontrollable, unpredictable, and irrational.

This view of the participants is at the root of police actions in the event. Lieutenant-General Venter, Chief Deputy Commissioner for the South African Police, clearly justified the response of his men by perceiving participants in this fashion. 'If we don't do anything the rioters will run amok burning, looting, killing and injuring innocent people.'[42] This view was supported the following day by the Minister of Police. Rubber bullets, he said, make the mob 'tame to the gun'.[43] The implication is clear: participants were a mob and therefore, as the only means to control them, Soweto students had to feel the cut of live ammunition. There is a deep irony to this. *Die Transvaler* once ridiculed 'African democracy' for its alleged intimidatory tactics and glorification of violence.[44] The police response in 1976 presents a picture of a government claiming a firmer allegiance to democracy, using violence to restrict democracy and to deny the rights of Blacks.

Mobilization

Arising from the first deaths was a spontaneous eruption of opposition—as spontaneous as any act can be in the context of the conscious resistance of people to a long history of oppression. It was spontaneous in the sense that the series of events were *ad hoc* responses to given circumstances rather than components of a premeditated strategy. In view of the number of participants arrested, interrogated, and charged, and with regard to the allegations made, it is significant to note that the Commissioner of Police, General Prinsloo, after 'intensive police investigation' found no evidence of conspiracy.[45]

As news of the events spread through the confines of Soweto, rapid mobilization increased the number of participants and spread the area of disruption. Thirty thousand people were amassed in Soweto by mid-morning and within twenty-four hours clashes with police and attacks on symbolic targets had occurred at Tembisa, Kagiso, Alexandra, Vosloorus, Katlehong, Mohlakeng, and the African universities at Turfloop and Ngoya. Eventually it was to envelop much of the Transvaal, Cape Province, and Natal. Initially mobilization was affected by what Blumer called contagion, and needed little stimulus from older students. The speed of the chain reaction in other townships virtually rules out the possibility of organization on any significant scale. It took nearly two months for the SSRC to emerge and with it came the decision to mobilize workers and parents. Following on this, Student Representative Councils were formed in Katlehong, Mamelodi, Atteridgeville, Sibasa, Seshego, and Port Elizabeth—and probably in other places too. None of these bodies achieved the degree of influence or sustained activity of the Soweto Council, nor is there any evidence of co-operation between them. The SSRC was the most developed and it remained an amorphous, unformalized body. For one thing, it was in a constant state of flux due to police harassment and imprisonment of supporters. It never constituted itself as a formal organization with decision-making structures, rules of procedure for the slection of membership, leadership, and so on. The role organization did play was to politicize many Representative Council members through their participation in organized politics with the South African Students Movement—a junior division of the South African Students Organization which formed part of the Black Consciousness movement, although those writers who wish to deny any role for Black Consciousness emphasize that the SASM was independent of Black Consciousness and linked to the ANC.[46] Black Consciousness did play a supportive role to the SSRC, especially through the Black Parents' Association, Black People's Convention, Black Priests' Solidarity Group, and SASO. Many attempted to channel the expression of anger by students through their own organization, especially the BPC, and all failed to do so initially. The reason for this is that while these organizations had a supportive role with the SSRC, the latter's leadership was far from complete. Support for it among workers and parents was variable, it was only slightly less so among students—even in Soweto.

A number of examples illustrate the point. The SSRC supported peaceful collective protest in all its leaflets but could not prevent more militant students from resorting to violence, and to arson and vandalism in schools, in an attempt to keep school children on the streets and active. These militant groups issued their own directives urging their 'countrymen not to retreat'. This slogan made reference to the major issue which divided students—whether or not to boycott examinations. It is significant that these internal schisms coincided with the dwindling of worker support—students turned inward and found division. The SSRC denounced the planned boycott. There was, never the less, a widespread boyott, refuting the claim by Khotso Seathlolo the new president of the

SSRC, that it was a shadow government in Soweto[47] When the schools reopened in January 1977 and the boycotted examinations were timetabled for February, the SSRC did then support a boycott. By this time student opinion had changed against such action. Showing an independent spirit, pupils at Naledi High School in Soweto said 'we would like to remind the SSRC that its duty is not to frustrate and dictate terms to students'.[48] Students at Musi High School and Diepkloof High School issued statements calling for the SSRC to change its decision. Modibane High School in Soweto supported the SSRC as did a statement issued in the name of 'African scholars of Cape Town'.[49] In spite of the SSRC's ban, the boycott of examinations was largely a failure. At the same time, there was a large enough minority in favour of it for crowds running into several thousand to demonstrate, and burn school-books and examination papers. Sometimes the protesters would be stoned by students wishing to continue their work.

COLLECTIVE ACTION SINCE 1976

The factors which made the 1976 collective behaviour so success-ful are the explanation for its relative demise since the uprising. By its nature collective action ebbs and flows, being intense one moment and then subsiding, and spontaneous collective action since 1976 has oscillated in this way. What made 1976 so success-ful was the emotion-charged precipitation and the quick mobiliza-tion which circumstances allowed. While incidents in 1980 and 1983–5 have been as intense as those in 1976, some incidents since have not had the effect of the Soweto uprising. As long as the structural conduciveness of South African society to collective protest remains constant, and the shared image of apartheid as evil still exists, collective action has the potential to become as intense as the 1976 incident. This has been the case on two occasions but elsewhere the incidents have lacked sufficient precipitation and failed to mobilize support outside the epicentre of the event and its immediate participants.

The reasons for this are legion. Many African students recog-nized the passport to future mobility that paper qualifications provide even for Africans. Principals and parents were also able to capture some of the initiative they had temporarily lost. They did so by identifying themselves with the student cause in the hope of then being able to direct it through organizational forms. In 1977 for example, the Parents' Committee in Port Elizabeth's New Brighton township took over care for detained students and organized grocery parcels, defence lawyers, and so on. The Teachers' Action Committee in Soweto urged its members to resign *en bloc* and seven hundred did so in forty Soweto post-primary schools. The Committee took up the students' case under the directorship of Curtis Nkondo, subsequently active in the Azanian People's Organization and detained during the April 1980 Coloured students' boycott. *The World* and *Ilanga* opposed school boycotts and criticized the SSRC. The newly formed Soweto Committee of 10 under Dr Motlana sought to mediate between the students and the authorities with the intention of getting students back to school. The students' elders, normally the African community's natural leaders, sought to express student opposition through themselves: having made their point, participants were urged to rely on more conventional modes of protest.[50]

Shackles were, therefore, being imposed on students from within the African community as well as from outside it. The government, through its ability to stifle opposition, was able to pressure parents to control their children. WRAB gave parents a simple choice—either be deported to their homeland with their rebellious children or to stay in Soweto without them.[51] Parents were also required to pay a 'riot deposit' which was forfeited upon their children being involved in any protest. Pressure was placed on students too. The SSRC was banned in 1977. Additionally, the Regional Director of Education demanded that pupils sign a 'contract' indicating their acceptance of school rules before they could continue their education,[52] and the government withdrew its subsidies to schools where unrest occurred.

A tough response was one of the government's measures. Yet paradoxically, the government demonstrated that it had partly learned the lessons of 1976. The police began to take a low profile in some incidents as well as attempting to lessen fatalities by using rubber bullets and bird shot. This process is evolutionary and the police response, like the incidents of collective action themselves, tends to oscillate between caution and repression. Many deaths occurred in 1977 but the incidents in 1980 showed some transformation in police action in the direction of caution; 1984–5 demonstrated a transformation in the other direction.

The decline in the frequency and scope in the incidents of collective protest after 1976 was a slow process. 1977 was a year of continued unrest. The SSRC was particularly active in organizing protest marches, propaganda campaigns, and general opposition to proposed rent increases in Soweto. The rent increases were postponed but not stopped. It was clear that the police had decided to adopt different tactics as, instead of attempting to halt demonstrations, they gave their permission for them. 'We are here to keep the peace,' one police officer was quoted as saying, 'we are not murderers.' The number of deaths in 1977 suggest that though this may have been a policy it was not yet a practice. It had not filtered outside Soweto. In Uitenhage seven were left dead and thirty-three wounded after police intervened in protest marches in June 1977.

Schools were a constant focus of discontent throughout the year. In Soweto alone, 27,000 students in forty state schools boycotted classes. Only three thousand signed to re-register at the start of the new school year. For the first time primary schools were affected. Violent incidents occurred: for example, police fired several shots when about six hundred students held a protest demonstration outside Orlando High School on 10 June, and stones were hurled in retaliation. However there were fewer clashes with the police. The worst scenes of violence came with the anniversary of the 1976 uprising. Commemoration services were held throughout the country. In Soweto's Regina Mundi church, a service attended by 7,000 people ended in chaos when, unprovoked, the police fired tear gas into the church. Whatever peace may have been ordered was tenuous. Nine Soweto people were shot at street barricades. The taint of tear gas hung over the township once more, and allegations of its indiscriminate use were printed by the *Sunday Tribune*.[53] The Regina Mundi service seems to validate this suspicion. A one-day stay-away was called, and met with limited success. A large demonstration was held in Johannesburg's John Vorster Square; the students outwitted police by dressing as workers while travelling into Johannesburg. Similar incidents were repeated elsewhere. Eight died at New Kabah and KwaNobuhle townships and twenty-three were wounded; schools were set alight in Queenstown and Daveyton.

In other words, the serious incidents measured in either deaths, damage or the number of participants, occurred when precipitating factors were sufficiently emotive—the 16 June anniversary and examination boycotts—and when the police responded with aggressive action. Only the examination boycott was sustained—all others lacked effective mobilization. The consequence of this was that participants came to be restricted mainly to school children, and Black education was the focus of protest: in October 1977 there were 196,000 students either boycotting classes or affected by closed schools.

The Port Elizabeth disturbances were also fuelled by Steve Biko's death and funeral (this was his native area). Only at the time of his funeral in King William's Town, in September 1977, did the collective action mobilize non-students and spread beyond education. Three died in Mdantsane and Dimbaza near King William's Town, two of them Black policemen killed at the hand of students when they tried to arrest mourners alighting from a bus. The following day a seventeen-year-old student was killed, and arson gutted schools in the area. By January 1978, every classroom in New Brighton, KwaZakhele, and Zwide was empty. The memory of Biko's death and the revelations which emerged at the inquest precipitated similar incidents. Surprisingly, in Soweto the schools opened in 1978 with attendance high, and it remained so until the 1984 incidents. A call for a boycott in February 1980 by AZASO and COSAS was unheeded. The explanation for this does not lie in any departure from Soweto's militancy but actually reaffirms it: because it had been the centre of student opposition it met with stringent police action, leaving older student leaders in prison or exile. Although this left Soweto schools three-quarters full, their complement of students was below half what it had been two years before.

In 1978 the anniversary of the uprising was quieter. The SSRC was now banned and the Soweto Students' League, formed to replace it, was of less independent spirit. The Soweto Action Committee, the Black Parents' Association and the Committee of 10—all formed to give organizational expression to student anger—had better relationships with the League. These bodies organized the anniversary and took the platform at Regina Mundi, not the students. There were no shootings, little tear gas and the church was not desecrated. Reverting to a conventional police role as peace-keepers was now the practice, but this was not the only transformation in police action. In the incidents of 1976 and 1977, police action was an impromptu response to given events, often precipitating further events to which they had immediately to respond. The Cillié Commission and the Minister of Police testified to the lack of police planning on 16 June 1976. The events shook Whites out of self-confident complacency. As a result, a new kind of strategy emerged within the police force. By prior preparation in 1978 they sought to control the initial events which could lead to any precipitation on their part. Their strategy was two-pronged—to avoid precipitation by channelling the initial events, and to take a low profile in them. Obviously their success in achieving the latter was a product of their success in doing the former. On the second anniversary of 16 June, the police were successful in channelling the events with their battery of emergency regulations controlling demonstrations, gatherings, and meetings, and, especially, culling from the community, permanently or temporarily, all potential student leaders. Through sweep and search tactics for two weeks prior to the anniversary, the police arrested up to three thousand Blacks in urban townships throughout South Africa. Emergent leadership, through which effective mobilization is conducted, was removed. Such a strategy has it weaknesses. Leaving aside the question of the ethics of totalitarian control, it depends upon the patience of policemen when faced with a vocal Black crowd. Nor does it work for spontaneous events which take the police by surprise. This is one of the reasons why the number of deaths during mass demonstrations oscillates, and has been high during the 1983–5 incidents.

The impression is fostered in the White press that the incidents of collective action which occur are motivated by mindless violence. This impression is one of their own making as they carry reports only of those incidents where violence erupts. The Black press is much less discriminating in its reporting. More incidents, and more peaceful incidents, have occurred than the White press suggests. For example, prior to 1980, collective action occurred on many occasions. In Eldorado Park Blacks picketed a White shop after a dispute over change. The police were called, and, losing patience, pointed guns at the pickets and so caused a fracas.[54] Collective protest was provoked by the hanging of Solomon Mahlangu on terrorism charges,[55] the appointment of certain school principals,[56] and by the government's policy of supplying free copies of South African Defence Force journals and pro-National

Party newspapers to schools.[57] These incidents are indicative that it only takes a simple, often small spark, to ignite collective action. Yet, in all cases, the precipitation was insufficient for further mobilization and remained confined to the immediate vicinity and participants. They did, however, have a cumulative effect which showed itself in 1980.

One of the largest incidents, in terms of both numbers participating and geographical spread, was the April 1980 boycott by Coloured students protesting against inferior education. Apart from studies at the University of Natal Medical School, and a few schools in Mamelodi, Kwa Mashu and Atteridgeville, African students did not join the boycott; Coloured students were among the first to join with Soweto students in 1976. In April 1980, Indian students joined their Coloured colleagues but Soweto students remained in class. This could be explained by a variety of reasons. No spontaneous eruption occurred and it is virtually impossible for other race groups to mobilize support in African township schools and even more so in rural areas. Moreover bad as it is *vis-à-vis* White education, Coloured education is far superior to that available to Africans. Perhaps there is also less of a common ethnic consciousness between Africans and Coloureds than Black Consciousness thinks. Maybe the answer lies also with those internal and external constraints on the African community discussed above.

African participation being what it was, the size of the boycott is all the more impressive. On the first day of the boycott, 21 April, 100,000 students at seventy schools on the Witwatersrand and in the Cape were boycotting. The following day all Coloured schools on the Reef and Pretoria joined—Natal had 11,000 Coloured and Indian pupils boycotting classes. In total, over 190,000 students made their protest, which enjoyed the support of some parents and teachers. There was little attempt to link up with workers or to transcend the issue of Coloured education, although in Cape Town students did link up with workers in the meat industry strike. This also occurred to a partial extent in Natal with its large Indian population. The students at the Indian University of Durban Westville combined the boycott with the Release Nelson Mandela Campaign. The numbers participating were immense.

Faced with this human swell, the actions of the police were cautionary. Up to the final day of the boycott, 1 May, there were only a few incidents of baton charging and tear gas being thrown; there was no shooting. It was not until the ninth day of the boycott that police made arrests and then only under the Riotous Assemblies Act, not the more rigorous terrorist laws. Demonstrations occurred every day in Durban, the Transvaal, and the Cape, and the police took to shepherding students while they marched and leaving them to make their protest speeches. Perhaps this is another explanation for the failure of African students to participate: the wounds of Soweto were not reopened by provocative police action. However, the response of the police in the 1980 incidents did have disturbing features. One possible explanation of their relaxed response exists which has its root in the racial prejudice of the police. It was significant that the police reserved their most vigorous action for African schoolchildren, and most of the tear gas and baton charging occurred at African schools. In Kwa Mashu, for example, police responded very vigorously at the one school where unrest occurred. The motivation behind this could be an unwillingness to see the collective action spread. Conversely, the hold on police patience could be more precarious when faced with African participants.

When schools reopened in January 1981 boycotts were being continued only in Cape Town. The Port Elizabeth Students' Committee was in favour of continuing the boycott until local students who had been detained in November were released and an equal education system introduced. COSAS considered that the boycott should end. The twenty-one students were released in February, and the students' committee disbanded, and the boycotts gradually petered out. Collective action was once again at a low ebb. One interesting incident occurred: Dr Koornhof addressed a lunchtime meeting at the University of Witwatersrand in March which was disrupted by 300 Black students on campus. The disruption of the speech marked a new development, for it saw the emergence of a well-organized, articulate, and powerful group of Black students on a White campus. They organized themselves into the Black Students' Society, and similar societies exist on other White university campuses. On 29 April the general election became a focus of student protest against apartheid, and in the period during the celebrations to mark the twentieth anniversary of the Republic of South Africa, student groups, among others, organized widespread campaigns of protest. There were further demonstrations in June to commemorate the uprising of 16 June 1976. In these ways students linked up with other groups and demonstrated on other issues than education.

The government's response was to make threats that students would forfeit the right to write examinations, lose study aids and grants scheduled for their schools, lose bursaries, be suspended or expelled. Threats were backed up by aggressive police action. As a result of the detention of a colleague, students staged a protest in the townships near Johannesburg which was violently opposed by the police with dogs, sneeze machines, batons, and tear gas. The authorities employed the police and army to search homes and forty children, some as young as seven and nine, were briefly detained. A massive stay-away followed in the local schools.

Constraints were also being applied from within the African community as adult organizations tried to channel the anger and protest of the young. For example, Bishop Tutu urged in 1980 that the government should negotiate with authentic representatives of affected communities, such as parents' committees. Indeed, there seems to have been a close relationship between the students and the many parents' committees which were themselves linked to a variety of political organizations in the townships. In 1982 it was the Port Elizabeth Parents' Action Committtee which negotiated on behalf of students at the University of Fort Hare when 500 students demonstrated against Chief Lennox Sebe and many were detained. None the less, student organizations were the subject of considerable harassment during 1982: of the total of those detained and whose occupation is known, 60 per cent were students, trade unionists and workers amounted to 15 per cent and constituted the second largest category, and only 9 per cent were political and community leaders. This is indicative of where the state saw the greatest threat to law and order arising. Yet despite this, school boycotts and unrest in 1982 were generally sporadic and concerned issues peculiar to the schools and areas where they occurred.[58]

After two years of relative calm, conflict in Black educational institutions increased in 1983 with boycotts affecting 10,000 pupils. Many grievances concerned particular local issues, among them opposition to certain teachers or headmasters, lack of communication between teachers and pupils, the transfer of teachers, lack of facilities, and dissatisfaction with the education and examination system. However, education protests also occurred in response to specific political circumstances, including the constitutional referendum and the repression of the transport boycott in the Ciskei. In September, the Director General of the Department of Education and Training warned that the continued unrest would result in stricter controls being applied. A number of Soweto schools formed a 'Committee of Concern' which gave the considered response of the students to the threat and negotiated on their behalf. It was through the Committee that the students advanced their demands for autonomous student representative councils, the re-opening of schools that had been closed, the unconditional readmission of students, and an end to police interference. In this way students were widening the organizational and issue base of their protests. Pule Monama, National Organizer of the Azanian Students' Movement, said school problems should not be seen in isolation from the political struggle or pursued without reference to wider organizations. This is not a surprising claim for Monama to make given the association between his organization and AZAPO, but the spontaneous and sporadic outbreaks of collective action which occurred in 1983 seemed to have followed this advice.

What is also significant was the extent to which students were aware that direct collective action was a useful strategy for pursuing even petty grievances; and the triviality of some of their grievances showed how sensitive and volatile the student body had become. For example, in February students boycotted classes to protest about Soweto teachers and an unpopular headmaster. In Huhudi pupils protested about what they described as 'problems between teachers and the student body'. The transfer of popular teachers was also an occasion for public demonstration and protest. But many issues were serious. The age limit and the readmission problem caused considerable unrest, as did the related problem of the pass rate. As higher standards are being applied with the increase in the number of African matriculation candidates, the pass rate has fallen. In 1979 73 per cent of African Standard 10 candidates passed and 28 per cent obtained an exemption; by 1983 the respective figures were 53.5 per cent and 12.8 per cent. Despite being a slight improvement on 1982, a great deal of unrest followed. If the attempts to raise standards continues to affect the pass rate, anxiety and the subsequent frustration will have serious consequences for stability among senior African pupils. Already anxiety over examinations has fuelled unrest. In June 1983 police were called to quell a crowd after four pupils were expelled from a Soweto school for cheating in examinations. The following day the four returned to school and stabbed the headmaster. After this other pupils cut the school's telephone lines, threw stones, damaged cars, and broke windows. Eight policemen were injured and tear gas was used.

Two points are striking about these educational protests. The first is the growing organizational maturity of the students as they themselves attempt to harness the force of the crowd through organizational and institutional forms. Often the parents attempt to do this through parents' support committees, but so do the students. During 1983 there emerged the Azanian Students' Movement and the Port Elizabeth Youth Congress, and the Candidates Crisis Committee was formed to investigate the possibility of legal action against the Department of Education and Training over the examination results. The earlier Committee of 61 and Port Elizabeth Students' Committee are examples of how the 1980 student boycott was channelled through organizational forms.

The second point to note is the link which students forged with other organizations to harness their own protest to wider concerns. The conflict surrounding the boycotting of buses in Mdantsane in the Ciskei, which began in July 1983, spread to schools in and around the Ciskei. On 4 August Ciskeian police fired at commuters trying to board trains, killed five and injured at least forty-five people. Immediately 1,000 pupils boycotted classes in one Mdantsane school and within three days boycotts affected half the student population in the township. During the course of the transport boycott, several schools were damaged by fire. COSAS linked up with the organizations involved in the transport boycott, who in turn formed the Detainees' Parent Support Group to work on behalf of the students.

It had been obvious to the state for some time that it needed to depoliticize education. The attempt to do this by increasing the access of Africans to education only increased the pool of alienated and politically disaffected African youths. The attempt to impose an age limit to avoid older and more politically conscious students from influencing younger pupils badly misfired, at least in the short term. It was in 1982 that the de Lange report on education was published. This was to make recommendations on how best simultaneously to improve Black education and to depoliticize it. The report advocated an increase in expenditure on Black education generally and, crucially, the formation of a single education department as the first step in desegregating education. The government's white paper on the report appeared in 1983. It supported the increase in expenditure on Black education but rejected the establishment of a single ministry. Separate departments and separate schools are non-negotiable in the government's view, with the emphasis being on co-ordination rather than integration. The white paper also rejected the report's recommendation that the Group Areas Act be waived to allow Black children to be accommodated in under-utilized White schools. Curtis Nkondo, former president of AZAPO and now president of the National Education Union of South Africa, claimed that the government's response entrenched apartheid in education and would be no solution to the crisis in African schools. The government's response to the report was no surprise, for it was based on the same principle as the new constitution: education is regarded as an 'own' group affair. This explains the existence of five separate education departments and five ministers. The 1984 National Policy for General Education Affairs Bill enacted the white paper. The Department of Education and Training, dealing with African education, has since been subsumed under the now much smaller Department of Co-operation and Development, which deals with urban African affairs under the new constitution.

The government's response to the de Lange report did little to prevent unrest in schools and universities. When schools reopened in 1984 widespread boycotts broke out and by April, 13,000 pupils in 24 schools were involved. Individual boycotts which began over issues such as the excessive use of corporal punishment, implementation of age restrictions and victimization, focused increasingly on the demand for elected student representative councils to speak on behalf of students. Alongside this was a notable unity between education protests and other community-wide collective action.

The first action was taken in defence of ninety pupils at Saulsville secondary school who were refused admission following disturbances there in 1983. The boycott spread to other schools and the police responded violently. On 13 February fifteen-year-old Emma Sathekge was killed by a police vehicle as tear gas was used to disperse a crowd. Fifteen thousand mourners marched to her funeral behind COSAS banners demanding free and compulsory education for all. Although the boycotts continued intermittently until May, Sathekge's death did not escalate the collective action to the extent that Hector Peterson's death had in 1976. For one thing it was an accidental death and, more significantly, there was a closer link with adult organizations who channelled the mobilization through community-wide organizations. This was facilitated by a more restrained response from the state. After Sathekge's death the Minister for Education and Training attempted to defuse the situation by co-operating with Bishop Tutu who negotiated on behalf of the students. However, unrest broke out again later in the year. The demands which sparked the second period of unrest called for the introduction of student representative councils, the control of corporal punishment, and the termination of 'improper relations' between male teachers and female pupils. After classes at five high schools were temporarily suspended, pupils set fire to cars, stoned the police, and harassed teachers. Eighteen people were injured in the clashes between the pupils and the police, and eventually the schools were closed. By closing the schools, the authorities placed 6,000 politicized children on the streets, which were already crowded with the unemployed and those protesting against the new constitution elections.[59] This gave added strength to both campaigns. By August 1984, the Minister for National Education announced proposals to improve communication between pupils and the school authorities. These included the setting up of democratically chosen class leaders and pupils' councils, liaison committees, whose members will be drawn from a number of schools in a specific area to discuss community problems, and regional committees that will work with the department to solve problems. The main short-term demands of the students had been met; but this announcement did not affect the more long-term demands outside Black education.

Incidents of collective action by students do show students to be concerned with this kind of issue. There is in fact another side to the link which students have forged with wider organizations and issues: school-based collective action has provided an example not only for other school protests, but also for adult organizations. There have been some incidents since 1980 which have extended the range of participants (and issues) beyond the school. In 1981,

African political organizations played a leading role in protesting against the twentieth anniversary celebrations of the South African Republic. African political groups joined with trade unions, Black Consciousness groupings, local community organizations, churches, exiled political organizations, and students in a countrywide campaign of protest which involved numerous incidents of mass collective action, the most effective being over transport.

South Africa has characteristics of both highly developed and underdeveloped countries. There is a sophisticated industrial and financial sector with high levels of motorization, and the associated congestion and infrastructure problems. Contrasted with this is a large sector concerned with basic needs and dependent on access to cheap and effective transport. This is particularly so given that apartheid compels the majority within this sector to be located in separate city fringe residential or border homeland areas far from both places of employment and shopping and recreational facilities. This has resulted in the politicization of Black transport, especially African transport, and transport boycotts in South Africa have a long history. A number of these boycotts occurred in 1982 and some lasted well into 1984. In December 1982 Putco in Inanda, Natal, announced a fare increase of 7.6 per cent on cash fares, and 16.6 per cent and 19.4 per cent on coupon fares. In general, 1982 was a daunting year for workers and commuters. In the second half of the year particularly, the economic recession began to bite deep. Retrenchment of workers in the Durban area was widespread. Food prices were increasing with the inflation rate and the increases in the general sales tax levied on food. It was also the third year of the drought and rural families were becoming increasingly dependent on remittances from migrant breadwinners. The high unemployment of the area and the low average income meant that many African youths were unemployed or that their parents could not afford to send them to school. Implementation of the fare increases led to boycotts in the affected areas. The Welgemoed Commission into bus transport issued two interim reports in 1983. It complained that public transport had become 'highly political', and recommended that smaller tariff increases be introduced and that an effective process of consultations be devised to eliminate protests. This did not bring an end to the boycott. Commuters used a cheaper alternative bus service but after fifteen months the government intervened and ordered the company to raise its fares to the Putco level or lose its government subsidy.

However, the most prolonged and violent boycott occurred in Mdantsane over a 10 per cent fare increase. It began in July 1982 and continued well into 1984. Although the township is in the Ciskei, it is a commuter township for East London. The Ciskeian police detained hundreds of commuters and many were physically assaulted when boarding trains. A leaflet issued by the UDF quotes an eyewitness who said that 90 people were shot on one occasion. As the boycotters defied the violence directed against them, a state of emergency was declared with a strict curfew. Nevertheless, the boycott was sustained even after the fare increase was reduced. Protests against the repression spread the collective action to schools, workplaces and the universities. Eleven independent trade unions, together with the UDF and the Detainees' Support Committee, organized the campaign against detentions and against the banning of the South African Allied Workers Union which was active in the area and in the boycott.

A degree of tactical agility was shown in involving the trade unions and political organizations like the UDF, and in harnessing the mass protest through organizational forms like the Detainees' Support Committee and the Mdantsane Committee of 10. The latter committee had a mandate to seek out and negotiate with another company to take over from the Ciskei Transport Corporation. In this way collective action was closely linked to practical politics. When the boycotts spread to Daveyton and Alexandra, the Alexandra Commuters' Committee performed a similar role to that of the Mdantsane Committee of 10. The boycott in Alexandra escalated considerably when the Commuters' Committee was banned. The active participation of students saw COSAS become involved in the transport boycotts, and many COSAS members were arrested for alleged intimidation. In August 1984 the fare increases were withdrawn.

The transport boycott spread rapidly to other townships where it became wrapped up with the campaign of opposition against service charge increases. Service charges can be quite high in comparison with wages. For example, the township charge for residents in Dobsonville in 1983 was R44.15 per month, R40.36 in Soweto, and R36.85 in Diepkloof. Yet the shortfall in rents received for Dobsonville was R1,873,000 per annum or R39 per house per month. The equivalent figure for Soweto was R14.90 per house per month. This led to pressure to increase service charges, which resulted in increases of 45 per cent in Bekkersdal and 51.8 per cent in Soweto. Protests followed and some community councils decided against introducing the increases. Similar protests against service charge and rent increases occurred at Mbekweni and around Durban. In April violence broke out in the townships of Lamontville and Chesterville, near Durban, when residents protested against proposed rent increases ranging from 40 per cent to 80 per cent. During the violence, Harrison Dube, a community worker, was shot and killed. The increase was shelved until August. Sporadic violence continued throughout the period to August and allegations were made that the police were assaulting residents for no reason and had handcuffed and blindfolded youths who were then forced to run behind police vehicles. The violence was also exacerbated by the government's announcement that the townships were to be incorporated in Kwa Zulu.

This kind of problem over service charge increases is inherent to the financial problems faced by African local township councils, which will be discussed elsewhere. In the midst of the unrest over service charge increases the government established the Van der Walt Commission to look into African rates and levies. The problems they face are immense and in order to redress the shortfall between monies received by the local councils and the enormous cost of providing even basic facilities, the new 'mayor' of Soweto argued in 1984, that the government should hand over all bottle stores in the area to the council. The present arrangement acts like a tax on the local councils and denies them considerable funds. The combined earnings of all the bottle stores in Soweto would provide the council with R100m. a year which could be used toward reducing rent and service charge increases. So desperate has the 'mayor' become that he has also recommended the introduction of toll gates in the townships and that the government give the council in Soweto two cents for every traffic ticket issued in the township.

During 1984 collective protests against rent and service charge increases spread. In August, rioting broke out in Tumahole, near

Parys, after police ordered 1,000 youths protesting against rent increase to disperse. Police used whips and tear gas to halt the disturbances. Service charge increases and elections to the new constitution formed a particularly explosive mix. Protests in the Witwatersrand townships led to fourteen deaths in Sharpeville, ten of which were perpetrated by the police. Four deaths were the fault of the protesters as they attacked members of African local councils and participants in the elections. The leader of the Sharpeville council was hacked to death by protesters. By 4 September, the day the new State President was elected, twenty-nine deaths had occurred and 300 injuries. Although most of the violence was directed by police against the demonstrators, those participating in the collective action had also attacked the shops and factories of Indians, besieged the homes of African local politicians, and harassed those voting in the elections to the new constitution. The police responded by using live ammunition.

In Sharpeville, the police subsequently moderated their response and began to negotiate with the protesters. Delegates were nominated from among the residents to speak with the police. The rent increases were deferred. This moderate response was not noticeable in other incidents; striking miners were shot by the police as they pursued their claim for a 25 per cent pay rise, and other deaths occurred in the major townships on the Witwatersrand. An effective one day stay-away took place on the Witwatersrand in September 1984 advancing grievances related to the new constitution, the detention of boycott leaders, and the ban on all political meetings, even those indoors. The use of the stay-away, which had not been seen since 1976, illustrates how intense collective action had become in 1984. However, this fact is perhaps better demonstrated by the increasing violence used by the protesters themselves.

In October 1984 the government escalated its repression of the township protests. In a joint police and military manoeuvre the townships of Sharpeville, Sebokeng and Boipatong were sealed off and 350 people detained. The intervention of the military in a civil incident was unprecedented even in South Africa. This again is testimony to the pressure the township protests applied. Unrest broke out in other townships as a result of the intervention of the military, but the three townships sealed off were quiet.

Dr Allan Boesak, president of the World Alliance of Reformed

Churches and a leading member of the UDF, criticized the actions of the police. During a speaking tour of Australia he spoke of the 'most unbelievable police atrocities'. The Minister of Law and Order asked the police to investigate a charge against Boesak under the Police Act which prevents publication of police atrocities. Boesak's claims were subsequently supported by the Southern African Catholic Bishops' Conference in a report on police actions from August to November 1984. The report accused the police of indiscriminate use of fire arms, birdshot, rubber bullets, tear gas, assaults, damage to property, and callous and insensitive conduct. These allegations were based on sworn affidavits from those who had suffered from, or been witnesses to, police brutality. On the basis of these sworn statements the report accused the police of 'wanton violence'. Their behaviour 'resembled that of an occupying foreign army controlling enemy territory by force without regard for the civilian population and without regard to the law'. The report was outspoken in its condemnation of police conduct. Like Boesak, the president of the Southern African Catholic Bishops' Conference, the Most Reverend Dennis Hurley, Archbishop of Durban, faced trial under the Police Act. Archbishop Hurley was due to appear in court in February 1985 for similar remarks made about police brutality in 1983, although all charges against him were withdrawn before the trial.

CONCLUSION: THE LIMITS OF COLLECTIVE ACTION

The government seems to have learnt very little from the 1976 uprising. The oscillation in police behaviour between violent repression and a moderate conciliatory response suggests that the government has not fully assimilated the lesson of 1976, that collective action is only intensified by a vigorous police response. Another lesson remains unlearned. The government still sees these incidents as the result of agitators urging participants to acts they would not otherwise commit—participants merely represent a suggestible mob. It sees the causes of these incidents as lying outside government policies and the society they create. Participants are not seen as making a case, for there is no case to be made; rather intimidators transform participants into a mob thinking they have a case. In this way the deciding factor in the occurrence of collective action is the existence and ability of agitators. Hence collective action is seen as transitory, *ad hoc*, and unpredictable.

As the other incidents of collective action since 1976 show, the progeny of 1976 was a new found confidence, a concomitant determination not to accept South African society as unchanging or unchangeable, and a psychological readiness to act in this cause. As long as the structural conduciveness of South African society remains as it is and Blacks share the image of apartheid as unjust, collective action needs only a precipitation. Rather than being transitory and *ad hoc*, collective action is therefore inherent to apartheid. As a form of opposition it is likely to continue and, undoubtedly, intensify given sufficient precipitating circumstances. Collective action has the distinct value of uniting communities in action. In the short term they are effective in registering collective anger and protest. The frustrations behind collective action can become blurred and overshadowed by the state's accusation that the collective action is either irresponsible or the work of intimidators, or by the obvious fact that many incidents do little to either appease or correct the root causes of the frustration and anger. Nevertheless, in the present circumstances, collective action is inevitable.

As a form of opposition, however, it has limitations. By its nature it ebbs and flows in its intensity, and in the degree to which it mobilizes people. It is also sporadic. If the anger expressed through collective action is ever to transcend immediate events or participants, or become permanently institutionalized, collective action must be translated into organizations and organizational forms. Through self-interest this tends to be the view of practical revolutionary leaders—Lenin, Mao, Castro, Cardenas. It is proof of the point that those who argue this are the successful ones. This view is not without its critics. In a study of working-class protest movements in the USA, Piven and Cloward attribute greater effectiveness to mass protest than mass-based protest movements.[60] A similar view is taken by Touraine in his account of the Popular Unity government of President Allende in Chile.[61] Many of these criticisms concern the over-bureaucratization and oligarchy which affects organizations. Organization can become a fetish so that its absence is an excuse for non-action. Nonetheless, organization is useful in opposition if it gives new expression to collective anger and protest. Without that, collective action remains a mere demonstration of opposition, what Luxemburg called an isolated revolutionary rupture, rather than a revolutionary challenge. This demonstration of opposition is in itself important, but the main means by which collective action should be judged is whether it raises the consciousness of participants and sympathizers to lead to organization and further forms of opposition. In this way collective action becomes a sign of wider revolutionary struggles which are themselves effectively pursued by other means.

Measured in this way collective action in South Africa has been successful. The initial demonstration in Soweto, and most of the subsequent incidents elsewhere, were organized independently by students. What has become apparent, is that school-based collective action has become effective in expanding the constituency for change, in winning people over to direct action, and in facilitating the expansion of their immediate concerns into a more generalized challenge to apartheid. Rudé's study of the French Revolution analysed the ways in which discontent through collective action was made specific in new definitions of rights, privileges, and programmes. The anger of working-class Parisians was traced to rising bread prices, and through a series of mass protests their opposition became defined in the ideology and organization of the revolution.[62] A similar process occurred in Russia after the initial February revolution in 1917, when Lenin was able to channel worker opposition through the Bolsheviks by his control of the soviets.[63]

The increasing tactical and organizational sophistication of collective action in South Africa particularly since 1980, reveals that this process is beginning to operate within Black opposition to apartheid. The formation of a variety of organizations to harness the power of the crowd and to push more effectively the demands of protesters is an example. These organizations channelled the protest and made it more concrete. Tactical agility is also evident. The various committees occasionally called a temporary halt to the collective action in order to provide time for their short-term demands to be met, and for a breathing space in which to consolidate their own organization and prepare strategy. Moreover, students became tactically astute in realizing the limits of working alone. This led them to forge links with workers and a number of community-wide adult organizations, in whose campaigns the students become increasingly involved.[64]

There is another way in which collective action has led to organization and further forms of opposition. The years since 1976 have seen a proliferation of organizations in African politics, sustained by the new circumstances and heightened resistance which collective action has helped to create. The list is mammoth and includes the Committee of 10, Soweto Students' League, Azanian People's Organization, Port Elizabeth Black Civic Organization, Writers' Association of South Africa (later reformed as the Media Workers' Association of South Africa), Soweto Civic Association, Soweto Action Committee, Soweto Residents' Committee, Teachers' Action Committee, Congress of South African Students, Azanian Students' Organization, and so on. Though localized, the township protests in 1983 over housing, transport, education, removals and the constitution created a climate of heightened resistance which contributed to one of the most significant developments in African opposition to apartheid, namely, the formation of the United Democratic Front. The establishment of the UDF has produced a national and legal organization as a means by which opposition and resistance can be co-ordinated and expressed. Together with a variety of organizations which pre-date 1976, such as Inkatha, the African National Congress, and numerous Black Consciousness groups, the UDF and these other organizations translate, codify, and co-ordinate African opposition to apartheid. The most effective opposition in the African community since 1976 has been through these organizations, not through collective action. The following chapters document this opposition, examining its expression through such organizations as the ANC, the trade unions, Black Consciousness groupings, the UDF, Inkatha, and press and literary groups.

Notes

1. See e.g. B. Hirson, *Year of Fire, Year of Ash*, London, Zed Press, 1979; T. Lodge, *Black Politics in South Africa Since 1945*, London, Longmans, 1983, Chapter 13; A. Mafeje, 'Soweto and its Aftermath', *Review of African Political Economy*, 11, 1978; R. First, 'After Soweto: A Response', ibid.; L. Mqotsi, 'After Soweto:

Another Response', ibid.; F. Molteno, 'The Uprising of 16 June', *Social Dynamics*, 5.1, 1979; F. Molteno, 'South Africa: A View from Within the Liberation Movement', ibid., 5.2, 1979; J. Saul and S. Gelb, *The Crisis in South Africa*, New York, Monthly Review Press, 1981, p. 101; L. Schlemmer, 'The Stirring Giant: Observations on the Inkatha and other Black Political Movements in South Africa', in R. Price and G. Rosberg, *The Apartheid Regime*, Berkeley, Institute of International Studies, 1980.

2. There is one exception to this, in the work of Smelser, who sees some purposive elements. See N. Smelser, *Theory of Collective Behaviour*, New York, Free Press, 1963; id., 'Some Additional Thoughts on Collective Behaviour', *Sociological Inquiry*, 42, 1972. He retains the view, however, that it has non-rational elements, likening it to magic.

3. These criticisms include its difficulty to operationalize; see E. Quarantelli and J. Hundley, 'A Test of Some Propositions about Crowd Formation and Behaviour', in R. Evans, *Readings in Collective Behaviour*, Chicago, Rand McNally, 1975. Its view that social movements are merely a type of collective behaviour is challenged by those who emphasize the rational, organizational elements to social movements. See R. Herbele, *Social Movements*, New York, Wiley, 1951; P. Wilkinson, *Social Movements*, London, Macmillan, 1971; J. A. Banks, *The Sociology of Social Movements*, London, Papermac, 1970. It has been criticized also for viewing collective behaviour as a response to change rather than a possible initiator of change; see R. A. Levitas, 'Some Problems of Aim-Centred Models of Social Movements', *Sociology*, 11, 1977; G. Lewis, 'The Structure of Support in Social Movements', *British Journal of Sociology*, 27, 1976; A. D. Smith, 'The Diffusion of Nationalism', *British Journal of Sociology*, 29, 1978.

4. See R. Evans, op. cit. p. vi.

5. This utilizes some of the terms in Smelser's work *Theory of Collective Behaviour*. Whereas Smelser sees his six-stage process as a general theory for all collective behaviour including social movements (if it persists and develops long-range tactics and goals), I see this as a descriptive tool to organize data in this case alone. Although Smelser offers a 'partial' structural–functionalist analysis, in the sense that he sees collective behaviour having purposive elements, involving participants 'reconstituting' their social environment on the recognition that their social environment is 'problematic', he still sees it as having strong non-rational elements. His vision of the participants' 'generalized belief' is akin, he says, to magic. He continues to see collective behaviour as a response to change rather than a possible initiator of it.

6. See *South African Outlook*, February 1977, pp. 19–32; Counter Information Service, *Black South Africa Explodes*, London CIS, 1977; SAIRR, *South Africa in Travail*, Johannesburg, SAIRR, 1978. However, the best is undoubtedly B. Hirson, *Year of Fire, Year of Ash*, in which he sets the chronology of the events in a structural context.

7. See J. Kane-Berman, *Soweto: Black Revolt White Reaction*, Johannesburg, Ravan Press, 1978, p. 27. (Also published as *The Method in the Madness*, London, Pluto Press, 1978.)

8. I do not use the term 'institutionalized', because the SSRC never became an organization following institutionalized behaviour. There were no rules of leadership, procedure, membership or decision-making. The *Weekend World* carried a series on the SSRC for four weeks beginning 31 July 1977. If anything, this points to the charismatic character of the body with a collection of mythologies surrounding it.

9. This is worked on the basis of J. Kane-Berman's estimate, op. cit., p. 6, F. Molteno, 'The Uprising of 16 June', *Social Dynamics*, 5, 1979, p. 54, and E. Webster, 'Stay-Aways and the Black Working Class since the Second World War', (mimo.), p. 18.

10. See *House of Assembly Debates*, vol. 81, 1976, col. 620.

11. This is discussed further in Chapter 3.

12. *Post Transvaal*, 11 March 1979.

13. The term 'Bantu Education' was dropped in 1978 when the Department of Bantu Education became the Department of Education and Training. However no other change than that of title occurred.

14. The one exception is E. G. Malherbe, *Education in South Africa*, Cape Town, Juta, 1979.

15. Quoted in L. Schlemmer, 'Education and Social Change in South Africa', paper delivered at Metzeral, France, 25–6 March 1983.

16. 'Education and Consociational Conflict Regulation in Plural Societies', in F. van Zyl Slabbert and D. J. Opland, *South Africa: Dilemmas of Evolutionary Change*, Grahamstown, Institute for Social and Economic Research, 1980.

17. A. Brooks and J. Brickhill, *Whirlwind Before the Storm*, International Defence and Aid Fund for Southern Africa, London, 1980.

18. The government could easily remedy the situation. To fulfil the purpose of apartheid it pays handsomely. The 'apartheid bureaucracy' gets a lion's share. The Department of Co-operation, for example, received R650m. in 1979, nearly 7% of the country's total budget: education commands less attention and less money and this is true even of White education. Those teachers in 1980 who protested about White teacher salaries did not criticize apartheid, but if they want more money they must face the need to get rid of apartheid. The

moral case of White teachers is seriously flawed by salary discrimination against Blacks. If White teachers have a case for higher salaries, the case for Black teachers is overwhelming. Black children are already the victim of the conditions White teachers threaten will come about in White schools if their salaries are not raised—shortage of teachers, high pupil–teacher ratio, merging of classes, a lack of specialist teachers.

19. These tables are compiled from figures given in K. B. Hartshorne, 'Black Education in Perspective', address to the Natal Region of the SAIRR, 16 March 1978. Mr Hartshorne is the retired Director of Education Planning in the Department of Bantu Education.

20. Based on figures provided in *South African Digest*, 30 July 1984.

21. *Daily News*, 6 February 1980.

22. *Post Transvaal*, 16 April 1978.

23. *House of Assembly Debates*, vol. 80, 1975, cols. 5472–7.

24. Department of Statistics, *South African Statistics 1976*, Pretoria, 1976, pp. 5.12 and 5.27. As a mechanism to ease the crisis in Soweto schools some principals are refusing to enrol those students 20 years of age and over.

25. Soweto's demographic structure is such that youth as a whole is numerically preponderant—52% of Soweto's (legal) population is under 25 year of age, and 63% under 30. These are taken from Kane-Berman, op. cit., p. 110.

26. The age breakdown of participants in the collective action mirrors this. In a sample of 1,200, 44% were between 13–16 years, 49% 17–23 years, and 7% over 24 years of age. Ibid., p. 7.

27. Quoted in IBR, op. cit., p. 65.

28. *The Citizen*, 27 July 1977.

29. *Sunday Tribune*, 8 August 1978.

30. R. Hitchcock, *Flashpoint South Africa*, Cape Town, Don Nelson, 1977.

31. IBR, op. cit., p. 13.

32. Quoted by J. Kane-Berman, op.cit., p. 47.

33. *Rand Daily Mail*, 7 May 1977.

34. F. Fisher 'Class Consciousness Among Colonized Workers in South Africa', in T. Adler (ed.), *Perceptions on South Africa*, Johannesburg, University of Witwatersrand Press, 1977.

35. Op. cit, pp. 18–19.

36. For example, see the debate between Mafeje, First, and Mqotsi in the *Review of African Political Economy*, 11, 1978.

37. *Rand Daily Mail*, 17 June 1976. The similarity of the police response in Sharpeville and Soweto is commented upon by R. W. Johnson, *How Long Will South Africa Survive?*, London, Macmillan, 1977.

38. IBR, op. cit., p. 11.

39. See *Rand Daily Mail*, 17 August 1976; *Sunday Express*, 20 June 1976; *Rand Daily Mail*, 24 September 1976; *Star*, 22 September 1976. The Mayor of Soweto, T. Makhaya, is reported in the *Rand Daily Mail*, 23 June 1976, as saying the children provoked nobody. Pathologists' reports quoted by J. Kane-Berman, op. cit., p. 29, show that 80 people had been shot from behind, 28 from the side, and 42 from the front. This was evidence from post-mortems carried out in Johannesburg.

40. Quoted by the *Daily News*, 29 February 1980. The report came out only in Afrikaans. The report of the judicial inquiry on the deaths during the 1985 unrest in the Eastern Cape, incidents which are not discussed here, avoided direct criticism of the policemen who first opened fire, arguing that it accepted their belief that they were under threat of attack. However, the report did criticize some actions of the police as provocative and it confirmed that the protesters who were first shot were not carrying petrol bombs as the police claimed.

41. *Sunday Tribune*, 2 March 1980.

42. *Rand Daily Mail*, 21 June 1976

43. Ibid., 22 June 1976.

44. 5 March 1980.

45. SAIRR, *South Africa in Travail*, op. cit., p. 68.

46. For example see B. Hirson, op. cit., p. 104 and A. Brooks and J. Brickhill, op. cit. Also see T. Lodge, op. cit., pp. 331–5.

47. *Weekend World*, 22 May 1977.

48. Quoted by J. Kane-Berman, op. cit, p. 136.

49. Quoted by SAIRR, op. cit., Appendix B. p. viii.

50. For example the *Weekend World*, in an editorial, wrote: 'The kids have made their point. Let them not push their luck too far . . . the ball is no longer in their court. Let the parents be given a chance. Let the Committee of 10 be allowed to go on with its work.' See the issue of 11 August 1977.

51. *Post Transvaal*, 14 September 1979.

52. *The Citizen*, 31 August 1979.

53. 19 June 1977.

54. *Post Transvaal*, 12 March 1979.

55. Ibid., 10 April 1979.

56. Ibid., 11 April and 30 April 1979.

57. Ibid., 19 April and 9 September 1979.

58. Based on figures contained in the SAIRR, *Survey of Race Relations 1982*, Johannesburg, SAIRR, 1983, p. 244.

59. The schools were still closed in October and the Department of Education and Training was concerned to reopen them as soon as possible. The Department wished the examinations to be sat and expected students to attend class six days a week and for longer each

day, in order for the syllabus to be covered in time. This itself became an issue in the protest as parents and children considered this schedule too rigorous. Some people expressed the idea that more trouble would be created if the children returned to school and failed their examinations than if the schools remained closed. The Department of Education and Training was in a dilemma. By leaving the schools closed it placed politicized students on the streets, but by opening the schools and forcing pupils to take and probably fail the examinations, it risked further protests.

60. E. Piven and R. Cloward, *Poor People's Movements*, New York, Pantheon, 1977, p. 36.

61. A. Touraine, *Vie et mort du Chili populaire*, Paris, Éditions du Seuil, 1973.

62. G. Rudé, *The Crowd in the French Revolution*, Oxford, Clarendon Press, 1959.

63. The works on this are legion. The best short introduction is J. Carmichael, *A Short History of the Russian Revolution*, London, Sphere, 1966.

64. See J. Saul and S. Gelb, op. cit., pp. 108, 113.

2

Racial Liberation and the Tactic of Terror

THE CONCEPT OF TERRORISM

In common with many concepts in the vocabulary of social science, the concept of terrorism originates with the French Revolution. It is a derivation of *terrorisme* and was first commented upon by Edmund Burke. Other antecedents have been identified as anarchism, nihilism, and existentialism.[1] Variety is also a feature of the contemporary meaning of the term. Clifford Geertz has shown, in his discussion of ideology, how those who control the language used to describe political objects (in the physical and non-physical sense of the word 'object') have enormous influence over those objects.[2] Governments are quick to label many acts of their opponents as terrorist, while these opponents prefer the term guerrilla. The last group to call itself terrorist was the Stern Gang in the former British mandate of Palestine. Trotsky often used the term 'Red terrorism': today it has a pejorative connotation. Some social scientists refuse to use the term in the context of racial liberation in South Africa.[3] This point is demonstrated in another way. Two Black reporters on the *Rand Daily Mail* publicly disclaimed responsibility for the word 'terrorist' in a story about one incident. They used the term gunman instead and they felt discredited when this had been changed in the published form.[4]

There is an assumption behind this objection which is erroneous, namely that terrorism is associated with an ideology or cause at odds with the idea of emancipation. Terrorism exists across moralities. There is the ultra-fascist terrorism of right wing groups in Italy, Spain, Chile, or Argentina and the ultra-left terrorism of the Red Brigade. Terrorism can be embedded within either a national liberationist ethos, as with the IRA, PLO or ANC, or an ideological one such as with the Baader Meinhof Gang, the Weathermen, or the Red Brigade. Very often it is a mixture of these elements. The IRA and the ANC are moving from being national to becoming ideological movements. Terrorism is not a cause or an ideology. It is a tactic; a tactic in a struggle which takes many political forms.

The work of Paul Wilkinson represents one of the best discussions of the nature of this tactic, distinguishing it from other forms of armed opposition. Its defining characteristics are that it is indiscrimate, arbitrary, unpredictable, denies any 'rules of war', and is free from conventional forms of moral constraint.[5] These qualities differentiate terrorism from guerrilla warfare. This distinction is recognized by political actors themselves. Che Guevara saw guerrilla warfare as deliberate and discriminate, striking at military targets and accepting conventional rules of war.[6] This is the basis of the distinction accepted by social science,[7] although Clutterbuck adds considerable confusion to the debate. In his book *Living with Terrorism* he continually used the term 'guerrilla', and in his work *Protest and the Urban Guerrilla* he refers repeatedly to terrorists — the terms are used interchangeably with no conceptual distinction between them.[8]

In a moral sense, the nature of an act is not altered by the name used to describe it. Fortunately there is a consensus on the nature of the acts labelled 'terrorism' by most people. It is these acts which are common across moralities even if the word is not. In the very broad sense used by Horowitz, terrorism describes the use of fear, subjection, and intimidation to disrupt the normal operation of a society.[9] This broad usage conceals quite different acts and Wilkinson found it necessary to distinguish political terrorism as the use of fear, subjection, and intimidation for political ends.[10] Since political ends differ, so must the types of political terrorism. A ruler-ruled dichotomy is common in discussing such a typology. Crozier distinguished 'terrorism' and 'counter terrorism',[11] Thornton referred to the former as 'agitational terrorism' and the latter as 'enforcement terrorism',[12] and Witten uses the categories of 'siege of terror' and 'regime of terror' respectively.[13] Wilkinson's typology has special advantages in circumventing this dichotomy. He distinguishes 'revolutionary terrorism', being the use of terror, fear and intimidation for the long-term object of bringing about political revolution and a fundamental change in the power structure and socio-economic order, and 'repressive terrorism' as the type used to protect society from such a change. These form the main contrast, but 'sub-revolutionary terrorism' is identified as a further type which lacks the intensity and indeed the intention to bring about political revolution.[14]

The notion of 'revolutionary terrorism' is useful because it avoids the pejorative connotations normally associated with the concept by making clear that behind the use of the tactic is a serious political judgement of that which it seeks to change and some vision of the future to be attained through it. Revolutionary terrorism is not mindless killing, although that is little comfort to the pacifist. Death is not the ultimate object. It may well be the result, but it is incidental rather than deliberate;[15] and incidental death, in fact, is the consequence of many political acts. Revolutionary terrorism is about publicity. Kropotkin once described terrorism as propoganda by deed. Death may well serve the interest of publicity, but it is publicity which is the ultimate aim.[16] This point is emphasized by Paust's contrast between the 'instrumental target' of terrorism, such as attacks on banks, offices, police stations, and specific individuals, and the 'primary target' which is to weaken the legitimacy of the dominant ruling group and the society it upholds.[17] The physical attacks on buildings and personnel normally associated with terrorism are not the primary purpose. This is true of even the most ruthless terrorist organizations and, while this does not excuse their brutality, it does place it in the context of all historical struggles for moral and political causes. This puts terrorism as a form of uninstitutionalized war, and it is only its uninstitutionalized nature that leads people to question its brutality but ignore the brutality of war. In fact, in those societies where the struggle over moral and political legitimacy is most fierce (colonial, sectarian, or ethnically divided societies), some ruling groups force their opponents to resort to physical attacks on buildings and personnel by denying them access to conventional forms of political opposition. This supports the view that terrorism is most often a weapon of the weak pretending to be strong — it is the last resort of the weak and powerless.

Herein lies the paradox of terrorism: by resorting to this tactic the weak often become weaker and the strong stronger. This is true for two reasons. Used in isolation from other forms of opposition, terrorism works less effectively because its success is based on a number of assumptions which Wilkinson rightly shows to be invalid: that people faced with threats will ultimately surrender their principles to save themselves; that terrorism invariably leads to psychological terror; and that those gripped by terror will submit.[18] The weak and powerless need to combine it with more conventional forms of opposition, and the irony is that these channels are denied them once they become terrorist. The weak can only hope that their revolutionary terrorism wins them a place at the negotiating table.[19] Until that happens they must see other opposition groups using conventional means reap the benefit of their tactic. This is even more so where the terrorist group lacks an internal political wing.

The only occasions where terrorism alone played the decisive role in political change were in colonial situations where the dominant ruling group lacked the will to continue colonial occupation. This was the case with Portugal in Mozambique and Angola, and Britain in Cyprus, Aden, Kenya, and Malaysia. Normally terrorism strengthens the resolve of the powerful not to bow to the demands of the weak. Very often it leads to an intensification of their power through emergency regulations, as well as the strengthening of the will to resist. In assassinating the Tsar, the Russian Populists only succeeded in replacing one monarch by another who was more autocratic. This historical precedent led Lenin and Trotsky to consider terror as merely an auxiliary weapon in the pre-revolutionary stage. In his list of factors necessary for change, the British socialist G. D. H. Cole rated a united ruling group resolved to keep its power and a ruthlessness within the group to use it as major obstacles.[20] South Africa is a good example. The revolutionary terrorism of the ANC has only provoked, in the short term, an intense repressive terrorism by the state which has increased its oppression.[21] The following section discusses some of the factors leading to the use of revolutionary terrorism as a form of resistance, including the historical and moral background to the use of this tactic, and its link with the escalation of repressive terrorism by the state.

THE ROOTS OF REVOLUTIONARY TERRORISM IN SOUTH AFRICA

Although the ANC is not the only organization utilizing this tactic, it is the largest and the most active, so the emphasis will be placed on it. It is necessary to examine the historical and moral background in order to understand the ANC's present use of revolutionary terrorism. It was temperamentally suited to Gandhi's passive resistance, on which it relied heavily in opposing apartheid in the 1950s.[22] Chief Luthuli, its President, actually condemned the use of violence. Then, in 1960, passive resistance was outlawed and major peace rallies were met with force of arms, culminating in the Sharpeville massacre. Nelson Mandela expressed the ANC's moral dilemma: 'If peaceful protests are to be put down by mobilization of the army and the police, then the people might be forced to use other methods in the struggle.'[23] The moral dilemma behind his plea is clear: when you feel you have a just cause and the legal pursuit of that cause is denied, do you resort to illegal means? Hamlet mused on this issue: 'To be or not to be. That is the question. Whether 'tis nobler in the mind to suffer the slings and arrows of outrageous fortune or to take arms against a sea of troubles and by opposing, end them.' History is replete with examples of those who chose illegality to right injustice. Barrington Moore defined two types of injustice: the feeling that an existing social rule is wrong and that a different one ought to apply, and that an existing rule recognized as legitimate is not being applied fairly.[24] The ANC's definition of the situation is in accord with the first type. The ANC felt that, in using violence against its subjects participating in passive resistance and peaceful protest, the South African government had abrogated any obligation to it. It was imposing punishment in violation of a social rule that was accepted by all its subjects — that peaceful protest was legitimate. By responding to peaceful protest with violent repression, it was imposing punishment in accord with a social rule that many subjects no longer held as legitimate — that Blacks had not the right to protest at their subjugation. In the face of this injustice, the ANC sought to change these social rules by illegal means.

The Afrikaner community gave an example to the ANC in this choice which is illustrated by the historical parallel of Israel. The Revisionist Zionists led by Jabotinsky, Begin, and Raziel rejected Ben-Gurion's diplomatic approach to an ending of the British mandate in Palestine and resorted to terror tactics. The extreme ruthlessness of the Stern Gang and the Irgun gave a lesson to the Palestinian terrorists who later followed them. The Ossewabrandwag functions similarly for the ANC in South Africa. Ossewabrandwag began as an Afrikaans cultural organization in 1938 to commemorate the centenary of the Great Trek, but quickly developed a political character and became a vehicle for national liberation from the British.[25] This ambiguity was reflected in its insignia — the ox wagon, as a symbol of the Afrikaner's trek, and the Nazi eagle. It used the sympathy and arms of Nazi Germany in the way that many terrorist organizations use the Soviet Union today: in a single haul in Lydenburg 200 lbs of gelignite were discovered, 1,000 rounds of ammunition, 1,000 detonators, hand grenades, bomb casings, fuses, vickers guns and bren-guns. It resorted to acts characteristic of organizations current today: terrorization of individual members of the armed forces and police, murder of informants, indiscriminate vendettas, bomb explosions, and the harassment of judges and witnesses in cases involving Ossewabrandwag supporters. The bomb explosions were indiscriminate and all focused on civilian targets: the Benoni post office was blown up, as was a cafe in Buxton and the *Bantu World* newspaper offices; bombs failed to explode at the Jewish synogogue in Boksburg and at Delmas railway station; powerlines were destroyed at Johannesburg, Krugersdorp, and Potchefstroom. Innocent civilians died in the Benoni blast and two dissident members were murdered. The Ossewabrandwag felt as removed from conventional moral constraint as some contemporary terrorists. What they saw as the moral justification of their acts was the justness of their cause for national liberation, seeing themselves as 'soldiers of the future republic'. This end justified their means. Their oath expressed this: 'I implicitly subject myself to the demands which my people's divine call requires of me. I shall be prepared to sacrifice my life for my people. If I advance follow me, if I retreat shoot me, if I die avenge me.'[26] This acted as the moral anaesthetic for all the brutalities they perpetrated; and this moral anaesthetic allowed the new government in 1948 to release all those responsible for committing murder, sabotage, bombings, and terrorist activities, and eighteen years later an ex-Ossewabrandwag member, B. J. Vorster, internee of Koffiefontein, became South Africa's seventh Prime Minister.

There are other factors to consider in understanding the ANC's choice of revolutionary terrorism as a form of resistance. We can condemn the use of illegal means such as this only if our conception of normality incorporates the idea of a peaceful order under the rule of law free from terror and fear. Africans have never possessed that in South Africa. Violence directed at them is endemic. It is physical violence, as with the nameless Bikos, or psychological violence, in the form of years of neglect and collective discrimination. In this regard, the repressive terrorism of the state has contributed greatly to a context where violence is beginning to be seen as legitimate.

Repressive terrorism takes many forms. In South Africa it is necessary to consider ideological repression. Apartheid as a ruling ideology preaches racial inferiority[27] and Whites act towards Africans as if they are incapable of responsible decision-making. This inferiority is entrenched every time White officials herd Africans this way or that, every time Africans are prevented from eating, sleeping, defecating, walking, and playing where they want. Even if not in the minds of Whites, African inferiority is entrenched in every statute of South Africa's legal code, in every decision they are not allowed to make for themselves. It is perpetuated in inferior education, housing, wages — in every facet of African life.

This is what Black Consciousness calls psychological oppression. It involves a dual orientation: of deference and fear towards Whites, and a lack of confidence and pride in themselves as Blacks. These orientations are severe constraints which are partly self-imposed; both the PAC and Black Consciousness recognized that before they could attack a racially discriminating system, Blacks themselves had first to deal with this problem. As we shall see, that is why Black Consciousness once mobilized support on a purely ethnic basis: it was a struggle unique to them as Blacks. These attitudinal constraints could not be so successful without two requirements being met: Africans recognizing the awesome power of the state, and, on occasions, witnessing it. In this sense then, fear is well grounded; police power, for example, provides daily lessons. The death in detention of Steve Biko is a good example. The response of White South Africans went through a number of stages. First came a denial that death was due to the police. The Afrikaans press spent some time in solving the riddle of when a knock is not a knock. *Beeld* announced Biko died from a stamp — 'an ambiguous word meaning a blow or knock but not a punch'; it refrained from editorial comment. *Die Transvaler* ignored reports that Biko died from head injuries. *Die Vaderland* criticized English-speaking press reports, arguing the matter was *sub judice*.[28] Once the cause of death was known, the Minister of

Police and *Beeld* provided reassurance by saying that brain damage is caused by many factors. When the evidence was overwhelming, much was made of Biko's alleged advocation of violence,[29] the implication being that some prisoners deserve it. Finally came the curious inquest verdict: in a five-minute appearance, the magistrate adopted the police version of events that Biko sustained injuries in a 'scuffle' with his interrogators. The verdict did not undertake to persuade. It did not clear away evidence against this theory nor did it offer a justification for rejecting defence submissions that Biko was an unwilling participant in any 'scuffle'. There was a complete lack of comment on the conduct of the police and their doctors. Nothing was said about Biko being kept naked in his cell in leg-irons and chained to a grille; or about the fact that this was not noted in the occurrence book, as is required by police standing orders; or about the doctor's admission that Biko should have been sent to hospital but the police initially refused permission; or about Biko being transported naked in the back of a van through the night for 1,200 km while on the verge of death; or about the fact that he had no medical supervision or supplies through this journey; or about the failure of a medical record to accompany him, so that a Pretoria prison doctor had no case notes to work from and gave a man dying of brain damage a vitamin injection and drip feed; or why the drip feed was later empty; or why the medical certificate admitting him was incorrect.

A committee appointed by the Medical Association of South Africa to investigate the issues concerning medical ethics which arose from the conduct of the two doctors involved in the treatment of Steve Biko published its report in August 1981. The committee found that it was undesirable that the security police headquarters in Pretoria should have the power to decide whether or not a detainee should be removed to a non-prison hospital. Medical practitioners should ask detainees themselves what their health problems were and could not absolve themselves of responsibility if their medical advice was rejected by the security police. In the event of being overruled, the doctor should report this to the Minister of Police and the local medical association. Because it did not have any subpoena powers, the committee did not attempt to establish whether the doctors involved were guilty of disgraceful or unprofessional conduct. However, the committee did find that a medical certificate issued was 'unsatisfactory and incomplete, if not a deliberate suppression of the facts'. The committee also found that Colonel Goosen, the security policeman in charge, regarded himself as being above the law. In October 1985 the two doctors were eventually struck off the medical register. In this way the medical ethics were well discussed, but other issues raised by Biko's death were ignored.

The issue of the treatment of detainees came to a head once more with the death in detention of Neil Aggett in February 1982. In March, the Detainees' Parents Support Committee approached 50 foreign medical associations to ask for support for a campaign to force the government to allow independent doctors to examine political detainees. In April, the committee sent a memorandum to the Minister of Law and Order alleging that detainees were being tortured. It presented statements from 70 detainees and ex-detainees claiming that systematic and widespread torture was being used. The claims included 20 cases of sleep deprivation, 22 cases of electric shock, 11 cases of mid-air suspension, 25 cases of suffocation, 28 cases of enforced standing for long periods, 54 cases of physical attack, 14 cases of attacks on the genitals, and 25 cases of being kept naked for long periods.[30] Similar allegations were made by a former detainee who brought a case of assault against the police for his treatment while in detention. The case was heard in August 1984 and revolved around whether the alleged victim was a police spy, the defence being that the allegations are untrue because the victim was a spy. The torture was said to have taken place during 1981, at the same time that Neil Aggett was detained. The inquest into his death began on 3 March 1982 and lasted for forty-four days. Evidence was presented that Aggett had made a statement on 19 January alleging assault and torture during interrogation. On three occasions, two magistrates and the Inspector of Detainees had tried to see Aggett but were told that he was 'unavailable'. It transpired that the district surgeon did not have free access to detainees and visited a detainee only when called by the police. The police official in charge of detainees, who had instructions to visit detainees every hour, did not do so on the night Aggett died because he was 'too busy'. In short, the weak monitoring system the police were supposed to operate was even weaker since they did not in fact implement it. It appeared that Dr Aggett underwent a 60-hour interrogation session and a fellow detainee reported that he saw him doing strenuous exercise and being beaten while naked.

When the inquest resumed in September 1982, evidence was provided by nine ex-detainees, with the lawyers for the Aggett family attempting to show that there was a pattern of interrogation used by the security police and that these detainees had experienced the same torture as Dr Aggett. Some of the nine had seen Aggett in the last days of his life and supported Aggett's claim that he had suffered electric shock treatment. One witness said that he had seen Dr Aggett just hours before his death when he was being escorted back to his cell—Aggett appeared to be in great pain, had a spot of blood on his forehead and walked with enormous difficulty. Another ex-detainee reported that Aggett claimed he was beaten and given electric shocks to his testicles. In evidence it appeared that the interrogators were neither aware of the rights of detainees nor that detainees were not to be subject to 'intensive interrogation'. Police evidence claimed that Aggett hung himself in remorse at having implicated friends in a statement concerning 'subversive activities'. Two expert witnesses disagreed over whether Dr Aggett was the kind of man to commit suicide.

In December, the presiding magistrate ruled that Dr Aggett's death was not brought about by any act or ommission on the part of the police and that he had died as a result of suicide. The magistrate accepted the evidence of more than thirty policemen as honest and reliable, while the evidence of former detainees was described as contradictory and unreliable. There was widespread condemnation of the verdict by human rights groups internationally and by various organizations inside South Africa. Also in 1982, Ernest Dipale died in police custody, Tshifiwa Muofhe died in detention in Venda, and Linda Dladla died shortly after being released.

It was in this context that the Rabie Commission of Inquiry into security legislation tabled its report in 1982. The report made mildly critical remarks, arguing that laws which were drafted to control unrest and violence could not eliminate the circumstances which led to unrest and violence. Yet the substance of the recommendations did not match this rhetoric. Their main conclusion was that, unwelcome as the Republic's drastic security laws were, they were to be retained in the interests of law and order. There can be no substitute for open court, and the fundamental flaw in the Rabie Commission's proposals was their entrenchment of the draconian measures to deny people access to the courts. The Commission tried to balance this by making other recommendations concerning the treatment of detainees. It suggested a board of review, the right to appeal, limited periods of detention, fortnightly visits by a magistrate and district surgeon, and the appointment of an Inspector of Detainees who would have access to the Attorney-General when pursuing cases of mistreatment.

Within five months of these recommendations being made another detainee died while in police custody. The liberal Afrikaans-speaking press heavily criticized the actions of the security police and pointed to the disastrous effects such incidents had on South Africa's image abroad. By the end of 1982 the Minister of Police had announced a new code for the humane treatment of detainees similar to that adopted by British governments in Northern Ireland. Responsibility for guarding detainees shifted from the security police to the uniformed branch and the code clearly stated that non-compliance would result in both criminal and disciplinary action being taken. The code is laudable in its sentiments: 'a detainee shall at all times be treated in a humane manner with proper regard to the rules of decency and shall not in any way be assaulted or otherwise ill-treated or subjected to any form of torture or inhuman or degrading treatment.' It became a disciplinary and criminal offence for interrogators to torture or mistreat detainees. But the system of control and monitoring remains weak. The main provisions of the code are that detainees held for more than six months can make oral or written representations to a board of review about their release; detainees should be informed 'as soon as possible after arrest' of the reasons for the detention. Unspecified provisions allow detainees to make complaints about their treatment and give them the right to immediate visits from the district surgeon, to regular visits, and to exercise and sleep. Two members of the police are to witness every interrogation and no degrading treatment or torture is to be administered. The code is weak because regular visits will be made by state medical or judicial officials, and it does not specify what procedure is to be allowed by which detainees can make complaints. Visits from the detainees' personal doctor are forbidden because of the risk 'of information being passed on'. Investigations of mistreatment are not to be independent but carried out by an officer of a branch of the police not involved in either the detention or interrogation. The chief advance in this code is that it prevents police officers pleading ignorance of the rules governing interrogation. During 1984 530 people were detained under the terms of the security legislation and in February 1985 the Minister of Law and Order announced that 1,611 visits had been made during 1984 to detainees by inspectors and 1,833 by magistrates. As a result 49 complaints of ill-treatment were received. However, during the state of emergency in 1985 the number of detainees rose to over 7,000 and the police were granted legal indemnity for their actions under the emergency powers. The code was temporarily abandoned and allegations were made of widespread torture of detainees.

It would be easy to argue that it took the death of a White detainee to wring this concession from the state. It is more complex than this, for the code must be linked to the state's need to present a humane face at that time, not only to the international community but also to the Coloured and Indian communities it was attempting to co-opt. Yet the repressive nature of the state has not been altered by the humane face it is trying to project. The allowance whereby magistrates and district surgeons visit detainees every two weeks, and the appointment of inspectors of detainees who make written recommendations, still mean that detainees are visited in private by officials reporting in confidence to the Minister concerned. Moreover, as will be emphasized shortly, the legislative implementation of the Rabie Commission's proposals led to the 1982 Internal Security Act, which, in the process of codifying many of the country's security laws, tightened up and strengthened the legislation. While it is also the case that the most flagrant excesses of police mistreatment have been pursued before the courts, few have ended in guilty verdicts for murder. Little has been done to introduce some kind of control over the number of deaths resulting from police action 'in the course of their duty' outside the detention cell.

The true number of those who die in detention is unknown; one only knows of those cases where the police are unable to pass it off as suicide or where relatives do not take the police at their word. Black Sash estimated there were forty-four cases of death in detention between March 1976 and July 1978.[31] The International Defence and Aid Fund in London estimated that there had been fifty-seven people killed while in police custody during 1983 although only two died while in detention. One of these was a thirteen year-old boy detained for the theft of pigeons. Five people died while in detention during 1984. In only a handful of cases was a charge brought before the courts where the police were found guilty. It may be significant that the majority of these charges are tried in Natal, the only province not under National Party control, although the central government still takes responsibility for the appointment of the judiciary. The Natal judiciary are noted for their independence. Judge Mostert, who made the first revelations regarding the Department of Information's secret projects and who later felt it necessary to resign, came from the Natal Bench. But even in these instances policemen are invariably acquitted of murder and found guilty only of culpable homicide. In one such case, the sentence was merely birching. This was after a pathologist had described the victim's injuries as the worst he had witnessed in forty years and after evidence had been given that the victim was suspended by his neck from a rope tied to a branch, then suspended by his wrists and beaten with a sjambok until he died; and that the policeman had refused him medical care out of fear of discovery. In 1979 there were 279 convictions of policemen for various crimes, but only 20 were dismissed from the force, of whom 17 were Black policemen.[32] In 1982, 286 policemen were convicted of crimes. Among them 55 White and 135 Black members of the police force were convicted of common assault, 10 White and 31 Black policemen convicted of assault with intent to do grievous bodily harm, and 5 White and 1 Black policemen convicted of culpable homicide. In 1983 the number of culpable homicide verdicts had risen to 14 and 3 officers were convicted of murder.[33] In short, only three deaths among the massive number for which the police are responsible have led to the accused being found guilty of murder, and these verdicts occurred precisely at the time when the government was attempting to project a humane face.

The police have no compunction in using a great deal of violence in performing their duties. The damages paid for assaults by the police through civil courts or an out-of-court sum have risen sharply since the Soweto uprising, as shown in Table 6. In addition to the information in the Table, in 1983 R168,701 was paid for unlawful arrests.[34] Even allowing for inflation and the greater availability of legal aid, the inference is still that the police are assaulting more people. This belief is reinforced by the 1977 Indemnity Act No. 13, which specifically excluded the liability of

Table 6. *Police Assaults*

Year	Claims	Accepted	Compensation (R)
1975	—	34	30,888
1976	312	39	33,666
1977	392	69	87,184
1978	—	78	178,725
1979	—	144	295,551
1980	—	173	370,000
1981	—	150	488,888
1982	—	190	418,914
1983	—	166	492,234

the Minister of Police and any officer of the government for wrongs committed by the police or armed forces. It is significant that with this protection the number of assaults drastically increased. As a response in order to reduce the monetary value involved, Section 32(i) of the Police Act now establishes a relatively shorter period in which to institute proceedings against the Minister. Normally a person is permitted three years to institute a claim for damages. In this case it is six months, which is effectively reduced to five months because one month's notice of intention to sue is required. The physical evidence of violence is partly obliterated by the press ban on publishing photographs and even sketches of prisoners. The 1978 Amendment Act No. 75 widens the ban to members of the public not criminally charged who die in police custody.

The attitude of the authorities to this is not condemnatory but protective towards the police. The perceived threat to law and order is seen as justifying vigorous police action. The Minister of Police excused the assault on Biko as 'following automatically from an arrest with a stroppy person'. The Minister was 'prepared to concede and accept that a policeman could lose his temper'.[35] The violence shown was 'hardly serious enough to justify a charge before a police court'.[36] South Africa is, admittedly, an extremely violent society, as is shown by the high incidence of crimes of violence. It could almost be argued that the aggression Blacks show to each other is a way of releasing tension, preventing aggression flowing outward to the dominant racial group. The police, however, do not seem to be a restraining factor, nor, as these figures indicate, are they immune to the use of violence. For example, a police constable, on being called to correct a fault in a parade, shot at his lieutenant;[37] on breaking up a fight between two policemen, a third was shot dead by one of the fighters.[38] Were it not for the fact that it reflected a serious 'security-complex' which glorifies the mechanisms of violence, one recent incident has all the comedy of theatre. During a civil defence practice in Estcourt, a group of policemen became over-excited and interfered with members of the public, holding several at gunpoint and commandeering their cars. Two members of the public were assaulted when they objected.[39] The divisional criminal investigating officer for Natal, Brigadier van der Westhuizen, reiterated this complex in a warning to Whites. 'Never expect a robber to act like a normal person. Never argue with a robber. Shoot first and ask questions later.'[40] The assumption behind this remark is alarming, the more so because it is held by those in positions of authority within the police who are called upon to control the excesses of police power. The assumption is that to threaten law and order is to be abnormal and to lose one's rights to human life.

However, at the root of this assumption is something worse than the assumption itself. The police recognize their omnipotence. A number of *ad hoc* incidents are further indications of this. The police recognize that they have enormous formal or informal power if they can prevent doctors from moving or treating Steve Biko; or force a fifteen-year-old African girl to have sex with them;[41] or assault a member of the public when he objects to their commandeering his car with a baby in the back seat just to transport them to the station;[42] or rape a nineteen-year-old African woman at gunpoint and say they had become sexually excited after watching semi-naked women dancing;[43] or charge an African for blasphemy because he said 'Oh God' when they arrested him;[44] or beat up a nightclub owner when he refused them free drinks;[45] or set their dogs on suspects and refuse hospital treatment until after their court appearance;[46] or instruct cell-mates to attack a prisoner 'like dogs' while they watched;[47] or force two Indians handcuffed together to run ahead of policemen on motor cycles for three kilometres;[48] or shoot an African because he has no pass;[49] or refuse a mother the right to lay a wreath at her son's graveside and fire tear gas when she persisted;[50] or kill an eighteen-year-old schoolboy when he ran away from a roadblock;[51] or shoot and kill a taxi driver for not parking his car properly;[52] or be responsible for the death of two babies as a result to over-exposure to tear gas;[53] or in 1984 shoot and kill two children aged four and six years respectively.[54]

Police attacks on members of the public and prisoners are common. The number of those members of the public killed or wounded by the police in the execution of their duty since 1978 is represented in Table 7.[55] Quite clearly the number of deaths as a result of police action is increasing, which reflects the growing intensity of Black opposition and the increased repression by the police. 1983 was a particularly active year politically for Black South Africans, and while an average 15 people were killed by the police per month in 1982, this increased by over 25 per cent. By 1984 it was over 29 people per month. During the seven-month state of emergency imposed in August 1985 to cope with township unrest, 780 people died up to the day it was announced the emergency was to end, which is an average of over 100 per month. Amnesty International also revealed that up to that day 7,878 people had been detained for some period of the emergency, 2,000 of which were children under fourteen years of age.

An argument used in South Africa to combat criticism of incidents such as the ones listed above, is that such incidents represent mainly acts by Black policemen in rural areas—presumably a type of area calling for tough measures and a kind of policeman who knows no better. The evidence only partly supports this. It is in the urban areas that the police consider law and order to be most threatened, and most incidents occur in police stations servicing Black townships. In 1980, in a police force of 35,000, Black policemen constituted 24.4 per cent and, in fact, are over-represented in those cases of assault which come before the court. This could well be explained by the marginality of the Black policeman; with high Black unemployment and a rigid racial status hierarchy, Blacks see in a police career both economic security and some degree of acceptance by the dominant racial group. Among their fellow Blacks, however, they have little respect. There is a high incidence of physical attacks on Black policemen and their relatives by Blacks.[56] Many Independent Churches also act as their own vigilante groups because of an unwillingness to rely on and a lack of confidence in the police.[57] Clearly this marginality is felt by

Table 7. *Deaths/Woundings in the Course of Police Duty
1978–1984*

Year	Race Group	Deaths		Woundings	
		Adult	Juvenile	Adult	Juvenile
1978	Black	190	12	464	47
	White	2	0	12	0
1979	Black	152	10	454	33
	White	1	0	8	0
1980	Black	148	28	354	61
	White	2	0	9	1
1981	Black	149	24	468	76
	White	2	0	7	0
1982	Black	168	20	460	73
	White	10	1	16	2
1983	Black	198	8	305	51
	White	4	1	12	0
1984	Black	327	21	1140	107
	White	4	0	33	2

Black policemen, and on their part it can result in a greater sense of frustration with Blacks and/or a greater identification with the dominant racial group. Both of these could explain their heavy-handed methods. Above all, Black policemen have a marginality within the police force itself, and this provides a better explanation. One sees this in the way Black policemen are ridiculed by their White colleagues, or in the physical attacks on them by their White superiors. This marginality perhaps means they cannot call upon the same sense of loyalty and support from the police hierarchy in allegations of assault; allegations involving Black policemen are thus more likely to be proceeded with and come to court.

Perhaps a more defensible argument would be that what is important for democracy in South Africa is not that such incidents occur but that judicial judgement is eventually passed upon them. Some of the more flagrant incidents are now being pursued in the courts, especially where the victim is White. But what is important is the number of guilty verdicts, and the conviction rate is low. Guilty verdicts are more likely if the charge is culpable homicide rather than murder. Only three policemen have been found guilty of murder in recent years. The policeman accused of murdering Saul Mkhize, the prominent community leader, was acquitted. One of the most chilling incidents involved three warders at Barberton farm prison. Twelve prisoners were murdered in one year and their bodies secretly buried. The six warders were found guilty of assault, with the longest sentence being eight years. Rather than bring the full weight of justice against the men, the state instituted another of its commissions. The Van Dam Commission recommended suspending the clause in the Prisons Act which placed a ban on the publication of information regarding the prison service. The Minister subsequently agreed that he could see no reason why the clause should be retained. No concession was allowed for the similar clause in the Police Act. It would be an error to suggest that police power is legally unrestrained, but there is a willingness on the part of the state to pay damages rather than restrain the powers that lead to the necessity for paying them. Many cases of death and assault do result in legal action, but one wonders about the size of the unseen part of the iceberg. Even in those cases which reach legal judgement, the quality of justice depends on the Bench and is often quite variable. Jury trials, never common, were abolished in 1969 on the consensus of opinion in the legal profession that all-White juries were prejudicial to Blacks. The presiding authority in most legal judgements is now a magistrate who is a civil servant vulnerable to governmental interference. Promotion of magistrates depends ultimately on the recommendation of the Minister of Police. Judges have security of tenure and need an Act of Parliament to unseat them. They are also drawn from the ranks of practising advocates with plentiful experience of appearing for accused persons. In contrast, most magistrates are drawn from Public Prosecutors and have never appeared for a defendant, their previous court experience being limited to appearances as prosecutors for the state.

The quality of mercy from magistrates is often strained. Their credulity is evidenced in the peculiar Biko judgement, for example, and the naivety of some is hard to believe. Dismissing a case of assault in which it was alleged that three policemen attacked an African for playing a radio too loud, causing him to be detained in hospital for examination and treatment for head injuries, the magistrate commented: 'I fail to accept that a policeman would assault a man or hit him over the head without reason.'[58] Another incident is revealing. After a ten-day inquest into the death of Lungile Tabalaza, who fell five floors while in the custody of the police, in which evidence was given by his relatives that the suicide note was not in his handwriting, the Deputy Chief Magistrate in Port Elizabeth concluded: 'it is not the function of this court to establish whether the involved persons contravened departmental instructions or whether disciplinary steps should be taken against them.'[59] The bias of magistrates in sentencing has long been suspected but is under-researched.[60] The following incidents provide no proof of this bias, although they do indicate that at least in some instances a proper detachment was lacking. A nineteen-year-old student, fifteen minutes late reporting to a police station while on probation, was fined R1,000 and sent to Robben Island, the maximum security prison. A White policeman who punched a driver was fined R10, whereas Black violence is severely dealt with in case it should spread to violence against Whites.[61] In 1976 members of the Soweto Students' Representative Council were sentenced for up to fourteen years for alleged conspiracy to effect violence, whereas a Namibian court sentenced a White right wing terrorist in possession of an arsenal of weapons to a suspended sentence. In June 1983 Eugene TerreBlanche, leader of the AWB, and Jocob Viljoen were charged with illegal possession of arms. Evidence was heard that the Afrikaans terrorist group had hidden caches of arms at various sites. Viljoen was fined and Terre-Blanche was given a suspended sentence. Four months later the two men appeared in court with two colleagues, again charged with terrorism and the illegal possession of arms and explosives. The arms included an Oerlikon missile. They received suspended sentences. Mr Justice van Dyk described the men as 'civilized and decent people' who 'were victims of an unfortunate set of circumstances' and added that the community 'certainly does not expect me to send them to jail for that'.[62] It was the same judge who had earlier sentenced Barbara Hogan to ten years without leave of appeal for collecting information for the ANC. This leniency toward the AWB came after Afrikaans terrorists threatened to blow up all PFP offices in Natal. A letter to PFP members described them as 'evil and verminous Black *boeties*' and went on to say 'long live the glorious AWB, heroes of the White race'.[63] Various incidents of tampering with cars have been ascribed to the AWB. In March 1983 the Dean of St George's Cathedral in Cape Town found a bomb attached to his car. The general secretary of the African Food and Canning Workers' Union found his tyres over-inflated. This had previously happened to other churchmen, and trade unionists. In 1982 several trade unionists and church men died in unexplained car accidents. In addition many prominent Black politicians have received death threats from the AWB.

These are some of the reasons why a number of lower-division court judgements are overturned in higher courts. Some judges have demonstrated surprising independence, granting acquittals in sensitive political trials. There is, however, one further restriction on racial equality before the law. In practice, the absence of an effective legal aid system seriously prejudices the prospects of Africans. In criminal cases, counsel is mandatory. But in contrast to Britain, where no one can be sent to prison without the benefit of counsel, more than 200,000 Africans are imprisoned each year without legal representation (mostly for pass offences). The legal aid scheme effectively excludes anyone with employment or a family member in employment. Most of those who get lawyers depend on savings or charity. (The United States-based Lawyers' Committee for Civil Rights Under Law has funded some security trials.) In fact Africans rarely apply. Through ignorance, fear, or the prejudice of officials, the system of legal aid seems to aid poor Whites more. For the year ending 31 March 1976, 8,996 applications for legal aid were received from Whites, 2,041 of which were refused, compared with 2,307 applications from Africans, 386 of which were refused.[64]

In 1979 the government established the Hoexter Commission to report on ways of improving the administration of justice. After the publication of a number of interim reports, the main report was published in April 1984. At the heart of the report is the principle that the judicial system must be independent of the state; from this flows a series of necessary recommendations. In regard to judges, these ran from the revision of the system of appointment, to the undesirability of the involvement of judges in commissions of inquiry. Significantly, it recommended the removal of the identification of magistrates with the state. So detailed were the commission's investigations that it even drew attention to the unsatisfactory practice whereby magistrates use the same cars as prosecutors to travel to court. Other aspects which the commission found disturbing were the low average level of experience of prosecutors, administrative arrangements which were incompatible with the standards of judicial aloofness expected of magistrates, and deficiencies in the offices of registrars. Yet in suggesting remedies the commission did not consider the possibility of professional advocates being briefed by the state to act as prosecutors, so prosecutors still remain civil servants. Independence was to be achieved by widening the background of magistrates so that they embrace all population groups in South Africa. The same sort of manpower crisis that has seriously lowered the efficiency of the private and public sectors of the economy is now threatening justice. It is largely the consequence of trying to run the country on the skills of the White minority. The remedy is a belated crash course of training in a proposed National Law School independent of the public service, providing intensive practical courses in civil and criminal law for all racial groups. The shortage of skilled staff has been made more acute by the parallel system of commissioner's courts for Africans and the report recommended a single hierarchy of courts for all without reference to race. Other recommendations to make the courts fairer to Blacks concern the extension of legal aid to all accused persons in all courts and the establishment of a council of justice to supervise and advise on the administration of justice. The government has yet to decide what it intends to do about the recommendations. The immediate problem is that many of the situations which the commission castigates are inextricably bound up with government policy. It is difficult to see how the penal sanctions of influx control can be scrapped while the government insists on implementing separate development and the homelands policy.

Although often over-zealous in the manner in which they carry out their duty, the police and the judiciary are merely law-enforcers. Repressive legislation forms an essential element in repressive terrorism, and South Africa's security laws are by far the most infamous part of the repressive legislation.[65] They promote three basic powers: to ban, imprison, and detain people; to prohibit organizations, publications, and meetings; and to harass with the threat of such sanctions anything falling within the terms of reference of the legislation. The key measure is the 1982 Internal Security Act, which was the statutory outcome of the Rabie Commission. This provides for four different kinds of detention.[66] The most drastic is the indefinite detention of persons suspected of committing either of two very broadly defined crimes of terrorism or subversion, or of persons suspected of having information about the commission of these crimes. Although provision is made for consideration of each case by a board of review where the detention is to exceed six months, the board is not independently constituted as courts of law are. The remedy of *habeas corpus* is specifically abolished, which denies the courts the right to pronounce on any detention under this provision.

Another clause within the Act allows the Attorney-General to detain any witness whom he believes will be either intimidated or tampered with, or will abscond. Again there is no control by the courts of this detention. Two forms of preventive detention are also authorized by the legislation which allows indefinite detention of persons thought by the Minister of Law and Order to be endangering state security. Although the Act provides for the consideration of such detentions by a review committee appointed by the Minister, who is responsible for the detention order in the first place, the safeguards are of limited value because referral to the Chief Justice only takes place if the review committee disagrees with the decision to detain on the grounds of ministerial bad faith or abuse of power, both of which are difficult to prove.

As conventionally seen, the rules of law require that any order depriving a person of his liberty should be made in terms of rules precisely defining the forbidden conduct and administered by an impartial tribunal. This is what Weber called formal rationality in legal systems. As Weber also recognized, legal systems can be substantively irrational, which is the case in South Africa. The provisions of the rules of law are not satisfied in most of the security laws. This creates the paradox Weber was trying to express: officials can operate in terms of the law, but in truth operate outside it. In South Africa they are operating outside it in the sense that they do not need to conform to any prescribed norms and are excluded from judicial regulation or control. Lawmakers have defined for the courts a very limited role and Tocqueville's ideal of the separation of powers does not exist in South Africa, for the executive have *de jure* and *de facto* judicial power.

Freedom of association is restricted by a number of laws, of which the most serious is that which allows the Minister of Law and Order to declare any organization unlawful on the grounds that it is a threat to state security. The safeguards which the 1982 Internal Security Act provides in such cases are the same as for the banning of individuals and are inadequate for the same reason.[67] As Professor Mathews shows, what is worse is that the 1982 Act confers upon the Minister the power, unfettered by any limited safeguards, to declare that any given organization is the same as one already declared unlawful. When he does this the courts are bound to accept this decision. That is to say, criminal proceedings can be brought against members or supporters of an organization on the grounds that they are really members and supporters of an unlawful organization.[68] The 1982 Internal Security Act confirmed the banning of all organizations still banned at the time of its enactment.

The right to public assembly is restricted under the 1982 Act. This gives both Ministers and magistrates the power to ban meetings. This power is absolute and empowers the Minister to ban either specific meetings or any meetings anywhere and everywhere in the Republic without independent check or control. It has been illegal for several years to hold outdoor meetings other than sports meetings without the permission of the Minister. In 1984 this ban was applied to indoor meetings in certain townships. One of its drastic effects is that outdoor meetings of workers to discuss grievances are illegal unless prior permission has been sought. The police have the power to disperse such meetings by force, and this power has often been exercised.

The 1982 Internal Security Act empowers the executive to suppress organizations, newspapers, and the expression of opinion, and to ban or impose house arrest on individuals without the regulation of such power by the courts. In the terms of the act, the State President is empowered to declare an organization unlawful and to prohibit the printing, publishing, or distribution of a periodical or other publication if he is satisfied that the organization or publication is a threat to national security. In a sense the wide terms of reference of this definition are superfluous because there are no procedures available to contest the State President's decision: an organization or publication is a threat if he believes it to be such, or simply if he states that he believes it to be such. Neither this belief nor the criteria employed to reach his decision can be challenged. This leaves the State President free to ban at will. Just as encompassing are the powers entrusted to the police and the Minister of Justice in the terms of Section 6 of the Terrorism Act. A police officer with the rank of lieutenant-colonel or above may order the detention for an indefinite period of a person whom the officer believes either to be a terrorist or to have committed other acts covered by the definition of terrorism. The detention is supervised by the Minister of Justice, not the courts, and the Minister is the only person with authority to order the release of detainees. The act expressly removes the jurisdiction of the courts. Not even the right of review remains. People so held are kept in total isolation without recourse to legal representation, without the right to be heard in their own defence, without protection against ill-treatment, and without the prospect of a trial. Like feudal chattels, their well-being is in the hands of the same political rulers who assign them their position.

These laws therefore provide wide powers of repression. In 1978 there were 105 people charged under the Terrorism Act, 56 of whom were convicted; but the number of detainees who had no trial was 98 adults and 252 juveniles. The number of people banned under the Internal Security Act was 145. In 1980 there were 768 people detained up to 30 November.[69] Banning is an effective control to suppress those for whom no evidence exists to charge under more serious offences, but who are none the less an embarrassment. It is possible to restrict people to a magisterial district, and thus deprive them of their means of subsistence if they work outside it. Temporary bannings of 12 to 180 days allow the detention of those who are short-term embarrassments. That is why all but one of the Biko family were detained after Steve Biko's death. This method of control is also used against strike leaders. One of the dangers of a banning order is that it immediately identifies the banned persons as government opponents and opens them up to risk of right wing violence. A political science lecturer, Dr Richard Turner, was assassinated while serving a banning order; the Black sociologist Fatima Meer has been shot at and her house fire-bombed; and Donald Woods, former editor of the *Daily Dispatch*, suffered an acid attack. This parallels the danger detainees run from police violence.

As a political dispensation in the run-up to the elections to the Coloured and Indian institutions established under the new constitution, the government allowed most banning orders to lapse in 1983. It only renewed five orders. However, detentions increased in tandem. The number of publicly known detentions increased in 1983 by 159 per cent in the 'independent homelands' and 31 per cent in the rest of South Africa, giving a total of 453 people.[70] Of those whose occupation was known, 52.8 per cent were pupils, students and teachers; 24.5 per cent were trade unionists and workers; 16.6 per cent were community and political leaders, and the remainder were journalists.[71] In 1984 the Minister of Law and Order stated that 530 people had been detained, although the SAIRR estimated the figure to be 1,129. Again over half were students and teachers.[72] During the seven and a half months in which the state of emergency was in operation in 1985–6, over 7,800 were detained.

REVOLUTIONARY TERRORISM IN SOUTH AFRICA

The relation between repressive and revolutionary terrorism is symbiotic, so that an escalation in one form of violence causes an increase in the other. Since 1976 there has been a definite upsurge in the use of revolutionary terrorism. This symbiotic relationship was commented upon by A. S. Mathews when he drew a parallel with Northern Ireland, believing that Northern Ireland provides support for the proposition that the denial of rights through harsh repressive laws and treatment is counter-productive to the goals of political order, for a counter-reaction has grown ugly in proportion to that repression. He wrote:

Whatever official assurances South Africans may be given, the security situation is undoubtedly serious and appears to be growing steadily worse. . . . During this whole period the laws have become progressively tougher in form and application. What seems significant is that the growth of violence and the toughening of the laws have run parallel with each other. The laws have not diminished violent opposition; instead, that kind of resistance has intensified in almost direct proportion to legalized repression.[73]

Black opposition has undergone the transformation which is characteristic of many dispossesed groups without rights, moving from civilized pressures to mass demonstrations and non-violent defiance, and eventually culminating in sabotage and terrorism. The weaponry exists for a large-scale onslaught. In August 1979 statistics issued by the police revealed the quantities of arms seized during the previous year. (These figures did not include the large quantity seized in Northern Zululand during February 1980.) In the twenty-six different caches covered by the figures, 61 assault rifles were discovered, 21 submachine-guns, 3 machine-guns, 14 hand carbines, 29 machine pistols, 32 automatic pistols, 2 rocket-propelled grenade-launchers, 304 grenades, 31,805 bullets, 235 kg explosives and numerous associated detonators, primers, cord, and safety fuses.[74] Assuming that police are unlikely to have discovered all the caches, and that the process of infiltration of munitions continues, as the find in Zululand shows, the availability of weaponry presents no problem for revolutionary terrorist organizations.

The manpower position is more complex. Early attacks evidenced a great deal of crudity in the use of weaponry and the manufacture of explosive devices. The training of manpower is the greatest problem, for there is no lack of willing recruits. Irrespective of the broad meaning of the term in security legislation, security trials in South Africa in practice define four types of act as terrorism: politicizing and propaganda; acts of sabotage; suspected infiltration; and recruitment of trainees. The ANC engages in all four acts as do other smaller organizations like the Soweto Students' League, the South African Suicide Squad, and the People's Organization Front for the Liberation of South African Blacks. Black Consciousness tends to concentrate on the first type, so many supporters are prosecuted for terrorism without engaging in sabotage attacks as such. Police estimated in June 1978 that 4,000 Africans were in external military training camps, 75 per cent of them under the banner of the ANC. At the same time, one hundred trained men were apprehended along with six hundred untrained recruits. However, Lodge has discussed how difficult it is to estimate the size of the ANC's military wing, with estimates varying between 2,000 and 8,000.[75] An SADF spokesman said that the higher figure of 8,000 was 'gross exaggeration'. The Rabie Commission gave a figure of 1,400.[76] These numbers have to be set against a backdrop of twenty thousand people who attended the funeral of a revolutionary terrorist in Soweto. Three out of four Africans questioned in a survey felt they had 'a strong or qualified sympathy' for the dead man and 39.7 per cent felt he was a hero.[77] The actual number of revolutionary terrorists should therefore be set against the numerical support base they enjoy, the sea of sympathizers who give them safe housing, and provide hideouts, food, and succour.

The influence on recruitment of recent political events in South Africa has been enormous. From 1960 until 1974 Morris shows that there were only 55 terrorist incidents, 89 per cent of which occurred in the first four years of the ANC's banning.[78] The most effective stimulus to an intensification of terrorist attack was the Soweto uprising in 1976. Clutterbuck once argued that terrorism is fostered by a sense of grievance which not only comes from impoverished social conditions but from the desire of educated people to express this grievance and translate it into some sort of concerted plan of action. It is no coincidence, he points out, that terrorists tend to come from the more educated sections of the community, and that terrorism is most common where there is disparity between deprived social conditions and a developed education system, causing some to emerge from that system with an awareness of the iniquities of their society and a desire to rectify them.[79] This process has worked only slightly differently in South

Africa. A mass of African students intensely aware of the iniquities of their inferior education came to attack the social conditions within which education exists in South Africa. The repressive response of the dominant racial group led to an exodus of these students, many of whom ended up in terrorist training camps. The ANC is accommodating this clientele by opening a school, the Solomon Mahlangu Freedom School, in Tanzania, with the intention of continuing the education of 900 students. In April 1983 they had 400 primary and secondary-level pupils.

The events of 1976 were not a planned affair with a fall-back strategy worked out in advance. The immediate response of many was flight. By November 700 students were in Botswana and 190 in Swaziland. The second anniversary of the events saw a 41.4 per cent drop in the number of Soweto schoolchildren available for schooling. Some were dead, in prison or in other schools; many were missing and in exile. These young recruits swelled ANC numbers; they returned to South Africa very quickly and in the early days were both ill-trained and unprepared. Solomon Mahlangu left South Africa in October 1976 and entered Mozambique. He returned within eight months lacking skills and the necessary dedication and obedience. On being discovered by police he panicked and shot wildly at anyone nearby, wounding members of the public. Mahlangu was hanged at the age of 19. He had not fulfilled the brilliant academic promise he showed at school, but the events of June 1976 had fired him with other ambitions. Many of the defendants at recent terrorism trials show the same career profile as Mahlangu. Occasionally a 'cell' leader of more mature years and experience may be caught and stand trial with them. Later attacks show more sophistication and skill, paralleled by increasing effectiveness and intensity.[80]

The intensification of revolutionary terrorist attacks in the wake of the Soweto uprising is evidenced in many ways. In the three years from March 1976 until February 1979 there were 260 convictions under the terrorism laws, although 450 people were awaiting trial in February 1979 alone, and of this number 57.7 per cent had been put there in the twelve months up to February 1979. Remembering that in the fourteen years that followed the banning of the ANC there were only fifty-five terrorist incidents, the number since 1976 shows how great a stimulus the Soweto uprising was. The number of incidents which are estimated to have occurred varies depending on the time-scale used, the particular definition of political violence employed, and whether incidents involving Namibia and right wing groups are included. A chronology of guerrilla activity made in 1981 records 112 attacks and explosions in South Africa between October 1976 and May 1981.[81] Statistics compiled by the Centre for Intergroup Studies at the University of Cape Town showed that between 1977 and September 1983 the ANC had undertaken 210 instances of political violence, killing 52 people in the process and injuring 286. Statistics given by the police in a security trial in October 1983 record 197 acts of political violence and 47 deaths.[82] The Minister of Law and Order put the figures at 220 incidents and 48 deaths, 67.7 per cent of which had occurred since 1981.[83] The Minister indicated the geographical spread of the incidents since 1981, showing their concentration in Natal (26.17 per cent), Soweto (18.9 per cent), and the border and Eastern Transvaal region (32.2 per cent).[84] According to the Centre for Intergroup Studies, more people were killed and injured in political violence in 1983 than in the previous six years, a vivid testimony to the escalation in the political struggle. An analysis by the Terrorism Research Centre in Cape Town showed that incidents of political violence rose from 59 in 1980 to 395 in 1983, although these figures include 'stoning, riot and mob situations'.[85] According to figures compiled by the Institute of Strategic Studies at the University of Pretoria, there were 55 attacks in 1983.[86] The Minister for Law and Order revealed that there were 58 attacks during 1984. Thus, whatever set of figures is used, political violence has escalated since 1976, and particularly since 1980–1.

The targets have been political and economic. In the former group are government offices, courts, military bases, police stations, and assassinations of policemen. In the latter category are attacks on railway stations, banks, oil depots, shops, and offices. The ANC declared 1980 its year of action, and the increase in attacks since then is a good barometer of the ability of the ANC to translate threats into deeds. There are more than numerical factors to consider. 1980 saw an intensification of the ANC's confidence and planning, and in the damage inflicted. The year began with the Silverton bank hostage siege,[87] and included the SASOL oil depot explosion and the attacks on the Transkeian Consul. Surprise attacks had been common on isolated police stations in urban townships, but the 1980 incidents marked a venture into White residential areas directed against carefully guarded targets. The SASOL target was particularly interesting because it struck a blow at South Africa's drive for economic self-sufficiency. It also occurred on Republic Day, a historic day for Afrikaners. The following day bombs failed to explode at the American-owned company that is building the SASOL II and SASOL III depots. None the less, damage amounting to R5.8m. was caused over the two days. Damage caused by armed action against the state since 1976 has been conservatively estimated at R600m.[88]

The increase in political violence since 1981 is attested to by the estimate that this period has seen between 46.6 per cent and 68.6 per cent of all attacks since 1976. In 1983 there were more attacks than in any previous year, and 1984 continued this trend. Predictions of such an escalation have been made for a considerable time,[89] but the escalation that occurred has provoked debate on whether there has been a change in the strategy of the ANC towards becoming more ruthless and indiscriminate. With the exception of the assassination of informers and other people regarded as collaborators, the ANC's strategy was to avoid civilian casualties. In November 1980 it became a signatory to Protocol One of the 1949 Geneva Convention which binds it to refraining from attacks on civilian targets. In August 1981, however, Oliver Tambo announced that the ANC would attack 'officials of apartheid' and that there could arise 'combat situations' in which civilians might be killed.[90] A few days later a bomb exploded in the main shopping centre of Port Elizabeth at a time of peak use. In May 1983 a car bomb exploded in Pretoria outside the South African Air Force Headquarters and opposite a building which housed military intelligence personnel. Nineteen people died in the explosion and 217 were injured. According to official sources, eight of those killed were African and only four were military personnel. Damage was estimated at R4m. After equivocating, the ANC claimed responsibility. Tambo repeated this view several times during 1984–5. It has been suggested that this change reflected the dominance of the younger guard within the ANC who had left South Africa in 1976, and that the older guard who opposed violence involving civilians was being ousted from leadership positions.[91] Even liberal Whites in South Africa feared the Pretoria car bomb marked the beginning of attacks on soft civilian targets. Some people have argued in defence of the ANC, pointing out that attacks are generally on unpopular targets like rent offices, police stations, and administration boards. Gwendolen Carter claimed that the ANC was more concerned with seeking civilian support than winning military victories and that terror campaigns were still subordinate to political mobilization.[92] This is also the view of Tom Lodge, who argued that the ANC's leadership sees indiscriminate acts of violence as counter-productive.[93] The ANC has denied there is a change in tactics.

Two points need to be identified. The ANC's use of political violence is still tied to wider political mobilization, but, while soft civilian targets are not the primary target, it is prepared to escalate its use of armed propaganda even if this incidentally involves civilian deaths. There is clear evidence to suggest that the ANC places considerable emphasis on co-ordinating its attacks with local mass struggles. Lodge indicates that many attacks occurred in 1980 to link with the popular campaign against rent increases.[94] This co-ordination was particularly evident in the political campaign against the new constitution. In November 1983, during the White referendum, a bomb exploded at a police station in Durban, in a Durban bus depot, and on many railway lines in Natal and the Witwatersrand. In December there were at least six bomb blasts, including attacks on the offices of the Department of Foreign Affairs, the Department of Co-operation and Development, and on law courts. In 1984 bomb explosions occurred on the anniversary of 16 June, on the signing of the Nkomati accord, on the opening of the new Parliament and during the elections to the Coloured and Indian parliamentary institutions. The South African Suicide Squad, an offshoot of the ANC, used fire bombs on 22 occasions during the Coloured and Indian elections in 1984, including attacks on the homes of African councillors in local government, school principals, and candidates in the elections. Two fire bombs exploded at the house of Lucy Mvubelo, the moderate African trade unionist.

Despite being linked to wider political struggles, the incidents do show an escalation in ruthlessness and in the involvement of innocent civilians. The Pretoria car bomb was clearly aimed at a political target, but the 1981 Port Elizabeth car bomb involved a crowded city shopping area. The repercussions following this particular incident temporarily persuaded the ANC to abandon attacking this kind of target. They came to be seen as legitimate targets again in 1984. In February, a bomb exploded on the fourth floor of Durban's major shopping complex at the height of the rush hour. The target itself was the Ciskeian Consulate, but the ANC was prepared to countenance injuring civilians in order to attack it. In April three people were killed and twenty-three injured when a car bomb exploded in the rush hour outside a shopping and office complex in Durban. The three people who died were civilians who had been walking past when the bomb exploded. The site of the explosion was 100 yards from the customs entrance to the docks, and diagonally opposite the Department of Internal Affairs, which was relatively unaffected by the blast. If this was the intended target a lack of expertise seems to have been shown, for the office and shop complex, which also included a nursery school, was most affected by the explosion. Similarly, a home for the elderly was severely damaged when an explosion occurred at an adjacent electricity transformer in Mus-grave Road, Durban, in June 1984. Five people were killed and twenty-seven injured when a bomb exploded on an industrial estate near Durban in July 1984. This is not just a cell active around Durban, for a powerful car bomb exploded in a car show room near a cinema in Johannesburg during June 1984. Pedes-trians were injured in the blast. There is then some change in ANC strategy. It is prepared to attack political and security targets, as it always has been, but will now do so even when this is likely incidentally to involve innocent civilians.

It is not possible to leave discussion of revolutionary terror attacks without considering the response of the government, which is, after all, the primary target. Lodge believes that the incidents up to 1981 were an attempt to inspire confidence amongst the dominated groups rather than to create terror within the White community.[95] This was still only slightly less true for the incidents occurring in 1984. Either way, confusion surrounds the govern-ment's response. On the one hand they exaggerate the strength, support, and potential destructiveness of the ANC so as to justify repressive terrorism against subordinate groups. Conversely, they underplay the likelihood of further attack so as not to weaken the resolve or confidence of Whites. The Commissioner of Police said that the worst South Africa could expect was sporadic attacks. All terrorism is sporadic; that is its very nature. If it were not sporadic it could be predicted and hence wiped out. Conversely, the Brigadier of Police warned of 4,000 Africans eager to cross South Africa's borders and merely waiting for the opportunity to wreak havoc. The state's failure to decide whether the ANC poses a serious threat or not could well explain the failure of the police to take more than rudimentary precautions in safeguarding police stations. It is this which probably made targets so easy to hit. The preparedness of security forces will now increase. In the past, despite being greatly outnumbered, terrorist cells were able to inflict injury and damage without sustaining much injury to themselves: this will not be the case in urban areas after 1984.

In a sense, terrorism is a subjective phenomenon because individual reactions to it vary according to individual susceptibility to terror. Whites are determined not to give in. The press have joined their role of reporting news with that of forming public opinion in this direction. Supposed conversance with terrorists is used as a convenient bludgeon to batter any opposition force the government-supporting press decide to feature. In character with its normally vituperative attitude, the *Citizen* threatened liberal newspapers, the PFP, Black Consciousness, White universities, and neighbouring countries not to become 'embroiled with those who perpetrate' terrorism. It wrote, 'we must not lose our resolve to fight: instead we must rededicate ourselves by dying if need be. We must not let the liberals and their press undermine our confidence and our ability'.[96] Behind this is an image of the ANC. It is invariably portrayed as a ruthless, amoral, violent organization striking civilian targets, seeking nothing more than to create panic and enjoy senseless killing. This is an opinion which unites the pro-government with the liberal press they condemn — it is, indeed, the popular image of the ANC among Whites.[97] It is necessary to assess how true this image is.

THE LIMITATIONS OF TERRORISM IN SOUTH AFRICA

The image of an ideology or the movement which espouses it is just as important as the reality behind the image. Yet an image can distort as well as reflect the reality it hides. The ANC could never conform to its popular image because there are structural limitations preventing it from doing so. These limitations are of two kinds — those emanating from the nature of the organization itself, and those that are imposed from the outside. External limitations tend to restrict the frequency of the ANC's attacks and the internal limitations provide important brakes on its ruthlessness.

The most obvious among the external limitations is the enormous power of the South African state. It is this which most commentators point to in dismissing violent liberation in South Africa.[98] The imbalance of finance, weaponry, manpower, and training is very great but one should also consider the topography of South Africa. The country's borders are easy to cross: apart from its long coastline, Natal has three frontiers, with Mozambique, Swaziland and Lesotho; and Botswana, Zimbabwe, and Namibia all have long borders with South Africa. However, because of the great distance from the borders to the densely populated industrial areas, the ANC cannot use neighbouring Black states as staging-grounds even if it were allowed to. In fact, the interwoven relationships of dependence on South Africa allow it to pressurize neighbouring states who give overt support to liberation forces. This pressure has been applied through economic, political, and military destabilization. Barber and Hill report that Presidents Machel and Mugabe share the view that change will come about largely as a result of pressure from inside the Republic and that guerrilla activity from neighbouring states is relatively insignificant.[99] This belief could well be one of the factors behind Machel's readiness to act so quickly against ANC bases in Mozambique. After the accord with South Africa Machel claimed that the ANC should give up its armed struggle and concentrate on being a civil rights movement. Tambo refuted the claim that the Nkomati diplomatic accord seriously damaged the ANC, referring to it as only a temporary set-back. Yet similar agreements have been signed with Lesotho and Swaziland, and by June 1984 36 bases had been moved from Mozambique.

Geography is against the ANC in another way. The communities in South Africa's great geographical expanse are not isolated or remote. White settlement is scattered throughout the Republic, thus allowing some rudimentary observation of infiltration. This is especially so in the fertile farming districts of Northern Transvaal, bordering on Botswana and Zimbabwe, and in Northern Natal, adjacent to Swaziland and Mozambique. Area defence units have been established in these places to check on infiltration. Some people argue that South Africa's own homelands could in future provide the logistic support-base which urban attacks require.[100] The homelands form a horseshoe around the White urban areas, making them possible springboards for operations in the urban areas. Some are very fragmented, making their borders difficult to control. In a less obvious way, the ANC faces limitations because of its distance from the masses in South Africa. This is true in a physical sense because over twenty-five years have elapsed since its banning, a whole new generation has been born, and there is a completely new array of social movements and ideologies competing for success. The ANC is still popular,[101] but it has lost the position of dominance it held in the 1950s as virtually the sole legitimate voice of Black opposition.[102] This is true also in an ideological sense. There is a great deal of evidence to show that the majority of Blacks do not want a violent solution to South Africa's problems.[103] Anger and militancy have increased, but this falls short of the systematic use of violence. This is less true of the younger generation fired by the loss of their peers in 1976. As one African schoolboy said, 'How can one eat food and then later say you don't want the food you've eaten? Violence does not mean the end of education, it means the beginning of a good education. Whites are not prepared to change their policy of apartheid. If we think we can change them we are mistaken'.[104] Desperation is growing among the young, but in the majority there is still a commitment to a peaceful solution. There was very little evidence to the contrary even in the Soweto uprising. Attacks on Whites were the exception; among the haunting death roll only two Whites were listed. The figures provided by the Institute of Black Research's study of the Soweto uprising, when conscientization through participation in armed struggle was at its height, reveal only 11 per cent supporting violence to achieve political ends, 34 per cent explicitly rejecting it, and the remainder feeling it justified in a variety of differing circumstances.[105] These circumstances do not seem to have arrived yet although they are near. A study undertaken by the Centre of Applied Social Sciences at the University of Natal illustrated that while anger had increased among adult urban Blacks, hope for the future and a general approval of the leadership of the Prime Minister had grown more.[106]

Table 8. *Urban Black Opinion 1977–1979*

Year	Anger (%)	Confidence in the Future (%)	Approval of the Prime Minister (%)
1977	39	15	6
1979	44	61	57

Survey material like this is very dependent upon the political and economic circumstances existing at the time of the survey. For example, in March 1984 39.4 per cent of a nation-wide sample of 2,648 Coloured and Indian respondents rated P. W. Botha the best prime minister, with only 3.9 per cent favouring Allan Hendrickse and 2.9 per cent selecting Allan Boesak. It is highly likely that after the heavy-handed repression of Black protest that occurred during 1984 and 1985, the number supporting P. W. Botha dropped. Nevertheless, it is possible to discern certain trends in a number of different surveys over recent years. Schlemmer has shown how the level of expressed anger and dissatisfaction has increased among Black South Africans between 1977 and 1981, but that this fell short of sympathy for the use of political violence.[107] Research for the Buthelezi Commission showed that in response to the statement 'it is best for Black South Africans to be careful in politics and not make trouble', the differences between those who agreed and disagreed was 2 per cent in favour of disagreement in Kwa Zulu and Natal, and 10 per cent on the Witwatersrand.[108] While 'trouble' is itself considerably different to political violence, the sympathy for political compromise and negotiations was strong. This feeling is confirmed by Table 9.[109] There appears to be a feeling that patience, negotiation, and the building-up of bargaining power will lead to reforms and concessions being granted peacefully. This probably explains the lack of support there is among most Blacks for disinvestment.[110] Schlemmer refers to this duality of attitudes towards increasing anger and dissatisfaction, and continued moderacy, as the 'dual consciousness' of Black South Africans.[111] He considers this to be the most important factor bearing upon the lack of sympathy for ruthless and indiscriminate terror.

None the less, this 'dual consciousness' contains a dynamic for

Table 9. *Percentage Endorsement of Alternative Choice Statements Relating to Black Political Strategy*

Statement	Percentage
'A leader must act strongly to win support' vs.	22
'He should wait in order to form a strong organization'	76
'A Black leader should never co-operate with the government' vs.	11
'He should criticize but co-operate where beneficial'	85
'Being patient does not help, a leader must make strong demands now' vs.	30
'He must be patient and work with the tools he has'	61
'There is no longer anything to be gained by being patient' vs.	19
'It still pays to be patient and plan carefully'	81

the future in that the anger and dissatisfaction which forms a part of Black political attitudes may increase to an extent that it militates against political moderacy. There is a depressing contradiction between current Black optimism for the future, and the current unwillingness of the Whites to reform. The result of rising expectations that are frustrated is relative deprivation, which may be the cause of long-term revolutionary violence.[112] While sociopolitical and economic reform may be effected piecemeal by the South African government, reform will not keep pace with the rising expectations of Blacks under the impact of external developments, job advancement, and the erratic advance of reform. Indeed, research for the Buthelezi Commission showed that Black patience should not be taken for granted. Respondents were asked what they expected in the future if the government did not introduce changes for Blacks in the next ten years. The results are contained in Table 10.[113] This point has not yet been reached for many Black South Africans and the majority are still prepared

Table 10. *Black Expectations of the Future*

'Definitely expect'	Rural Kwa Zulu (%)	Kwa Zulu Natal Cities (%)	Witwaters-rand (%)
Blacks will be too frightened by army/police to act	21	9	17
Many more Blacks will leave country for military training	44	56	51
Mass strikes by Black workers	60	65	64
Bloodshed/war/revolution	80	80	80

for the moment to place emphasis on peaceful political compromise.

While it is true that over 20,000 people attend the funerals of young revolutionary terrorists, two different kinds of acts are involved. Sympathy with a teenager hanged for a cause they also believe in is quite different from acceptance of the violent means chosen to realise that cause. Research for the Buthelezi Commission revealed that 48 per cent of respondents in Kwa Zulu and Natal felt that 'most or many' people would try to help ANC insurgents. Fear of police rather than disagreement with the aims of the ANC was the main reason why the respondents felt some people would not help the ANC.[114] Clearly there is support for the ANC, but this does not suggest that there is support for the use of political violence. South Africa is a very violent society, but the violence is not inter-racial or directed at political change. Statistics on crimes involving violence attest to this. For the year up to 30 June 1978, only 5.62 per cent of murders of White victims were committed by Blacks. Whites were charged with six times as many inter-race murders and twenty times as many inter-race culpable homicides per 100,000 of population. The same applies to rape and attempted rape — only 5.28 per cent of White victims were raped by Blacks.[115] A further index is provided by the numbers in the Black community perceiving Whites as a fundamental part of a peaceful future. A 1980 survey pointed out that only 16 per cent of urban Blacks in South Africa felt Whites in Zimbabwe should be forced to leave upon independence.[116] Studies confirm that this reflects their opinion on the position of Whites in South Africa.[117] The research for the Buthelezi Commission and the Quail Commission has shown that, despite the high levels of discontent and dissatisfaction, the minimum political demands of a wide cross-section of Blacks are surprisingly moderate. Schlemmer reports that between 60 per cent and 70 per cent of Blacks declare themselves prepared to accept socio-political arrangements which amount to a substantial compromise with White interests. In particular, majorities of Blacks in various surveys are willing to accept consociational arrangements in which Whites have an equal power with Blacks in a future dispensation.[118] The Buthelezi Commission not only found that 70 per cent of Black South Africans would oppose discrimination against Whites, but also indicated that they valued White participation in South Africa.[119] Clearly mass Black opinion is in favour of peaceful coexistence.

The irony of the position of the ANC is that its vision of the future is much the same, but it has chosen revolutionary terrorism to realize it, feeling that future peace can only be earned through present strife. It visualizes order coming through conflict but none the less aims at stable, ordered, and just racial coexistence.[120] However, these means and ends do not hang happily together and their incongruence provides an important internal limitation on the ANC. Its vision of the future prevents it being utterly ruthless. The seeds of this vision are firmly planted in the history of the movement, and although it chose to use revolutionary terrorism on its banning, the organization has been unable completely to overthrow its tradition of pacifism, pluralism, and social democracy. The early leaders of the ANC were non-violent men. Meer has shown how in leading the defiance campaign as President of the ANC Luthuli never deliberately violated unjust laws;[121] and, surveying 129 speeches made between 1952 and 1956, Meer discovered that only 11 per cent made reference to violence.[122] The organization was temperamentally suited to non-violence and passive resistance, and actually condemned the use of violence on those occasions when the masses went ahead of them and resorted to it. There is an additional element — a deep sense of moral superiority among the leadership of the organization, what Meer called a 'cult of suffering', and Barrington Moore in another context termed asceticism.[123] The ANC was pervaded by a feeling of the moral superiority of its cause, that it had the support of the world, and that eventually right would win over might. In this way the move to revolutionary terrorism in the early 1960s was predicated on the temperament of martyrs, not ruthless saboteurs. It was an organization more used to words than to violence.[124] The men who went underground were radicals, but they were not revolutionaries. They lacked what Stone called the 'obsessive revolutionary mentality'.[125]

Unlike the Vietcong, SWAPO, and the Zimbabwean liberation forces, this has meant that the ANC has not resorted to political gang terror or the killing of village headmen. It has never wanted to intimidate the indigenous civilian populace. Thus, for example, it does not extract 'dues' from Black businessmen, Blacks working within government posts, and the like. Its assassination attempts have been directed against former ANC members who have turned state's evidence, or started working with the South African Police. In this respect the ANC parallels the early IRA, which advocated a very selective use of terror against the security system, believing that general terror would alienate popular support. There is a danger that a spiral effect may work for the ANC as it did for the IRA forcing it to become more ruthless in order to compete with more ruthless rivals (or factions) or to match the escalation of the state's repressive terrorism. There is some evidence that this has already happened. There have been civilian deaths, and civilian targets have been the object of attack where the public were open to threat. However, if it really wished it, a very effective campaign against distant powerlines, dams or agricultural production could totally disrupt civilian amenities. There would be less risk to itself since these tend to be isolated targets and nearly all unguarded. A host of easy civilian targets present themselves, but the ANC still prefers to attack the more difficult political–security targets. In other words, the 'primary target' still remains the upholders of the present system of power in South Africa, in preference to wreaking death or destruction for their own sake. None the less, the statistics reveal an escalation in ruthlessness, though it remains to be proved that this marks any long-term shift in attitude.

One final limitation on the effectiveness of the external liberation forces is that they are not cohesive. The intensity of their opposition to apartheid is deflected by conflicts among themselves.

Energy, effort, and manpower are depleted in unnecessary duplication and squabbling. The nature of these divisions is twofold: the lack of unity between the ANC and PAC; and the conflicts within each, especially within the ANC, over their ideological or nationalist character.

Historically these two sets of divisions are related. The PAC was formed in 1959 after conflicts within the ANC over its identity as a Marxist or Black nationalist movement. These differences have simmered ever since. The two movements were careful not to denigrate each other in public, but at the Libreville OAU conference in 1977 mutual tolerance was abandoned. The racial exclusivism inherent in Pan-Africanism caused the ANC to portray its rival as being run by Black racists.[126] The timing of this statement was no coincidence. It was partly due to the heightening of competition in the wake of the Soweto uprising, and partly to the increasing global competition of China and the Soviet Union, the former backing more the PAC and the latter supporting more the ANC. Each world power is seeking to portray its surrogate as the sole authentic representative of the liberation struggle in South Africa. A Lisbon conference in 1977 formally recognized the ANC as such and so have the states which border South Africa. The West has yet to choose between them and the United Nations has asked the two organizations to settle their differences amicably.

The conflict between the rival organizations is complicated by the schisms within each movement. The PAC has been disunited since the death of Sobukwe. In 1978 seven members of the Central Committee and sixty rank-and-file members were expelled from Swaziland for 'dishonest practices', and in the following year they formed a breakaway group called the Azania People's Revolutionary Party, led by Sibeko, Make, and Ntloedibe. Sibeko was then shot dead and Make seriously injured in Dar es Salaam by allies of Leballo who had been instrumental in expelling them from Swaziland. Tanzania has since expelled Leballo, and Make was elected chairman of the PAC in Dar es Salaam. This division tends to have ideological differences overlaid by personal ambition: within the ANC personal ambition is less obvious.

Historically, ideology has always been a source of schism in the ANC. On the one level this has given it an ambiguity as the influence of the Marxist and Black nationalist factions alters. Conflicts between the factions have periodically broken out. A breakaway group, calling itself the ANC of South Africa African Nationalists, has committed itself to Africanism and rejects support from non-Blacks. In 1979 it was reported as saying 'we hate the communists'.[127] Thus some people have claimed that the ANC is a petit bourgeois organization advancing national liberation and bourgeois democratic rights but not class struggle.[128] Such a view was denied by First, who pointed to the ANC's 1969 statement 'Strategy and Tactics', in which the organization's commitment to a class struggle is explicit.[129] In other ways, the links between the ANC and the South African Communist Party have been strengthening. Speaking on British television, Oliver Tambo said that the struggle is no longer one of satisfying Black interests but of furthering the aims of communism. In 1979, however, a group of British-based Marxists were expelled. The schism is thus a very complex one and cannot be commented upon without a more extensive examination of the external liberation forces than this study undertakes. Although the factions within the ANC often act as if they were opposed to one another, in a theoretical sense the frames of reference they advance, based on race or class, are reconcilable. Chapter 3 shows how opposition in the workplace reveals that it is a false dichotomy to separate race and class.

One of the most important divisions within the ANC is over the role of armed conflict. In the past the ANC has been criticized for an overemphasis on armed struggle. Mafeje feared that this growing militarism would eventually submerge politics to the detriment of the organization.[130] The British-based Marxists who were expelled in 1979 felt that the movement was not active enough in underground political and trade union activity. They believed that guerrilla activity was less important than mobilizing the masses to political and economic action. The ANC has always seen itself as doing both. The 1969 statement 'Strategy and Tactics' argued that 'the continued support of the mass of the people has to be won in all-round political mobilization which must accompany the military activities'.[131] First's response to Mafeje emphasized that the dominant view in the ANC was that militarization for its own sake was meaningless and that military activities should always have a political context.[132]

Yet the relationship between military and political activities has been difficult to decide and, in practice, there have been occasions when the ANC's involvement in political struggles was slight.

However, since 1976 the rapidly expanding political struggle inside South Africa has been such that the ANC has been forced to involve itself politically as well as militarily. It has chosen to use revolutionary terror, yet there are internal and external constraints preventing it from using this tactic to its fullest effectiveness. Therefore it opens itself up to all the criticism and pejorative evaluation reserved for terrorists and subjects itself to the repressive response of the South African state, without fully justifying it. This may well be acceptable to the ANC. If not, the movement faces a moral dilemma as important as the one it faced on choosing revolutionary terror upon its banning. In the face of the moral and physical sacrifices of the present strategy, does it abandon the use of revolutionary terror or escalate it to make the sacrifice worth while? The second answer seems more likely, and 1980, its year of action, was the watershed at which the choice was made. In August 1980 an unexploded mortar bomb was discovered against the wall of Emmerentia dam, and two young children were injured when a bomb exploded near Heatonville, Empangeni. The bomb attacks in city centres throughout the Republic injuring innocent passers-by could well be evidence of how the ANC resolved its dilemma. But the evidence is contradictory. When we consider the open political struggle that is taking place for leadership of the urban townships between the community councils and a number of their critics, it will be shown that the ANC is seeking an internal political wing in order to participate in this open political challenge. The ANC is hoping to be able to feed politically off the increased pressure it is applying through the tactic of revolutionary terror. This has enabled some political organizations inside South Africa to forge a strategy based on revolutionary terror and the mobilization and articulation of political grievances.

In recent years there has emerged a much closer link between armed struggle and political mobilization. Not only does this distinguish the ANC's use of revolutionary terror from other groups like the IRA and Baader–Meinhof, but it increases the pressure which internal politics generates in South Africa. This pressure is added to by pressure from workers, and it is to opposition in the workplace that we now turn.

Notes

1. Noted by P. Wilkinson, *Political Terrorism*, London, Macmillan, 1973, and R. Clutterbuck, *Living with Terrorism*, London, Faber and Faber, 1975.

2. 'Ideology as a Cultural System', in D. Apter, *Ideology and Discontent*, Glencoe, Free Press, 1964.

3. G. Moss, *Political Trials in South Africa: 1976–79*, Development Studies Group, University of Witwatersrand, Information Publication no. 2; B. Davidson *et al.*, *Southern Africa: The New Politics of Revolution*, London, Penguin, 1976; M. Morris, *Terrorism*, Cape Town, Timmins, 1971.

4. *Rand Daily Mail*, 16 April 1978.

5. P. Wilkinson, *Terrorism and the Liberal State*, London, Macmillan, 1977, p. 52–3.

6. Quoted by P. Wilkinson, *Political Terrorism*, p. 79.

7. This is discussed fully in M. Morris, op. cit., p. 16 ff.

8. R. Clutterbuck, op. cit.; *Protest and the Urban Guerrilla*, London, Cassel, 1973.

9. 'Transnational Terrorism, Civil Liberties and Social Science', in Y. Alexander and S. Finger, *Terrorism: Interdisciplinary Perspectives*, New York, MacGraw-Hill, 1977, p. 283.

10. P. Wilkinson, op. cit.

11. B. Crozier, *The Rebel*, London, Chatto and Windus, 1966, p. 72.

12. 'Terrorism as a Weapon of Political Agitation', in H. Eckstein, *Internal War*, New York, Free Press, 1964, pp. 71–99.

13. J. Witton, *Terrorism and Resistance*, New York, Oxford University Press, 1969, p. 7.

14. P. Wilkinson, op. cit., pp. 36–41. See also his *Terrorism and the Liberal State*, pp. 52–6.

15. There are exceptions to this but it is doubtful whether these conform to what Wilkinson means by revolutionary terrorism, where the political aspect is manifest.

16. B. Singh, 'An Overview', in Y. Alexander and S. Finger, op. cit., p. 10, identifies four other functions — morale-building within the movement, disorientation of the populace, elimination of opposition forces, and provocation of the government.

17. J. J. Paust, 'A Definitional Focus', ibid., p. 21.

18. P. Wilkinson, *Terrorism and the Liberal State*, p. 50.

19. It could be argued that terrorism is by nature self-defeating because it forfeits the right to participate in or influence a constitutional process. The IRA faced this rejection in the British government's discussions on Ulster. But more examples exist to the contrary, the most recent of which are the cases of Zimbabwe and Namibia. The examples of Kenya and Malaysia also come to mind.

20. 'The Anatomy of Revolution', *Africa South*, April–June 1969, p. 9.

21. This explains the pessimism of L. H. Gann, 'No Hope for Violent Liberation: A Strategic Assessment', *Africa Report*, 17, 1972.

22. Histories of this period cover these events well. See: E. Feit, *African Opposition in South Africa*, Stanford, Hoover Institute Press, 1967; G. Gerhart, *Black Power in South Africa*, Berkeley, University of California Press, 1979; T. Karis and G. Carter, *From Protest to Challenge*, 4 vols., Stanford, Hoover Institute Press, 1972, 73, 77; E. Roux, *Time Longer Than Rope*, Madison, University of Wisconsin Press, 1966; P. Walshe, *The Rise of African Nationalism in South Africa*, Berkeley, University of California Press, 1971.

23. Quoted by F. Meer, 'African Nationalism: Some Inhibiting Factors', in H. Adam, *South Africa: Sociological Perspectives*, London, Oxford University Press, 1971, p. 148.

24. B. Moore, *Injustice: The Social Bases of Obedience and Revolt*, London, Macmillan, 1978, p. 4.

25. The only known source of any length on this is G. Visser, *OB: Traitors or Patriots?*, Johannesburg, Macmillan, 1976.

26. Ibid., p. 27.

27. I use the term 'race' here in its conventional sociological sense of referring to cultural as well as biological differentia. In this sense, the term 'ethnic' is synonymous with that of 'race', as Rex argues forcibly. What is meant by this is that some ethnic groups are in a subordinate group position and face inequalities and differentiation related to the physical or cultural qualities of their *ethnie*. See J. Rex, *Race Relations in Sociological Theory*, London, Weidenfeld and Nicolson, 1970, p. 25ff.

28. See the *Daily News*, 28 October 1977.

29. See the *Citizen*, 16 November 1977.

30. See SAIRR, *Survey of Race Relations 1982*, Johannesburg, SAIRR, 1983, p. 253.

31. Quoted by the *Daily News*, 11 July 1978.

32. Taken from SAIRR, *Survey of Race Relations 1980*, Johannesburg, SAIRR, 1981, pp. 230–1. The incident referred to is that of Paulus Cane, widely reported in the press during 1978–9.

33. See SAIRR, *Survey of Race Relations 1983*, Johannesburg, SAIRR, 1984, p. 534.

34. Compiled from statistics provided by the SAIRR. See *Survey of Race Relations 1980*, p. 230, and *Survey of Race Relations 1983*, p. 536. Earlier figures provided by the Minister of Police: see *Republic of South Africa, House of Assembly Debates*, vol. 84, nos. 1–19, cols. 1–1095.

35. *Daily News*, 18 May 1978.

36. Ibid., 22 October 1977.

37. *Citizen*, 3 December 1977.
38. *Post Transvaal*, 2 April 1979.
39. Reported in the *Daily News*, 21 November 1978.
40. Ibid., 12 January 1980.
41. Ibid., 13 September 1979.
42. Ibid., 19 September 1978.
43. Ibid., 12 July 1979.
44. *Sunday Tribune*, 30 July 1978.
45. *Daily News*, 3 October 1978.
46. Ibid., 16 April 1978.
47. *Sunday Times*, 20 August 1979.
48. *Daily News*, 23 October 1978.
49. *Post Transvaal*, 1 April 1979.
50. Ibid., 15 April 1979.
51. SAIRR, *Survey of Race Relations*, p. 214.
52. SAIRR, *Survey of Race Relations*, p. 535.
53. Ibid.
54. BBC television news report, 30 July 1984.
55. Statistics compiled from various editions of the SAIRR's annual survey of race relations.
56. In October 1985 the Minister of Law and Order announced that fourteen policemen had been killed in the previous eighteen months of unrest, and 500 homes of policemen had been burnt and gutted.
57. See for example, J. Kiernan, 'Public Transport and Private Risk: Zionism and the Black Commuter in South Africa', *Journal of Anthropological Research*, 33, 1977.
58. *Sunday Times*, 16 September 1979.
59. *Daily News*, 3 October 1978.
60. As a beginning see: J. Jackson, *Justice in South Africa*, London, Penguin, 1980; J. Dugard and W. Dean, 'The Just Legal Order', in S. van der Horst and J. Reid, *Race Discrimination in South Africa*, Cape Town, David Philip, 1981.
61. *Voice*, 14 October 1978, and *Daily News*, 24 April 1979 respectively.
62. Quoted in SAIRR, *Survey of Race Relations 1983*, p. 567.
63. Ibid., p. 571.
64. Quoted by SAIRR, *Laws Affecting Race Relations in South Africa*, Johannesburg, SAIRR, 1978, p. 404.
65. For an excellent survey of South Africa's legal code see SAIRR, *Laws Affecting Race Relations in South Africa*, and A. S. Mathews, 'Security Laws and Social Change in the Republic of South Africa', in H. Adam, *South Africa: Sociological Perspectives*; id., 'Legislation and Civil Liberties in South Africa', *Optima*, 32.1, 1984.

66. The following discussion is based on A. S. Mathews, 'Legislation and Civil Liberties in South Africa', pp. 10–12.

67. A. S. Mathews, 'Legislation and Civil Liberties in South Africa', p. 11.

68. Ibid., p. 12.

69. See SAIRR, *Survey of Race Relations 1980*, p. 265.

70. SAIRR, *Survey of Race Relations 1983*, pp. 2, 549.

71. Compiled from figures ibid., p. 549.

72. SAIRR, *Survey of Race Relations 1984*, Johannesburg, SAIRR, 1985, pp. 758–60.

73. Op. cit., p. 14. This escalation is denied by government supporters who believe that the rise in revolutionary terrorism is not linked to the repressive nature of the South African state. As one example, see K. Campbell, 'Prospects for Terrorism in South Africa', *South Africa International*, 14.2, 1983, p. 403. Indeed, to Campbell any suggestion that there is a link should be vigorously denied in order to avoid delegitimizing the police (p. 404). For a more balanced view see J. Brewer and J. Smyth, 'Political Violence and Conflict Management in Northern Ireland and South Africa', in T. Hanf, *Deeply Divided Societies: Violence and Conflict Management in South Africa, Northern Ireland, Israel and Lebanon*, Munich and Mainz, Kaiser and Grunewald, 1986.

74. Reported in M. Morris, 'South African Security: Some Considerations for the Future', Terrorism Research Centre, Special Report, 1980, p. 13. The Terrorism Research Centre is an organization run by Morris single-handed in Cape Town. It claims financial and political autonomy from the government, which is probably true, but Morris is a notorious right wing academic, an ex-policeman, and a naive political opportunist with literary ambitions. The Centre's publications are useful for obtaining semi-official information and attitudes.

75. SAIRR, *Survey of Race Relations 1983*, p. 45.

76. Ibid.

77. By Marplan for the *Johannesburg Star*: see the edition of 26 May 1980.

78. This is worked out from the discussion by M. Morris, *Armed Struggle in Southern Africa*, Cape Town, Jeremy Spence, 1975, p. 282.

79. R. Clutterbuck, *Living with Terrorism*, p. 23.

80. Also noted by T. Lodge, *Black Politics in South Africa Since 1945*, London, Longman, 1982, pp. 340–1, and SAIRR, *Survey of Race Relations 1983*, p. 568.

81. See *Work in Progress*, Development Studies Group, University of Witwatersrand, no. 18, 1981, pp. 22–6.

82. Quoted by SAIRR, *Survey of Race Relations 1983*, pp. 567–8.

83. Ibid., p. 567.
84. Compiled from figures provided by the Minister of Law and Order, quoted ibid., p. 567.
85. *Cape Times*, 11 January 1984.
86. Quoted by SAIRR, *Survey of Race Relations 1983*, p. 568.
87. This was not directed at supplementing ANC funds, for the organization is very wealthy. According to T. Gulick, policy analyst of the Heritage Foundation in Washington, USA, the ANC received R118m. in the first six months of 1983. This came from the World Health Organization, the United Nations, and from other organizations and governments in West Germany, Sweden, Finland, and the Netherlands. Quoted in the *South African Digest*, 24 June 1983, p. 4.
88. International Defence and Aid Fund, op. cit., p. 10.
89. For example see P. van den Berghe, *South Africa: A Study in Conflict*, Middletown, 1965, p. 263; S. Nolutshungu, 'The Impact of External Opposition on South African Politics', in L. Thompson and J. Butler, *Change in Contemporary South Africa*, Berkeley, University of California Press, 1975, p. 371.
90. *The Times* (London), 13 April 1981, p. 14.
91. C. Coaker, quoted in SAIRR, *Survey of Race Relations 1983*, p. 45.
92. Ibid., pp. 45–46.
93. T. Lodge, 'The ANC and Violence', University of Natal, Forum Lecture, September 1983.
94. *Black Politics in South Africa Since 1945*, p. 340.
95. Ibid.
96. *Citizen*, 7 April 1980.
97. In this respect the South African press have drawn a parallel between the ANC and the IRA, likening the Brighton bomb blast to the bomb blasts which occurred in South Africa since 1982. The liberal *Beeld* wrote, 'take a look at some of the points they have in common. Both the IRA and ANC plan to overthrow legal governments and replace them with Marxist systems. Both commit acts of terror to achieve their aims. There is no difference between terrorist organizations' (15 October 1984).
98. See R. Stokes, 'External Liberation Movements', and J. Daniels, 'Radical Resistance in South Africa', in I. Robertson and P. Whitten, *Race and Politics in South Africa*, New Jersey, Transaction Books, 1978; P. van den Bergh, *South Africa: A Study in Conflict*, Berkeley, University of California Press, 1967; L.H. Gann, op. cit.; G. D. H. Cole, op. cit.; K. Campbell, 'The Prospects for Terrorism in South Africa', op. cit.
99. J. Barber, J. Blumenfeld, and C. Hill, *The West and South Africa*, London, Routledge and Kegan Paul, 1982, p. 17.
100. M. Hough, *Financial Mail*, 19 January 1979; J. Saul and S. Gelb,

The Crisis in South Africa, New York, Monthly Review Press, 1981, p. 21; S. Duncan, 'The Effects of the Riekart Report on the African Population', *South African Labour Bulletin*, 5.4, 1979; H. Giliomee, 'Crisis and Co-option in South Africa', European Consortium for Political Research, Freiburg, 20–5 March 1983.

101. The mammoth longitudinal study of the Arnold Bergstraesser Institute in Freiburg discovered that 19 per cent of adult urban Blacks still rated Mandela as their most popular leader. See T. Hanf *et al.*, *Südafrika: Friedlicher Wandel*, Munich, 1978. The Free Mandela Campaign is gaining a great deal of support in South Africa from leading Black politicians, the liberal press and, especially, the young generation of radical Black students. It is very poignant to sit in the midst of a Free Mandela meeting and see the surge of South Africa's present young generation cheering a man they have never seen or heard. The mantle of the ANC is one which all contemporary Black political movements wish to pick up. An English edition of the Freiburg study was published in 1981 in London by Rex Collings as *South Africa: The Prospects of Peaceful Change*.

102. In one sense it could be argued that the ANC never possessed that position because of the competition of the PAC, but the latter was always the smaller and less influential body.

103. This point was also a prominent finding of the Arnold Bergstraesser Institute's study; see T. Hanf *et al.*, op. cit., pp. 16ff. An excellent summary of the attitude surveys on African opinions which point to this is H. Lever, 'Attitudes and Opinions of Africans', in id., *South African Society*, Johannesburg, Jonathan Ball, 1978. All contemporary forces in African opposition, including Inkatha, Black Consciousness groups, the South African Council of Churches, the Committee of 10, and the Black media, are committed to a peaceful solution, at least as a first option.

104. In an interview with the author, 11 November 1979.

105. IBR, *Soweto: A People's Response*, Durban, IBR, 1976, p. 11.

106. See L. Schlemmer, V. Möller and P. Stopforth, *Black Urban Communities*, Centre of Applied Social Sciences, Document and Memorandum Series, March 1980, p. 10.

107. L. Schlemmer, 'Conflict in South Africa: Build up to Revolution or Impasse?' European Consortium for Political Research, Freiburg, 20–5 March, 1983. The original research undertaken for the Buthelezi Commission.

108. Ibid., p. 19.

109. Ibid., p. 28.

110. See *Indicator: Political Monitor*, May 1983, pp. 10–11; *Indicator: Political Monitor*, September 1984, special issue on Black attitudes.

111. L. Schlemmer, 'Conflict in South Africa: Build up to Revolution or Impasse?', p. 30.

112. In saying this I am passing no judgement on the merits of the socio-psychological theories of revolution (and the rise of social movements) called the 'rising expectations', 'dissatisfactions' or 'relative deprivation' theories. The complexities of these theories go beyond what is said here. See J. Davies, 'Toward a Theory or Revolution', *American Sociological Review*, 27, 1962; T. R. Gurr, *Why Men Rebel*, Princeton, Princeton University Press, 1970; J. Geschwender, 'Explorations in the Theory of Social Movements and Revolutions', *Social Forces*, 47, 1968.

113. Taken from L. Schlemmer, 'Conflict in South Africa: Build up to Revolution or Impasse?', p. 20.

114. Ibid., pp. 20–1.

115. See M. Morris, 'South African Crime Trends', Terrorism Research Centre, Cape Town, 1979.

116. *Daily News*, 25 May 1980.

117. This is another of the significant findings in T. Hanf *et al.*, op. cit., part 3. Schlemmer has found this to be true even for young Black Consciousness supporters; see L. Schlemmer, 'Black Consciousness: Pride and Dignity or Militancy and Racism?', *South African Journal of Sociology*, 20, 1979.

118. See L. Schlemmer, 'Conflict in South Africa: Build up to Revolution or Impasse?', p. 28; L. Schlemmer and D. Welsh, 'South Africa's Constitutional and Political Prospects', *Optima*, 30.4, 1982.

119. Quoted by L. Schlemmer, 'Conflict in South Africa: Build up to Revolution or Impasse?', p. 29.

120. A good example is Mandela's 'Address to the Court before Sentence', 7 November 1962, in *We Accuse*, Christian Action pamphlet, no. 25, London, n.d.

121. F. Meer, 'African Nationalism: Some Inhibiting Factors', p. 141.

122. Ibid., p. 142.

123. For Meer's use, see ibid., and for Moore see *Injustice: The Social Bases of Obedience and Revolt*, p. 50.

124. Noted by R. Stokes, op. cit., p. 69.

125. L. Stone, 'Theories of Revolution', *World Politics*, 1966, p. 68.

126. Reported in SAIRR, *Survey of Race Relations 1978*, Johannesburg, SAIRR, 1979, p. 38.

127. Reported in SAIRR, *Survey of Race Relations 1979*, Johannesburg, SAIRR, 1980, p. 56.

128. A. Mafeje, 'Soweto and its Aftermath', *Review of African Political Economy*, 11, 1978, p. 27; D. du Toit, *Capital and Labour in South Africa*, London, Routledge and Kegan Paul, 1981; J. Saul and S. Gelb, op. cit., p. 41; A. Callinicos and J. Rogers, *Southern Africa After Soweto*, London, Pluto, 1966.

129. 'After Soweto: A Response', *Review of African Political Economy*, 11, 1978, pp. 98–9.

130. 'Soweto and its Aftermath', p. 29. This view is supported by J. Saul and S. Gelb, op. cit., pp. 103, 142.
131. 'Strategy and Tactics of the ANC', reprinted in *ANC Speaks: Documents and Statements of the African National Congress 1955–1976*, London, ANC, 1977, p. 179.
132. 'After Soweto: A Response', p. 99.

3

Opposition in the Workplace

INTRODUCTION: THE RACE–CLASS ISSUE

It is not surprising that South Africa elicits strong emotions in view of its social, economic and racial injustice. There is a wide variety of conceptualizations of this injustice. Some see the situation as one of straightforward class struggle under capitalism. Others argue there are either two separate working classes or two economies. Yet others suggest that there is an irreducible ethnic or racial element involved. What defeats understanding is the vituperative emotion aroused in protection of preferred interpretations of this injustice. Robert Davies prefaced his interpretation by charging those who would disagree with being 'bourgeois ideologists'.[1] In an unusual piece of invective, Luckhardt and Wall accuse the liberal Edward Feit of deliberate malice and of being motivated by hostility to the working class.[2] The implication of these remarks is clear: to offer anything other than a Marxist analysis of social and political change is to oppose a change that benefits the disenfranchised, impoverished majority in South Africa. This assumption is unwarranted and the invective has been equalled in response. Kantor and Kenny referred to the 'poverty' of this theorizing,[3] while Johnson questioned its usefulness when it 'flattened out lived experience into bloodless manoeuvres of categories'.[4] In an important sense such passion between Marxism and liberal–pluralism is pointless: they are wrong to present themselves as mutually exclusive.

If anything, the South African government fears African workers more than the terrorists, and Black workers generally are aware of their potential. Winnie Mandela once said that it is Black hands that have made South Africa what it is. Irrespective of who directs the hands to work in any particular way, if those hands are withdrawn the work does not get done. African trade unions know that they wield what André du Toit called 'Black muscle power'.[5] This power comes from various sources—from the sheer number of African workers, their strategic place in the economy, the shortage of all forms of White labour, and the growing politicization of the Black community generally. The government has responded by conceding some liberalizations in the economy,[6] although it remains adamant in refusing to grant political rights to Africans. So, at a juncture when African workers are gaining some relative freedoms in the workplace, the workplace is the focus of vociferous opposition. This conundrum is not difficult to explain: the idea of political liberation has permeated down to the workplace. Mobilization of African workers is done on a variety of social bases. The Black trade unionist, W. Mahlangu, who was killed in the 1978 Sigma strike, conjoined political, economic and ethnic aspirations. Under the mobilizing banner of 'We shall overcome', the aims in the Sigma strike were not exclusively class or plant-based. A shop steward said, 'we cannot draw a distinction between trade unions and guerrillas . . . they are on the same side. The trade unions aim at political liberation'.[7]

Just what rank is to be assigned to political mobilization is a source of tension within the trade union movement. This was most evident in the conflicts between the Federation of South African Trade Unions and the group of independent unregistered unions who are unaffiliated. The latter accused FOSATU of ignoring politics in favour of narrow factory concerns. The South African Allied Workers' Union described itself, for example, as a trade union dealing with workers who are part and parcel of the community. The problems of the workplace were seen as going outside the factory, and wider community problems, such as transport, rent, citizenship rights, and segregated facilities, were described as worker issues. FOSATU rejected this degree of politicization of the workplace. This rejection does not in itself involve an inability to recognize the relationship between the workplace and its socio-political context. It could be argued that FOSATU's attempt to draw a line between plant-based and political issues provided a chance for the trade unions under its affiliation to develop before the government could proscribe them for political meddling. But despite the stand taken by some trade unions, it will be argued that there is pressure from African workers to bring community-wide issues into the factory, and where the trade unions are reluctant to do so, community-based organizations are drawn in to the workplace to fill the void.

This illustrates clearly that in the mind of the main participants themselves, it is a false dichotomy to separate race and class, politics and economics; race and class are inextricably interwoven in South Africa, irrespective of whether theoreticians from the Marxist or liberal–pluralist camps wish to separate them and give priority to one over the other. The complexity of African opposition in South Africa defeats an exclusive concentration on one frame of reference over the other for on the ground, African workers are pragmatic enough to utilize every platform and to form opposition groups on a number of social bases and material interests. Rather than advancing a preferred theoretical position, a more intellectually worthwhile exercise has been undertaken, *inter alios*, by Rex, Adam, and Mason,[8] who offer attempts at a synthesis of the two approaches. The nature of these syntheses will go without comment. The following discussion of opposition in the workplace seeks to show how at the level of practical action the two frames of reference based on class and race are inextricably interwoven and cannot be separated or presented as dichotomous. What is unique about South African capitalism is that African workers are not simply members of an economically defined group, but members possessing a skin colour which has significance for their economic, social and political relationships. Theoretically it has been possible to accommodate this fact within the terms of each doctrinal position without threatening the validity of that position. Again this accommodation will go without comment. The discussion of opposition in the workplace in this chapter will simply show how, in practice, African workers operate with a model based on both frames of reference. Mayer's pioneering work on class and ethnicity among Africans in Johannesburg demonstrated this.[9] His findings repeated those of Leggett in Detroit,[10] and were confirmed by Geschwender.[11] This will be returned to in the conclusion to this chapter.

AFRICAN LABOUR AND TRADE UNIONS PRIOR TO 1979

African labour legislation evolved in an *ad hoc* fashion in response to a number of exigencies, and as a result, was extremely complex.[12] African workers were never legally denied the opportunity to form collective bodies, but although there were no statutes formally preventing unionization, both employers and the government placed obstacles inhibiting workers from doing so, and many apartheid laws conspired to prevent it. The right to strike in law was accorded in 1973, providing that the correct procedures in calling for industrial action had been followed. What has been denied such bodies is formal legal recognition as trade unions, and hence the institutionalized right to participate in collective bargaining. The legislation that followed the 1979 Wiehahn Commission accorded this privilege, but the recognition by African workers of the potential of collective action and corporate identity pre-dates Wiehahn by half a century.

The South African trade union movement began in the last century.[13] Initially there were too few Africans in industry to organize. The Industrial Workers of Africa was founded in 1917 to mobilize African workers, but the major thrust towards African unionization came with the Industrial and Commercial Workers' Union in 1919. Founded by Clemens Kadalie, its political affiliations were openly to African nationalism.[14] Shula Marks documents how in Natal, the ICU gained most response from African wage-labour and labour-tenant farmers.[15] At its height ICU's membership was 100,000,[16] almost double that of the Council of Non-European Trade Unions, which was active during and after the Second World War, and SACTU which was prominent in the 1950s and 1960s. Each of these three thrusts to African unionization were trammelled by the state. Until 1979 the Industrial Conciliation Act denied Africans formal collective bargaining by excluding them from its definition of 'employee'. Africans could not be members of registered trade unions, although they could belong to unregistered unions, which had no role in collective bargaining. Thereby any protection the Africans had against exploitation and victimization was removed.[17]

In 1979 there were twenty-three African worker organizations, representing nearly 75,000 members,[18] and affiliated to a number of co-ordinating bodies. The government established the Trade Union Council of South Africa, which accepted the affiliation of parallel African organizations in 1974. Pressure from right wing White unions had delayed this acceptance for nearly twenty years. As a result of this, few African worker organizations affiliated when the opportunity arose. The major exception was Lucy Mvubelo's National Union of Clothing Workers. In 1983 TUCSA had 453,906 members, of which less than a quarter were African. Many African unions have since disaffiliated from TUSCA and became affiliated to other federations. In 1984 27,000 members had been lost by the spring. Even from 1982 a shift to the right by the TUCSA leadership was noted.[19] In 1983, for example, motions at the annual conference were passed which called for a prohibition on independent unions. This led to the South African Boilermakers' Society withdrawing from TUCSA: the society went on to elect its first Black president in April 1985. However, all through its history TUCSA has been against politicizing the workplace and consequently few Black unions ever affiliated.

To accommodate pressure for a wider co-ordinating body from organizations not affiliated to TUCSA, Eddie Webster founded the Trade Union Advisory Co-ordinating Council.[20] Affiliated to it were the African Metal and Allied Workers' Union, the National Union of Textile Workers, the Chemical Workers' Industrial Union, and the Transport and General Workers' Union. This co-ordinating body lasted until it was incorporated within FOSATU, which was established in October 1978, and operative from April 1979. All the TUACC unions affiliated to FOSATU, including a number who were at that time unaffiliated, such as the Glass and Allied Workers' Union, the Sweet, Food, and Allied Workers' Union, the Coloured Jewellers', and Goldsmiths' Union, and the Coloured Chemical and General Workers' Union (neither called themselves 'Coloured').

On a narrow Africanist line, the South African Association of Black Trade Unions mobilized among Africans alone. Most leaders of Black Consciousness supported FOSATU when it was formed, including the pro-Black Consciousness newspaper, *Post Transvaal*.[21] Only two unions affiliated to SAABTU, the Food Beverage and Allied Workers' Union and the South African Chemical Workers' Union. FOSATU insists on non-racial unions and has a number of Coloured and Asian unions as affiliates. Often it has non-Africans in leadership roles—its General Secretary up to 1980 was Alec Erwin, a White ex-economics lecturer from the University of Natal in Durban. FOSATU took over the role of SACTU in mobilizing workers on non-racial lines, and SACTU was critical of the potential threat to its own legitimacy as the only internationally recognized co-ordinating body of trade unions in South Africa.[22]

In 1980 a new co-ordinating body was established called the Council of Unions of South Africa, with nine all-African unions affiliated to it. CUSA was born out of the old Black Consultative Committee of Trade Unions, formed in 1973. It first emphasized the importance of Black leadership and control of any union federation, and its leading officials claimed that CUSA supported Black Consciousness, although it was not associated with AZAPO. However, CUSA has undergone a process of radicalization and moved away from orthodox Black Consciousness, which resulted in it opening itself up to membership of all races during 1985. Accordingly there were meetings that year among the Black Consciousness unions to form a new union federation. Eventually the Azanian Confederation of Trade Unions was formed. It linked itself with AZAPO and espouses the beliefs of orthodox Black Consciousness. But while in the Black Consultative Committee, the nine unions within CUSA were not confrontationist. Bonner emphasizes how their vision of the role of trade unions was comparable to that of the registered unions, since they stressed relatively specialized and bureaucratic leadership, little mobilization from below and the benefit functions of unions.[23] Many of its affiliated unions were registered with the state industrial machinery, but in 1982 it announced that it would support any of its member unions who refused to register. It has also launched a strong attack on official industrial courts. Likewise it has urged its affiliates to increase their support for sympathetic community organizations through participation in wider political activity. This process of radicalization led in 1983 to CUSA pronouncing on many non-plant issues, such as influx control, removals, shack clearance, and housing shortage. It also endorsed the call of the Soweto Anti-Community Councils Committee for a boycott of Soweto's elections, stating that it rejected community councils as being in conflict with its belief in a common citizenship in an undivided land.

In 1983 the membership of unions affiliated to CUSA was 100,000. Its fastest-growing affiliate was the National Union of Mineworkers, which began recruiting in October 1982 and whose membership had risen to 55,000 within twelve months. The NUM gained official recognition from the Chamber of Mines during the year, as a result of which it became the first Black union in the country's history to participate in wage bargaining on behalf of Black miners.

Among Black workers in South Africa, of all these co-ordinating bodies FOSATU was once undoubtedly the most popular. Within six months of its establishment, four Coloured and Asian unions had affiliated to it, and, with the nine African unions, it represented 48,000 members. Its African members constituted 48.5 per cent of all African unionized labour.[24] In 1979, of African unionized labour 28.5 per cent affiliated to TUCSA, and 22.6 per cent was unaffiliated. The unaffiliated unions included the fiercely independent Black Allied Workers' Union, the African Garment Workers' Union, the African Leather Workers' Union, the African Food and Canning Workers' Union, and the Western Province General Workers' Union. The remainder were affiliated to SAABTU.

Because of FOSATU's original stand against becoming politicized and engaging in wider community action, which it has since been forced to alter, CUSA is fast overtaking FOSATU. In 1983 FOSATU's total membership was only 6,000 more than CUSA's, the latter having trebled its membership in two years, and by 1984 CUSA had more than double FOSATU's signed-up membership. CUSA's phenomenal growth can be attributed to the fact that it satisfied the demand of Black workers to politicize the workplace. This forced FOSATU to take a stand on several non-union issues, especially on the constitution. FOSATU disbanded in December 1985 with the formation of the Confederation of South African Trade Unions. The division within the trade union movement will be discussed further, but first it is necessary to discuss the situation facing the African trade union movement as it existed prior to the legislative changes recommended by Wiehahn.

The position as it existed prior to the 1979 legislative changes presented fundamentally two problems for African trade unionists. There were a number of organizations prepared to undertake the traditional role of a trade union, but legislation denied this right to Africans. As it existed, the legislation forced no obligation on employers to consult with African trade unions or involve them in collective bargaining even if the union was allowed to function in the plant. However, an even greater problem existed. African worker organizations were allowed to represent only a fraction of

Table 11. *Racial Composition of Unionized Labour**

Type of Union	1972	1978	1979	1980	1981	1982	1983
Racially Exclusive:							
White	88	83	79	80	77	71	54
Asian and Coloured	48	50	49	54	51	46	38
African	—	—	—	12	23	26	19
Mixed:							
White, Coloured, Asian	42	41	39	40	36	16	23
Coloured, Asian, African	—	—	—	—	7	10	13
All groups	—	—	—	2	6	30	43
Total Membership	637,480	692,102	808,053	808,053	1,054,405	1,226,454	1,288,748

* Taken from SAIRR, *Survey of Race Relations 1983*, Johannesburg, SAIRR, 1984, p. 177, and *Survey of Race Relations 1984*, Johannesburg, SAIRR, 1985, p. 308.

economically active Africans, because the legislation denied unionization to three major sectors of African employment— migrant labour, agriculture, and domestic service. Vast sections of African labour were isolated and atomized in their workplaces. In 1979 the government's statisticians estimated the African indus- trialized workforce at 3,135,000, which represented 47.8 per cent of all those economically active in the African community. The unionized sector of the African industrial workforce was a meagre 2.3 per cent, and only 1.1 per cent of the total population of economically active Africans. This compares with a unionized sector of 30.5 per cent of those economically active in the Col- oured and Asian population groups.[25] By way of comparison with the situation as it exists after the 1979 legislative changes, in 1983 the total membership of all unions comprised 12.4 per cent of the economically active population, which is still very low compared with Sweden (83 per cent), the United Kingdom (50 per cent), West Germany (38 per cent), and Japan (33 per cent). While this is an increase, greater change is evident in the composi- tion of the membership, for since 1979 there has been a significant decrease in the number of mixed unions for Coloured, Asian, and White workers, and a move towards unions representing either all population groups or African workers only.

It was not until the Durban strikes among Zulu stevedores that some form of official representation was defined for Africans. The 1973 Bantu Labour Relations Regulation Amendment Act pro- vided for a system of liaison and works committees. Represent- ation was plant-based, not industry-wide, providing an important restriction on their effectiveness. More important restrictions were placed on their scope. No committees were allowed in companies with less than twenty employees, or for those in government or local authority employment. By far the greatest constraint was the prohibition on representing workers in the mining industry. In consequence, there was little use of the system, as Table 12 demonstrates. African workers could refuse to participate in the system, and the figures suggest that many did so. Employers could also refuse to co-operate with the committees once established. The Minister of Labour, as he was then called, now the Minister of Manpower Utilization, initially inserted a clause in the 1973 Act obliging employers to co-operate in forming these committees, but the Minister announced in the House of Assembly that he was

Table 12. *Works and Liaison Committee Representation**

Year	Liaison Committees	Works Committees	Members Covered	% of African Industrial Workforce	% of Economically Active Africans
1973	773	128	312,541	9.9	4.7
1974	1,482	211	521,629	16.6	7.9
1975	2,042	292	617,597	19.7	9.4
1976	2,382	307	715,056	22.8	10.9
1977	2,552	313	771,160	24.5	11.7
1978	2,673	311	771,015	24.5	11.7
1979	2,683	312	779,150	24.6	11.8

* Taken from *South Africa 1980–1*, Department of Information, Pretoria, pp. 433–4.

deleting this clause 'under pressure from employers' organizations.'[26] It was not until 1977 that the committees were allowed to negotiate over pay.

In fact employers are eager to co-operate so as to prevent workers establishing the more powerful works committee. The liaison committee is by far the most widely used because half its members are chosen by management, thereby denying the workers private discussion, and the chairman is also appointed by management. There is no obligation on management to accept the committee's suggestions. In comparison, works committees are composed entirely of workers and deliberate in private. However, these committees cannot be established where a liaison committee exists already, and the low number of works committees suggest that employers have chosen overwhelmingly, where they do decide to allow representation at all, the system where they have greatest influence.

The committees are no substitute for trade unions and have not reduced the pressure for representation.[27] This is attested to by the high number of strikes that occurred in plants where the committees operated.[28] Industrial action has increased during the 1970s according to a number of different measures, such as the total of man-hours lost, the number of shifts lost, and the number of workers involved. This is so despite the legal prohibitions on African strikes. The legal position on strikes prior to 1979 was that once an agreement between employers and workers' representative committees was made and ratified by a government-instituted Industrial Council, it was legally binding and strikes for the duration of the agreement were illegal. In 1978 there were 99 such agreements covering 539,397 African workers.[29] In the absence of an Industrial Council, strikes were illegal unless an application for the appointment of a consultative board to conciliate in the dispute had been made and this had been reported to the Minister (or thirty days had elapsed without agreement since the appointment of the board, or a longer period fixed by such a board, or thirty days had elapsed since the application but no board had been appointed). These procedures do not preclude the occurrence of illegal strikes or other forms of industrial action; neither do they preclude the harassment through other forms of repressive legislation of strikers on a legal strike.

The whole issue of strikes and industrial action will be con-

sidered shortly. First, the issue of the limitations in labour legislation prior to 1979 needs further explanation. Employers were
dissatisfied because the legislation did not prevent illegal stoppages
or industrial action other than strikes. The obvious iniquities of the
representative system as it existed for Africans meant that pressure from African workers for a more equitable system was
undiminished. There was another even more important pressure
for legislative change. During the 1970s the workplace became a
battleground within a wider struggle. This is true in two senses. As
will be argued later, the workplace had always been used by
African workers to press for political liberation, and they were
doing so throughout that decade. During this period also, the
government was utilizing the workplace as one mechanism to
procure Black *embourgeoisement*, either by creating a Black middle class or by improving the conditions of African workers. The
changes in labour legislation initiated by the Wiehahn Commission, and the consideration by the Riekert Commission given to
the status of urban Blacks who worked in the White industrial
areas, are examples of this attempted *embourgeoisement*. Before
the issue of industrial action for wider political aims is considered,
it is necessary to outline the broader context given to the workplace in government policy.

BLACK *EMBOURGEOISEMENT* AND THE WORKPLACE

Dr Jan Marais, National Party MP for Pinetown and a former
Trust Bank Chairman, was explicit when he said in 1978 that what
South Africa need was to create 'a Black middle class and a happy
working class'.[30] After the chaos of the 1976–7 events in urban
townships, what was needed, he argued, was stability. Stability
means many things. To *Die Vaderland* it meant maintaining White
political supremacy: 'By so adjusting circumstances that the quality of life for Blacks is made acceptable, the demand for political
rights could be lessened to a degree.'[31] For private enterprise in
South Africa it meant higher profit and more investment. An
unprecedented investment boom in 1978–9 fuelled by the price of
gold created new demands for skills which Whites could not
satisfy. In the past immigration had filled the gap—from 1961
until 1979 there was a new inflow of 651,743, of whom 16.5

per cent were artisans and 18.2 per cent were professional, administrative, and managerial.[32] The Soweto uprising in 1976 saw a drastic reduction in this flow. Legislation was needed which eased discrimination and enabled Blacks to satisfy the demand. A survey of 166 companies in Johannesburg during 1978 revealed that two-thirds desired that employment discriminations be removed.[33] This pressure was added to by Afrikaans newspapers and some Nationalist politicians.

The effect of such pressure was uneven. Fixed investment in South Africa rose in 1980 by 5 per cent in real terms, and Black unemployment fell between 1978 and 1979 by 6 per cent.[34] The wage gap between the race groups diminished: from 1970 to 1975 Black wages grew at an annual rate of 6.6 per cent compared with a 1.1 per cent growth rate for Whites. This trend increased in the second half of the decade;[35] but this should not disguise the shortfall to be made up. In 1975 per capita income for Whites was R3,192, compared with R376 for urban Blacks and the increase in Black wages has not eroded this differential substantially.[36] Additionally many international firms, under pressure from the EEC or USA codes of conduct were going part of the way towards ending discrimination in employment. Some city councils have abolished salary discrimination on a racial basis for their salaried staff.[37] Barclays Bank made a disclaimer against the allegation of racial discrimination in salary.[38] Some improvements have been made, but this confuses the issue by ignoring the inequality that exists in employment opportunities, with Blacks having special difficulties to overcome before they become salaried staff. None the less, in an *ad hoc* manner certain employers were slowly beginning to provide a better working environment for their Black employees. Transgressions in job reservation were becoming more frequent and there had been an increase in Black management roles.

Up to 1979 employers tried to alleviate the racial restrictions within the workplace to some degree, and the government made some concessions concerning those operating outside. Prior to labour legislation changes in 1979 their greatest efforts were directed towards establishing community councils as an expression of limited local government autonomy, and tampering with land tenure rights.[39] Urban Blacks were not allowed to own land in the White industrial areas where they lived and worked because of their *sojourner* status. The Bantu Urban Areas Amendment Act of

1978 introduced a ninety-nine year lease system where Blacks could own the walls of their house but not the land on which it stood. Discussing the Act in Parliament, H. J. Coetsee, National Party MP for Bloemfontein West, and later Minister of Justice, now envisaged a new Black middle class. The limitations inherent in not granting freehold failed to win Blacks to the system. Their citizenship in the rural areas was not revoked by owning a house in the urban areas and, unless a wife or her children qualified under the system in their own right, the family could be evicted on the death of the husband. Many workers were not in a financial position to afford to buy their own home. Finally, an intricate series of forms had to be completed by the applicant, effectively denying ownership to those who were politically active, to the many illegal residents and to those who did not have Section 10 rights under the Bantu Urban Areas Consolidation Act.[40] In a survey conducted by Market Research Africa in 1979, 71.8 per cent of the 1,419 urban Africans questioned did not intend to buy their homes. Up to June 1979, only 94 people had availed themselves of the opportunity to buy their home in the whole area covered by the West Rand Bantu Administration Board.[41] Outside the immediate Soweto area the numbers were somewhat higher; Orange Vaal Bantu Administration Board reported 2,000 applications. However this is well below the potential numbers. The Minister for Co-operation and Development said in 1983 that 49,809 houses in the nine main urban areas were available for purchase under the ninety-nine-year leasehold scheme and 57,200 in 'White' South Africa as a whole, while the figures for a thirty-year scheme were 22,184 and 282,951 respectively. On the West Rand 18,679 houses had been sold under both schemes, while the East Rand Administration Board had received 996 applications, the East Transvaal 274 applications, the Orange-Vaal area 425 applications, and the Western Transvaal only 20 applications. As part of its policy of limiting state responsibility for housing and encouraging greater participation by Africans in housing provision and ownership, the government launched a grand sale in 1983 at discounts of up to 40 per cent. In Soweto 48,849 houses went for sale, and by the end of the year 560 had been sold.[42] This demonstrates how unpopular the system is.

In 1979, for the first time Building Societies set up office in African areas to satisfy the expected demand for house purchase.

There was some lack of co-ordination between them and the government, as the Association of Building Societies in South Africa imposed their own restrictions on lending, denying loans to purchase homes of the poorer 51/6 quality with four rooms and a toilet outside. The Urban Foundation, financed by Anglo-American, provided some of the cash instead. There is an irony in this. Anglo-American are one of the main financial backers of the Progressive Federal Party, the chief opposition party, but find themselves funding government policy in order to ensure its effectiveness. However, to facilitate the sale of houses in 1983, some Building Societies said they would provide mortgage loans for those buying under the ninety-nine-year scheme, including 51/6 houses. The downturn in the economy, which has resulted in a mortgage rate of over 20 per cent, prevented many Africans from taking up the offer of mortgages. By 1985 the government had acknowledged the unpopularity of the leasehold system, enshrining, as it did, the temporary *sojourner* status of urban Africans. As part of the government's attempt to convince urban Africans of their permanency, P. W. Botha announced in February 1985 that they could have full freehold rights. He justified this policy shift against right wing critics by pointing out that President Paul Kruger had advocated the same policy. In April and December 1985 Botha indicated that freehold rights were to be granted in 1986.

But all those *ad hoc* changes which had been introduced up to the late 1970s were not the main point, as perceived by the *Post Transvaal*, the African community's main national daily newspaper at the time. It linked acceptance of these reforms to legislative changes and called for co-ordinated revision of legislation controlling labour, and the status and rights of Blacks working in urban areas.[43] This kind of review is inherent in the dynamic of stability: economic growth, the maintenance of White political supremacy and Black *embourgeoisement*, are incompatible with out-dated legislation. The government's awareness of this was reflected in its initiation of two Commissions under Wiehahn and Riekert to investigate such changes.

These Commissions were to provide the government's main platform of reform. Opening the first meeting of the Wiehahn Commission on 11 August 1977, the Minister of Labour, as he was then known, spoke of the government's intentions: 'The outcome of your investigations will not only directly effect the labour scene, but will certainly spill over into the economic, social and other spheres of daily life. Sound labour relations must provide the firm basis for a peaceful and prosperous society.'[44] The Commission's terms of reference were to examine the effectiveness of current labour legislation and suggest reform with a view to making the system more effective, to aid the prevention and settlement of disputes, and to eliminate labour problems.[45] The Riekert Commission was established in the following week, to examine the auxiliary problem of the effective use of labour and to assess the restrictions placed on optimal manpower use by discriminatory legislation.

It was clear at the beginning what the Commissions were to recommend. A month before the Wiehahn Commission was initiated, Wiehahn called for the ending of labour discrimination. He repeated this call on many occasions.[46] Commission members were predominantly businessmen, whose preference for stability through reform has already been noted.[47] Effectively the government was attempting to placate the opposition on its ethnic-based right by instituting reform through the more neutral procedure of government commissions. A statement by the Minister of Mines was an excellent barometer of the government's intentions. The maintenance of White privilege, F. W. de Klerk said, could contribute to terrorism. The Commissions were intended to alleviate the political and economic risks associated with the radicalism of the left. Yet, as so often in its pledge for reform, the government was held back by refusing to break completely with the right wing of Afrikaner nationalism.

Both reports were tabled in 1979, to much acclaim in South Africa.[48] Some critical opinion was won over; Heribert Adam feels it unjustified to dismiss the reports as 'cosmetic or insignificant', believing that they constitute the 'deracialization of the work place'.[49] The legislative changes that immediately followed these reports were hardly that. The Industrial Conciliation Amendment Act of 1979 solved only one of the two problems that were identified earlier as central to African trade unionism. It gave Africans the right to form trade unions, but failed to solve the more severe problem of low unionization. It will be demonstrated in the following section that this failure made it unlikely that the government would depoliticize the workplace. Therefore, in a further amendment to the Act in 1981, the government ended all restrictions on access to trade union membership. In so doing it strengthened its political control over trade unions.

CHANGES IN LABOUR LEGISLATION

The Wiehahn Commission made a number of recommendations: statutory props for racial discrimination in industry must be removed; a long-term commitment should be made to freedom of association at work with the ending of segregated facilities; Blacks should have the right to join registered trade unions; they should be able to supervise White employees; racial discrimination in wages should be stopped; and Africans should be able to be apprenticed in jobs previously reserved for Whites. The government's implementation of these recommendations was limited. In the Industrial Conciliation Amendment Act of 1979 it restricted African trade union rights to Section 10 workers: those who qualified under the Bantu Urban Areas Consolidation Act either by having worked for the same employer for ten years or having had legal and continuous property rights in urban townships for fifteen years. Trade union rights were not extended to three major sections of African employment—farming, domestic service, and migrant labour. Responsibility for moving away from discrimination was placed on the White trade unions themselves: the government abrogated responsibility by leaving it to them to decide whether they wanted to accept Blacks. Without this acceptance Blacks had to form parallel unions. The South African Boiler Makers' Society quickly announced it would not accept African members. A number of parallel unions were created by the Motor Industry Workers, the Engineering Industrial Workers, the South African Electrical Workers' Association, the Textile Workers, and the Radio Television Electronic and Allied Workers. This was no commitment to racially mixed trade unionism but was disguised segregation.

The 1979 Act provided two forms of control over radical African unions. Some right wing White unions did attempt to organize their African workers. The Brewery Employees Union is an example. In so doing they refused to recognize legitimate and viable African unions within the industry. The radical Sweet Food and Allied Workers' Union was faced with a difficult choice—either to integrate and conservatize or to segregate and politicize. In instituting a requirement for African unions to register with the Department of Manpower Utilization, as the Ministry of Labour became under the Act, the government effectively immobilized the radical unions under the co-ordination of FOSATU. The dilemma the Act presented was either to refuse to register and thereby isolate themselves by being unable to engage in collective bargaining, or to register and open themselves up to supervision. Registered unions were not allowed to 'engage in politics' and their constitution had to be vetted by the government, with the Minister deciding which workers it could organize. Legal restrictions on strikes remained with a 'labour court' being established as the arbiter. This Industrial Court had the responsibility of overseeing the practice of the new unions. It was very clear that the government intended to 'strengthen' the African trade union movement, but only in such a way as to restrict demands emerging within it to economic ones.[50]

In November 1979 FOSATU decided not to register unless certain conditions were met. Unions should be allowed to integrate fully without separate branches for each racial group, and they should not be forced into excluding any existing members. These conditions vitiated the whole tenor of the government's legislative response to Wiehahn and FOSATU's dilemma remained. The African Food and Canning Workers' Union and the Western Province General Workers' Union rejected registration. The Consultative Committee of Black Trade Unions at first rejected registration but reversed this decision in July 1980. Lucy Mvubelo's National Union of Clothing Workers welcomed the opportunity and registered immediately. The Commercial Catering and Allied Workers' Union refused. By November 1980 nineteen African unions had applied for registration and nine of them had been accepted. At that juncture, therefore, the African trade union movement was disunited as bickering erupted between parallel unions and those who refused to register. FOSATU's attacks on parallel unions were widely reported and seconded by *Post Transvaal*.

No commitment was made in the legislation to ending segregated facilities in the workplace, although Blacks were allowed to be apprenticed in jobs previously reserved for Whites and to be in positions of authority over them. Trade union rights were

Table 13. *Frontier Commuters 1977–1980*

Homeland	1977	1978	1979	1980
Bophuthatswana	148,200	151,800	155,400	161,200
Ciskei	34,600	36,200	37,100	38,100
Gazankulu	6,300	6,700	7,800	8,800
KaNgwane	25,200	28,500	33,100	35,600
KwaNdebele	1,100	1,300	3,500	5,900
Kwa Zulu	291,300	321,700	352,300	363,900
Lebowa	46,600	54,400	57,900	65,800
Qwa Qwa	2,100	2,000	2,500	6,800
Transkei	7,100	8,600	8,900	9,000
Venda	4,500	5,100	5,600	5,600
Total	567,000	616,300	664,100	700,700

extended to a minority. The African working class was divided between the privileged Section 10 workers with union rights and the rest. The very size of the numbers excluded from trade union rights, however, worked against the depoliticization of African trade unionism. Extra-workplace demands emerging from within it were likely to increase. 'Frontier commuters', i.e. African workers living in homeland townships but travelling daily to work in the White industrial areas (as artisans) or residential areas (as domestics), were excluded. The vast majority of residents in homeland townships like Kwa Mashu, Umlazi, Ga-Rankwa, Mdantsane, and Mabopane were denied trade union representation. Tables 13, 14, and 15 demonstrate the extent of this exclusion.[51] Issues like homeland citizenship, political decision-making in the homelands, township property rights, and so on would still have been live issues for these workers. The same applies to migrant workers who were excluded from the 1979 legislative dispensations. Table 15 shows the extent of the workers affected.[52] In addition to the exclusion of some workers, others would lose their existing trade union rights. The President of the Commercial Catering and Allied Workers' Union, Henry Chipeya, estimated that tens of thousands of African workers would lose their trade union rights because those African unions seeking registration would have to force

Table 14. *Frontier Commuters from the African Homelands (1979)*

Homeland	Number	% of Total	% of Population Resident in Homeland
Bophuthatswana	161,900	22.5	12.9
Ciskei	37,100	5.3	6.7
Gazankulu	7,800	1.2	2.2
KaNgwane	33,100	4.6	15.1
KwaNdebele	3,500	0.5	—
Kwa Zulu	400,600	55.3	13.8
Lebowa	57,900	8.2	3.9
Qwa Qwa	2,500	0.3	2.6
Transkei	8,900	1.3	0.4
Venda	5,600	0.8	1.5
Total	718,900	—	—

these excluded workers from their rolls[53] This only exacerbated the pressure within the African trade union movement.

The Riekert Commission on Black manpower utilization was of even more doubtful value. The following recommendations were made: influx control was to be outlawed, and 'passes' were to disappear; night curfew regulations for Blacks in White residential areas were to be relaxed; trading rights were to be granted to Blacks in 'free trade' city areas; and Blacks were to be allowed as managers, supervisors, and professional employees outside their own group area. The ending of job reservation, which as a practice was declining anyway, and the abolition of employment restrictions on Blacks will undoubtedly affect the occupational structure of South Africa. With the shortfall of skilled Whites and the growth of Black business this was what Riekert was designed to do. There is little of positive merit apart from this. Three Bills were published by the government—the Black Community Development Bill, the Local Government Bill, and the Laws on Co-operation and Development Amendment Bill, designed to implement the proposals of the Riekert Commission that had been accepted by the government in its 1979 White Paper. On 6 February 1980 Piet Koornhof, the then Minister of Co-operation

Table 15. *Estimated Extent of Migrant Labour from the Homelands 1977–1981 (000s)*

Homeland	1977	1978	1979	1980	1981
Bophuthatswana	175	178	185	197	197
Ciskei	54	54	54	56	60
Gazankulu	43	45	46	50	58
NaNgwane	34	37	44	48	57
KwaNdebele	27	33	35	44	63
Kwa Zulu	244	244	245	261	280
Lebowa	155	159	163	175	186
Qwa Qwa	34	37	38	43	51
Transkei	301	302	302	308	336
Venda	28	29	33	35	41
Total	1,095	1,118	1,145	1,217	1,329

and Development, withdrew the Bills for review by a multiracial committee to 'ensure the final product maintains the spirit of the White Paper on the Riekert Commission'. Two points should be noted: the Bills were not to be judged against the original recommendations, only those which the government accepted; and no such committee was established for the Wiehahn Commission, whose 'spirit' was emasculated in the 1979 legislation. Each of these points warrants further consideration.

In the White Paper on the Riekert Commission the government again abrogated its responsibility. Influx control was to remain for migrant workers, frontier commuters and domestic servants; only those with Section 10 rights would have the burden relaxed. The burden was not removed: free movement between urban areas for Section 10 workers was made conditional on the availability of housing and employment. Control was shifted, therefore, to employers and housing authorities. In effect the 'passbook' for this privileged section within the African community was replaced by a certificate granted at the workplace and place of residence, granting them a job and a home. The 'pass book' and influx control remained for those without Section 10 rights. Legislation was envisaged which required all employers of Black labour to register with the newly formed Department of Manpower Utilization, and employers were to suffer prosecution and financial penalties for the employment of 'illegal Blacks'—i.e. those Blacks without the necessary certificate or pass allowing them to be where they were. These penalties were severe; the penalty for 'unfair practices' against Black workers was R250.

The basic assumption of Riekert was that there was a settled and permanent African urban population outside the homelands as distinct from those Africans with homes in the rural areas but who work in the urban areas temporarily. The proposals related to defining these two groups and making mobility between them more difficult.[54] Practical steps were taken in this direction immediately after the Riekert Report. In November 1979 a moratorium was placed on Africans working illegally in the urban areas. Regulations gazetted in June 1980 for the first time allowed Africans with permanent residence qualifications to move from one prescribed area to another. This measure facilitated occupational mobility among qualified African workers. Attached to this concession was the proviso that free movement was subject to the availability of approved accommodation. Since the shortage of approved accommodation in most areas is critical, this concession had limited practical consequences. The three Koornhof Bills, which were eventually withdrawn, were directed to this question. The Grosskopf Committee, which reviewed the Bills, recommended that full property rights be granted to Africans in urban areas which the government announced it intended to do in 1986. Other recommendations of the Grosskopf Committee included that the right of residence in urban areas should be made conditional on 'approved housing'; that the provision preventing Africans being in an urban area for longer than 72 hours be scrapped; that pass controls should be exercised at the place of work and residence rather than on the streets; and that employers and householders should be severely punished for providing employment and housing illegally. The 1982 Orderly Movement and Settlement Bill replaced the three earlier Bills. It defined 'authorized' and 'unauthorized' persons. 'Authorized' persons had the right to remain in 'prescribed areas' of the urban centres if they had approved accommodation. 'Unauthorized' persons were to be permitted to remain in the urban areas for only seventeen hours. Citizens of independent homelands were not to be allowed permanent residence rights under the Bill unless they could claim ten years of residence in a particular area and both their parents could do the same. No unauthorized persons were allowed to seek or take up employment in the urban areas. The penalties available to enforce those restrictions were severe. This Bill was finally scrapped in May 1984 after considerable opposition both inside and outside Parliament. A weaker Bill, the Urbanization Bill, was promised and was expected to be introduced in the first session of the new tricameral Parliament. It has been suggested in the *Johannesburg Star* that this is a sign that the future strategy might be to co-opt township residents into an alliance against rural Africans.[55] Certainly influx control regulations were tightened in 1983, particularly those preventing migrant workers from bringing their families to live with them, or changing their jobs. Parliament also amended legislation to counteract two court rulings which would have allowed migrants who had worked for ten years with one employer to acquire permanent residence rights in the urban areas and to be joined by their families.

These court rulings would have had far-reaching effects. Major multinational companies had welcomed them, as had the Association of Chambers of Commerce. The Conservative Party had condemned them as likely to cause a flood of Africans to the city, although Charles Simkins estimated that the ruling only applied to about 130,000 workers. The government figure was 143,802.[56] Despite the ruling, Administration Boards delayed in implementing it, awaiting, no doubt, the amended legislation which circumvented the court rulings. In July 1983 the Amendment Act No. 102 was passed, which introduced strict controls on the entry of the families of migrant workers who qualified under the ruling. Although the ruling was not technically nullified, those who qualified would have great difficulty in bringing their families to the urban areas with them. By the end of 1983, 24,688 workers had elected to leave their families behind and move to the city permanently.

When combined with the Wiehahn legislation extending trade union rights to Section 10 workers, the Riekert Commission proposals for an ending of influx control and freedom of movement for Section 10 workers produced a privileged class of insiders. For the remainder, it became more difficult to escape the poverty of the rural areas. This strengthening of control coincided with structural changes in the economy which added to the problems of 'outsiders.' The centripetal geographical forces pulling to the urban areas are partly a result of changes in African employment due to capital-intensive farming and consequent agrarian depopulation.[57] These African workers are not allowed to enter the urban townships, but they are not needed in the only place they are allowed to be. The special camps established in Kwa Zulu, the Eastern Cape, and in East and West Transvaal are used to house displaced agricultural workers. These camps are densely populated ghettos in isolated rural areas with little productive land to maintain the numbers there. There is no shortage of residents, however, for as the agricultural areas de-populate under structural changes in agriculture, these camps at least provide a home as a base from where employment as a migrant worker may be sought. Wilson calls this 'urbanization-at-a-distance'.[58] The Riekert Commission and subsequent legislation have made it more difficult for these people to find work in the cities as the migrant labour system itself slowly retracts. Structural changes in the economy have shifted its base away from mining, the traditional employer of migrant labour, towards manufacture. In 1911–12, mining accounted for 27.1 per cent of Gross Domestic Product and manufacture only 6.7 per cent. In 1979 manufacturing had risen to 22.6 per cent with mining dropping to 18.1 per cent.[59] In 1978 three-quarters of the work force in manufacture was Black—but predominantly Asian, Coloured, and Section 10 urban Africans. In combination with this trend, the government's enactment of the Riekert Commission's proposals isolates residents in the resettlement camps. Therefore, in addition to the schism within the African working class over access to certain privileges, the geographic and social gulf between urban and rural dwellers is widening. A great deal in the future will depend on whether Black politicians in the urban and rural areas are prepared to let this gulf grow.[60] Certainly another crucial extra-workplace issue was provided for African trade unionists to incorporate in their process of interest articulation. On this basis there is no potential in the reforms for ending the politicization of the workplace.

This was even more the case in the legislation implementing certain proposals of the Wiehahn Commission. In this regard the 1979 Act was only tepidly received by businessmen.[61] In implementing the Wiehahn report, the government acceded to pressure from its right. Fears expressed by White unions, leading to a White miners' strike and an electoral swing to the HNP were a brake which led to only partial implementation of Wiehahn's proposals. Senator Anna Scheepers, and White trade unionists like J. R. Altman and Tom Neethling, expressed fears for the White trade union movement when the Commission was first announced in 1977.[62] Neethling was actually a member of the Commission. A minority report in the Wiehahn report by Niewoudt found greater implementation in legislation. The *Sunday Times* in Johannesburg correctly stated in its editorial that the majority lost.[63] The fears expressed by Niewoudt, and to a lesser extent by Neethling and Piet van der Merwe, the Pretoria University economist, were twofold: that African trade unions would swamp White workers, and that the trade unions would be used for political purposes. These fears met with satisfaction in the government's rejection of the majority report's view that trade union rights should be extended to migrant and frontier commuter workers. This attitude won the support of the Afrikaner establishment in the universities and Parliament, the Afrikaans press and Afrikaner unions. *Die Burger* felt that South Africa should now have a 'contented population'.[64] *Oggenblad* referred to it as a 'giant step towards establishing as a right the dignity of the Black man'.[65] *Rapport* believed that race relations had now been normalized in South Africa,[66] and *Beeld* thought it would help maintain law and order in Black residential areas.[67]

It was more correct to say that polarization of an ethnic kind was increased by the legislation. The government's ethnic right wing succeeded in denying Africans their legitimate trade union rights, and those privileges which were accorded only exacerbated the permeation of wider ethnic, political, and nationalist issues throughout the workplace. Very few African trade unionists were satisfied, and some took the risk of remaining unregistered to avoid the degree of supervision which the Act defined. These problems lay behind the government's 1981 amendment to the Industrial Conciliation Act. It was an attempt to strengthen its control over trade unions in order to restrict demands from it to economic ones only. The depoliticization of the workplace had not been achieved in the 1979 legislation for two reasons: its exclusions increased the likelihood of extra-workplace issues being incorporated in trade union demands; and some trade unions took the decision to remain unregistered and therefore immune to the controls on their extra-workplace activities which the legislation provided. The 1981 Act threw open trade union membership to all Africans, including foreign migrant workers. It did away with the prohibition on mixed trade unions which the 1979 Act only partly treated. However, the main thrust of the Act was to extend to unregistered unions the same controls as govern registered unions. This amounts to a form of compulsory registration, and the more radical unregistered unions will now be subject to all the controls on their extra-workplace activity which the 1979 Act defined. The controls are manifold. They include the keeping of proper books, statements of income and expenditure, minutes of meetings, and so on. Their constitution will be vetted by the state. Unregistered unions, like their registered counterparts, will have to submit a register of members. Inspectors will have wide powers to investigate the affairs of the union, to examine and confiscate any union document and to question any person about the union's affairs. It is an offence to refuse to answer any questions asked. Unregistered unions will not be granted stop order facilities for the deduction of membership subscription fees. Unregistered unions, like registered unions, are barred from either granting financial assistance or incurring any expenditure aimed at assisting any political party or candidate for election to a legislative assembly, and from granting 'other' assistance to any such party or person. The government's desire to clamp down on political involvement may be seen in the new provision which makes it obligatory for all unions to have their head office in the Republic (excluding the homelands): the provisions for control of the affairs of a union would be meaningless if its head office were inaccessible. Finally, no union, registered or not, is allowed to give strike pay to workers on an illegal strike—a measure obviously designed to channel strike activity through formal state-sponsored machinery and to starve workers back where this procedure is by-passed.

The radical unions—a small but militant minority—have decided to defy the restrictions, although it is difficult to see what form this defiance can take given that these controls are initiated by the Act itself rather than a union's decision to register, as existed under the 1979 Act. These independent trade unions have effectively been emasculated. Whether or not this will result in their demands being restricted to plant-based issues is difficult to judge. Looked at another way the unregistered unions emerge without any rights, so they have nothing to lose by politicizing the workplace. Certainly a review of industrial action up to 1983 shows that extra-workplace demands are intricately entangled with plant-based issues to influence opposition in the workplace. Clearly the Wiehahn reforms are contradictory. The intention is to control by drawing the independent unions into the official bargaining process. This requires the granting of rights in the form of official recognition of African trade unions. As a result of this change the independent unions have grown rapidly and are now permanently established. Furthermore, workers have become more assertive as they attempt to challenge the economic and political injustices they face. The granting of rights to African workers has enabled them to make permanent gains. A brief survey of industrial action from 1976 to 1983 shows how contradictory the Wiehahn reforms are.

INDUSTRIAL ACTION 1976–1983

Industrial action takes many forms. The conventional contrast in a South African context is between plant-based strike action and more general stay-aways, i.e. an *en masse* refusal to work by various kinds of workers in a national or community unit over non-plant-based issues,[68] such as occurred in Soweto in 1976 and often during the defiance campaign. Industrial action can also take the form of industrial sabotage of either machinery or plant, or, as occurs frequently among migrant workers, of their hostels and catering facilities.[69] It can be what Africans call *ukubamba amadolo*—the go-slow. There are disputes of various kinds which may or may not involve a stoppage of work. Those that do involve a stoppage of work may disrupt either part or whole of a shift. These disputes are not legal strikes under South African legislation. The extent of this kind of industrial action is represented in Table 16.[70] Government statistics of this kind can only be a rough calculation. They lack reliability because of the variable extent to which companies inform the Bureau of Statistics,[71] and the ambiguous nature of what constitutes such a thing as a stoppage. Strike action of one kind or another is much more common than industrial sabotage, more visible than *ukubamba amadolo*, and is more reliable in its documentation. The concentration hereafter will be on strike action.[72]

Table 16. *Non-strike Action 1965–1982* *

Year	Stoppages (all races)	Shifts Lost, excluding Strikes (Africans only)
1965	84	2,492
1966	98	3,797
1967	76	1,812
1968	56	3,161
1969	78	3,980
1970	76	3,051
1971	69	3,316
1972	71	13,724
1973	370	229,136
1974	384	98,395
1975	274	18,559
1976	245	22,190
1977	90	15,069
1978	106	10,536
1979	107	16,515
1980	203	148,192
1981	342	206,230
1982	394	—

* From SAIRR, *Survey of Race Relations 1983*, SAIRR, p. 200.

Strikes among African workers have a long history despite the legal restrictions imposed and the human deprivations which result.[73] The conventional wisdom[74] is that the 1960s were a period of quiescence in South African industrial relations due to the banning of SACTU which did not alter until the new decade saw the dock strikes in Durban[75] and the Ovambo workers' strike in Namibia in 1971. At least two criteria are involved in making a judgement of this kind—either the total number of strikes or the number of employees involved. Tables 17 and 18 provide figures for the number of strikes since 1965 and the size of the workforce affected, and Figure 1 shows how variable the relationship between these two criteria can be.[76]

The statistics in Table 17 require some clarification. First, the figures are from the government's Official Yearbook and cover

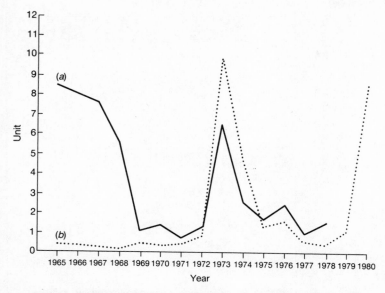

FIGURE 1. Graphical presentation of the relationship between total numbers of strikes (all races) and participants (African) 1965–1980

industrial disputes which are defined by the government as strikes. Official statistics are ultimately the source of all estimations of strike activity but the legal distinction under South African law between 'stoppage' and 'strike' is not taken account of in some estimations, which give a much higher incidence of strike activity among African workers. The fact that the total number of workers involved remains more or less constant across the various estimations suggests that the difference is merely one of classification. This emphasizes that in the literature there is a somewhat discretionary designation of a dispute as stoppage or strike. The designations used here follow those of the government. Secondly, the Official Yearbook labels some strikes by African workers as legal for a period before 1973 when all strikes by African workers were illegal. It is difficult to know quite what was 'legal' about such disputes before the 1973 legislation. The strikes entered in the Official Yearbook for this period may be disputes which employers reported to the Bantu Labour Boards, established under the 1953 Bantu Labour (Settlement of Disputes) Act. These

Table 17. *Strike Action 1965–1983*

Year	Strikes (all races)			Strikes (African)			% Strikes that are African	Africans involved
	Legal	Illegal	Total	Legal	Illegal	Total		
1965	38	46	84	34	38	72	85.7	3,540
1966	26	72	98	17	50	67	68.3	3,253
1967	35	41	76	28	39	67	88.1	2,874
1968	21	35	56	19	33	52	92.8	1,705
1969	7	4	11	3	2	5	45.4	4,232
1970	5	9	14	3	3	6	42.8	3,303
1971	5	3	8	4	1	5	62.5	4,196
1972	6	7	13	1	5	6	46.1	8,804
1973	56	9	65	52	7	59	90.7	98,029
1974	18	9	27	14	7	21	77.7	58,925
1975	11	7	18	9	7	16	88.8	23,130
1976	13	11	24	5	11	16	66.6	26,846
1977	5	5	10	4	5	9	90.6	15,060
1978	11	4	15	11	4	15	100.0	14,095
1979	—	—	—	—	—	46	—	21,000
1980	—	—	—	—	—	—	—	95,000
1981	—	—	—	—	—	—	—	84,706
1982	—	—	—	—	—	—	—	122,481
1983	—	—	—	—	—	—	—	61,331

Table 18. *Number of Man-days Lost*
1972–1983

Year	All workers	African workers
1972	14,167	—
1973	229,281	—
1974	98,583	95,327
1975	18,709	18,275
1976	59,861	22,014
1977	15,471	14,987
1978	10,558	10,164
1979	67,099	16,515
1980	174,614	148,192
1981	226,554	226,230
1982	365,337	298,256
1983	124,596	—

Boards were charged with the settlement of work disputes and the aim of officials generally was to facilitate a quick return to work. The prosecution of African workers involved in a dispute was resorted to only when workers proved more than usually obdurate. It is possible that strikes were recorded as 'legal' or 'illegal' according to whether a conviction was made or not.[77] They could also represent the number of African workers affected by legal strikes by White workers. This highlights the discretion which compilers of official statistics have in designating disputes, and reinforces the point made earlier about the limitations of official statistics and how they should be taken only as a guide to the level of industrial action.

Two facts emerge from these tables. Beyond the earlier peak associated with the Durban strikes, the numbers of African employees involved in strike action has risen progressively. This is despite the fact that the total number of strikes has often been low in comparison with the period 1965–8. This would suggest that many strikes after 1970, at least, are occurring in large multinational companies and involving numbers in excess of the immediate plant workers. A brief review of strike action for the years 1978–83 confirms this impression. It also indicates the significance of plant-based strike action.

The fourteen thousand African workers who engaged in strike action in 1978 lost between them R42,166 in wages, totalling 59,711 man-hours.[78] In January and February, 1,800 African building workers went on strike over discriminatory pay. Issues on which other workers were mobilized included, in February, October, and November, dissatisfaction over unfair dismissal. In April and May, 3,500 workers at Carletonville and at Sigma's site in Silverton were on strike demanding higher pay. The same issue was the basis of strike action among 400 Vaal Transport Corporation drivers, bus drivers in Alberton, timber workers in Mobeni, Transkei, Hillmead weavers, at Escom's Germiston plant, at Klip power station, at Indomeni colliery, and at Langberg canning factory. Union recognition was the issue for 800 strikers in South African Airways. In April, 1,000 workers went on strike protesting against increases in township service charges, and discriminatory treatment by White workers caused fifty Africans to strike in Johannesburg during July. The biggest strike of the year was at the Ever-Ready works in October.[79] It began in Port Elizabeth and won mass support among many workers and township residents. Effective mobilization was aided by the dismissal of workers for what was a legal strike. FOSATU organized an effective boycott of Ever-Ready products in the Eastern Cape. FOSATU had yet to be fully inaugurated and this was the first test of its loyalty among workers and of its organizational ability. These two qualities were of benefit to FOSATU in the 1979 strikes.

That year began with the Rainbow Chicken workers' strike in Hammersdale, Natal. A subsidiary of Anglo-American, Rainbow Chicken refused recognition of African union representatives and workers combined this issue with the demand for higher pay and better working conditions. There was a strike in the meat industry in Cape Town which evidenced excellent collective solidarity, with money being collected for strikers, positive discouragement given to scabbing, and an effective boycott of meat products. The Frametex strike in Pinetown won the support of Asian township residents in Claremont and African residents in Kwadebeke, other workers came out in sympathy, and schoolchildren boycotted classes. This solidarity was intensified by the murder of Samson Cele, the Frametex liaison committee member. This dual strategy of boycott and extra-workplace mobilization either in sympathy strikes or in more general collective action, was evident in the

Fattis and Monis strike in Cape Town. Support was widespread in African townships and the complex matrix of ethnic, class, and political aspirations among its participants was commented upon by Frank Molteno, a Cape Town Marxian social scientist: 'workers stood together as Black brothers for workers unity and more broadly still for solidarity for all oppressed men and women.'[80] This point is perhaps better made by considering in more detail the much larger Ford strike at the end of 1979.

Ford were pioneers of mass production in South Africa during the 1920s and were one of the first companies to recognize unregistered African trade unions. The dispute erupted in November 1979 and lasted into the first months of the New Year. It began over allegations of racial discrimination against the company in their Port Elizabeth plant and eventually engulfed most of the townships surrounding Port Elizabeth. Thozamile Botha, leader of the Black Consciousness organization PEBCO, was dismissed by Ford for being too frequently absent from work due to his political activity. A statement on the same day by PEBCO conjoined Black Consciousness rhetoric with a denunciation of multinational companies and worker exploitation. Botha's political work in the community seemed to have been respected by the workforce and the entire African workforce left the following day. This illegal strike lasted three days. This expression of solidarity with PEBCO was responded to by White workers who went on strike, objecting to the lack of power to control African workers. This counter-strike shows how real ethnic mobilization can be in the workplace. Subsequent strikes by African workers broke out on 13 November and the list of demands included higher pay, better working conditions, especially canteen facilities, objections to unfair dismissal, racial discrimination, and segregated facilities. When an ultimatum to return to work was ignored, the entire African workforce was sacked.

Under Botha's direction, PEBCO took a leading role in organizing the sacked workers, with the African trade union, the United Automobile Rubber and Allied Workers' Union, not becoming involved. Its General Secretary, Freddie Saul, argued in defence that PEBCO were the community's leaders and they should therefore organize the strike.[81] In its mobilization, PEBCO incorporated plant-based issues, urging benefits for strikers, official recognition of the union, the provision of channels of communication with management, and reinstatement of all sacked workers. This was in addition to the usual Black Consciousness rhetoric against police brutality and the detention system. (Botha was detained briefly and eventually fled to exile in Botswana during 1980.) In linking the strike with the philosophy of Black Consciousness, strikers won the support of students, businessmen, the African *petite bourgeoisie*, parents, and other workers. This was not the only reason for the rapid spread of support. PEBCO's mobilization coincided with increases in the cost of living for Africans in the Port Elizabeth area. In the year up to October 1979, it had jumped overall by 10 per cent with King William's Town having an increase of 17.5 per cent. This occurred in a society which was once relatively immune to the ravages of Western inflation. Starting from a much lower base of earnings, inflation hits the African community hard: there had been general increases in transport, fuel and lighting, township services charges, and food. Paraffin, for example, had increased by 70 per cent up to the year ending October 1979. In the face of widespread support, three and a half months later the workers were reinstated.

The most significant strike of the year—for a number of reasons—was the municipal workers strike in July, which involved 10,000 workers in the Johannesburg area. The numbers involved made this the largest strike against a single employer. Again Black Consciousness involvement was evident through the Black Municipal Workers' Union, which is a union with strong sympathy for the ANC and Black Consciousness. It evidenced great solidarity among municipal workers over the sacking of some colleagues at a power station who were repatriated to the homelands. It is perhaps most significant for the fact that Black Consciousness organizations became involved, through the BMWU, after workers became dissatisfied with the conservative response of the company union, the Johannesburg Municipal Workers' Union. This was a repetition of the 1979–80 experiences of PEBCO in the Ford strike. The trade union movement, in all its diversity, shows great political muscle, especially in the Eastern Cape and the Witwatersrand. The Natal-based unions lag a little behind in comparison. This can be explained partially by the greater opportunity of involvement by community-based organizations in the Eastern Cape and on the Witwatersrand because of the greater support for Black Consciousness in these two areas. The role of

Inkatha in moderating some Zulu workers in Natal should also be taken into account. In short, strike activity seems to be greater when the nature of the community-based organizations is such that they encourage the politicization of the workplace. It is probably this which explains Schlemmer's findings, during a survey of 532 African workers in five Natal companies, which indicated that two-thirds would not support a strike call from either political or union leaders. He concluded from this that political and ideological factors were not a priority of workers and that workers were not becoming politicized or radicalized.[82] He made this claim elsewhere,[83] but he must only have had Natal in mind, for strike action since 1980 does not bear this claim out.

In 1981 large-scale industrial unrest was sparked off by the government's proposed Pensions Bill and the strikes led to the Bill being dropped. Another of the major strikes in 1981 occurred in May, when 1,500 workers in the Eastern Cape downed tools in solidarity with 150 Firestone workers who were dismissed after a strike. This indicates considerable ideological development. The largest strike of the year was at the Sigma factory in Pretoria, involving 4,500 workers who demanded a minimum wage treble that which the company was offering. Union recognition led to a number of other strikes in the year. The South African Allied Workers' Union launched a boycott of Rowntree products after the company dismissed workers following a strike. The consumer boycott was very successful and was supported by students at the universities of Cape Town, Durban Westville, Natal, Witwatersrand, and Rhodes, and by COSAS, the Natal Indian Congress, AZAPO, FOSATU, the General Workers' Union, and the Soweto Chamber of Commerce and Industry. Overtly political strikes were linked to mass campaigns such as the Anti-Republic Day campaign, protests against Ciskeian independence, and Anti-South African Indian Congress election campaigns. These led the Minister of Defence to allege that the ANC were promoting labour unrest.

In 1982 a major confrontation occurred between the South African Transport Services and the General Workers' Union over the recognition of the union as the representative of dock workers in the Eastern Cape. Workers were dismissed, placed on buses and told to return to the homelands. It is possible that this hard line approach was taken to prevent a backlash from the 115,000 White workers whom SATS employs. The Federal Council of the seven unions representing White workers publicly thanked SATS for its strong stand against the recognition of 'an outside union'. On 5 February 1982, Neil Aggett, an organizer for the Food and Canning Workers' Union, died while in detention. His death led to many political strikes and a considerable amount of trade union unity. The Food and Canning Workers' Union called for a nation-wide stoppage on 11 February in honour of Dr Aggett. It was well supported throughout the country and led many unions to attack the detention system. The General Workers' Union said that Aggett's death would lead the union to intensify its struggle against the state. The unions were strongly condemned by TUCSA. Other strikes in the same year occurred over retrenchment.[84] Mention should also be made of the mine strike in July, which involved 70,000 miners in Transvaal gold mines and Natal colliers, making it the largest labour action on the mines since the 1946 miners' strike. Police intervened in force and shot dead two miners. Over 3,000 miners were sent back to the homelands.

There were more strikes in 1982 than ever before, which counteracts the belief that in times of recession workers are automatically less willing to engage in strike action. There was a 45 per cent increase in the number of African workers on strike and the number of man-days lost increased from 1981 by 61 per cent. A survey of strike trends from 1975 to 1982 by Eddie Webster concludes that the broad trend was towards strikes becoming a normal part of the collective bargaining process in South Africa, although the strike figures are still well below those of other advanced industrial societies.[85] In contrast, the National Man-power Commission argued that the relatively high level of strike action that has accompanied the Wiehahn reforms is a transitional phase and not an indication of what lies in the future.[86] In view of the repressive action taken against the labour movement, this moderate and cautious approach by the NMC suggests there is a tension between state apparatuses, with some sections wishing to repress industrial action while others seek to institutionalize it.

The attempt to institutionalize industrial conflict continued into 1983. The Director General of Manpower said, towards the end of 1983, that more unions than ever were now using the official disputes machinery, either in the form of conciliation boards or industrial courts. The use of conciliation boards increased fourfold in comparison with 1981. However, this was often only a prelude to calling an official strike, for strike activity also increased in 1983 to above the 1982 peak. A strike at Natal Thread over wages was the second largest legal strike by African workers in South Africa's labour history. Workers at all three plants of Autoplastics went on strike in concert, which is an unusual occurrence in South Africa. In September 1983, 89 Black workers at the Liberty Life Association of Africa were dismissed when they went on strike over the company's refusal to recognize their union. A successful consumer boycott of Liberty Life and associated companies was launched. This action won international support with pressure being put on Guardian Royal Exchange in London, who hold Liberty Life shares. In 1984, the new African National Union of Miners was very active. It won recognition at eight mines, and by June 1984 strikes were reported in a number of mines following the rejection of a 25 per cent wage increase by the Chamber of Mines. A 40 per cent increase had been suggested by an inquiry in 1982 as necessary to bring the lowest-paid workers up to subsistence level. The police responded aggressively to the striking miners. In June, two miners were shot dead by 'unknown persons' from a nearby White residential area, in response to which a Colonel in the South African Police said that the Whites had 'all the reason' to shoot the miners.[87] In September seven striking miners were shot dead by police.

Clearly there is some confusion in the state's response to the industrial unrest. On the one hand, the liberal NMC is committed to a liberal reform policy based on a free enterprise approach which stresses the non-interference of the state in labour issues. In November 1984 the Minister of Home Affairs, F. W. de Klerk, reiterated his view that politics should be kept out of the employer–employee relationship. He had government interference as well as political strikes in mind when he said this. The NMC expresses the same commitment, as revealed in the following policy statement: 'the government is committed to the principles of maximum self-governance by employers and employees, the maximum decentralization of negotiation and decision making, a minimum of government interference in what is essentially a private relationship.'[88] The Commission's position on strikes is liberal, stating that 'we must guard against regarding every strike as virtually a national crisis. This is far from the truth . . . a strike is a normal feature of the bargaining process that takes place in a free market'.[89]

Conversely, there is a considerable police and security harassment of trade unions and workers. This harassment extends beyond detentions and includes raids on union offices, pressure on landlords to deny premises, arrests of strikers and union officials, and bans on meetings. The South African Allied Workers' Union was particularly hard hit, being harassed by both the South African security police and the Ciskeian police. It was eventually banned in the Ciskei. At a time when the government is seeking approval for its labour reforms, the repeated detentions, raids, and harassment to which trade unions are subject can only further undermine the confidence of workers in the reforms. Certain sections of the state apparatus work against the reforms by seeing industrial unrest and trade union activity as subversion. The Minister of Police claimed, in 1982, that trade unionists were 'involved in terrorist activities, sabotage, arson and disruption of the economy'.[90] The Minister of Defence in introducing the 1984 defence White Paper in Parliament referred to labour unrest as being linked to the ANC's use of sabotage.

With these twin beliefs, the institutionalization of industrial conflict through liberal machinery goes hand in hand with severe state repression of trade union activity. This is an attempt to restrict demands emerging from the unions to economic ones only. The government is imposing a framework of institutional controls on the unions while limiting the extent to which unions can participate in broader issues, especially the extent to which unions can play a part in the mobilization of political opposition to apartheid. The repression of non-institutionalized and political activity is severe. According to the Minister of Police, during 1981 and 1982 police were called to industrial disputes on 358 occasions. Many deaths and injuries were inflicted on strikers, and many more have been charged under various laws. One manifestation of this attempt to restrict non-institutionalized union activity is the strengthening of the laws affecting industrial relations. The 1982 Internal Security Act and the 1982 Intimidation Act constitute some of the most draconian pieces of trade union legislation in the world. Any trade unionist who 'cripples, prejudices or interrupts' industrial production with intent to 'achieve, bring about or promote any constitutional, political, industrial, social or economic aim or change' can be convicted of subversion or sabotage. The punishment for either is up to twenty years' imprisonment. Those who either withdraw labour or advocate the withdrawal will be liable to arrest on the grounds that they are a threat to national security. To this form of legalized repression must be added another. Since the 1981 Labour Relations Amendment Act, the government has sought to prevent unregistered unions from acting outside the institutional controls it imposes on registered unions. In 1983 new legislation admitted unregistered unions to the conciliation board machinery. This form of compulsory registration was enhanced by the Labour Relations Amendment Bill, announced in June 1984, which limits the collective bargaining rights of unregistered unions and extends the rights of those who do meet the minimum legal requirements. The unregistered unions are to have the same state control as registered unions but few of their privileges.

It may seem paradoxical, but this repression can strengthen the independent and unregistered unions. For a period, repression may restrict the growth and effectiveness of the independent and unregistered unions, yet it also produces further waves of alienated workers who have little option but to turn to other forms of resistance and opposition. It was this which the Wiehahn reforms were designed to prevent, but as a result of the continued repression Black workers experience the state as an instrument of racial and economic oppression, an entity which traps and ensnares them at the pass office, the police station, the segregated township, and in the workplace. In this regard, the hope of the Wiehahn reforms, that industrial conflict will be institutionalized, economic issues thereby separated from political ones, is unrealistic.

This truncated review of industrial action in the years up to 1983 has highlighted a number of points. The longitudinal study by the Arnold Bergstraesser Institute reported that 83.7 per cent of urban Blacks, in three industrial centres, believed workers solidarity would give them a strong position in disputes but that only 47.8 per cent actually supported trade unions. The surprise was that support for trade unions was higher among the professional Black middle class.[91] The truth of this is very clearly demonstrated in the collective action by Black Consciousness organizations such as PEBCO and MWASA and the support given to workers on strike by African businessmen, schoolchildren, and university students.

In 1978, for example, the Western Cape Traders' Association, representing 600 Asian, Coloured, and African businessmen, declared a 'war on racial discrimination' and used the boycott weapon for extra-workplace ends. Their President, Dawood Khan, said: 'we are going to use the only legal weapon we are able to use—our economic muscle.'[92] *Inter alia*, this muscle was used to reinstate dismissed workers in companies which members of the Association had dealings with, to end segregated facilities, and even to force the organizers of an all-White dancing competition to open it up to Blacks. The relatively younger, more radical, better-educated section in the African community was most active in the Ford strike. It is this section which Mayer's research indicates has what he calls the 'racial model' of South Africa's system of social relations. This point is relevant to the argument in Chapter 4: Black Consciousness is undergoing a shift towards operating with a class model, with a consequent shift away fom an exclusive race model.

The reluctant conservatism of some African trade unions has been commented upon in the past many times,[93] and was evidenced in many strikes in 1979–80 for example. The obvious politicization of the workplace that has occurred in more recent industrial action reflects that fact that African workers want wider issues expressed through the unions. For the most part the unions do become involved in this politicization; where this does not happen extra-workplace organizations are drawn into the workplace. The attempt to differentiate between ethnic and class aspects of either workers' consciousness[94] or collective action[95] seems on this evidence to be futile. It is erroneous for Webster to argue, for example, that stay-aways involve these general issues while strikes are plant-based.[96] This brief review has shown how strikes in his terminology involve extra-workplace issues. The refusal of some workers to participate in a number of stay-aways organized by the Black Consciousness movement, or their reluctance to participate in 16 June anniversaries, do not reflect their rejection of politicization of the workplace. The extreme economic pressure on workers not to lose pay and not to lay themselves open to security harassment could well explain this refusal. The collective nature of strikes is a psychological encouragement to participate, whereas the decision to participate in stay-aways organized outside the plant is not a collective decision by workers in the plant. The stay-aways which are successful may be those where a collective decision to participate was made beforehand: Webster does show how successful well-organized stay-aways have been.[97]

There are both theoretical and practical advantages in strictly demarcating political and economic struggles. The practical advantages are many. Historical example shows SACTU went underground for its political activity. In bringing extra-workplace issues into the plant, extra-workplace divisions are also introduced. In the Cape Town meat industry strike, for example, Coloured butchers would not support the strike by African workers, while African butchers did. The Frametex strike in Pinetown saw conflicts between Xhosa and Zulu over scabbing. In effect what happens in politicizing the workplace is the blurring of class-based consciousness and of the specific nature of plant-based issues. This creates theoretical problems with the conceptual framework through which industrial action is categorized. None the less, certain Marxists welcome this politicization,[98] realizing that class consciousness may well develop from it.[99] Molteno has argued against those who dismiss Black Consciousness by indicating that ethnic mobilization has a potential to develop into class solidarity.[100] This may or may not be the case, although Chapter 4 will demonstrate how the Black Consciousness movement is moving away from an exclusive racial model.

Those that welcome this politicization have at their base Lenin's notion that the proletarian struggle must be transformed from a purely economic one to a political one. The historical example most readily recalled is the conflict in the German Social Democratic Party over the German Free Trade Unions' policy of restricting itself solely to economic issues.[101] In South Africa, widening the struggle in this way has theoretical consequences which were absent from Lenin's Russia and Bernstein's Germany. It is not only Black workers who can engage in political opposition, and therefore Black workers are not the sole carriers of change. David Hemson, for example, recognized that workers have used the workplace to offer political resistance and have engaged in political strikes.[102] He does not explore the implications of this but it leaves open the possibility that classes are not the only motors of change because other groups can offer political resistance and engage in political boycotts. The value of Hemson's argument is its recognition that no simple distinction can be made between the economic interests of African workers in the workplace and the wider interests of African workers treated as a racial category outside the workplace. Once such a recognition is made it is no longer possible to argue, as many have done, that industrial action is either caused by ethnic (i.e. non plant-based) issues or class (i.e. plant-based) issues. This belief is implicit in Webster's contrast of stay-aways and strikes. In reality a strike which starts as one quickly becomes expressed as both. The history of the ANC's early mobilization in the defiance campaign and PEBCO's role in the 1979–80 Ford strike demonstrates how both kinds of issues become simultaneously wrapped up in industrial action.

It is true that wage demands formed the basis of numerous strikes during the period under review—the South African Institute of Race Relations estimated in 1983 that 47.2 per cent of African strikes in that year were over wage increases.[103] However, it is impossible to separate the ethnic connotations associated with low pay or segregated facilities for African workers. The documented evidence identifying which social problem Africans perceive as their priority is contradictory. Many studies show economic issues, such as low pay and the high cost of living, to be paramount,[104] although studies showing the establishment of political equality as the priority can easily be found.[105] Despite this, the inference drawn from these studies is erroneous: it is impossible to separate political equality from economic improvements. The ending of ethnically structured inequality in one necessarily leads to pressure for its abolition in the other. In its drive for Black *embourgeoisement* this is something the government has not yet appreciated. Equal pay across the ethnic divide presupposes ethnic equality *per se* because equality is indivisible. Hence, the demand for wage increases necessarily involves the abolition of racial restrictions on earnings, employment, and occupational opportunity. All of this has ramifications for educational provision and social welfare. In themselves these issues challenge the present distribution of political power. It is worth considering the extent to which the trade union movement is prepared to fit the workplace and plant-based issues into their wider context, for this forms one of the major divisions within the South African Black trade union movement.

POLITICAL UNIONISM AND THE DIVISIONS WITHIN THE TRADE UNION MOVEMENT

Unlike the 1960s, when a similar purge of Black trade unions and workers reduced union membership to 3 per cent of the Black workforce, the repression of the 1980s has been accompanied by soaring membership. There are two reasons for this. First, South Africa's burgeoning industrial sector needs a more stable, skilled workforce. Such a workforce is not easily replaced in a short time and is thus less vulnerable. Secondly, the need to build and maintain good industrial relations has meant that a well-organized union movement has been able to achieve notable economic advances. Yet, in a country where genuine Black progress is restricted the unions tend to become channels for frustrations of all kinds. Duncan Innes has divided Black trade unions into three types according to how they respond to this challenge.[106] The first are the TUCSA-affiliated unions, which see the state as neutral and assiduously avoid politicization. These contrast with the independent unions, which are of two types. The first is the unregistered unions and the CUSA-affiliated unions, some of which are registered, which see the state as repressive and incapable of granting genuine reforms, and which therefore use the workplace as a means to political liberation; the other type of independent union is affiliated to FOSATU: they see the state as repressive but as also able to introduce concessions of benefit to workers. These concessions must not be endangered by precipitous political action. Indeed, this must be avoided in order for the trade union movement to grow and establish itself in the workplace.

However, the extent to which unions are prepared to politicize is not the only basis of division between Black unions in South Africa. Phil Bonner defined a number of issues which divide Black trade unions.[107] Some of these he described as internal issues, such as different assessments of the optimal organizational scale and the question of union democracy. Other issues he described as external, such as the differing attitudes towards wider political mobilization in the factories and the relationship with political and community organizations. Other issues cut across this simple internal–external dichotomy. Registration, for example, generates both internal organizational and administrative issues, and has implications for the politicization of trade union activity. The externally located divisions will be discussed further.

'Political unionism' is a term used by Saul and Gelb to describe the stance taken by some trade unions who use the workplace to advance political claims.[108] Others have noted this tendency within some sections of the Black trade union movement. Nolutshungu referred to the 'political mindedness of workers',[109] Lodge used the term 'political trade unions',[110] and D. K. Smith referred to the 'nationalist mindedness of trade unions'.[111] While some analysts see this tendency as regrettable, it is nevertheless clearly taking place. A survey of attitudes among employers and workers showed that each believes that there is a growing overlap between political and economic issues.[112] This overlap was predicted even after the 1973 dock strike.[113] It has led to a rift in the Black trade union movement between the FOSATU faction, which believes in widening its power-base by strong shop-floor and industrial organization and developing stable and disciplined negotiating procedures, and the opposing so-called 'radical' faction, which tries to become powerful by mobilizing the community and refuses to make any compromise with the state. FOSATU's position was reiterated in 1982, when at its April congress Joe Foster, acting general secretary, stated the federation's policy of building a workers' movement independent of all political organizations'. He criticized many of the activities of the community-based unions, referring to building up unions in the factories as the fundamental political task. Relations with other unions were not improved by Foster's remark that those unions who restricted their membership to Africans alone were racist.

However, politicization has two elements which need to be distinguished. Politicization can be evidenced either by associations with political organizations or by the articulation of political grievances. FOSATU was once against both, but with the obvious increase in worker pressure for politicization of some form, and with the increasing intensity of political resistance, it came to identify itself with political issues and to articulate political grievances. What it refuses to do is to identify with wider political organizations. For example, Joe Foster made plain at the 1982 congress that FOSATU was committed to wide-ranging political change. The federation rejected the homelands policy and called for a democracy based on universal franchise and majority rule. The campaign against the constitution saw FOSATU become highly involved in the articulation of Black political demands, and it described the proposals as undemocratic, racist, and anti-worker. On 2 November 1983, FOSATU members were instructed to wear one-man-one-vote stickers to work and to ask their employers what their attitude to the constitution was. Thus, FOSATU strategists argued for a 'deeper understanding of the interrelatedness of workplace issues and political structures'.[114] The clearest indication of a change in attitude toward politicization came with the 31 October stay-away in 1984, when FOSATU collaborated with the UDF, CUSA, and COSAS in organizing a one-day protest against the repression of the township protests and the use of the military to suppress political opposition.

Yet this degree of politicization is still far below that adopted by some other unions. For example, the position on the constitution taken by the unregistered and unaffiliated General Workers' Union was far more extreme. Its general secretary warned employers that so far workers had used the factory floor as a political base with great restraint, but if employers voted 'yes' in the referendum the General Workers' Union would feel no compunction in using the shop-floor to achieve political rights.[115] This was also the stance adopted by the CUSA-affiliated unions, and CUSA has involved itself in such issues as relocation, township housing, and the campaign of opposition towards the community council system. It also identified itself unambiguously with political organizations, including Black Consciousness organizations, the UDF, and the ANC. CUSA's inauguration was attended by a large number of Soweto politicians who work outside state-sponsored politics, including members of the Soweto Civic Association and the Committee of 10. This reflects the growing interest of Black Consciousness in worker and trade union issues.

The phenomenal growth of CUSA provided a lesson to FOSATU as did the success of the South African Allied Workers' Union and PEBCO in earlier periods. The South African Allied Workers' Union was formed in 1979 as a result of splits in another union. SAAWU's growth was in contrast to the careful professionalism of FOSATU. Its membership was drawn from almost every form of working-class employment in East London and it eschewed the cautious plant-based approach of FOSATU.[116] Much of its recruitment took place at mass political rallies. The union operates at the community level not in the factory, and it has eaten into FOSATU's support in the Eastern Cape. Further inroads into FOSATU's support in the area were made by PEBCO when the FOSATU-affiliated United Automobile Workers' Union refused to support a spontaneous strike in support of PEBCO's leader Thozamile Botha. PEBCO's community-wide support led to the formation of a rival union at Ford's, the Motor Assembly and Component Workers' Union, which is active in community issues. The position of the FOSATU-affiliated union in the plant was weakened. As Lodge makes clear, it was in response to challenges like these that FOSATU strategists argued for a closer relationship between plant-based issues and wider community action.[117] In some union rivalry disputes, FOSATU-affiliated unions lost to CUSA-affiliated ones when employers organized ballots among workers to resolve the issue of which of the two the employers should recognize.[118]

It is divisions such as these which explain the trade union movement's varying response to the formation of the UDF and its various political affiliates. The UDF has many unions affiliated to it and it has taken a high profile in many strikes. FOSATU pledged its support for the UDF and co-operated with it in some political campaigns, but is not an affiliate. Critics of the UDF who advance a strict worker- and plant-based form of mobilization accuse the UDF of blurring the working-class struggle because it does not agitate exclusively on class issues. Thus, it has been referred to as 'radical *petite bourgeoisie*' by some opponents.[119] Relations between the UDF and the Black trade union movement will be subject to further debates such as this, and opinions on the UDF will vary according to whether politicization of the workplace is supported or not.

Registration is another divisive issue within the Black trade union movement. Some unions, like those belonging to CUSA, registered on the basis of racially exclusive membership for Africans only, while others, such as the FOSATU unions, decided to apply for registration on condition that it was on a non-racial basis. A third group, notably SAAWU and the General Workers' Union, decided not to apply for registration. Although the Minister of Manpower has appealed to employers not to deal with unregistered unions, the success of these unions in mobilizing workers has led many employers to recognize them. However, their role in collective bargaining is to be restricted by the proposed new industrial relations legislation. Not surprisingly, it tends to be the unregistered unions who are seen as politically the most militant. This makes the stand of the radical unions within CUSA interesting.

The CUSA group had no difficulty in registering, and this undermined their credibility with non-collaborationist Black Consciousness groups. It was for this reason that CUSA has announced that it will support those unions who wish to deregister; some of its affiliates have done so. This deregistration occurred at a time when the FOSATU unions, who once opposed registration, began to register once that it was clear that they could register on non-racial lines, after a court ruling to this effect was obtained by FOSATU. After considerable hesitation, FOSATU supported registration and advanced two basic arguments for doing so. The first is that registration strengthens the unions against the employer. Secondly, the Wiehahn reforms involved concessions which FOSATU believed would strengthen the working-class struggle as a whole. The unregistered unions, however, are totally opposed to even conditional registration because it involves 'becoming a part of the system'.

In a series of articles in the radical *South African Labour Bulletin* during 1982, strident critics of apartheid argued the case for registration on the same grounds as those advanced by FOSATU.[120] Registration is particularly appealing to those who advance the idea of a class struggle, for it does strengthen the position of the organized labour movement. It is less appealing to those who see the liberation struggle in more political terms, for registration involves a curtailment of the political involvement of unions. It is for this reason that the unregistered unions are in a strong position. There are two underlying causes of this strength. They are the unions which most unambiguously represent the pressure for political unionism that exists among Black workers. Paradoxically, employers are also willing to sign recognition agreements with unregistered unions. In part this is because employers may be responding to pressure from foreign investors or multinational companies, but they are also motivated by the success of the unregistered unions in mobilizing amongst the workforce. This may make the unregistered unions seem a better protection from industrial unrest. If this is so, the unregistered unions need to be cautious in their willingness to politicize the workplace, for this may lose them the confidence of employers, which is one of the strengths of the unregistered unions at the moment. This power-base might also be taken away by the state as it tries to stop employers dealing with the unregistered unions. Yet, if the state harasses and represses them, this will affect how workers view the labour reforms and it may pressurize unions to deregister.

There is considerable uncertainty in the Black trade union movement at this juncture. The divisions and rivalry between the unions add to this. The unions have shown themselves to be aware of the problems generated by this uncertainty and a series of unity meetings have been held since 1981. At Langa in August 1981 FOSATU, CUSA, and unregistered unions, like SAAWU and the General Workers' Union, formed a united front in rejection of registration, industrial councils, Ciskeian independence, bannings and detentions. There was agreement on resolutions and, in an attempt to maintain the unity, delegates decided to form *ad hoc* solidarity committees in the regions in order to work out plans for concerted joint action. Yet major policy differences hindered the formation of one over-arching federation to which they could all belong. FOSATU's acting general secretary criticized a unity based either on a 'loose federation' or on a 'united front' where the organizations remain autonomous. At a second unity meeting in Wilgespruit April 1982 more than 200 trade unionists pledged their support for the launching of a more permanent programme for unity. Plans were mooted for further regional meetings to discuss possible alliances at the local level. However, the radical Motor Assembly and Components Workers' Union walked out and neither this meeting nor the next, at Port Elizabeth, could agree on forming one federation of unions. The Port Elizabeth meeting ended in deadlock when seven unregistered unions identified certain principles which they said were non-negotiable. These included non-racialism, worker control, no registration, no industrial councils, increased community involvement, no links with reactionary organizations, and the need for a tight federation of unions. They rejected any alliance with unions who could not support these principles.

While a united front seemed unlikely, the potential of unity had already been demonstrated. In February 1982 most of the independent unions came together as a body to protest against the death of Neil Aggett. It was a major historical event, for it was the first instance of industrial action of a political nature organized on a national scale and centred at the point of production rather than the traditional form of a stay-away. This unity was again demonstrated in the form of a stay-away in October 1984 when all the independent unions and political and student organizations came together in support of the township protests. Common purpose and belief was evident again in response to the government's constitutional proposals. There are also some instances of close alliances being forged at shop-floor level between rival unions. In March 1983 for example, the General Workers' Union and a FOSATU affiliate met to discuss common grievances against one company.

It was in this atmosphere that at the fourth unity meeting, in April 1983, it was agreed to set up a feasibility committee to consider the structure and policy of a new encompassing trade union federation. The general secretary of the unregistered General Workers' Union said that the committee had not been set up to discuss whether a new federation was desirable but when and how this should happen. The unions and federations committed to this goal included FOSATU, SAAWU, GWU, and CUSA. The union which had earlier walked out was undecided on whether to support either this proposal or a federation of all unregistered unions. At it was, the potential membership of the proposed federation was 300,000. FOSATU's general secretary even said that FOSATU would disband and deregister if wider unity would be achieved by it. Meetings of the feasibility committee were held regularly throughout 1983 without agreement emerging. A further meeting in November 1983 was postponed until February 1984. In March unions representing 300,000 workers agreed to form a new federation before the end of the year. They included FOSATU's nine affiliates and CUSA's twelve, but not SAAWU. CUSA and FOSATU agreed they would disband when the new federation came into being. But the debate was intense and sometimes acrimonious. The NUM, affiliated to CUSA, withdrew from one meeting with CUSA officials complaining of what it saw as the officials' lack of commitment to the new federation. SAAWU left talks after being informed they could have only observer status. It was not until the end of the following year that the disputes were

resolved and the new federation was announced. The Confederation of South African Trade Unions was inaugurated in
December 1985, to represent 34 trade unions with 450,520 paid-
up members and a signed-up membership of 520,000. Neither
CUSA nor the orthodox Black Consciousness unions in AZACTU
joined COSATU. FOSATU disbanded when its unions affiliated
to COSATU. CUSA's major affiliate, the NUM, also joined the
new federation and disassociated itself from CUSA. NUM officials, in fact, played a major role in the formation of COSATU:
the NUM's former president, Elijah Barayi, is president of
COSATU, and the NUM's general secretary, Cyril Ramaphosa,
attended COSATU's launch. CUSA was involved in the negotiations up to June 1985 but withdrew because of COSATU's
commitment to strive for a single union per industry. The
AZACTU unions objected to COSATU's commitment to non-
racialism. While the latter dispute is likely to be irresolvable, the
schism with CUSA is not unbridgeable.

The commitment to non-racialism is part of COSATU's wider
support for the aims and policies of the ANC; Barayi was a
stalwart of the ANC in the 1950s. At its inauguration Barayi
likened COSATU to SACTU, the union federation linked to the
ANC in the 1950s and 1960s. The general secretary of COSATU,
Jay Naidoo, also has former connections with the ANC. In
speeches at the launch in Durban, Barayi and Naidoo committed
COSATU to political unionism, and within this to support for the
goal of universal franchise within a unitary and non-racial state
which is associated with the ANC and UDF. However, with
respect to affiliation to the UDF, COSATU took a similar position
to FOSATU's stating that it would not affiliate to one single
political organization because its members supported many organizations. However, many of its affiliated unions are also affiliates
of the UDF and it has openly expressed support for the aims of the
UDF.

CONCLUSION

The nature of industrial action among African workers provides
contemporary evidence to support the arguments of those who
claim that African workers are an economically exploited class
defined in ethnic terms. In South Africa class is a racially struc-

tured phenomenon. This does not mean, as Leftwich argues, that African workers are first reacting as Africans and secondly as workers.[121] Rather it implies that class and race are so intertwined in consciousness and action that each becomes an expression of the other. 'Political unionism' is the outcome of this intertwining. Kuper has argued this point previously, when he maintained that consciousness of class is contained within ethnic groups rather than across them.[122] Leggett uses the term 'race-class consciousness' and means by it the marriage between an economically exploited class which is defined on ethnic terms.[123] Giddens refers to Leggett's conclusions in suggesting a general theory to the effect that under certain conditions ethnic characteristics offer a very strong source of what he calls 'class structuration'.[124] Weber argued a similar position for the caste system and its influence on what he called Indians' 'life chances' and 'market situation'.[125] This leaves open the possibility that in the future, under changing circumstances, African workers who now do not see themselves as members of a non-race working class, will develop a working-class consciousness. This is so because an end to the appropriation of power, wealth, and prestige on ethnic lines will prevent group identity being an ethnically structured phenomenon. At present, however, opposition in the workplace involves both of these two central frames of reference.

Chapter 4 argues that what is significant in South Africa at the moment is that the two main political opposition forces, Black Consciousness and the ANC, are slowly coming to realize the futility of maintaining separate allegiances to different frames of references.

Notes

1. R. H. Davies, *Capital, State and White Labour in South Africa*, London, Harvester, 1979, p. 2.
2. K. Luckhardt and B. Wall, *Organize or Starve*, London, Lawrence and Wishart, 1980, p. 440.
3. B. Kantor and H. Kenny, 'The Poverty of Neo-Marxism: The Case of South Africa', *Journal of Southern African Studies*, 3, 1976.
4. *New Society*, 13 December 1979.
5. A. du Toit, 'Emerging Strategies for Political Control', in R. Price and G. Rosberg, *The Apartheid Regime*, Berkeley, Institute of International Studies, 1980, p. 2.

6. Some of these are discussed in the following section.
7. On BBC's *Panorama*, 15 June 1981.
8. H. Adam, *Modernizing Race Relations*, Berkeley, University of California Press, 1971; 'Minority Monopoly in Transition: Recent Policy Shifts of the South African State', *Journal of Modern African Studies*, 18, 1980. With H. Giliomee he has written *Ethnic Power Mobilized*, New Haven, Yale University Press, 1979 (published as *The Rise and Crisis of Afrikaner Power* in South Africa, by David Philip). D. Mason, 'Industrialization, Race and Class Conflict in South Africa', *Ethnic and Racial Studies*, 3, 1980. J. Rex, *Race Relations in Sociological Theory*, London, Weidenfeld and Nicolson, 1978; *Race, Colonialism and the City*, London, Routledge and Kegan Paul, 1973. See also M. Lipton, *Capitalism and Apartheid*, London, Temple Smith and Gower, 1985.
9. 'Class, Status and Ethnicity as Perceived by Johannesburg Africans', in L. Thompson and J. Butler, *Change in Contemporary South Africa*, Berkeley, University of California Press, 1975, and 'Good and Bad Whites', delivered at Queen's University, Belfast, January, 1983.
10. *Class, Race and Labour*, New York, Oxford University Press, 1968.
11. *Class, Race and Worker Insurgency*, New York, Cambridge University Press, 1977.
12. For a review see S. Duncan, 'The Central Legislation of South African Labour Exploitation', *South African Labour Bulletin*, 3.1, 1977.
13. See E. Gitsham and J. Trembeth, *A First Account of Labour Organizations in South Africa*, Durban, Durban Commercial Printing, 1926. Also H. and R. Simons, *Class and Colour in South Africa 1850–1950*, London, Penguin, 1969, p. 353.
14. B. du Toit, *Ukubamba Amadolo*, London, Onyx Press, 1978, p. 14. See also C. Kadalie, *My Life and the ICU*, London, Humanities Press, 1970.
15. 'Natal, The Zulu Royal Family and the Ideology of Segregation', *Journal of Southern African Studies*, 4, 1978, p. 185.
16. E. Webster and J. Kuzwayo, 'A Research Note on Consciousness and the Problem of Organization', in L. Schlemmer and E. Webster, *Change, Reform and Economic Growth*, Johannesburg, Ravan Press, 1978, p. 232.
17. For a study of victimization, see P. Galt, 'Security of Employment and Victimization in South African Law', *South African Labour Bulletin*, 3.1, 1976. Other relevant articles include: H. Cheadle, 'Reflections on the Right to Strike and the Contract of Employment', ibid. 5.1, 1979; F. Hayson, 'The Right to Strike in South African Law', ibid.

18. Taken from *South Africa 1980–81*, Official Yearbook of the Republic, Department of Information, Pretoria, 1981, p. 433. Figures do tend to be contradictory on this point. According to F. de Clercq, even in 1976 there were 26 trade unions with a total membership of 110,000. See 'Apartheid and the Organized Labour Movement', *Review of African Political Economy*, 14, 1978, p. 73. Whichever figure is taken, both the number of unions and the proportion of unionized labour remain small.

19. For example see the *South African Labour Bulletin*, 8.3, 1982, p. 4.

20. Durban has always been a stronghold of trade unionism. The ICU was strongest in Durban, and the militancy of Asian and Zulu workers was attested to in the 1969–74 strikes. The TUACC was established in Durban, as was FOSATU. However, in recent years Durban's strike record lags behind that of other areas.

21. In its review of 1979, *Post Transvaal* ran a series of four articles on trade unionism in South Africa, where its support for FOSATU was made plain. When Black Consciousness organizations began to co-operate with the ANC, the *Post Transvaal* began to support strongly the ANC, as does its successor, the *Sowetan*. It uses the term 'pro' to the extent that the newspaper gave publicity to Black Consciousness over other organizations which it ignored or treated critically.

22. See K. Luckhardt and B. Wall, *Organize or Starve*, pp. 462–3. This conflict is also shown in the opposition which SACTU has offered to the establishment of direct links between British trade unions and their counterparts in the independent unions in South Africa. Motions calling for direct links at the Annual General Meeting of the Anti-Apartheid Movement in London, in November 1981, were defeated by a 2 to 1 majority on the grounds that SACTU still represented the whole of the Black working class. The Anti-Apartheid Movement took this position as the official stance of SACTU, notwithstanding that the FOSATU unions already had informal links with unions in Britain. Acting general secretary Joe Foster made several criticisms of SACTU at the 1982 Congress. His address is reproduced in the *South African Labour Bulletin*, 7.8, 1982.

23. 'Black Trade Unions in South Africa Since World War Two', in R. Price and G. Rosberg, *The Apartheid Regime*.

24. *South Africa 1980–81*, Department of Information, Pretoria, p. 434.

25. Ibid., pp. 433–4.

26. *Hansard*, 18, col. 8776, 1973.

27. For example, the *Weekend World* wrote 'this country needs Black trade unions. A trade union is the only effective way of ensuring

workers get their rights ... Certainly the government-sponsored works' committees are no alternative,' 28 July 1977.

28. See A. Erwin, *et al.*, 'Case Study: The Function, Nature and Effectiveness of the Statutory Liaison Committee: Pinetex', *South African Labour Bulletin*, 2.9–10, 1976; on Industrial Councils see ibid., 3.10, 1977.

29. *South Africa 1980–81*, Department of Information, Pretoria, p. 430.

30. *Citizen*, 14 April 1978.

31. *Die Vaderland*, 25 September 1979.

32. *South Africa 1980–81*, Department of Information, Pretoria, p. 254.

33. Reported in the *Daily News*, 29 June 1978. Job reservation had almost ended as a practice. An inspection in 1973 of 2,501 Johannesburg building sites revealed contraventions of job reservation on 62.7 per cent of them. See J. Kane-Berman, 'Rejoinder to the O'Dowd Thesis', in L. Schlemmer and E. Webster, op. cit., p. 53.

34. *Standard Bank Review*, Johannesburg, 1980, p. 16; *The Economist*, 8 March 1980.

35. Reported in P. Bonner, 'Black Trade Unions in South Africa Since World War Two', in R. Price and G. Rosberg, *The Apartheid Regime*, p. 188.

36. Taken from M. D. McGrath, 'The Problem of Cyclical Unemployment in South Africa' (mimeo.), p. 9. The figures are calculated on 1975 prices. For comparative figures, see M. D. McGrath, 'The Racial Welfare Budget in South Africa', conference paper, Economics Society of South Africa, Cape Town, September 1979, p. 34. Also see S. van der Horst, 'Employment', in S. van der Horst and J. Reid, *Race Discrimination in South Africa*, Cape Town, Philip, 1981, pp. 40–2.

37. For example, Pietermaritzburg City Council. See *Daily News*, 12 July 1977.

38. *Sunday Tribune*, 29 May 1977.

39. See Chapter 4 for community councils. On land tenure see P. Morris and S. van der Horst, 'Urban Housing', in S. van der Horst and J. Reid, *Race Discrimination in South Africa*.

40. This is discussed further below.

41. *Post Transvaal*, 24 June 1979.

42. SAIRR, *Survey of Race Relations 1983*, SAIRR, pp. 270–1.

43. *Post Transvaal*, 3 April 1979.

44. *Citizen*, 22 August 1977.

45. Ibid., 9 July 1977.

46. Ibid., 15 July 1977. See also the *Sunday Tribune*, 15 May 1977, and the *Daily News*, 13 May and 17 May 1977.

47. The Riekert Commission was a one-man commission; Riekert was P. W. Botha's national economic adviser. Members of the Wiehahn Commission were: Professor van der Merwe, labour economist at Pretoria University; Dr Drummand, of the Steel and Engineering Industries Federation; C. W. du Toit, of the Federated Chamber of Industries; T. Steenkamp, General Mining and Finance Corporation; R. Sutton of SA Breweries; A. Nieuwoudt, President of the Confederation of Labour; J. Grobbelaar, General Secretary of TUCSA; C. Grobler, of the Railways Artisans' Staff Association; T. Neethling of the Confederation of Metal and Building Unions; N. Hechter, Department of Labour; G. Munsook, South African Indian Council; C. Botes, National Union of Furniture and Allied Workers; B. Mokoatle, School of Business Leadership, University of South Africa.

48. See the *South African Labour Bulletin*, 5.2, 1979, 'Focus on Wiehahn', and 5.4, 1979, 'Focus on Riekert'. Also see S. van der Horst, 'Employment', in S. van der Horst and J. Reid, *Race Discrimination in South Africa*, pp. 34 ff.

49. See 'Minority Monopoly in Transition', *Journal of Modern African Studies*, 18, 1980, pp. 617, 619. Also S. van der Horst and J. Reid, 'Introduction', in S. van der Horst and J. Reid, *Race Discrimination in South Africa* op. cit., p. xi, where the changes are described as significant, profound and substantial. This view contrasts with that of L. Schlemmer, who wrote in 1980 that the government 'does not intend to devolve one iota of real power at this stage'. See 'Postscript 1980' in the English edition of T. Hanf *et al.*, *South Africa: The Prospects of Peaceful Change*. London, Rex Collings, 1981, p. 443.

50. See H. Giliomee, 'Structural Change and Political Options in the 1980s', lecture given at the Centre of Applied Social Sciences, University of Natal, 13 May 1980.

51. Table 13 is taken from SAIRR, *Survey of Race Relations 1982*, Johannesburg, SAIRR, 1983, p. 138. The figures in Table 14 are from *South Africa 1980–81*, Department of Information, Pretoria, 1981, p. 214. The figures for homeland population in 1979 are from SAIRR, *Survey of Race Relations 1979*, Johannesburg, SAIRR, 1980, p. 70. Note that the figures for frontier commuters in 1979 do not correspond in the two tables because of the different calculations used by the two different sources.

52. SAIRR, *Survey of Race Relations 1983*, p. 137.

53. *Rand Daily Mail*, 23 May 1979.

54. See International Defence and Aid Fund, Briefing Paper no. 13, 1984, p. 2, from where the following analysis is taken.

55. 7 May 1984.
56. Quoted in SAIRR, *Survey of Race Relations 1983*, pp. 265–7.
57. See F. Wilson, 'Current Labour Issues in South Africa', in R. Price and G. Rosberg, *The Apartheid Regime*.
58. Ibid., p. 162.
59. *Africa South of the Sahara 1980–81*, London, Europa Publishers Ltd., 1980, p. 925. Also see S. van der Horst, 'Employment', in S. van der Horst and J. Reid, *Race Discrimination in South Africa*, pp. 36–9.
60. The urban response is considered in Chapter 4, and the rural response in Chapter 6.
61. See S. van der Horst, *Sunday Times*, 11 November 1979.
62. *Sunday Tribune*, 12 June 1977.
63. 6 May 1979.
64. 22 June 1979.
65. 27 June 1979.
66. 24 June 1979.
67. 22 June 1979.
68. This is Webster's term: see E. Webster, 'Stay-Aways and the Black Working-Class since the Second World War—The Evolution of a Strategy' (mimeo), p. 1.
69. For example see the *Citizen*, 23 May 1978, where the rampage left fourteen injured and damage estimated at R1m.
70. Department of Information, Pretoria, *South Africa 1980–1*, p. 431; *Survey of Race Relations 1983*, p. 183.
71. That is why statistics of this kind differ greatly in the literature. E. Webster, 'Stay-Aways and the Black Working Class', p. 22, provides figures for the years 1973–7, which vary considerably. The total number of disputes without stoppages was 126, involving 12,275 workers. The figures for stoppages, excluding strikes, totalled 621, involving 71,025 workers—742 stoppages below the government's figures. This is discussed below.
72. There is no reason to assume that this delimitation will affect the argument because the go-slow is no more likely to be used in plant-based issues than any other strategy of industrial action.
73. For a summary see *South African Labour Bulletin*, 2.8, 1976; 3.7, 1977.
74. For example, see P. Bonner, *Strikes in South Africa*, p. 186; B. du Toit, *Ukubamba Amadolo*, p. 113.
75. E. Webster, *The Durban Strikes*, Johannesburg, Ravan Press, 1976.
76. Department of Information, Pretoria, *South Africa 1980–1*, p. 431; SAIRR, *Survey of Race Relations 1983*, p. 200.
77. This inference was drawn by Roseinnes Phahle, a Black trade unionist in London, and made in a private communication to the

author, dated 13 November 1982. C. J. Bezuidenhout, of the South African Embassy in London, has refused to clarify the meaning of the term prior to the 1973 legislation.

78. SAIRR, *Survey of Race Relations 1979*, p. 286.
79. See R. de Villiers, 'Ever-Ready Strike', *South African Labour Bulletin*, 5.1, 1979.
80. 'South Africa 1976: A View From Within the Liberation Movement', *Social Dynamics*, 5.2, 1979, p. 76.
81. Quoted by G. Maree, 'The 1979 Port Elizabeth Strike and an Evaluation of the United Automobile Rubber and Allied Workers' Union', *South African Labour Bulletin*, 6.2–3, 1980.
82. Quoted in SAIRR, *Survey of Race Relations 1983*, p. 202.
83. See 'Conflict in South Africa: Build Up to Revolution or Impasse?', European Consortium for Political Research, Freiburg, 20–5 March 1983.
84. For an analysis of retrenchment see R. Lambert, 'Strike Action in 1982—the Politics of Reform', and C. Albertyn, 'Retrenchments and the Law', in *Indicator: Urban and Industrial Monitor*, 1.1, 1983.
85. Quoted in SAIRR, *Survey of Race Relations 1983*, pp. 202–3.
86. Quoted by R. Lambert, 'Strike Action in 1982—the Politics of Reform', p. 23.
87. Quoted in the *Rand Daily Mail*, 30 June 1984. Also see the issue of 3 July 1984.
88. Quoted in R. Lambert, 'Strike Action in 1982—the Politics of Reform', p. 23.
89. Ibid.
90. SAIRR, *Survey of Race Relations 1982*, p. 251.
91. See T. Hanf *et al.*, *Südafrika; Friedlicher Wandel*, Munich, 1978, p. 262. (Page numbers differ from the 1980 English edition.) See also L. Schlemmer, 'Change in South Africa', in R. Price and G. Rosberg, *The Apartheid Regime*, pp. 276–8.
92. *Sunday Times*, 21 May 1978.
93. For example, see H. Adam, 'Minority Monopoly in Transition', p. 623; F. Fisher, 'Class Consciousness Among Colonized Workers in South Africa', in L. Schlemmer and E. Webster, op. cit., pp. 202–3.
94. For such attempts see F. Fisher, ibid., and P. Mayer, 'Class, Status and Ethnicity as Perceived by Johannesburg Africans'.
95. For example, see E. Webster's contrast of stay-aways and strikes. This draws upon Hyman's distinction between confrontation strikes and demonstration strikes. See R. Hyman, *Strikes*, London, Fontana, 1971. (But Webster adds the dimension of class-race, by making stay-aways ethnic and racial in character, and strikes class-based.)

96. E. Webster, op. cit., pp.1 ff.
97. Ibid., pp. 13 ff.
98. D. Hemson, 'Liberation and the Working-Class Struggle in South Africa', *Review of African Political Economy*, 9, 1978.
99. See P. Bonner, *Strikes in South Africa*, p. 184.
100. Molteno, op. cit., p. 72.
101. One of the most interesting discussions of this, both for its novelty and originality, is Barrington Moore's *Injustice: The Social Basis of Obedience and Revolt*, London, Macmillan, 1978. Among others see: P. Gay, *The Dilemma of Democratic Socialism*; C. Scherske, *German Social Democracy 1905–17*; A Berlau, *The German Social Democratic Party 1914–21*.
102. D. Hemson, 'Liberation and the Working Class Struggle in South Africa', p. 79.
103. SAIRR, *Survey of Race Relations 1983*, p. 202.
104. For a summary of these studies see H. Lever, 'Attitudes and Opinions of Africans', in H. Lever, *South African Society*, Johannesburg, Ball, 1978; 'Public Opinion and Voting', in A. de Crespigny and R. Schrire, *The Government and Politics of South Africa*, Johannesburg, Juta, 1978.
105. In addition to the above see L. Schlemmer, 'Change in South Africa', in R. Price and G. Rosberg, *The Apartheid Regime*, pp. 276–8, and L. Schlemmer, 'Conflict and Conflict Regulation', in A. de Crespigny and R. Schrire, op. cit.
106. See the series of articles with R. Fine in the *South African Labour Bulletin*, during 1982–3, especially 'Trade Unions and the Challenge to State Power', ibid., 8.2, 1982, p. 60.
107. 'Independent Trade Unionism since Wiehahn', ibid., 8.4, 1982, pp. 16–36.
108. *The Crisis in South Africa*, New York, Monthly Review Press, 1981 p. 116.
109. *Changing South Africa*, Manchester, Manchester University Press, 1983, p. 127.
110. *Black Politics in South Africa Since 1945*, London, Longman, 1983, p. 346.
111. 'Unions and Politics: The Acceptance of Reality', *South African Journal of Labour Relations*, 7.1, 1983. This issue was a special issue on politics and trade unionism.
112. E. Ardington and J. Nattrass, Occasional Papers no. 11, Economic Research Unit, Department of Economics, University of Natal, 1981.
113. L. Thompson, 'White over Black in South Africa: What of the Future?', in L. Thompson and J. Butler, *Change in Contemporary South Africa*, p. 412.

114. See, for example, J. Maree, 'The UAW and the 1979 Port Elizabeth Strikes', *South African Labour Bulletin*, 6.2–3, 1980, p. 29.
115. Quoted in SAIRR, *Survey of Race Relations 1983*, p. 84.
116. Noted by T. Lodge, *Black Politics in South Africa Since 1945*, pp. 348–9, from which this analysis is taken.
117. Ibid., p. 349.
118. For example see SAIRR, *Survey of Race Relations 1983*, p. 189.
119. See I. Silver and A. Sfarnas, 'Debates: The UDF', *South African Labour Bulletin*, 8.8, 1983, pp. 98–104. Also see 'Briefings: Trade Unions and the UDF', in the same issue.
120. For example see D. Innes and R. Fine, 'Trade Unions and the Challenge to State Power'; P. Bonner, 'Independent Trade Unionism Since Wiehahn'; R. Lambert, 'Strike Action in 1982—the Politics of Reform'.
121. Ibid., p. 163.
122. See: L Kuper, *An African Bourgeoisie*, Yale University Press, 1965; 'Class and Colour in South Africa', *Race*, 12.4, 1971; *Race, Class and Power*, London, Duckworth, 1974.
123. J. C. Leggett, *Class, Race and Labour*.
124. *The Class Structure of Advanced Societies*, London, Hutchinson, 1973. pp. 111–17.
125. 'Class, Status and Party', in H. Gerth and C. Mills, *From Max Weber*, London, Oxford University Press, 1946.

4

Political Opposition in the Urban Areas

The struggle for influence between the different tendencies in African opposition is played out in the urban areas. By interest, inclination, and support base, the trade union movement and Black Consciousness are urban. The ANC's revolutionary terrorism always hits militarily more difficult targets in the urban areas. Outbreaks of collective protest occur almost exclusively in urban areas. Even homeland-based organizations like Inkatha are unwilling to restrict activity to the rural areas. It is in the urban areas that the government has chosen to experiment with limited liberalization and to create a relatively privileged group of Black insiders.[1] One manifestation of this has been the development of new government-sponsored African politicians to administer the urban townships. There are other characteristics which explain why the urban areas are the epicentre of opposition. One third of all Blacks live and work in the urban environment, in an ethnic mix which is uncharacteristic of the rest of South Africa. Most urban residents, as workers, occupy a strategic place in the White economy. This is why extra-workplace movements mobilize for support in the workplace and, as Chapter 3 demonstrated, are being drawn in by workers on those occasions when the trade union movement is reluctant to push extra-workplace issues. It is in the urban areas that Africans have closest contact with apartheid: the rural areas are uniformly African, while the cities generate a relative deprivation that comes from the daily experience of segregated and inferior facilities.

The government realizes the importance of the urban areas. This is shown in their unusual policy of repression and relaxation. On the one hand the state's experiments with liberalization have occurred in the urban areas, while its repressive apparatus operates there more severely. Despite the conduciveness to opposition of the urban environment, it is impossible for Africans to organize there politically and stay out of prison unless they utilize government-sponsored political machinery, such as the homeland organizations or the community councils. This gives Inkatha and the township councillors an advantage in any struggle to represent the urban areas. As alternatives to using apartheid platforms,[2] African opposition has been forced into spontaneous outbreaks of collective protest, into underground terrorist insurgency and into a relatively cautious trade union movement which hesitates to move beyond workplace demands. The first two alternatives emasculate African opposition by opening it up to all those limitations earlier identified as associated with these strategies. Chapter 3 documented how the response of some sections of the trade union movement tended, in the short term,[3] to be conservative and how the government's liberalizations attempted to reinforce this by restricting activity to the workplace. In the long term this is unlikely to be successful, for there is little potential in the liberalizations for depoliticizing the workplace. However, the alternative chosen by Black Consciousness constituted something of an exception until the formation of the UDF in 1983. That is why it assumes so much importance when political opposition in the urban areas is considered. For a long time it was unique among tendencies in African opposition for two reasons. Black Consciousness organizations maintained their right to organize openly by conventional political means, which distinguished them from the clandestine tendencies such as the student radicals urging collective protests and the military wing of the ANC, and from the cautiously conservative sections of the trade union movement. They functioned in an open, recognizably political, fashion, using traditional strategies for mobilization and for the articulation of grievances. Yet they do so without participation on government-sponsored platforms. Like the later UDF, this differentiates them from a variety of collaborators such as Inkatha and the community councillors. The costs of this unique strategy have been enormous. Black Consciousness organizations have been banned and their personnel hounded, imprisoned, and killed. This is also true now of the UDF.

For a long period the struggle for political leadership in the urban areas that took place above ground was therefore fought between a variety of collaborators and disadvantaged Black Consciousness organizations. This changed in 1983 with the formation of the UDF, but before this struggle is discussed in detail, it is necessary to understand the philosophy of Black Consciousness.

The chapter's final section concentrates on what is interpreted as being a developing co-operation between the ANC and certain sections of Black Consciousness within the umbrella of the UDF: among other things, some Black Consciousness groups have recognized they need the kudos of the ANC and the clandestine politics of exile have forced on the ANC the realization that it needs to be a part of the open political struggle for leadership in the urban areas.

THE PHILOSOPHY OF BLACK CONSCIOUSNESS

The name 'Black Consciousness' adequately describes its nature. There are two essential components: the ideological contents contained in this .consciousness, and the common ethnic identity associated with being Black.

The ethnic identity is a contrived one in view of the fundamental cleavages separating all those who share that skin colour. As a broad philosophy, Black Consciousness has become popular among certain sections of the African, Coloured, and Asian communities.[4] The longitudinal study of the Arnold Bergstraesser Institute revealed that two-thirds of a sample of over 1,000 Africans in Pretoria, Soweto, and Durban replied affirmatively to the statement that 'Africans, Indians and Coloureds should be one people compared to Whites'.[5] The available evidence is contradictory: clashes between workers on strike are often ethnic in nature; African students in the main refused to participate in the Coloured students' boycott of 1980; football hooliganism shows evidence of ethnic hositility.[6] The complicated network of informants the police operate with sometimes functions on ethnic lines.[7] In Natal, the Indian community is frequently the object of crimes of violence committed by Zulus.[8] Inter-ethnic faction-fighting is extremely prevalent among the Zulus. Yet having said all this, there is no reason to suppose that ethnic hositility is the main or only cause of such incidents. Faction-fighting in the urban areas, for example, has been explained as the inevitable product of the inhuman conditions of migrant hostels.[9] In the rural areas it is often the consequence of personal and private vendettas. Ethnic groups are in conflict, but the conflict is caused by the political and economic differences which divide the three Black communities, not ethnicity. The clashes either between strikers and students or between strikers and strike-breakers, may be related to these differences. In Natal, any Indian–Zulu hostility is overlaid by economic differences which come from the relative prosperity of the Indian community and the position of Indian businessmen as large employers of Zulu labour.[10]

It must be emphasized that ethnic divisions are positively encouraged by apartheid and are often reinforced as a result by the cultural traditions within each community, but the mere existence of ethnicity is not important. Ethnicity becomes important only if it predisposes pejorative evaluations of other ethnic groups: there is a fundamental distinction between ethnicity and ethnocentricism.[11] Ethnocentricism is the conviction of the innate superiority of one's own ethnic group. Theodor Hanf's study is one of the first to discuss ethnocentricism among Africans. In response to a question asking about the intelligence of other ethnic groups, one-third of African respondents gave the non-racist reply that they were all equal; one-fifth were convinced of their own inferiority, and a slightly larger group put their own ethnic group first. The clearest indication of ethnocentricism among Africans was the deprecatory evaluation of Coloureds and Indians, who were ranked as the least intelligent groups by one-fifth and one-quarter respectively.[12] What Hanf discovered, however, was that this tendency was strongest in the more economically and education-

Table 19. *Ethnic Composition of Three African Communities*

Ethnic Group	Soweto (%)	Durban (%)	Pretoria (%)
Ndebele	2.0	0.5	10.0
Pedi	9.0	—	36.0
Shangaan	5.0	—	16.0
South Sotho	14.0	—	6.0
Swazi	6.0	2.0	7.0
Tswana	17.0	1.0	16.0
Venda	5.0	—	4.0
Xhosa	10.0	5.0	1.0
Zulu	31.0	91.0	4.0
Other	1.0	0.5	—

ally deprived sectors of the African community. This confirms what others have discovered about racial prejudice in Britain and the United States—that it relates to competition over scarce resources and is more prevalent among the poorer sections of the population who are in the fiercest competition.[13] Among the better educated and economically privileged sections of the urban African population, ethnocentricism was lower than among White South Africans.[14] This in part reflects the 'liberalizing' tendencies normally associated with education and income. It also reflects the peculiar nature of African urban townships in South Africa which have a high inter-ethnic composition.[15] In these circumstances inter-ethnic relations have fostered inter-ethnic tolerance. In Hanf's study, only 27 per cent of urban African respondents wished their children to marry within their own ethnic group, only 19 per cent preferred to be with people who speak their own language, while 95 per cent did not care which ethnic group their neighbour came from.[16] This opinion extended to Whites, Coloureds, and Indians.[17]

The philosophy of Black Consciousness has traditionally won greatest support among the urban, better educated, economically privileged sector who are the least ethnocentric. This has allowed some critics to decry them as *petit bourgeois*, but this is the sector who have found it easiest to throw off the vestiges of their tribal ancestry in order to support a new contrived ethnic identity. The ideological contents of the philosophy of Black Consciousness owe a great deal to the composition of those social groups who form its main constituency. Ethnic tolerance is a direct reflection of its support base in the better-educated, economically privileged sections of the African community. There is a more important example. Apartheid is presented primarily as a psychological problem. There is an underplaying of the quite varied ways in which apartheid is physically experienced due to the different locations of Blacks in the socio-economic system. The divisions that might arise in Black politics as a result of these different socio-economic statuses are seen as counterbalanced by the unity which arises from the shared psychological consequences of apartheid. Black Consciousness portrays this psychological experience as involving the dual orientations of deference to and fear of Whites, and lack of pride and dignity in being Black. These orientations are the consequence of oppression, and exist whatever the socio-economic

Belief	Policy implication
Psychological oppression ——————▶	racial exclusivity
	universal franchise in a unitary state (Azania)
	non-collaboration and non-participation with Whites
Black awareness ——————————▶	underplaying of class, awareness through culture and politics
	self-reliance, self-help initiatives
Pacifism ——————————————▶	liberation through Black self-awareness

FIGURE 2. The philosophy of Black Consciousness

status of Blacks. Such an argument can be viewed negatively, as a belief which masks the relative economic privilege of those who utter it. The positive connotations are, however, more important, for it can be seen as an attempt to transcend whatever differences separate Blacks in order thereby to forge a political unity. Quite revolutionary consequences follow from the argument that class and status differences should not be an obstacle to political unity for Blacks.

This is not the only tenet of Black Consciousness, whose major beliefs and policies can be presented diagrammatically (Figure 2).[18]

Psychological oppression

The political hiatus that followed the Sharpeville massacre greatly reduced morale: it is an accepted generalization that morale is related to political activity, and as activity declined in South Africa, spirits fell accordingly. By 1968–9 this hiatus provided a fertile reception for Fanon's arguments about the psychological consequences of colonialism, and for the American Civil Rights theme of self-confidence and dignity in being Black. Interest was resurrected in the writings of Diop and Senghor on negritude, Kaunda on African humanism, and Nyerere on African self-reliance. The PAC's notion, drawn from Nkrumah, that oppression was first of all a psychological problem became the central belief of young Black intellectuals.[19]

It was no coincidence that these arguments took root in the tribal universities, eventually leading to the formation of SASO.[20] From SASO emerged the first enunciations of the philosophy which has since been translated by dozens of organizations. What has been emphasized about these first progenitors is the tribalism of their education—in seeking a response to ethnic campuses they arrived at Black solidarity.[21] This only forms a secondary influence, however. The major impetus to the central tenets of Black Consciousness was the social marginality of this young educated élite.[22] This worked in two ways. Here were social groups with a number of obvious privileges but with their prospects severely curtailed compared to Whites. The theme of psychological oppression solved this marginality, as it indicated that privilege counted for nothing. By being Black the psychological consequences were still a burden—and the relative deprivation of this young educated élite *vis-à-vis* Whites convinced them of their oppression irrespective of whatever privileges they enjoyed compared to the African working class.

A number of imperatives followed from this marginality. It became important to stress the similarity between African students and the masses. SASO wrote on many occasions that Black students were part of the Black oppressed before they were students.[23] It was also necessary to portray education as a community resource, not a means of personal advancement. In this way their immediate élite status was irrelevant; they were the servants of the people and their only role was to galvanize the masses.[24] The theme of psychological oppression became the unifying link between them.

From this theme came the antagonistic rejection of whiteness. SASO's original language was extreme and provoked the view that Black Consciousness was a form of reverse racism.[25] This is far from the case. There are two reasons for rejecting such a view, both of which relate to the theme of psychological oppression. Inherent in this theme is the realization that race relations involve a sense of group position. Herbert Blumer argued this in America,[26] and Black Consciousness writers recognized its truth in South Africa. When Biko argued that Black Consciousness involved a sense of group pride, and Mtimkulu portrayed it as a collective group response, they were conveying Blumer's point.[27] The racial terms 'black' and 'white' were not biological–genetic labels so much as shorthand descriptions referring to a group's position within a social structure. The term 'white' in Black Consciousness terminology is not a reference to colour but to the structure of social relationships that colour symbolizes. To be anti-White is to be anti-racist; the 'white man' ceases to be 'white' once relations of oppression and discrimination have been replaced. This is the reason why SASO could argue that there were no Black policemen.[28] Propping up the system in this way made them 'white' irrespective of biological–genetic skin colour.

A distinction also needs to be drawn between a racially exclusive struggle to end oppression and the non-racial society that replaces it. This distinction is premissed on the theme of psychological oppression. Because psychological oppression is unique to Blacks as the oppressed, the overthrow of oppression is something only Blacks can achieve. In this way they rejected the assistance of liberal Whites. Racial exclusivism does not extend to the future society. Its vision of the future is of a multi-racial, free, politically egalitarian society.[29] They use the term 'Azania' to describe the qualitative break that the new society represents from the old.[30] So aware are Black Consciousness leaders that universal franchise in a unitary state means *de facto* Black superiority, that some have argued that while Azania must have universal franchise the rights of minorities will be constitutionally guaranteed.[31] This has the support of the greater part of the urban Black population.[32] None the less, to achieve this non-racial future, Black Consciousness is racially exclusive. From this follow a number of political imperatives. It requires rejection of contact with liberal Whites working for change, and of any form of consultation with the state or participation on apartheid platforms. The liberation struggle is a Black one, not just because Blacks are the only group to suffer psychological oppression, but also because the struggle is an opportunity to promote Black awareness and Black self-reliance.

Black awareness

Black Consciousness operates on two complexly related levels simultaneously—the socio-cultural and the political. The theme of psychological oppression shows that the struggle is one ultimately against the distribution of power in a racist social structure. This ridicules attempts by critics to portray it as having semi-official status.[33] Black Consciousness also operates on another level. Culturally, Blacks were called upon to assert their Blackness and to resist powerful attempts to denigrate Black history and Black culture. This itself was not without political implications, for it generated Black awareness as the first logical step towards Black solidarity.

Inasmuch as Black life generally was geared to promoting this awareness and eventual solidarity, race, not class, became the main ideological theme in Black Consciousness. As Chapter 3 demonstrated, class and colour are coextensive to a high degree in South Africa. Black Consciousness generally saw colour as more important: class was the dependent variable. Sol Variava once wrote that it should be accepted that the struggle in South Africa is not a class struggle but a race struggle.[34] Irrespective of what the regime might be in its 'essence', in its 'appearance' it was a racial group which was dispossessed, and racial barriers worked against any unification with White workers. The rejection of class by early Black Consciousness supporters was neither arbitrary nor ideological—it was a rational judgement of the 'appearance' of the regime. The 'appearance' of the regime was that those who Pityana called the 'have-nots' were Black. Racial oppression forced the 'have-nots' to assert themselves, which necessarily took the form of colour awareness.

Changes in this emphasis will be discussed shortly, but even at this time Black Consciousness writers drew a distinction between class and the economic context within which class existed. While class was seen as irrelevant, economic considerations dominated Black Consciousness. Black awareness was closely tied to redistributing scarce resources to alter the equation of Blackness with dispossession. In this way Black Consciousness organizations supported disinvestment by foreign capital,[35] and welcomed the oil boycott of South Africa.[36] Multinational companies were uniformly seen as willing participants in racial oppression for profit.[37] Along with this awareness cam rejection of the materialist values and private enterprise associated with foreign and domestic capital.[38] Attention was given to workplace issues. Drake Koka led Black Consciousness involvement with the trade unions: strike activity was closely followed and supported.[39] The Black Renaissance Convention in 1974 made wage demands and the recognition of African trade unions important elements of its original declaration of intent.[40]

There were limitations to this focus which arose from the assumed dependence of class on colour. Black Consciousness organizations won little support from Black workers or the trade union movement until 1979, when they changed the exclusive concentration on racial issues. Until 1979 'race' was the primary theme, as the notion of Black awareness suggests it should be. Workers were mobilized primarily as Blacks, and mobilization in the workplace took no precedence over other areas of social life. Black awareness in the workplace existed alongside awareness programmes in the home (through the African Housewives' League and the Domestic Workers' and Employers' Project), in education, art, theology, and community work. The cultural diversity of those in South Africa who qualify to be termed 'Black' does not make this emphasis on culture impossible, as Afrikaner academics like Kotzé have claimed.[41] Diversity in this sense is in custom, tradition, and belief, a different definition of culture than that employed by Black Consciousness, which emphasizes Black fine and performing arts. Black awareness was to be achieved through the propagation of Black theatre, literature, and fine arts, which gave their arts an immediate political intent. The promotion of Black awareness through theology equally politicized religion.[42] The priests who took up Black Theology like Manas Buthelezi and Desmond Tutu, had different interests from those of the Black Consciousness radicals who took it up. SASO's Black Theology Conferences were not without clashes of emphasis, but the two elements were easily reconciled. The liberationist element to Black Theology (and Christ was portrayed as the primordial liberator) was situationally specific to the White racism which generated it: as White racism was overthrown, the message of Christianity could be reinterpreted.

Black awareness programmes in community welfare had the additional function of promoting self-reliance. The South African Black Social Workers' Association represented one avenue through which this self-reliance was fostered. Community self-help projects were another. From its inception SASO initiated community projects. An extract from the SASO Executive Committee Report in July 1972 shows that at the time field projects existed at Phoenix, Winterveld, and Dududu, and in addition to the education and literacy projects there were leadership training schemes and student benefit schemes.[43] Community welfare projects were co-ordinated in 1973 with the formation of Black Community Programmes. The BCP extended SASO's work into worker projects, church programmes, work with youth groups, health education schemes, crèche schemes, and a women's programme.[44] On its banning four years later, the government revealed that the BCP ran clinics at King William's Town and Adams Mission, a health clinic at Zanempilo, a shoe factory at Njwaxa, and a mobile clinic operating in Soweto. Its funds totalled R60,000.[45] This must negate the idea that Black Consciousness was 'apolitical',[46] engaging in 'endless philosophizing',[47] a view which misunderstands the dialectic relationship between welfare, culture, and politics, and fails to appreciate the political implications of self-help community schemes or protest poetry. With the formation of the Black People's Convention in 1972, Black Consciousness was given a political organization to spearhead the liberation struggle. Gail Gerhart's excellent narrative of this period emphasizes the involvement of M. T. Moerane, editor of *The World*, who focused greater attention on cultural factors.[48] SASO saw the BPC entirely differently. Its newsletter announced: 'The move was instituted at a conference which originally set out to form a national organization that would cater for the cultural needs of the "African" people. The conference was well attended and that idea was quickly thrown overboard. The rationale behind a Black political movment was investigated . . . SASO sees the necessity of this new organization.'[49] SASO was so enthusiastic because it broadened the appeal of Black Consciousness and disputed the claim that it was élitist[50] or liberal do-gooding.[51] The direct political challenge represented by the BPC was met with stiff repression, and within a year the BPC leadership was culled, with the organization eventually being banned in 1977.

Pacifism

This concentration on psychological oppression and its overthrow through practical Black awareness programmes, contains a view of the process of liberation as having political, cultural, and economic dimensions. Implicit also is a theory of how liberation will be realized. It is in this that Black Consciousness shows its greatest limitation. Liberation is seen as the automatic consequence of Black awareness. That is, Black awareness involves the end of psychological oppression and this produces a sense of dignity and pride in being Black, from which follows Black solidarity. Black awareness and Black solidarity are the motor to liberation: physical liberation, in other words, flows from psychological liberation.

Durban's Black Students' Society in 1980 explained this belief in the following way: 'The consequences of psychological liberation are very far-reaching. People cannot be kept in subjection if they do not believe they are of an inferior situation.'[52] This adumbrated the view of BPC in 1974: 'if we are a united Black people, no minority group of Whites is going to push us around like sheep. Once we achieve this Black solidarity and nothing will stop us getting freedom.'[53]

Three consequences follow from such a view. Inasmuch as it shifts the achievement of liberation on to Blacks themselves, in many ways it also shifts on to them the blame for oppression. The BPC's newsletter *Inkululeko yeSizwe* continually advanced this belief—Blacks had let the White minority kill their spirit and pride.[54] The implication is that developing spirit and pride would erase the consequences of past faults. Quite often the master–slave relationship was used as an analogy. It was frequently stated that there can only be a master where there is a slave, and that being a slave is largely a matter of passive acquiesence. This analogy illustrates the extreme naivety of Black Consciousness writings. (It could be argued that such a view was tactical in order to avoid state repression but I think it was inherent to the Black Consciousness view of change.) There was a failure to realize the complicated procedures necessary to translate awareness into liberation, and from this came their failure to specify the mechanics of liberation. Steve Biko, for example, put his faith in 'mutual respect' somehow developing once psychological oppression had ended and Blacks respected themselves. 'One does not have to plan for or actively encourage integration. Once the various groups have asserted themselves to the point of mutual respect, you have the ingredients for integration.'[55] Perceiving oneself as another's equal solves only part of the problem. Steve Biko's own death testifies that something more has to be done before the dominant racial group is prepared to accept Blacks as their equals. His death clearly demonstrates that the power and interests of the 'master' form an important part of the equation. Such an unrealistic view could only arise in a society like South Africa, where the 'slaves' assume that they have few economic, military and political resources to achieve liberation and can only rely on their determination.

Perhaps the most important consequence of this view is its

emphasis on peaceful means. This was not so much as a result of a principled support for pacifism—Black Consciousness protagonists in exile urged violence, some students in 1976 returned as revolutionary terrorists, and moral support was given to the use of terror tactics by the the PLO, SWAPO, the Eritrean Liberation Front, and the Vietcong. However, the connection between Black Consciousness and the Indian community did mean that it held Gandhi in high regard. The reliance on pacifism is partly explained as a realistic perception of the repressive measures which the advocation of violence would provoke, as well as a rational judgement of what the Black community supports, which has always been a peaceful solution. Largely, however, it is explained by the view that violence was unnecessary. In a manner reminiscent of Marx's early writings, Black Consciousness believed that change would occur from the automatic realization of its need. For Marx this occurred in a state of class consciousness, for Black Consciousness it occurred when the Black population had achieved full awareness and solidarity. While violence may contribute to the development of Black awareness (as the Soweto uprising did), Black awareness itself was the motor behind change. This made violence incidental to the process of revolutionary change—as Marx claimed it was to class consciousness.

Practical revolutionaries trying to implement Marx's theory realized that consciousness was not enough. This was the point behind the conflicts within the Russian and German Social Democratic Parties. Black Consciousness protagonists too have come to realize that Black awareness is insufficient. The state's response to the Soweto uprising and its wake cruelly crushed a young 'solidaristic' and 'aware' Black generation. Participation in the struggle for leadership in the urban areas since the uprising seems to have convinced current Black Consciousness protagonists that something more is needed to achieve liberation than merely awareness and solidarity. A survey of this struggle illustrates that it presented Black Consciousness organizations with a number of problems. It showed, for example, that to be successful Black Consciousness needed to engender a broader recognition of its legitimacy; to develop, specifically, a constituency among the trade unions; to put more pressure on the government than peaceful non-collaboration generates; and accordingly, to develop new strategies of opposition which allow some contact with Whites so as to benefit from this increased pressure.

THE FIGHT FOR LEADERSHIP IN THE URBAN AREAS

For a long time residents in the urban areas were the most politically marginal section of the Black population. Political rights were exercised in the homelands and there was little opportunity for political representation and participation in the urban areas. This effectively disenfranchised them, for they had few political rights in the place they called home and in which they lived, worked, and made emotional investments.[56] Administration of these millions of urban dwellers was by the White Bantu Administration Boards in association with the Urban Bantu Councils, on which Africans had representation. UBC's were established in 1961, as an extension of the Native Advisory Boards set up in 1923. The powers formally given to the councils were minimal.[57] The Minister of Bantu Administration was given the right to decide which council was to be granted the powers defined in the legislation. In no case did the Minister pass the appropriate regulation enacting the powers and the UBCs played a subservient role to the White BABs. They were purely advisory bodies: no mechanisms were defined to guarantee the representativeness of their membership and no statutory obligation was imposed on local authorities to respect UBC advice and opinion. They were incapable of doing anything to ease the problems of township life.

The first Soweto UBC election was in 1968 and drew a poll of 32 per cent; by 1974 this had fallen to 14 per cent. These figures suggest that at first residents were prepared to give the council a chance. After the township uprisings in 1976–77, the UBCs were discredited institutions. Their offices were the first to be attacked. The Soweto Council suffered heavily under SSRC pressure. The rent increases it was forced by WRAB to impose eventually led to the resignation of most of its members. The Soweto Council sought to forestall its demise by forming a junior council on which students were invited to sit; they refused and WRAB suspended the council. This left Soweto as the epicentre of the uprising without any government-sponsored African leadership. The phenomenal growth of social movements after the uprising produced many non-sponsored organizations offering to fill the vacuum. They based their campaign on impressive improvement and redevelopment schemes for Soweto. These competing political leaders spoke with no agreement. The major contrast was between those organizations who urged stronger powers for apartheid institutions and those who wanted their abolition. The Soweto Residents' Committee saw the solution as increasing the power of elected bodies, the main problem being their failure to satisfy African expectations. The Makgotla Party wanted to return to tribal ways and to have its judicial powers increased. Siegfried Manthatha announced that the Makgotla Parties were prepared to take over where the UBC left off. Letsatsi Faction Makgotla subsequently participated in township elections. The Sofasonke Party led by former UBC members, T. J. Makhaya and David Thebehali, closely allied itself to Inkatha, giving this homeland organization some representation in Soweto's leadership struggle. The Soweto Federal Party, Mamati Greater Society, and the Masingafi Party played minor roles. Conflicts developed between the Sofasonke Party and Inkatha, and between the Soweto Residents' Committee and Inkatha, over the role a homeland organization should play in the urban areas. Opposing these organizations was an array which advanced the more radical solution of abolishing apartheid institutions. Among them were the Teachers' Action Committee, the Soweto Civic Association, the Soweto Council for Justice, the Committee of 10, the Tembisa Committee of 20, and the various Black Consciousness organizations which pre-dated the uprising. The Soweto Committee of 10, later reorganized into a revamped Soweto Civic Association, became the most influential organization to push this solution.

Not only did this plethora cause confusion among local residents, it gave radical organizations some cover to propagandize and develop support which in itself encouraged the growth of new organizations wishing to participate in the leadership struggle. As a calming promise, in the midst of the 1976 uprising, the Minister of Bantu Administration announced that the government was considering devolving greater powers of self-government to African townships. The Chairman of the Soweto Council looked favourably on this and felt that it marked the end of a puppet role for African township politicians. The leadership vacuum left by the fall of the UBC's and the proliferation of social movements and political oranizations to fill it convinced the government that it should implement this change quickly. A Community Councils Bill was enacted in June 1977. Within six months of this enactment the first community council was in operation and within a year 92 had been established. By December 1980 elections had been held in 193 and by November 1981 1,227 councils had been set up. The rapidity with which they were introduced showed how the government realized that the post-1976 situation was different from the earlier one. There was no legal obligation on the government to institute UBCs and very little political pressure either, for in the first twelve years of the Act only 23 councils had been established. The community councils were instituted with greater speed and have already become a part of the institutional framework. Community councils on the East Rand have established a co-ordinating group, and this is being repeated elsewhere. An Urban Community Councils Association has also been formed.

The original 1977 Act placed community councils in a similar position to the old UBCs because the Minister had first to make a special ruling granting individual councils the powers which the Act allowed. Various other qualifications were written into the Act. The legislation bequeathed no powers at all as of right; the Minister could withdraw any powers he conferred and dissolve a council. The old BABs were retained as 'agents' until the community councils reached full municipal autonomy. Until then Koornhof announced that he had no intention of disbanding these White-appointed bodies. His Deputy Minister, Frans Cronje, opening a seminar on the community councils, said, 'I would like the community councils to accept BABs as a fact of life. Not to do so would be like burying one's head in the sand—chaos would result'.[58] Government spokesmen emphasized the need for Africans to be trained to use this responsibility, enshrining the role of White 'agents'; Africans were seen as incapable of responsible decision-making. The Chairman of the Atteridgeville Council spoke to the *Nation* of the powers he actually possessed: 'I've no power over Whites. We can never have direct dealings with the government, we have no legal right to make final decisions.'[59] There is evidence of the BABs overruling their political 'masters'. For example, Mamelodi Council decided to increase rents by R4.50 but the Central Transvaal BAB increased this figure to R9.30. Complaints were lodged by Kagiso residents over the rental of R54.26 for new houses; it was alleged that WRAB had delayed and suspended talks on several occasions.[60]

A comparison of the Community Councils Act with the Urban Bantu Council Act shows that the new councils were a poor disguise. They met with acclaim from the Afrikaans-speaking press. *Die Burger* called them important developments, *Die Vaderland* felt that meaningful powers had been transferred. They were supported by most former UBC members. David Thebehali, Chairman of the Soweto Council, felt that trust had been restored between the African community and the government, while his Vice-Chairman said 'we now have the powers for which we asked and have proved all the doubters wrong'.[61] The community councils provided such politicians with an outlet, however inadequate, for their personal ambitions. More qualified support came from those councillors who felt the councils had the potential to become more powerful bodies. The original Act did have problems in addition to the dependence on the Minister and his appointed White agents. Finance was an important limitation. Community councils cannot be self-financing, and as mere dormitory cities townships cannot develop far without government financial support. Moreover, the poverty of so many of their citizens imposes a low ceiling on the amount which can be levied from residents. The major sources of finance are the government and overseas loans. At present the electrification of Soweto is being financed by foreign capital at high rates of interest. Shelving its responsibility to pay for apartheid, the government helped the Soweto Council to negotiate a loan of R1.6m. The Soweto Council received an annual grant from the government of R21.3m. in 1979, but this leaves a massive shortfall which can only be financed from overseas loans. It was estimated that R126m. was needed for housing, R50m. for housing improvement, R101m. for electrification, R41m. for water and sewage, R70m. for transport and roads, and R87m. for the provision of amenities. The devolution of functions without the devolution of control over finance to support these functions strangles the community councils. Control over the remaining finance of the councils gives the government a powerful lever. Threats to slash the budget of Greater Soweto in order to force the council to implement unpopular decisions have been uttered many times by the government.

The third problem faced by the councils is their lack of legitimacy among the main opposition forces in African politics. Inkatha is the only exception to this: after some initial caution, Buthelezi came out in support of the councils. Among the urban African community as a whole, however, election polls suggest greater support. In 1978 the government was claiming an average poll of 30 per cent which had increased to 41.9 per cent by April 1980.[62] The average poll in all elections up to November 1981 was 39 per cent. A number of qualifications need to be made. Polls of 60 per cent and over have been obtained in elections for rival organizations outside sponsored platforms. Residents in Alexandra township cast 65,929 votes in a poll, slightly above 60 per cent.[63] Polls for the councils are much lower in townships on the industrial and population centre of the Witwatersrand. These average figures conceal the much greater support for community councils in the rural townships bordering homelands. The government has been successful in deflecting some of the criticism about the councils' ineffectiveness, and the polls reflect this. Those council members who saw the councils as only the start of a greater devolution have been justified because the pressure of events has forced the government since 1978 to 'experiment' with granting full municipal status to some councils. As these liberal measures fail to satisfy African expectations polls may decline as they did for the UBCs.

The limited transference of greater power in some instances, and the relatively high electoral polls, present the critics of the councils with their own problems. Since 1978 it has been impossible to portray some councils as little different to the UBCs or as irrelevant to township residents. This makes the case against the councils a complex one and provides practical dilemmas for the opposition forces advancing it. This can be illustrated by looking in detail at the struggle for leadership in Soweto, which is the second largest Black city in Africa and the one used as a yardstick to evaluate the position of Blacks in South Africa.

The Soweto Community Council elections were one of the first and the most eagerly expected. Only twenty-nine candidates came forward for nomination, sixteen of whom were disqualified for technical reasons. On polling day, 18 February 1978, nine candidates were returned unopposed, while nineteen of the thirty wards had no candidates at all. Only two wards were contested, mustering 500 votes between them on an average poll of 5.55 per cent. The new council fell short of a quorum and by-elections were needed in order for it to function. Fifteen of the nineteen wards were contested, with an average poll of 6 per cent. Only the support of Inkatha gave this high a turnout; the candidate receiv-

ing the most votes (896) was an Inkatha representative. Only ten
candidates got more than 100 votes. In one ward the percentage
poll was 0.4 per cent with three candidates sharing just thirty-
seven votes. David Thebehali, leader of the council, was elected as
Soweto's Mayor with the support of ninety-seven of his con-
stituents.[64] The government did not trust the electorate in Soweto
again until 1983; the 1980 elections were postponed until that
year. In many ways, however, Soweto is the exception. In nearby
Katlehong, the first poll was on average 23.18 per cent and polls
elsewhere on the Witwatersrand have been much higher. This did
not go without notice in Soweto: in a protest rally in 1979 against
the Soweto Council called by its critics, only 200 people turned
up.[65]

Because of this untypical level of electoral support, the first
experiments with granting full municipal status to the community
councils took place in Greater Soweto. In June 1978 the Soweto
Community Council was renamed the Soweto Council and had
certain powers transferred to it. It was made responsible for all
housing matters, the combating of unlawful occupation of land and
buildings, and the administration of sites for churches, schools, and
trade. It was allowed to consider building plans, promote welfare
and moral matters, beautify and tidy the environment, and
administer a community guard. In adjacent Dobsonville and
Diepmeadow, the provision and allocation of housing and evictions have been transferred, as well as the regulation of animals,
the collection of dog levies, and the administration of sport and
recreational facilities.

A number of points need to be emphasized. Some 'real power',
as the *Citizen* called it, was transferred in comparison with the
1977 Act, but only in the area of housing. With an acute housing
shortage and low wages, the responsibility of providing and
allocating housing and carrying out evictions is quite damaging. It
seems that the government is shifting the administration of the
worst effects of its policies on to Africans themselves in an attempt
to blur the racial discrimination inherent in them. Soweto is the
creation of apartheid, of which its problems are a direct consequence. It is a greatly overcrowded city and the shortage of land and
houses has led to much illegal occupation. The Soweto Council
could not cope with these problems. Unable to alter apartheid, the

root of Soweto's immediate difficulties, the council could only tamper with symptoms. It acted as a buffer between Africans and the government, carrying all the odium attached to the administration of apartheid while being helpless to change it. Important issues which affect the daily lives of Soweto residents, such as the provision of essential services, wages, employment, and labour influx control, remained the province of the government. The promotion of moral and social welfare was therefore undertaken without the authority to touch the major factors undermining it, such as excessive drinking and the dissolution of family life through the migrant labour system and discriminatory pay.

As part of the constitutional proposals whereby Coloureds and Asians were given limited parliamentary representation, urban Africans were given even more extended powers of local government during 1982–3. It is through this level of government that the urban African population is linked to the new constitutional structures. An upgraded form of local government was introduced for urban Africans in 1982 by means of the Black Local Authorities Act. The legislation arose out of the Riekert Commission. It provided for the establishment of two tiers of local authorities, town councils and village councils, with the former having the higher status and the greater powers. The Minister of Co-operation and Development had the power to establish the councils; to alter their names and bestow the status of city council upon a town council; to alter the council's area of jurisdiction; and to dissolve councils if the need for them no longer existed. If a local authority was established in an area where a community council existed under the 1977 Community Council Act, the minister had the power to dissolve the community council and transfer its assets and personnel to the new local authority. The number of members of the new authority was to be determined by the minister, although elections would be held at intervals between three and five years. The basis of the elections would be determined by the minister. Mayors and deputy mayors would be elected from successful candidates. The powers conferred by the legislation allowed the council to employ people; hire, acquire, hypothecate, let, sell, and dispose of movable property; acquire immovable property in its area; and develop any use of such property subject to the provisions of any other law. This denied the councils the ability to establish industry in the locality. With the approval of the minister the council could acquire debentures, sheets, or securities; borrow money and invest money; make or accept donations; and impose levies for specific purposes. All these financial rights were in the control of the Minister of Co-operation and Development. Inasmuch as the legislation did not tackle the problem of African freehold rights, there is inadequate provision for the financing of the new authorities. Revenue from rateable values, as the normal source of local authority finance, cannot apply to the African municipalities, as long as freehold rights are denied to African residents. With freehold being promised by the government in 1986, it set up the Van der Walt Commission in 1984 to investigate the question of Black rates and levies. But the unrest over service charge increases during 1984 showed that there is a low ceiling on the amount which can be levied on African residents.

A town council would be invested with all the rights and powers of the administration board except that it would not have the power to allocate land for housing. It could make recommendations to the minister concerning matters outside its powers which affected it, such as education, transport and electricity. Contact with representatives of the homelands was also envisaged. The act also allowed the local authorities to appoint persons for the maintenance of law and order in their areas.[66] In July 1984 the government granted this right to thirty-two township councils. Officers of the police force, however, have to be drawn from either the rank of inspectors now serving with the administration boards or local or regional authorities.

One difference between the community councils and the new local authorities is that the former had none of their own powers; powers were handed to them over time by the Minister of Co-operation and Development. The new authorities have been invested with specific powers at the outset. They are responsible for such services as waste disposal, sewerage, electrification, preventative health programmes, control of health hazards, sport and recreational facilities, housing administration, the prevention of illegal occupation, welfare services, including poor relief, granting of educational bursaries, construction and maintenance of roads, and the employment of staff. Yet a large degree of control remains with the Minister of Co-operation and Development, who is to authorize the following functions of the councils: the making of by-laws, the drawing up of budgets, the determination of levies, and the investment of monies. Administration boards will also retain some important control functions. They will be responsible for township and housing developments. The new authorities will also inherit the financial problems of the community councils. As they have no rateable property under their control, administration boards rely heavily on the sale of alcohol. In the financial year 1981–2, 70 per cent of the income of the boards came from this one source. In the same year, over half of the boards showed a deficit. While taking over a variety of the functions of the administration boards, the new authorities do not have comparable sources of income. They have service charges paid to them but house rents go to the administration boards. While they received revenue from beer sales (R183m. in 1981–2), the new councils did not receive revenue from liquor sales (R337m. in 1981–2).[67] The government has not indicated what plans it has to ensure the economic viability of the new councils. This is what the Van der Walt Commission has to confront.

In March 1984 Soweto became the country's first African township with city status under the act. The Minister of Co-operation and Development gave the council a cheque for R10,000 'to show the world we are going to assist you in every way we can'.[68] More than this will be needed, but there is an atmosphere of expectation surrounding the new authorities, for it has been suggested that they could form the basis of some possible future parliamentary representation for urban Africans. As head of the commission on whose recommendation the authorities were formed, Riekert warned in 1983 against the local authorities being a stepping-stone to African participation in central government.[69] This conflicts with the *verligte* Afrikaner newspapers. *Rapport* emphasized that the government's view was that reform was not over, and *Die Vaderland* said categorically that urban Africans must be given a 'say in matters which affect' them. This could mean anything, but the Minister of Constitutional Development and Planning said in Parliament during July 1984 that the last word on constitutional change had not been written.[70] In April 1985 the government announced the establishment of the Special Cabinet Committee on Black (i.e. African) Constitutional Advancement, which is to act as a multiracial forum to discuss how Africans outside the homelands can be incorporated into the constitution. All White opposition parties accepted the offer to participate with the exception of the Conservative Party. African politicians were invited, although the government refused to divulge the identities of the 135 people and organizations who made representation to the committee. A survey by Mark-en Meningsopnames showed that 80 per cent of White respondents were in favour of this forum. A fourth parliamentary chamber may be the recommendation to result from the forum's deliberations, but it is more likely that if urban Africans are to be linked more firmly to the constitutional structures than at present, it will be through the new local authorities. All elections to African municipal authorities have been postponed until 1988, which might be the time scale which the forum has in order to make recommendations.

This prospect has done little to endear the councils to Africans, for electoral polls were lower than for the earlier community council elections. Community council elections due in 1982 were postponed until November and December 1983. The criteria for voters under the Black Local Authorities Act are broader than under the 1977 Community Councils Act, resulting in a theoretical increase in the number of eligible voters. The new legislation even allows for migrants to vote. Prior to the elections an Anti-Community councils Election Committee was formed which consisted of COSAS, AZASO, the SCA, and a variety of trade unions. AZAPO would not join the committee but gave its support. The body held various meeting and rallies attacking the elections and called for a boycott. The campaign culminated in a rally at Regina Mundi church in Soweto. Oscar Mpetha, president of the UDF, addressed the meeting and urged the audience to remember that their children had died in 1976 because the children had wanted to do away with apartheid institutions like the community councils and town councils. Inkatha hesitated in giving its opinion on the boycott. Participation by Inkatha in the elections was made conditional on satisfactory arrangements being made for the financing of the councils. Other conditions were laid down, but Buthelezi finally decided against participating. This was a good tactical decision for the boycott was very effective. In October 1983 a survey by Markinor on behalf of the Urban Foundation indicated that between 38 and 40 per cent of Soweto residents who were eligible to vote intended to do so.[71] In the event the overall poll in the twenty-nine elections was 21 per cent compared with 30 per cent in 1978, while in Soweto it was 10.7 per cent, although this was an increase from the 1978 figure of 5.9 per cent. The detailed results are contained in Table 20.[72] Cape Town's African communities went to the polls in November to re-elect their community council. The percentage poll was 11.6 per cent compared with 27 per cent in 1977. In only seven cases was the percentage higher than it had been in 1977. It is true that many registered voters were excluded from voting because 28.2 per cent of all wards were uncontested. However, the UDF claimed that the percentage polls were even lower because many people were not on the electoral roll. It claimed that in Kasigo, for example, 15,000 people were not on the roll, giving a true percentage poll of 3 per cent, not 36.6 per cent.

A very high percentage of sitting councillors stood for re-election. In only two townships was this below 60 per cent. However, a much smaller percentage was re-elected. In only half the councils did old members comprise more than 50 per cent of successful candidates, while in seven councils this figure was as low as 25 per cent. Clearly, many people thought little enough of the system to bother to vote, while many of those who did vote thought little enough of serving councillors to return them to power. This might be another reason why further municipal elections were postponed until 1988. David Thebehali was defeated in Soweto. The new 'mayor' was Ephraim Tshabalala, a well-known businessman, who won 1,115 votes in the election compared with 35 received by his opponent. Tshabalala's Sofasonke Party fought the election on a radical manifesto promising to reduce rents, to work for the transfer of houses to their occupants free of charge, to press for the extension of freehold rights to Africans, and to urge the development of a business and industrial base in Soweto itself. This is an example of how the radical critics of the community council system have forced some of the councillors to move to the left themselves. Such a radical programme is impossible to fulfil given the web of constraints the councils are caught in, and a series of disputes occurred within the council over the extent to which the council system should be destroyed from within. Tshabalala was eventually ousted from his position as mayor. Hours before his successor, Edward Manyosi, was due to take up his office, he was

Table 20. *African Local Authority Elections*

Township	Uncontested seats in 1983	% Poll 1983	% Poll 1978
Alexandra	no election		79.0
Atteridgeville	0	14.8	22.8
Bohlokong	0	24.4	—
Daveyton	4	18.6	19.6
Diepmeadow	7	14.6	16.0
Dobsonville	2	23.5	42.0
Evaton	7	5.9	10.0
Galeshewe	1	26.9	36.4
Ikakgeng	1	24.5	40.3
Jouberton	0	31.7	23.9
Kagiso	8	36.6	48.0
Katlehong	2	22.7	23.0
Kayamnandi	1	13.7	11.0
KwaGuka	8	29.6	25.1
KwaNobuhle	no election		—
Kwa Thema	1	20.7	19.7
Lekoa	6	14.7	—
Lingelihle	no election		15.6
Mamelodi	1	27.8	24.7
Mangaung	5	24.8	—
Mhluzi	no election		46.0
Rini	6	6.0	26.0
Seeisoville	0	35.1	—
Soweto	3	10.7	5.9
Tembisa	7	16.9	13.2
Thabong	0	29.7	34.4
Thokoza	0	20.4	29.2
Vosloorus	5	11.9	16.0
Wattville	1	16.0	16.6

assassinated. It is not known whether Manyosi's death is connected with the bitter in-fighting on the Soweto Council.

In certain areas, the Soweto Council was given more powers as a result of the 1982 legislation than White local authorities, which testifies to the extent of the government's desire to see the reform succeed. In January 1985 it was given control of traffic, fire-fighting services, and health services. It had already been given permission to employ its own police force and had 270 officers at that time. Its total expenditure on security services was R1.7m. per annum. This has created problems for the councillors over the extent to which they use their increasing powers outside local government issues. Problems have also been created for the critics of the local government system. However inadequate their powers, the Soweto Council, like all those granted municipal status, is now in a position to distribute some scarce resources to African residents and to meet, however unsatisfactorily, some local needs. The councils, and those who co-operate with them, like Inkatha, have taken the gamble that in the long term the constraints that apartheid imposes in carrying out this role will not rebound against them. The critics can only rely on the long term, hoping this short-term disadvantage will be of no consequence. This tends to push the critics into a more radical position since the long-term ideal of a non-racial Azania is their only case. In order to isolate the critics still further, the government may well in the future ease the constraints on the councils and devolve even greater powers to its sponsored politicians. Internal conflicts within the critics may emerge as some respond to their isolation from immediate resource distribution by urging contact with or even participation in the councils. This is the choice that Inkatha has made. In March 1980 Buthelezi announced his backing for the system and his intention to participate in Soweto Council elections and invited individual councils to join the Black Alliance. Inkatha and the Soweto Council have become closely identified—Thebehali, who is a member of the organization, said when he was mayor that Soweto belonged to Inkatha. There are dangers to the government is this. Although it is comforting to have Inkatha further enmeshed in sponsored politics, inasmuch as the local councils are means by which urban 'insiders' are allowed to pursue their interests as 'insiders', if a mass movement based largely on migrant workers and rural dwellers won the contest for the control of African councils, institutions set up to co-opt African 'insiders' may come under the control of organizations geared towards promoting 'outsider' interests.

However, by becoming associated with the local government system, Inkatha is giving itself some role in urban politics and a number of short-term advantages in discharging that role. It is

worth looking in detail at those critics who refuse such inducements and the problems this refusal causes them.

When it was first formed it was left to various Black Consciousness organizations to oppose the Soweto Council openly. Dr Motlana's Committee of 10 was the main organization involved. It
decided that it would concentrate on local civic affairs in Soweto
rather than become involved in national politics. It was intended
only to be a rival to the Soweto Council; national politics was left
to other Black Consciousness organizations. However, the pressure of events made it impossible for Motlana to stick to this
intention.

The Committee was established in June 1977 out of the Soweto
Local Authority Liaison Committee, a group supporting the view
that Soweto should be made into a municipal authority. The
Committee of 10 was supported by all the Black Consciousness
organizations, including the SSRC, and Motlana was voted as its
Chairman. He had been active in the ANC and subsequently
became involved in Black Consciousness. He led a walk-out of
eighteen Black doctors from Baragwanath hospital, where he
worked as a houseman, in protest at low salaries for Black doctors.
Motlana is very much the professional middle-class Black to whom
Black Consciousness appeals. Among other things, he is on the
Board of Directors of New Africa Marketing, a company dealing
with cosmetic products, although he has claimed that the company
ploughs back the profit into the community.[73] The other members
of the Committee have similar profiles: Ellen Khuzwayo was a
teacher and qualified social worker; Mazibuko was a former
member of SASO and National Secretary for the BPC; Mosala
was an executive member of the Soweto Black Parents' Association; Mothabathe was a teacher on the Soweto Teachers' Action
Committee; Revd Mayathula was one of the original founders of
the BPC; Ramokgopa is a physics graduate and was on the branch
executive of Transvaal BPC; Lolwane was the national organizer
of the African Chambers of Commerce; Manthata was a member
of SASO and BPC, and Kraai was President of the Soweto
Traders' Association and sat on two school boards. All were
heavily involved in Soweto politics and have at times been banned,
although the organizaton itself remains unbanned.[74]

The government quickly perceived the threat the Committee
posed to the credibility of the community council. WRAB claimed

it had a Committee of 13 comprising 'prominent and known' Soweto leaders; this was later revealed as a hoax. It also engaged in a smear campaign against the Committee of 10, alleging that these local businessmen and professional people were bringers of darkness, death, chaos, and suffering and were paid by communists.[75] In one sense all the Committee wanted was local government for Soweto, which was consistent with state policy;[76] what it represented, however, was a threat to the credibility of the sponsored politicians lobbying for the same aim.

The original aims of the Committee were no more than the government eventually gave the community council. The case made by the Committee therefore was not simply a negative one. The council was making some of the decisions and distributing some of the resources the Committee of 10 originally said that it should. While this did not go as far as the Committee would have liked, it did mean that the Committee was forced to emphasize more long-term ideals. Its schemes of redevelopment all presupposed realization of a non-racial Azania which took the Committee away from the immediate concerns of Soweto's residents trying to cope with apartheid. Grandiose schemes for the future are appealing but they do little to solve rent arrears or homelessness. In relying on the moral justification for Azania, the Committee found it impossible to make a case against the council and stick to local civic issues in Soweto. The administration of a township cannot be removed from the apartheid context that townships are located in, and the Committee's response is valid. But concentrating on the long-term change in this context isolated the Committee from satisfying residents' needs, dispensing patronage and distributing scarce resources in order to ensure some advantage to itself. The Soweto Council was in a position to allocate houses, to waive evictions, pass building plans, decide on electrification, and so on: some socio-economic needs could be met by the council.[77] In Soweto, for example, 32,000 residents replied to the council's questionnaire on electrification. Residents are obviously prepared to associate themselves with apartheid institutions when they have some role in satisfying immediate needs. The council's critics can do nothing to prevent this.

To avoid being totally isolated from these immediate needs, Black Consciousness organizations have campaigned against bus fare increases, rent and service charge increases, housing conditions, and so forth. PEBCO did this effectively in Port Elizabeth during the Ford strike of 1979–80 and after, and this is the Committee of 10's responsibility in Soweto. Expressing opposition to increases does not prevent the eclipse of the Committee's relevance by the councils, who have the power to decide on and implement them. Outlining blueprints for Soweto's development is little better when the council has at least some say in how development actually proceeds and is seen to raise overseas loans in order to finance it. The Committee's respose to this dilemma has been to rely on the moral case for a non-racial, egalitarian Azania. Hence it has called for total autonomy (sometimes less radically, for Soweto to be made a constitutent part of the White Johannesburg City Council), with direct responsibility to Parliament, and control over education, police, transport, employment opportunities, and the power to raise taxes. This requires the total restructuring of South Africa, presupposing a unitary state with universal franchise and the abolition of apartheid institutions.[78] To make this ideal seem more immediately relevant and to have more practical effect, Motlana has predicted that South Africa will become Azania in under ten years, while Bishop Tutu reduced this to five.[79]

Long-term schemes do not satisfy short-term needs. An equal commitment by Soweto residents to a non-racial Azania does not resolve the immediate problems of living in apartheid's cities. What prevents the Committee from fighting elections, and perhaps assuming control of the Council and changing it from within, is its commitment to the main pillar of Black Consciousness' philosophy of non-participation and non-negotiation with White institutions and initiatives. In 1980 Motlana reiterated the position he has taken since 1977 in saying that he would negotiate with the government only when it had made a commitment to a non-racial unitary state with universal franchise. As to participating on the Soweto Council, he declared that he would only do so once the whole political superstructure had been overthrown and Blacks were represented in central government.[80] For an organization expressly concerned with Soweto's civic problems, this is a difficult position to take, making, as it does, any involvement in these problems conditional on wider long-term changes. While correctly linking up Soweto's situation with the racist context outside, short-term problems are created for the Committee. There has been pressure from some residents for the Committee to become involved in the satisfaction of their immediate needs. On 1 April 1979 the Committee held a rally for the purpose of seeking a mandate from the people on whether they should speak with Koornhof. Announcing this rally, the *Post Transvaal* felt the Committee should do so.[81] That the police permitted this rally when all others were banned under emergency regulations shows how much Koornhof wished to meet the Committee. The majority opinion at the rally was against consultation. A week later Motlana said he would meet Koornhof only when the pass laws were abolished.

Nevertheless, this remained a troublesome dilemma for the organization. During June 1979 the *Post Transvaal* conducted a survey which showed that of the 521 respondents 54.2 per cent believed that their leaders should serve on government committees discussing future political initiatives and 82.2 per cent believed that there should be consultation between Black leaders and the government. Support for negotiation was greater among the old, trade unionists and the working class.[82] Research for the Buthelezi Commission in 1981 found that 85 per cent of respondents agreed with the view that Black leaders should criticize the government but co-operate when this was beneficial.[83] The Soweto-based *Post Transvaal* initially supported negotiation but rescinded, so as not to isolate Motlana and the Committee (according to Qobozo). Whether or not to respond to this pressure was a matter which caused internal conflicts within the Committee. After the initial rally, Lolwane argued that instead of following the people the Committee should 'lead'—that the Committee had let the people down by failing to give guidance and direction. He was expelled from the Committee, and responded immediately by writing to the *Post Transvaal*, claiming that the Committee had lost much support over the years because of its stand and urging it to do something about alleviating the short-term problems which Soweto residents faced. Lolwane's own responsibility was to them, not to the Committee, he said.[84] Lolwane's expulsion was unfair, given the ambiguity on this issue. It seems more that his expulsion came for making public the internal disputes within the Committee, for Motlana was not averse to negotiating or participating in apartheid structures. The pressure to do so had led to an *ad hoc* policy of negotiation: Lolwane was expelled for making public his support for a more systematic approach. Motlana, for example, has met with Anglo-American, the Urban Foundation, and White opposition politicians in the PFP. At one meeting with Colin Eglin, the then Leader of the Opposition, Motlana told his White audience that constitutional models could be negotiated. He has met *verligte* Afrikaners like Williem de Klerk—in 1978 Motlana was a member of de Klerk's 'think tank'—and Stoffel van der Merwe. Contact with Whites is maintained through regular meetings with the PFP and through the Domestic Workers' and Employers' Projects whose National Chairman is Leah Tutu, Bishop Tutu's wife.

This *ad hoc* policy of consultation with Whites is the result of pressure from three separate sources. African opinion in Soweto supports some consultation and certain representatives within Black Consciousness urge the Committee to reflect it. Political dynamics suggest it also. The struggle for leadership in the urban areas requires the Committee not to be out-manoeuvred by the Soweto Council in satisfying residents' expectations and needs. Their short-term needs do constitute an inducement to participate in apartheid structures. Finally, the pressure of wider political developments must be considered. More and more incentives are being offered by the state to lure its radical opposition into negotiation. It is the strenuous attempt to resist this latter pressure which probably prevents the Committee caving in to the two more acceptable pressures. The conflicting directions in which these pressures pull the Committee have led to some inconsistency over the issue of negotiation. The Committee has met with the Broederbond in a tripartite discussion with the Greater Soweto Council, but Motlana refuses to talk with P. W. Botha, Koornhof, and Buthelezi. Meanwhile, this *ad hoc* approach does little to persuade residents that it is responding to the first two pressures. A letter in the correspondence columns of the *Post Transvaal* summed up Motlana's dilemma. Noting his refusal to speak with various people, the correspondent asked, 'So who does Motlana speak to? If he is supposed to do something for his people, then surely he must speak to somebody.'[85] This correspondent correctly perceived that if the Committee is seriously contesting the struggle for leadership in Soweto it must influence the immediate lives of residents, and for that to happen a change in strategy was necessary.

The Committee's first grudging moves on consultation with

Whites were a signal that Motlana recognized this. An additional sign was provided by the internal reorganization which the Committee underwent in September 1979. For its first years the Committee was a small interest-group of prominent and wealthy Sowetoeans. Thus, so as to be seen to represent a wider power bloc and thus add more authority to its campaigns, the Committee reorganized itself into the Soweto Civic Association. It opened itself up to membership from the public for R2.50 per annum. The ten members of the Committee became the Executive of the SCA, with smaller branch executives covering different townships in Greater Soweto. Bishop Tutu attended their inauguration, along with a crowd of one thousand residents. By opening itself up to public membership, it found it easier to legitimate any changes in strategy by arguing that it was merely reflecting its grass-roots support. What proved to be the greatest evidence of a change in strategy was the formation of AZAPO one month later, which took over from the SCA the responsibility for wider political concerns restricting the SCA to its original brief of struggling for the leadership of Soweto.

The formation of AZAPO to replace the Black Consciousness organizations banned in 1977 had been discussed since 1978, but it was not inaugurated until 1 October 1979. Curtis Nkondo was elected President (through the Soweto Teachers' Action Committee, Nkondo had led the teachers' support for students in 1976–7). The executive committee of the new organization reflected the stable constituencies from whom Black Consciousness drew its support: Nkondo was a teacher and after the uprising was employed as a teacher of English to Black management trainees in a Johannesburg company; Mrs Melane was a university graduate; George Wauchope worked in the personnel department of a Johannesburg company; Mosala was a company representative; and Tloubatla was a student. All were young—the average age was 32, with Nkondo's fifty-one years greatly enlarging this average. Except for Nkondo, all had emerged to political maturity during the SASO generation of the 1970s and had strong links with Black Consciousness politics. Wauchope was also Secretary to the SCA and Nkondo had been a member of the ANC Youth League with Motlana, Tutu, Thozamile Botha, and Mandela.

The formation of the new organization represented a demarcation of responsibility between the various Black Consciousness organizations. AZAPO took over responsibility for wider national politics from the SCA, whose responsibility now lay in Soweto, as PEBCO's lay in Port Elizabeth. Various other civic associations were formed to agitate on local issues in other urban areas. This paralleled the formation of AZASO, an organization representing university students, and COSAS, representing secondary school-children. With the addition of WASA (later MWASA) which catered for the interests of Black writers and media workers, these organizations represented the main Black Consciousness groups in 1979. There was a variety of associations guarding the interests of Blacks in the professions—for example, the Transvaal Black Attorney Association, Black Doctors' group, the Black Priests' Solidarity group, and the South African Black Social Workers' Association. Each was responsible for Black awareness and self-reliance schemes in the area of life they represented. AZAPO was defined as the only national political body. This clearly showed the SCA, and Soweto residents, where the SCA should devote its attention in the face of declining support and enthusiasm in Soweto for the old Committee of 10. The suggestion is clear that Black Consciousness leaders realized that they were temporarily losing the struggle for leadership in the urban areas. Tom Lodge reports that by the end of 1980 the SCA had lost its momentum.[86] At the beginning of the year its thirty-three branches had spearheaded an extremely effective campaign against proposed rent increases, which had succeeded in delaying the implementation of the new tariffs for over a year. By the year's end Lodge notes how its inability to be directly involved in 'bread-and-butter' issues caused it to lose some ground.

To be fair to the SCA, its problems in engendering support in Soweto merely reflected the problems in Black Consciousness generally. It was fighting the leadership struggle while enunciating a philosophy which hampered its strategy. This philosophy prevented open contact with platforms which could be used to affect immediately the provision of services and the satisfaction of the needs of residents. It cut the SCA off from contact with Black workers and involvement with the trade unions, where Black Consciousness never had much legitimacy. The support among Soweto residents, and particularly the Black working class, for consultation has already been noted. The respectable polls which the community councils received (although not in Soweto) could not have gone without notice. The growing, albeit inadequate, powers delegated to the Soweto Council nurtured an interest in it by residents, who were personally affected by it. The local authorities were also making some headway in establishing a more radical image for themselves. The Urban Community Councils' Association requested that Africans be granted the legal right to own land. It also recommended the abolition of influx control, freedom of Africans to trade anywhere, abolition of administration boards, provision of additional land for urban development for Africans, South African citizenship for all Africans, and the abolition of segregated education. Some of the demands formed the platform of the Sofasonke Party in the Soweto elections of 1983, which saw it take control of the council. By 1985 some of the demands had been granted by the government. The old Committee of 10 had little response to its campaigns. In the first half of 1979 the *Post Transvaal*, strongly supportive of the Committee, ran a poll asking readers to express their support for the Committee or the Soweto Council. In two months only 338 votes were cast, although 96.4 per cent were for the Committee. The *Post Transvaal's* explanation on 3 June had some truth: 'It is only those who felt strongly about their preference who bothered to vote.' This was an admission that the SCA did not generate strong feelings. Just over a month later a protest rally called by the Committee against the council mustered only 200 people.

There are constraints working against the open expression of support for radical organizations. Theodor Hanf and his colleagues add another caution. Historically, Black Consciousness is not 'leader'- or personality-oriented, but Motlana has none the less been able to generate some personal support. In Hanf's study, Schlemmer presents two interesting tables, reproduced here as Tables 21 and 22.[87]

A lot of the support for homeland leaders is inflated by including rural peasants in the count. Leadership trends in Soweto and East Rand townships show significant differences. The support for Winnie Mandela confirms the continued strength of the ANC. Buthelezi's support, like that of the ANC, is more evenly distributed across the country than the Soweto- or Witwatersrand-based support of Black Consciousness organizations. Schlemmer warns against misinterpreting surveys like this. They only tap transitory support and show the influence of whatever symbolic protests the

Table 21. *Percentages of Respondents giving 10 out of 10 to various Black Leaders (1979)*

Leader	Urban Xhosa in TVL and W. Cape	Eastern Cape Xhosa	Urban Ciskei	Rural Ciskei	Xhosa migrant workers	Soweto Sotho	Soweto Zulu	Durban Zulu
Bishop Buthelezi	15	10	11	9	11	11	17	13
Chief Buthelezi	18	26	27	22	25	23	48	45
Winnie Mandela	21	38	38	12	25	29	37	19
Chief Matanzima	5	27	33	26	18	12	5	5
Dr Motlana	33	18	16	12	10	51	59	15
Chief Phatudi	—	—	—	—	—	44	—	—
Chief Sebe	24	47	48	60	53	—	—	—
Bishop Tutu	30	22	19	11	7	29	31	12

Table 22. *Leadership Popularity in Soweto and East Rand Townships*

Leader	Most popular figure		% giving 10 out of 10	
	Apr. 1977	Apr. 1978	1979	1980
Chief Buthelezi	28	5	19	12
Winnie Mandela	27	21	19	18
Dr Motlana	0	61	28	26
Curtis Nkondo	5	7	—	11
PAC (various)	11	1	—	—
Bishop Tutu	0	—	17	33
Other homeland	14	3	17	—
Other	15	2	—	—

leaders are engaged in at the time. There is one very significant pattern to these figures, however. Buthelezi's popularity declines while his critics are involved in public confrontation with the government. Clearly, also, the various Black Consciousness figures are demonstrated to be protest spokesmen rather than leaders as such: if they are either quiescent or fail to deliver on promises, their position is quickly eroded. The only stable constituency which Black Consciousness can depend on is that of the young, educated, professional middle class. What Black Consciousness fails to retain is the support of Black workers and trade unionists, who, the *Post Transvaal*'s survey showed, supported the idea of consultation with Whites. Support for the idea declined in inverse proportion to age and socio-economic status. The young and the professional middle class are sections of the population which are not so immediately affected by the paucity of resources which the local councils can distribute. Among those materially interested in influencing this distribution, there is little support for the SCA. Its loyalty to the philosophy of Black Consciousness ensures that it is cut off from this power bloc. Baruch Hirson correctly summarized the SCA's position in the Soweto leadership struggle: 'The leaders of the Black Consciousness movement did make people "dream dreams". There was however a deep gulf between dreams and reality.'[88]

The ineffectiveness of the SCA in the struggle for leadership in Soweto impressed upon Black Consciousness organizations the need to change strategy. In short, it was realized that Black Consciousness organizations needed to engender a broader power-base, specifically to develop a constituency among African trade unionists, to produce more pressure on the government than peaceful non-participation creates, and, accordingly, to develop new strategies which allowed some consultation with Whites to benefit from this increased pressure. The reorganization of the Committee of 10 into the SCA and the formation of AZAPO in October 1979 were stages in the development of a new approach, which finally culminated in the formation of the UDF. But while Black Consciousness organizations remained loyal to the philosophy, little progress could be made to correct this ineffectiveness. With the formation of AZAPO came other changes—changes which point to the beginnings of co-operation between some Black Consciousness organizations and the ANC within the umbrella of the UDF, although AZAPO itself is opposed to any co-operation. Not only does this co-operation allow some Black Consciousness groups to be seen to take up the legitimate mantle of the ANC and to profit from its kudos, it opens it up to the ANC's support among African trade unions and the Black working class generally. It is not just the leadership struggle in the townships which made Black Consciousness supporters realize that a closer relationship was needed with workers. One of the consequences of the events of 1976 was to demonstrate to the students that this closer relationship was necessary.[89] Some Black Consciousness adherents have subsequently toned down their race approach in the light of ANC advances, structural changes in the economy which have seen the development of Black economic power, and their own failure in contesting the leadership struggle in the urban areas. Some Black Consciousness students came under the protection of the ANC when they fled into exile in 1976, and they have since returned to South Africa as ANC insurgents.

The problem with the urban spokesmen within Black Consciousness is that they are prolific articulators of grievances but fail to build viable structures and organizations around their high reputation. The powerful rhetoric often hides their real powerlessness in making decisions and distributing scarce resources which affect their constituency in the townships. The ANC has a viable structure and organization and is using co-operation with some

Black Consciousness groups in order to reinstate itself in the country. Regarding themselves as the sole and authentic representative of the oppressed in South Africa, the ANC could not entertain co-operation with organizations which appeared to oppose it. Hence Black Consciousness has undergone considerable ideological and organizational change to make this co-operation possible. This has caused divisions between Black Consciousness groups, some of whom reject contact with the ANC. The political association between them is very briefly referred to by Tom Lodge in his account of politics in the post-1976 period,[90] and was predicted by all those who have suggested that Black Consciousness either would become or was becoming more radical. Such a view is held by Horsch, Nolutshungu, and Saul and Gelb.[91] Saul and Gelb point out that the ANC is now also more willing to 'reach out' toward Black Consciousness groups.[92] The dynamics of this association will be outlined here in two sections. The first discusses the co-operation as it developed up to 1982. The second examines the co-operation as it has existed since the 1982 campaign against the constitution and the formation of the UDF.

THE BLACK CONSCIOUSNESS MOVEMENT AND THE ANC 1979–1982

Historically, the exclusive concentration on race by Black Consciousness led to antagonism with the ANC, which had always placed more emphasis on class (although race has not been ignored). The ANC saw in Black Consciousness the racial exclusivism it has always opposed and which had earlier led to the formation of the PAC. They referred to it as carrying the dangers of Black racism.[93] At a meeting in Lusaka during August 1979 the ANC rejected the formation of the exiled Black Consciousness Movement of Azania (formerly the Black Consciousness Movement of South Africa) as divisive. Black Consciousness organizations have never questioned the respect with which the ANC is universally held in the African population. When it was first enunciated, Black Consciousness newletters never underemphasized the earlier role of the ANC. Sharpeville massacre anniversary rallies were annually held, and despite pacifism some early literature ended with the ANC's call of *Amadla Ngawethu* and 'Long Live the Guerrillas'.[94] Nkwenkwe Nkome, National Organizer of the BPC, pencilled into the minutes of one BPC meeting which mentioned Mandela the phrase 'Black Prince of Azania'.[95] Support for the PAC was more reticent. One SASO newsletter called for the reprimand of a Natal Indian Congress representative who described SASO as propagating the policies of the PAC.[96] It described this as audacious, naïve, and irresponsible: the fear of state reprisals did not prevent acknowledgement of SASO's links with and support for the ANC. The closer ideological affinity between Black Consciousness and the PAC could well have contributed to SASO's efforts to distance itself from the PAC. Without doubt, therefore, what hostility there has been between Black Consciousness and the ANC has come from the latter.

The peculiar politics of exile have changed this. To reap the benefit of revolutionary terror tactics, guerrilla organizations need an internal wing. John Kane-Berman has claimed that the ANC, in a meeting with Buthelezi in London during 1979, admitted that 'working within South Africa for a political solution was necessary and needed to be pursued'.[97] Both Buthelezi and Kane-Berman see this as justification for Inkatha. Buthelezi's own relationship with the ANC is problematic. In April 1980 he argued that the Free Mandela Campaign was a deliberate ploy by the ANC to destroy his own credibility and, consequently, Inkatha members were instructed not to support the campaign. In criticizing the ANC, Buthelezi did make a perceptive appraisal of its difficulties. The ANC, he said, had lost touch with the feelings of Blacks. It had to be disabused of the illusion that the blowing up of a refinery was all they needed to do in order to communicate with the people of South Africa.[98] Not only do terror tactics isolate terrorists from political events in South Africa, but the general ineffectiveness of these tactics in South Africa, for the variety of reasons identified earlier, means that the best the ANC could hope for is to win a place at the negotiating table. The government has steadfastly refused that: having ANC surrogates at the negotiating table is the next best option.

The ANC seem to have first courted Buthelezi's Inkatha movement, with Tambo inviting him to London in 1979 to discuss 'common concerns'. At the same time, Tambo remarked in a letter circulating in South Africa's underground that participation on apartheid platforms was justified, so long as it was done for the right reasons. Many interpreted this as a legitimation of Inkatha, but an alliance with Inkatha was not a serious possibility. After vociferous criticism from supporters in South Africa the ANC played down the meeting. Later Buthelezi issued a diatribe of abuse against the ANC. By the autumn of 1979 the ANC turned to Black Consciousness organizations, some of whom were more than enthusiastic in their response, in view of the limitations that were evident in their struggle for leadership in the urban areas.

The co-operation emerged quite suddenly, or at least it took time to become public. In August 1979 the Lusaka-based ANC rejected the formation of the BCMA. By October 1979 they were meeting to discuss 'a common strategy'. After its April 1980 conference in London on 'Redefinition and Rededication', the BCMA established an interim committee to work more closely with other exiled movements. This coalition in exile paralleled developments inside South Africa. Unlike the case of organizations in exile, there has been no formal acknowledgement of the co-operation; this would be counter-productive because it would encourage state repression and the removal of organizations acting as internal political surrogates. In July 1980 there were fears that AZAPO would be banned after the Minister of Police accused it of furthering the aims of banned organizations and of being inspired and financed by the ANC. This is an example of how the co-operation creates its own problems. The two sides have to be closely identified in the public image for it to function in the way that the interests of each require, but they have to be distant enough in the state's view to prevent the alliance crumbling with the banning of Black Consciousness organizations. Maintaining this fine balance is problematic.[99] AZAPO announced that it recognized the importance of the ANC but that it was independent and had its own constitution and policies. None the less, there is evidence contradicting AZAPO's disclaimer.

Evidence of an emerging, if still embryonic, link exists on ideological and organizational grounds. Most of the movement has occurred on the side of Black Consciousness. The major ideological change coincided with the formation of AZAPO in October 1979, when it closely linked its new responsibility for the wider national political struggle to the theme of class. The once exclusive focus on race in Black Consciousness, with its attendant ambivalence concerning the role of workers in change, has been supplemented by a class analysis which places workers at the forefront of the liberation process. AZAPO seems to have been created specifically to represent this new development. At its inauguration meeting the President, Curtis Nkondo, said that the main instrument of liberation must be Black labour and the liberation process primarily requires a militant system of Black trade unions and the abolition of discriminatory labour legislation. No mention was made of the usual Black Consciousness themes.

This new interest took many forms. At the practical level, AZAPO established labour committees to investigate the problems of workers and to hold classes and study the economic and labour situation. During the latter part of 1979 and throughout 1980, AZAPO became involved in the campaign against bus fare increases in Soweto and Seshego, and rent increases in Soweto. It also gave support to the Coloured schools boycott and the strike by the Johannesburg municipal workers. The organization representing Black writers, WASA, opened itself up to print workers in an attempt to forge links between professional writers and media workers, and later became the Media Workers' Association of South Africa. The most impressive effort in this direction came in the 1979–80 Ford Strike in Port Elizabeth, which was organized and led by the Black Consciousness group PEBCO. During these months also, the *Post Transvaal* began to focus on work issues for the first time. It carried reports of trade union affairs, which it had never done before. The paper campaigned against the Wiehahn and Riekert Commissions for their effects on trade unions. A new vocabulary was provided, with the term 'Black working class' as its centre-point. It initiated a 'Workers Watch' to replace 'Dignity Watch', focusing on discrimination in the workplace. A series of articles were carried outlining the history of the trade union movement in South Africa, and it announced that it was to monitor the codes of conduct issued by the United States and the EEC for foreign firms in South Africa. It was very significant that at the same time the *Post Transvaal* was able to report that the ANC in London had denied any official contact with Buthelezi—Tambo only 'dined' with him. The newspaper quoted from an ANC pamphlet referring to Motlana as a 'patriot' and to Buthelezi as 'a betrayal of the South African struggle'.[100] Motlana's son is in exile and he has publicly supported the ANC and armed struggle.

This growing support for the ANC among some Black Consciousness supporters is demonstrated in other ways. The Coloured students at the University of the Western Cape played a big role in the school and university unrest in 1980. They linked their boycott to support for the ANC and the flag of the ANC was frequently raised at meetings to the cheers of the students. Similar unfurlings of the ANC flag occurred during the Anti-Republic Day campaign, where the Republic's flag was often burnt before being replaced by the ANC's emblem. (Burning the Republic's flag was subsequently made into a criminal offence.) Trade unions, local community groups, church groups, and student organizations showed their support for the ANC in this way. A member of the Black Students' Society at the University of Witwatersrand objected to the appearance of Dr Koornhof on the campus: until ANC leaders were released and allowed to exercise their democratic rights to speak on campus, students would object to Koornhof speaking. The ANC's anthem was sung twice during Koornhof's speech, which he eventually abandoned. The Free Mandela Campaign is another example of how the ANC is being associated with internal political struggles by some Black Consciousness organizations and by other groups. Free Mandela meetings and rallies have been organized by traditional Black Consciousness groups and supporters, such as students, church groups, community organizations, and by Black Consciousness political organizations. Many of these meetings were banned. In October 1983 the Free Mandela Committee, which organizes meetings, was to hold a rally to commemorate the banning of Black Consciousness organizations in October 1977. The meeting was banned, but the intention behind it was plain: ANC and Black Consciousness commemorations were being merged.

This is perhaps better evidenced by the support that has been expressed for the ANC's famous Freedom Charter. During 1980, the twenty-fifth anniversary of its adoption, dubbed by the ANC the Year of the Charter, there were reports in the press of the widespread circulation of the charter. Several editions were banned and there were many attempts by the police to prosecute people who had the charter in their possession. In January 1984 the Publications Appeal Board ruled that the charter was not an undesirable publication. The thought that the charter might be undesirable had not stopped anyone expressing their support for it. In 1982 the anniversary of the charter was commemorated on the Witwatersrand in a meeting organized by the Black Consciousness student organization COSAS. The thirtieth anniversary of the defiance campaign and the seventieth birthday of Walter

Sisulu were commemorated at a mass meeting held in the University of Witwatersrand. The meeting was addressed by AZASO, the Black Students' Society and the university's student representative council. The third anniversary of the execution of Solomon Mahlangu was marked by church meetings organized by COSAS. Black Consciousness organizations were again active in commemorations of ANC events and personnel in 1983, as were some unregistered trade unions like SAAWU and the General and Allied Workers' Union. The march by women protesting against the pass laws in 1956 was also celebrated by Black Consciousness groups and various women's federations. These events in South Africa's political history had not been marked by such celebration and support prior to 1980, and the fact that they have been celebrated since is an illustration of the ANC's resurgence as a political organization inside the country. What is more, it is various Black Consciousness organizations and personnel who have been taking the lead in re-establishing the ANC's position. This is more clearly demonstrated in the important campaign of opposition to the constitutional proposals during 1983–4, which will be treated separately in the following section.

At the level of belief rather than action, most Black Consciousness groups now link the themes of race and class (rather than replace race with class). In the peculiar South African economy this is highly realistic and a proper corrective to their former exclusive focus on race. Within five days of its inaugural meeting, AZAPO's President wrote in the *Post Transvaal* about the relationship between race and class in South Africa: 'Every morning in town I see young and old men with heavy dust bins on their shoulders running after moving trucks. Only Blacks do this. Those who sweep the streets are Black. Why? Those who clean windows are Black. Why?' He gave no answer in this interview, being content to present the equation of Blackness with working class status. In an interview in the *Sunday Post* two days later, he did advance the answer. Nkondo is worth quoting in length on this.

The worker is the vanguard of the organization. We have to shift from the idea that race is the main issue. Race is used as an instrument of economic exploitation and words such as apartheid are only excuses. The problem is not necessarily a racial one but an economic one. A worker is a Black man and no White is a worker. Blacks are workers because they are exploited with no opportunity for advancement or to own the means of production and distribution. Blacks are just part of the machinery. Black people want complete liberation. We do not want to remain part of the machinery and we do not want to remain reservoirs of cheap labour.[101]

A number of points are worth emphasizing which highlight the change in Black Consciousness. The equation of Blackness with being working class is the result of class, not racial, factors—it is the result of economic exploitation, not racial discrimination. Blacks are seen as working class before they are Black: the position of Blacks is not the result of racial categorization but has come about because they do not own the means of production and distribution. Liberation, therefore, does not merely imply liberation from White oppression: it primarily means liberation from capitalist exploitation. While Marxist analyses of South Africa are more sophisticated than Nkondo's own analysis, his statement relies on Marxist ideological categories. There is one ambiguity: at one point this emphasis is qualified when he says that the problem in South Africa is not *necessarily* a racial one. None the less, there is an unmistakable recognition that race and class coincide in South Africa and that class dominates—Nkondo's qualification suggests only that he is reluctant to ignore race altogether. The past concerns of Black Consciousness may have had some psychological hold, and, as we shall see, these changes were resisted by some elements within Black Consciousness.

In a policy statement in May 1980 AZAPO felt that it needed to reaffirm its allegiance to the philosophy of Black Consciousness. It described this as a process of self-understanding and self-assertion, a philosophy which expressed and ensured Black solidarity. Significantly, new clauses were added to the usual rhetoric. Economic exploitation was now added as an essential factor that would bring about Black solidarity and make them into a class-for-themselves. They were a class-for-themselves and not a race-for-themselves because, the statement continued, 'the political and economic exploitation of Blacks has created a rigid class structure in which Blacks constitute a class'. White workers formed a labour aristocracy which benefited from and defended the capitalist system in South Africa. The policy statement went on to outline the nature of Azania. There would be a redistribution of capital and property, with the trade unions bringing about this redistribution of power.[102] Without the terms themselves being used, for obvious tactical reasons, this had a strong socialist flavour. The BCMA in exile faced no similar tactical inhibitions. At its London conference in April 1980, a statement declared that the BCMA was moving ideologically closer to the ANC and that Black Consciousness as an ideology must be based on the principles of socialism.[103]

Frequently throughout 1980 Nkondo referred to Blacks as 'wage slaves'—forced labour power. In a New Year message, printed in the *Post Transvaal*, Nkondo complained of the dehumanizing consequences of forced labour, of merely being a commodity and an extension of a machine.[104] The symbolic enemy was no longer White oppressors but capitalist oppressors. The Revd Buti Tlhagale wrote a paper called 'A Further Direction of Black Consciousness' for one of the planning sessions in 1978, discussing the formation of AZAPO. Nkondo took up this theme directly from Tlhagale. Quarish Patel's paper, 'In Search of Ideology', also formed a part of the later emphasis, and both papers urged the development of a class analysis. The eventual President of AZAPO admitted the fundamental change that had occurred in Black Consciousness. Quoted by Zwelakhe Sisulu, in his review of a decade of Black Consciousness, Nkondo said that it was with AZAPO that the significance of the Black worker had been realized and that it had 'brought about a change in thinking'.[105]

While AZAPO was inaugurated to represent this change, other Black Consciousness organizations inside South Africa took it on board. PEBCO and MWASA are examples of this at the level of practical action. For reasons that will be discussed shortly, Motlana's SCA has remained silent. Having said that, Black Consciousness literature also reflected this new emphasis, and the magazine *Frontline*, to which Motlana contributes a regular column, is heavily committed to the change. Its first issue in December 1979 gave a great deal of attention to the BCMA in London, and the call for a class approach that had been made the previous October. The *Post Transvaal* was just as heavily committed, and its editor, Percy Qobozo, is a close friend and political ally of Motlana. In fact, the *Post Transvaal*, before its banning, acted as an excellent barometer of the changing nature of Black Consciousness with changes in editorial policy and copy reflecting these wider developments.

One of the factors that may have made an ideological reconciliation easier has been the internal debates within the ANC, which have resulted in the faction pushing a more nationalist policy, gaining some temporary ascendancy over those advancing an exclusive class approach. Opposition to a reconciliation from the latter faction has therefore been truncated. There has always been this tension within the ANC and while after its banning the movement moved more towards a class approach, the nationalist element has always remained a force. There were indications of this conflict when four White Marxists were suspended in January 1980, reportedly over the direction of the movement's internal operations. Documents allegedly belonging to the International University Exchange Fund were made public by the exposed security agent Craig Williamson, and revealed conflicts between the Black nationalist and Marxist factions within the ANC. Barend Schuitema, former leader of the Dutch anti-apartheid movement, alleged that there was conflict within the ANC and he claimed that the exiled South African Communist Party feared that the Black nationalist element were setting up an alternative ANC inside South Africa. The Black nationalist faction, led by Makiwane, opposed the decision to include White Marxists. However, a message from Nelson Mandela, allegedly smuggled out of Robben Island, is reported to indicate that he has maintained his own commitment to the involvement of Whites in the liberation struggle. Most significantly, this message was printed on a pamphlet that was distributed at the funeral of a Committee of 10 and SCA member, the Revd Mayathula, in September 1980.[106]

In distributing this pamphlet at a Black Consciousness occasion, Mandela was clearly distinguishing between two issues—contact with Black Consciousness and contact with Whites. Although the move towards a combined race–class strategy was facilitated by the conflicts with the communist faction within the ANC, this move was not to be achieved at the expense of the ANC's historic commitment to racial inclusiveness. In fact the ANC has been able to win from some Black Consciousness organizations a further change in ideology: to function as an internal wing for the ANC, Black Consciousness organizations need to participate and negotiate with Whites of all political persuasion. Some Black Consciousness groups now argue that the liberation struggle must be a racially inclusive one in which Whites can participate. Perhaps, with its experience of competing for leadership in Soweto, the organization which has moved furthest to this position is Motlana's SCA. The pressure among Soweto residents for the SCA to be drawn into consultation with Whites was noted earlier: it was met with an *ad hoc* policy of consultation. This consultation extended to radical White trade unionists in FOSATU, through the liberal

PFP to the Broederbond, covering all political opinions. In an issue of *Frontline* in 1980, Motlana penned an important passage: 'Progress', he wrote, 'is progress, even if it is very limited and we should not refuse to upgrade our environment or co-operate in upgrading it just because this it not answering the principal problem.'[107] This strongly suggests that taking a hand in Soweto's redevelopment justifies departure from the theme of non-negotiation and non-participation. Motlana, who after all does send his children to a White private school, implies that the conditions necessary to initiate consultation with Whites are slowly being satisfied. In April 1980 he set out the formal conditions necessary when he said that he would be prepared to negotiate with Whites once they had made a commitment to majority rule. But that these conditions were laid out at a multi-racial conference in the Afrikaans University of Stellenbosch suggests that the minimum conditions in practice fall below this. Moreover, when Lolwane was expelled from the Committee of 10 for demanding a more open and systematic policy on negotiation, Motlana retained him as a member of the SCA executive.

The rising importance in Black Consciousness of Bishop Desmond Tutu has been fundamental in influencing this particular shift in belief. The stand that the World Council of Churches took on the Soweto uprising and later on Zimbabwean independence, and the role that Tutu has played through the Black Caucus of the South African Council of Churches in the South African liberation struggle, has seen him emerge since 1977–8 as one of the main Black Consciousness spokesmen. Tutu was considered by *Post Transvaal* as one of the major Black Consciousness leaders. His position on various opinion surveys on Black leadership reflects his wider support. Bishop Tutu came to Black Theology primarily as a theologian. The demands of his faith always made him call for cross-colour contact. For example, in a 1973 paper entitled 'God Given Dignity and the Quest for Liberation', he clearly stated that 'the object of the exercise is to get together and to try and work out together the best and most just society'.[108] This 'working together' is exemplified in his own political career and that of his wife. As National Director of the Domestic Workers' and Employers' Project, Leah Tutu works with liberal Whites, advancing the case for one category of the Black working class. During a seminar in Durban, she outlined another purpose. Domestic labour, she thought, had an important role in breaking down the group barriers between Black and White since this was one of the few areas where workers and employers made contact at a social level.[109] It is her ambition to develop this contact as a stage in the process of liberation.[110] She has since joined the multi-racial, liberal South African Institute of Race Relations as Assistant Director of Programmes. Both the DWEP and the SCA are examples of how this move to limited negotiation and contact is translated in practice. If some Black Consciousness organizations are to act as internal political surrogates for the ANC, this contact can only increase, and both Motlana and Bishop Tutu are arguing the case that it should.

None the less, this particular ideological change has won less support in Black Consciousness than the other. The issue of involvement with Whites has led to some internal disputes within Black Consciousness organizations, and involvement has been limited to the political arena, which is where the ANC requests it anyway. This has not infringed Black Consciousness emphasis on racial exclusivity through awareness and self-reliance schemes in arts, sport, and the media particularly. This may be a deliberate strategy: Black solidarity is generated at the level of ordinary every-day life, and is then used as a lever in negotiation at the wider national political level. This is too easy a solution, however, for the idea of consultation with Whites has caused disagreement and division within Black Consciousness organizations. At the moment some Black Consciousness figures have not thought through the logic of the universally acclaimed new emphasis on class, which by nature requires contact with Whites. While Whites are by defini-tion one antithetic colour, they are not of one antithetic class or ideological position.

Before these internal disputes are discussed, it is necessary to consider the additional evidence of an embryonic link that arises at the organizational level. The organizations have not formally merged, nor could they, but Black Consciousness leaders like Tutu, Botha, Motlana and Nkondo are all ex-ANC. They were with Mandela, Sobukwe, and Robowoko in the ANC Youth League; Motlana was Secretary to the Youth League and it is reported that Botha has joined with the ANC now that he is in exile. Motlana worked with Winnie Mandela on the Black Parents' Association, which was formed during the 1976 disturbances.

These figures are not from the younger student generation who first enunciated the philosophy of Black Consciousness and who led its organizations. While the organizations which Botha, Motlana and Nkondo headed (Tutu is not a leader in that sense) are dominated by this kind of constituency, the actual leaders were from an earlier ANC-dominated generation. There seems to have been a power struggle within Black Consciousness which has seen the leadership wrested away from the younger student generation who first enunciated the philosophy. Since the murder of Steve Biko there has been no strong personality in Black Consciousness and the takeover has been facilitated by the fact that many of the younger generation are in exile or lost in South Africa's prisons and graveyards. It has also been helped by the fact that Black Consciousness students who fled the repressive response to the Soweto uprising came under the protective guidance of the ANC which had the most efficient organization in exile. The ANC is now completing the schooling of those students who fled before matriculation; some of them have also returned as revolutionary terrorists for the ANC. In the absence of this SASO generation, and perhaps with the acquiescence of some of their number, ex-ANC figures have taken over leadership of Black Consciousness organizations despite the fact that the organizations themselves have a heavy input of ex-SASO and ex-BPC figures on their executives. The age structure of AZAPO's executive in 1979 gave this away. The average age of the four members, excluding Nkondo, was twenty-seven years. Nkondo himself was fifty-one.

The quartet of ex-ANC figures committed Black Consciousness to the Free Mandela Campaign in 1980. That they did so reflects an important belief of theirs. All of them have frequently announced that they are no more than Mandela's surrogates. During the Ford strike Botha said that Mandela was the only person who could negotiate an end to it. All see Mandela as the only person who can negotiate with the government. The 'real leaders', they argue, are on Robben Island (although Mandela has now been moved to the mainland): they present themselves as only surrogate leaders pushed to the fore in Mandela's absence. At the beginning of 1979 the *Post Transvaal* cautioned against the veneration of 'old style' movements and leaders and wrote about the new generation who had only 'vague notions' of Mandela and about new circumstances since the exile of the ANC. It praised

Dr Motlana as the representative of this changed situation: a man brave enough to risk a lucrative career for the 'Idea'.[111] By the end of the year it joined in supporting the quartet's view of themselves as only Mandela's surrogates, describing Mandela as the 'real leader'.[112]

The legitimacy of the ANC in African opposition politics has meant that from its inception Black Consciousness never denigrated the organization or its leaders. Calls were frequently made by the younger student generation for the release of Mandela, Sisulu, and Mbeki. The BPC refused to meet President Carter's UN Ambassador in 1977 unless he first saw Mandela. The present situation, however, is fundamentally different. Three differences separate past concern from present statements. Today's statements do not come from younger students merely because they wish to legitimize their own position or because they recognize the ANC's past relevance. They arise out of a new ideological agreement with the ANC. Today's younger student generation tends to be much more unambiguous in identifying Black Consciousness figures as only temporary surrogate leaders. Audiences at Free Mandela Campaign meetings bear this out, and the figure of Mandela is a unifying link between the generations. Perfunctory genuflections in the direction of the ANC have been replaced by a greater political loyalty to its policies, practices, and personnel. The BPC once remarked that although it recognized the ANC's relevance, it did not agree with the organization.[113] Nkondo has never been so ambivalent over his support for the ANC nor have the remaining figures in the quartet of Black Consciousness leadership. This even extends to the role of armed struggle of liberation. There is now a wider awareness in Black Consciousness that a peaceful solution is well-nigh impossible. It is never said to be completely impossible, because that might be seen as threatening violence and provoking state repression. There is always said to be one last alternative to violence, which the government is invited to adopt, while the ANC's revolutionary terrorism illustrates how short time is. Dr Motlana expressed this as follows: 'In South Africa we hope violence will come to stop. But often it is a response to violence. External training of terrorists is a response to government unwillingness and inability to negotiate. We do not want violence but one way to make sure it does not continue is to create a system in which all people can come together in a democratic all-embracing power structure.'[114] Made in 1980, the statement alludes to Motlana's willingness to negotiate, and ties this to the ANC's armed struggle. As it was intended to, the alliance between some Black Consciousness organizations and the ANC has allowed the leverage of armed struggle to become a part of Black Consciousness's open political challenge, while they themselves avoid threatening or engaging in it.[115] Finally, perhaps the greatest difference about the present situation is that those making the genuflections are, as already explained, ex-ANC members.

These shifts in the ideological and organizational nature of Black Consciousness have not been uniform. Ideological changes are more pronounced than organizational ones, and within these changes in ideology the movement to a class approach is the more advanced. They have caused disunity and disagreement within Black Consciousness. Motlana and the SCA have remained silent over the new emphasis on class and labour issues. This may be because it falls outside the ambit of the organization in its struggle for the leadership of Soweto, but then Soweto is no more than a dormitory for Black workers. In truth, Motlana is a supporter of the free enterprise system and is involved in the management of several Johannesburg companies. His own vision of Azania as stated in July 1979 is capitalist: a country that is dedicated to wipe out poverty, that is certain to have a department of state solely devoted to the development of the small businessman, a country committed to the free enterprise system, where free market forces determine the type and siting of factories, where there is free mobility of workers, and where a person's labour is valued according to its intrinsic work not the colour of his skin.[116] There is no mention even of African communalism as a brake on unfettered capitalism—even Inkatha makes this qualification. Such a view contrasts markedly with that of AZAPO and the BCMA in exile. The 'chief villain', as the BCMA saw it, was capitalism and this must therefore include Motlana and the SCA.

There is presumably a free flow of ideas within Black Consciousness, and Motlana seems willing to accede to the majority view. He still contributes to *Frontline* despite the magazine's support for the views of the BCMA. He has neither criticized the new emphasis nor threatened resignation from Black Consciousness organizations. Nkondo's position is also slightly different from Thozamile Botha's. Nkondo identified AZAPO's first tasks as the education of workers, since the real problem is economic. PEBCO's role in the 1979–80 Ford strike seemed a practical application of that. Botha saw the problem slightly differently: 'The problem is political and you cannot separate the interests of the worker in his work situation from those outside.'[117] Both see race and class as inextricably combined but Thozamile Botha emphasized the influence of wider racial restrictions on political rights over and above workplace issues. Nkondo suggests that wider political rights will follow on from mobilization in the workplace. The emphasis, if not the policy, is different. Certainly the practical implications of the policy differ: Nkondo places emphasis on trade unions; the role of PEBCO shows that Botha emphasized community-based mobilization.

Whereas AZAPO has shown the greatest movement towards a class approach, it has been the most reluctant to depart from the Black Consciousness tenets of non-participation and non-negotiation with Whites. No White journalists were allowed at its inauguration, during which Nkondo argued that 'AZAPO has no intention of requesting for assistance from Whites . . . we shall not negotiate.'[118] On this aspect of the ANC's legacy, Motlana has shown the most advance. In May 1980 AZAPO and WASA (as it was then) held a seminar to review Black Consciousness in the 1980s. Some protagonists said it should abandon its exclusivity and welcome Whites. This was rejected by AZAPO. Integration and racial inclusivism belonged to the post-liberation era, not to the struggle.[119] While Nkondo argues that race and class are synonymous in South Africa, his stance on contact with Whites suggests that 'class' is given the same ascriptive characteristics as 'race' in this relationship. Just as Whites cannot experience 'Blackness', it is impossible to develop an identification with the workers' struggle unless one is a member of the working class. Contact and co-operation with White Marxists is excluded, despite the emphasis on class. So is contact with Whites in negotiating the end of apartheid. The irony is that the element in Black Consciousness most disposed to contact with White Marxists is that which is least disposed to Marxism. This effectively prevents Black Consciousness from reaping the maximum benefit from its ideological emphasis on class. It illustrates well how much Black Consciousness has been left in disarray by its co-operation with the

ANC. If this were to remain the dominant view in Black Consciousness, it would leave the ANC with the dilemma of choosing between power and its principles.

The ANC may be saved from making this choice, for the cleavages and tactical alliances within Black Consciousness cut across a simple division. The conflicts within PEBCO and AZAPO illustrate the point. After the banning and exile of Botha, PEBCO underwent a leadership crisis. On 12 March 1980 a new executive was elected with representatives from Indian and Coloured townships around Port Elizabeth, and Skosana was chosen as President. He announced that the policy and practice of the organization would be reviewed and said that he wished to push the organization to a more moderate position than Thozamile Botha: PEBCO was essentially a civic body dedicated to improving living conditions, and was not a political organization. Resignations followed and Skosana himself was forced to resign in August 1980. He was criticized for two main reasons which indicate the constituencies within Black Consciousness who opposed him. The first was his departure from the policy of non-negotiation—Skosana had initiated contact with the community council and the East Cape BAB, not much different from the kind of consultation which Motlana's SCA was initiating. Secondly he was criticized for not sufficiently emphasizing work issues. In September the new President, Moodliar, reaffirmed PEBCO's commitment to the one ideological change dealing with work issues but rejected the other.[120] What is interesting is that Motlana's position within Black Consciousness is revealed as unassailable. Despite being similar to Skosana in negotiating with Whites and being unenthusiastic about work issues, his position has not been challenged. In this rests the ANC's hope of partaking in any possible future negotiation. But in Motlana's opponents rests the ANC's other constituency of the Black working class and trade union movement.

As the representative of this particular constituency, Nkondo's stand on negotiation is crucial. In January 1980 Nkondo was suspended from the presidency by a vote of nine to five. The reasons given included his nullification of the policy of non-negotiation through his contact with Helen Suzman of the PFP, a White United States Senator, and with White journalists.[121] The support which Nkondo received was surprising. Despite their own stand on the issue of negotiation, Motlana, the SCA, PEBCO, and the *Post*

Transvaal did not support Nkondo. His support came from WASA, COSAS, and AZASO—significantly those organizations most strident at that time in upholding the Black Consciousness tenet of avoiding contact with Whites. This meant that the main defenders of the figure who symbolized the new emphasis on class, but who was not averse to negotiation in private, were the representatives of the faction whose support for non-negotiation was strongest. The conclusion to draw from this is that the non-negotiation faction are prepared to forgo this tenet in order to retain the emphasis on class. In fact, Motlana, as the main critic of a class analysis, was instrumental in Nkondo's suspension. Rather than back Motlana, the non-negotiation faction preferred to back the figure who at least combined his *ad hoc* negotiation with an emphasis on class and labour issues. What makes these schisms more cross-cutting is that as further evidence for Nkondo's suspension Motlana listed Nkondo's description of African trade unions as 'spineless'—in other words, Nkondo's departure from the new ideological emphasis on class and labour issues which Motlana himself has never publicly supported.[122] The new President, Mrs Melane, reaffirmed AZAPO's commitment to the policy of non-negotiation and the development of a better relationship with the trade unions. In a interview with the *Sowetan* on 1 July 1981, the Publicity Secretary of AZAPO confirmed these two beliefs. For this she had the support of those elements in Black Consciousness who were then negotiating and consulting with Whites of all political opinion and those who were ambivalent on the issue of class.

This suggests that either Motlana's position on class is not as ambivalent as it seems or (more likely) that there is a process of retrenchment by the moderate elements taking place, to claw back ideological gains won by the radical element by first having the symbolic figurehead of this radical element suspended on grounds acceptable to the radical element. The *Post Transvaal* sought to silence any defence of Nkondo by arguing that now he was suspended Blacks needed unity.[123] Motlana's position, therefore, seems unchallengeable; he was not censured for sending his children to a White school, a fact which emerged at the same time as Nkondo was censured for limited contact with liberal Whites. The constituency within Black Consciousness which Motlana represents is the faction which has gone furthest in trying to accommodate the ANC's need for internal political surrogates but has gone the least distance in finding an ideological accommodation with the ANC over class.

At a crucial meeting of the main Black Consciousness organizations Motlana got Nkondo's suspension confirmed. In May 1980 Motlana explained that these differences with AZAPO were the result of competing for the same constituency. Several meetings had been held to discuss the problem but no agreement had emerged over a demarcation of responsibility or role. This implied that the reorganization of 1979 restricting Motlana and the SCA to a local civic role in Soweto was being reopened for further consideration. In which case, in assuming responsibility for the wider national political role, Motlana would be in a position to advance the cause of negotiation and act as the ANC's internal wing. Despite the exiling of Botha and the suspension of Nkondo, the organizational dimension to this alliance will become stronger if Motlana's leadership position within Black Consciousness strengthens in the way that it seems Motlana wishes it to, for Motlana's earlier links with the ANC are the strongest. It seems unlikely, therefore, that the ANC will be faced with the choice of jettisoning its racial inclusiveness.

The oddity is that Motlana's critics in Black Consciousness are also unlikely to jeopardize any co-operation with the ANC because of their ideological agreement with the ANC over the issue of class and labour problems. The co-operation seems assured whichever faction in Black Consciousness is in the ascendency. What may jeopardize it is the ANC's unwillingness to be tethered to a philosophy which contradicts its basic class approach. This will depend on how much the ANC wants an internal political wing. The description of Motlana as a 'patriot' suggests that the ANC supports him and the faction he represents: the willingness of an organization to act as internal political surrogates comes above any ideological difference. But this does tend to make the alliance very dependent on ideological debates within each side, in addition to its dependence on the non-intervention of the state.

These internal conflicts continued after 1980, but in such a way as to strengthen the link with the ANC. At a meeting in May 1981 to discuss 'the interpretation of Black Consciousness ideology', 200 representatives of Black Consciousness organizations sought a compromise on the race and class issue by declaring that race was a class determinant. Quite what this means is uncertain: one suspects it was designed to be vague. None the less, the meeting remained committed to forging a link with workers and the trade union movement, describing them as 'the hub of the South African struggle'.[124] More significantly, COSAS and AZASO thought through the logic of a class analysis and, in 1981, came out in favour of consultation with Whites of all political persuasions. They rejected contact with Blacks working in 'apartheid structures', presumably Inkatha and the community councils. At Lenasia township near Soweto in June 1981 they bitterly attacked AZAPO as a reactionary body because of its stand on negotiation. At a joint meeting, the SCA, COSAS, AZASO and the South African Council of Churches committed themselves to the ANC's famous Freedom Charter. Two tenets from the Charter show the extent of the change in Black Consciousness ideology which identification with the ANC has forced upon it. The Freedom Charter above all sees the liberation struggle as a racially inclusive one in which all races can share and is committed to a negotiated settlement where possible. The ANC has won a great deal from Black Consciousness to enable some of its present exponents to argue in support of these two beliefs. In conjunction, before it was banned in 1985, COSA opened itself up to membership from all races and supported the SCA in its limited moves toward consultation with the dominant racial group. Ever since the suspension of Nkondo, AZASO has split with AZAPO and refuses to have any contact with it. Motlana's position has strengthened. He has won a powerful constituency within Black Consciousness and now has radical student representatives on his side. Motlana is furthering the identification of Black Consciousness with the ANC. He read the eulogies at two ANC funerals in 1981. None the less, the link with radical student organizations can only be tactical and remains a potential source of schism, for the young students are committed to a class analysis, while Motlana's public pronouncements at least ignore this and he has come out in support of private enterprise. The link with the ANC seems to be more important than such differences at the moment. It should be emphasized that the decision by COSAS to open itself up to membership from all races was a token gesture, for legislation prevented Whites from becoming members, but it was not an empty one, for it clearly identified COSAS as desiring racial integration. The same applies to the

PFP's decision in December 1984 to open itself up to membership from all races, although this has caused some internal disputes, with four PFP MPs resigning their portfolios in protest. The gestures by COSAS and the PFP became even more significant in 1985 when it was announced that the Prohibition on Political Interference Act was to be repealed in 1986, but COSAS was banned before this could happen. The repeal does not open up the possibility of Africans being elected to one of the Houses of Parliament by standing for a multiracial party, for the new constitution provides that a candidate for election to one of the three Houses of Parliament must be a member of the population group of that House. This effectively bars any African from standing for election, but they can be a member, organizer or campaigner for any party.

In 1981 efforts were made by the Committee of 10 and the South African Council of Churches to achieve a reconciliation between Black Consciousness groups and 'non-exclusivist democratic groups' committed to the principles of the Freedom Charter. This, unfortunately, excluded AZAPO as its leaders remained committed to a position where they refused to negotiate with 'non-equals'. This excluded contact with Whites, although they were prepared to meet with other Black organizations. The insistence of these other organizations on non-exclusivism ruled out any contact with AZAPO. COSAS and AZASO accused AZAPO of being reactionary, although AZAPO did argue that 'historic' political organizations like the ANC, PAC, and Black People's Convention should be unbanned. There was pressure from within AZAPO to moderate its stance on racial exclusivity. Speaking at the national conference in 1982, Strini Moodley, a former publicity director of SASO, said that Black Consciousness had to realize that the oppressor was capitalist as well as White. This suggests that capitalism could be the focus of attention rather than Whites alone, yet AZAPO's leadership at the conference committed the organization to a simple policy of avoiding contact with all Whites. At the funeral service of a leading AZAPO official, the role of Whites in the struggle for meaningful change was criticized by many speakers and described as hypocritical. This was at the same time as COSAS was holding its annual congress, at which the theme of worker–student action was dominant. Representatives were there from the White student union NUSAS. AZASO's congress in 1982 was attended by delegates representing all the English-speaking White campuses.

The commitment of the student organizations to racial inclusivity has led some commentators to argue that student organizations have progressed beyond Black Consciousness and can no longer be taken as representative of this tradition.[125] This is correct if we assume that Black Consciousness itself has not progressed. When such a claim is made Black Consciousness is viewed in its traditional form whereas the themes of Black Consciousness philosophy have progressed and the student organizations are typical representatives of that change. It is for this reason that AZAPO has established a student organization more in accord with its view of Black Consciousness. The Azanian Students' Movement was inaugurated in July 1983 at a meeting addressed by a former SASO official and the President of AZAPO. The President of AZASM said that its establishment was a reaction to the movement of AZASO from Black Consciousness to non-racialism. AZASM adopted a Black Consciousness stance, recognizing AZAPO as the legitimate liberation movement for Black people and advancing the theme of worker contact but no contact with Whites. It recognized the importance of Black community projects as a viable and effective method of promoting Black self-awareness and self-reliance.[126] This view of Black Consciousness is itself a departure from its traditional form because of the emphasis on worker and trade union activity, but clearly this view of Black Consciousness is more orthodox than that held by COSAS and AZASO. These two organizations find themselves in conflict with the more orthodox sections of Black Consciousness, who have not so easily overthrown some of the earlier concerns; also in conflict are those community groups who represent the more radicalized Black Consciousness faction, such as PEBCO and the SCA. In 1982, for example, PEBCO, COSAS and other community organizations in Port Elizabeth commemorated the defiance campaign and the foundation of the Freedom Charter, and stressed the need for 'different race groups' to co-operate in order to achieve democracy in South Africa. In that year also the Black Students' Society at the University of Witwatersrand co-operated with the White Students' Representative Council to nominate Nelson Mandela as chancellor of the university.

In 1980 MWASA, the unaffiliated union representing Black

workers and journalists in the media, reaffirmed its belief in Black Consciousness. It was not clear what precisely the union meant by the term for in October the annual congress stressed that the union could not work without co-operating with other unions. By the next annual congress pressure was being applied from delegates for the union to open itself up to membership from all races. It was agreed in principle that this should be done and a special conference was convened in 1984 to rewrite the constitution to allow this. Until the repeal of the Prohibition on Political Interference Act in 1986 trade unions were among the few politically active organizations which could be multiracial. Clearly MWASA's reaffirmation of Black Consciousness was reaffirmation of a radicalized version. Thus, in its calendar of holidays for a future Azania, the union celebrates Black Consciousness figures like Biko and Heroe, and the banning of Black Consciousness organizations in October 1977, but also Labour Day, the foundation of the Freedom Charter, and the banning of the ANC.

All these conflicts within Black Consciousness groupings centre around the extent to which organizations which once expressed support for Black Consciousness philosophy in its orthodox sense are prepared to accept an ideological and organizational change which more clearly identifies Black Consciousness with the themes, support base, and organizational structure of the ANC. There is universal agreement that Black Consciousness should progress to the stage of adopting a class analysis of apartheid and its overthrow. Some organizations within the Black Consciousness tradition have thought through the logic of this analysis and are ready to accept contact with Whites. Others are resistant to this degree of change. Consequent upon this schism, the former faction within Black Consciousness is identifying itself more clearly with the ANC through a series of political campaigns and policy statements. This is the case even when this faction is divided within itself over a number of other issues. These internal conflicts seem to be less important than the united front they wish to present in their conflict with the other faction in Black Consciousness centred on AZAPO.

The conflicts which closer association with the ANC has brought for Black Consciousness groups are more clearly shown in the campaign against the constitutional proposals during 1982–4. This is because certain factions within Black Consciousness identified even more closely with the ANC through the formation of the UDF which was established to co-ordinate opposition to the constitution. The other faction, centred around AZAPO, rejects the UDF and its emphasis on the Freedom Charter and supports instead the more orthodox Black Consciousness themes advanced by the National Forum Committee.

POLITICAL OPPOSITION TO CONSTITUTIONAL CHANGE

In May 1982, after two years' deliberation, a government commission published its constitutional proposals.[127] They included the establishment of the office of Executive President, chosen by an electoral college composed of members from the legislature, for a term of seven years. The Executive President would appoint a Prime Minister and an Executive Cabinet. Members of the Cabinet need not be elected members of the legislature but could be the Executive President's personal appointees. The Executive Cabinet was to be multiracial with no fixed ratio of representatives from the White, Asian, and Coloured communities. There was to be a single legislature, similarly multiracial. However, in the legislature a distinction was made between matters of common concern, which were to be discussed by that group alone. Below this was to be a second tier of provincial government constituting eight multiracial metropolitan authorities. Coloured and Asian representation would come from Coloured and Asian members of the third-tier local councils, which are not multiracial. The municipal authorities were to be nominated, but by whom was unclear. They were to replace the present provincial councils, elected by voters in the four provinces. Africans were included in the structure only at the third-tier level, having their own segregated local councils. It was not envisaged that any representatives would be nominated by Africans to the second-tier level.

The proposals provoked considerable debate in South Africa. Among the English speaking newspapers and the liberal Afrikaans press fears were expressed about the dictatorial powers of the President. As the country's chief executive officer the President has the power to appoint and dismiss the executive; not being elected on the popular vote, he was accountable to no one. No mechanism was provided for his removal from office in mid-term. It was also noted that there was a diminution of representative government at the executive and provincial levels, with members from both being appointed nominees. The degree of power held by Coloured and Asian members of the executive or legislature was unclear, but the proposals did not specify a fixed ratio of members in each, to avoid the possibility that Whites would have a numerical majority in both and hence enormous *de facto* power. No participation was defined for Africans, thus excluding the largest Black community and 67.3 per cent of the citizenship of South Africa in 1980. In contrast, the right wing of Afrikaner nationalism and the conservative Afrikaans-speaking press dismissed the proposals as power-sharing with Blacks and a threat to White self-determination. However, it was made clear that the proposals were only interim and that the government invited debate upon them.

The differences that emerged with the publication of the government's proposals in August 1982 are an indication of the lobbies which the government had listened to in the intervening months. The Executive President was to have a term of five years. Fixed ratios were defined for the electoral college, with Whites having 50 members, Coloureds 25, and Asians 13, thús ensuring that Whites had the permanent right to elect the country's chief executive officer. The Cabinet was to be only partially appointed by the President. There are to be 35 members elected from the legislature, but on a fixed ratio—20 White, 10 Coloured, and 5 Asian. In addition the President would nominate 25 members who need not be elected representatives. There was to be a single legislature, but now divided into three separate chambers, one for each of the population groups. Elections were to be on separate rolls. The size of each chamber was at first to be equal. Yet the real power of the legislature lay in the electoral college, where Whites had a permanent numerical majority. Subsequently the size of each chamber was varied, with Indians having 40 seats and Coloureds 80. Their representation on the electoral college is proportional to the number of seats, thus assuring Whites a permanent majority. Control has been institutionalized in another way. The legislative function is divided between matters of common concern, to be discussed by each chamber separately, and matters of community concern to one or other of the groups, to be discussed by that group alone. The Executive President will decide which matters are of common concern. Joint sessions of the three chambers were originally to be allowed for ceremonial purposes only. Matters of common concern were to be discussed separately and when there was disagreement between the three chambers the Executive Cabinet would arbitrate. In 1984, however, legislation was introduced to permit joint sessions 'within the terms of the joint rules and orders' of Parliament. It is not clear what this means and ambiguity still surrounds the nature of those issues which can be discussed jointly.

It was specifically stated in the proposals that the President and the Cabinet will not be subject to motions of censure and no confidence from the legislature. This constitutes a diminution of role for the White English-speaking opposition parties (a point which van Zyl Slabbert made when he resigned as leader of the Official Opposition in 1986), although it is more an attempt to prevent radical parties within the Black chambers from utilizing their position to challenge the government. This isolates even further one half of the White voters in South Africa who do not support the National Party. A greater isolation is felt by Africans. Apart from some exceptions at the local level, Africans remain excluded from the proposals. The Prime Minister has categorically confirmed that there will not be a fourth chamber for Africans, although in 1985 they were given seats on the non-elected President's Council, chaired by Koornhof, who has hinted at the eventual possibility of Africans being incorporated in the constitution at the executive level. This tends to obscure the real powerlessness of the Asian and Coloured chambers. There is no sharing of power, merely an unequal division three ways: it is not a shared Parliament but three separate ones. The fixed racial rations constitute a permanent entrenchment of White power.

The dynamic behind this framework is clear. The constitution over emphasizes ethnicity. While ethnicity is undoubtedly one of the realities of South African society, there are other factors at work which provide possible sources of cleavage. The constitution institutionalizes ethnicity despite the reality of common problems requiring an inter-group approach. It assumes that matters can be divided into two unambiguous categories—those that relate to one ethnic group only and those that are common. Very few issues in practice can be categorized as ethnically exclusive. Most issues involve some aspect of inter-group relations. Moreover, in excluding Africans, the constitutional rearrangements completely fail to deal with the central issue of the relationship between Whites and Africans. This exclusion reveals the assumption that White and African interests are irreconcilable. Inter-group relations therefore remain dominated by fear and mistrust. Thus, the existing White Parliament remains the arbiter of change and has retained the important functions for Whites. In many ways, the process of constitution-making is as important as the final constitution. Blueprints are largely evaluated on the basis of the method by which they are formulated. The present constitution is the product of the existing White Parliament and does nothing to engender African support.

With regard to the two Black communities which are allowed some participation, the policy of the government remains fixed around two principles: that co-operation takes place at an executive level only, and that Whites remain the senior partner. Neither principle is the basis of a just political system. The rearrangement of the political system does not in any way prejudice the hold which the National Party has on power. The criteria for enacting this rearrangement are not the moral claims of the majority, but the interests of the minority. The Prime Minister admitted that 'the White group's feelings of security and permanence have to be considered'.[128] Even the liberal Afrikaans newspaper *Beeld* wrote that the criterion must be 'the fears of the Afrikaner that the loss of self-determination will mean abdicating from our own back-yard'.[129] Therefore, the constitution is an uneasy reconciliation of two opposing forces, one rising from the tide of Black expectations, the other from White reaction. Yet it is impossible simultaneously to extend civil liberties to excluded groups and retain a White monopoly on political power. With the present constitution White monopoly has not been breached and there is no threat whatsoever to White self-determination.

The Labour Party's decision to participate in the Coloured assembly came after a long period of vacillation. This probably reflects the considerable degree of pressure the party came under from the government and radical critics in the Black communities. It was also mindful that without its platform in the disbanded Coloured People's Representative Council the party would shrivel and die. In the run-up to its national congress in January 1983, it seemed that the Labour Party members were evenly divided over participation, but in the final vote only ten delegates opposed it. According to an internal poll conducted among 1,000 party members in 1982, 75 per cent believed that the proposals could be a useful tool in achieving reform; 82 per cent believed that the party should continue to negotiate with the government; and 78 per cent rejected the view that the party should remove itself from sponsored platforms.[130] The party's decision was condemned by its partners in the South African Black Alliance, which is dominated by Inkatha. Strong tensions were aroused, especially in the Western Cape, and the party was subject to considerable harassment from its opponents. Many of its meeting were physically disrupted and it eventually stopped holding public meetings in the Cape. Clearly the party did not take the Coloured community with it but, although it was branded as an apartheid collaborator, the decision was generally in line with the party's longstanding strategy of reform from within the system. Just as the party stood for the old CRC as a means to its destruction, Hendrickse professes himself fully committed to the destruction of the new constitution. He is committed to evolutionary politics and he recognizes that, while from a Black perspective the constitution is only a small step, from a White perspective it is a greater leap. It is understandably difficult for Hendrickse to persuade Blacks that they need to look at the constitution from the White perspective.

Similar optimism is expressed by a variety of Indian parties who agreed to participate. Dr J. N. Reddy, leader of Solidarity, emphasized that the party's commitment to the constitution did not mean that it would stop pushing for further and more meaningful change.[131] Amichand Rajbansi, leader of the Indian National People's Party, reassured audiences at election rallies that the Indian House of Delegates would oppose all legislation which was discriminatory. Without taking in the consequences of the remark, he did none the less explain the emptiness of such a reassurance: the White House of Assembly 'can regularly outvote us, and deadlocked issues, matters and bills which we reject can be adjudicated by the President's Council where we will be outnumbered'.[132]

The election campaign did little to win the Coloured and Indian communities over to the constitution in view of the evident powerlessness of the Indian and Coloured legislatures. The government managed to reinforce the strongest arguments of the boycott campaign by rounding up more than 100 leaders and activists in the boycott on the eve of the poll. The final results showed that 29.5 per cent of registered Coloured voters turned out, representing an estimated 18 per cent of the total number of Coloureds qualified to vote. The Labour Party took 76 of the 80 seats in the Coloured House of Representatives. Hendrickse had predicted a poll of at least 60 per cent in his own constituency but had to be satisfied with 46.5 per cent. The most telling results came in the heartland of the Cape, where a dozen seats were won with polls below 10 per cent. No party had a clear majority after the elections to the Indian House of Delegates; Solidarity and the National People's Party had 17 and 18 seats respectively. The percentage poll was 20.2 per cent. Polling was marked by violence in several parts of the country, and police used tear gas and rubber bullets to disperse demonstrators opposed to the elections.

In order to justify the claims of Asian and Coloured politicians who participated in the new Parliaments that they were meaningful institutions, the government announced a number of changes which the new Parliaments finalized or ratified. During 1984 it announced the introduction for 1986 of a uniform identity document for all races which abolished the African 'pass'; it indicated that the 'labour preference' in the Cape which protected Coloured workers from African competition, and which has been criticized by both Coloured and African politicians, was to be abolished; that Coloureds and Indians were to have greatly extended local government powers; and that the Mixed Marriages and Immorality Acts were to be scrapped, which they eventually were in April 1985. None of this assuaged the opposition of most of the African community to the constitution.

The political debate about the constitution which had taken place from 1982 onwards proved to be a tremendous political stimulus for both supporters and opponents of the change. It was this issue which split the National Party and led to the formation of the Afrikaans dominated Conservative Party. Within the Indian and Coloured communities there has been an explosion of new political parties fighting with the established parties for a place in the new Parliaments. In all a dozen new political parties were formed or old ones resurrected. In the election to the Coloured

House of Representatives, 207 candidates were nominated for 80 seats. This heightening of political activity is likely to be short-lived, for the Parliaments will probably experience the same deflation of interest and activity which characterized the homeland legislatures once they were demonstrated to be ineffective institutions.[133] The Conservative Party, however, is likely to be a permanent feature barking at the heels of the government. This has proved to be one of the unintended consequences of constitutional reform. One other unintended consequence was the effect the constitutional debate had on the excluded African community. These consequences are also likely to be permanent. Inkatha opposed the plans and its South African Black Alliance split. Buthelezi warned his fellow partners in the alliance who were considering participation that they were risking African violence against Coloureds.[134] FOSATU condemned the proposals and was moved for the first time to comment openly and directly on an overt political issue. This itself has reduced the conflict between it and the more politicized unregistered unions. A number of local alliances occurred among opponents of the reforms. Bodies like the Eastern Cape Co-ordinating Committee and the Transvaal-based Ad Hoc Anti-President's Council Committee were formed.

Attempts by the Black Sash in 1981 to hold a national convention of all Black political and community groups had failed. Motlana said such a convention would be futile. The constitutional proposals were obviously more persuasive than the arguments of the Black Sash, for in addition to the local political alliances which occurred in 1983 Black political unity emerged within two broad factions centred on the UDF and the NFC.

The UDF originated in the campaign for a boycott of elections to the South African Indian Council at the end of 1981. The boycott succeeded in keeping the polls down to 10 per cent. The Anti-SAIC committees formed to mobilize the boycott were instrumental in reviving the Transvaal Indian Congress and the Natal Indian Congress in early 1983. In January 1983 a steering committee was set up to establish the UDF, following a call by Allan Boesak, president of the World Alliance of Reformed Churches, at the Transvaal Anti-SAIC congress, for progressive forces to unite in resistance to the government's constitutional proposals. Regional structures were formed in Natal, Transvaal, and the Cape during the summer. The national organization was launched in August at a meeting attended by 12,000 people, and with the support of over 500 organizations. Delegates representing 575 organizations attended the inaugural meeting on 20 August 1983. The delegates came from community and civic organizations, trade unions, sporting bodies, women's and youth organizations and political organizations. These included AZASO, Soweto Committee of 10, the SCA, Soweto Residents' Association, Release Mandela Committee, COSAS, PEBCO, MWASA, General and Allied Workers' Union, SAAWU, South African Mineworkers' Union, Detainees' Parents' Support Committee, and various Black Students' Societies. Messages of support came from SWAPO, the UN Committee Against Apartheid, international labour movements, and in South Africa from FOSATU, the GWU, and other trade unions and organizations. The patrons of the UDF elected at the conference included Hassan Howa, Nelson Mandela, Helen Joseph, Dennis Goldberg, Martha Mahlangu, mother of Solomon Mahlangu, Beyers Naude, and Johnny Issel. The elected presidents were Archie Gumede, a prominent ANC activist in the 1950s and chairman of the Release Mandela Committee; Albertina Sisulu, another former ANC activist; Oscar Mpetha, of the African Food and Canning Workers' Union; and Popo Molefe, a member of the Soweto Committee of 10. Other elected office-bearers had been involved in such organizations as SASO, the Black People's Convention, the Natal Indian Congress, and the Soweto Civic Association. Terror Lekota, publicity secretary of the UDF, was a former organizer of the GWU. Allan Boesak, of the World Alliance of Reformed Churches, is also a very prominent figure in the UDF.

The aim of the UDF, according to Gumede, was to achieve maximum unity among all democratic people, including Whites. This was emphasized by the election of a multiracial set of patrons. Boesak said that the 'politics of refusal', that is of non-collaboration, needed a united front. The national committee emphasized that although the UDF articulated the viewpoint of a wide cross-section of people, 'the main burden of exploitation and discrimination' fell on the working class and the main thrust of the organization should be towards class issues and the participation of working people.[134] Thus, at the national launch of the UDF resolutions were passed which condemned British and American imperialism, expressed solidarity with workers in their fight for a fair share of the wealth they created, attacked the migrant labour system, and expressed concern over relocations. The conference adopted a declaration which stated that its aim was to create a united democratic South Africa free from homelands and group areas and based on the will of the people. There was a need for unity with all democrats regardless of race, religion and colour. In a subsequent meeting Boesak reacted to criticisms of the UDF for its inclusion of Whites by saying that Blacks should not let their anger become the basis of a blind hatred of all White people. Not all Whites supported apartheid. Gumede called for a unity between all democratic organizations. At the same meeting, the president of the General and Allied Workers' Union presented the problem as one of class. It was a case of one class oppressing another rather than of one race oppressing another. Thus the need was for a powerfully based mass political organization which was non-racial and capable of waging a political struggle on behalf of all the oppressed and exploited.[135]

The UDF is a popular front rather than an organization, and this has a number of consequences. As a front the UDF cannot make policy for its affiliates. The affiliates take up UDF campaigns in ways suited to their own activities and constituencies. The UDF emphasizes the importance of a strong grass-roots organization provided by its affiliates. It has learnt this from Inkatha. Secondly, because of its structure, the voting power of the UDF's affiliates is not proportional to their membership. All affiliated groups have equal voting power within the front. Thirdly, its overall size is very large. The UDF claims a membership of two million, which makes it the largest political movement in South Africa's political history. This total represents the membership of all its affiliates, and it is difficult to gauge the commitment which members of affiliate organizations have to the umbrella organization of the UDF; but UDF meetings draw enormous crowds and the harassment it is subjected to from the state suggests that it takes the UDF very seriously.[136]

The NFC is open to membership from Blacks only and thus restricts its contact to exclusively Black organizations. In June 1983, 800 Blacks representing about 100 organizations met in Hammanskraal following a resolution at the February AZAPO conference which called for a common front among Black organizations against the government's constitutional proposals.

AZAPO was also concerned about the decision in January to form the rival front centred on the UDF. The meeting was convened by a committee whose members included Phiroshaw Camay from the South African Council of Churches, Bishop Tutu, and Tom Manthata, a member of the Soweto Committee of 10. Saths Cooper, formerly of SASO, was convener of the meeting. He said that the NFC was launched in response to the crisis facing the oppressed and exploited Black masses. There was the same concern with oppression and exploitation as with the UDF, but the NFC emphasizes race more than the UDF. Speakers at the launch included Manas Buthelezi, of the Evangelical Lutheran Church, Neville Alexander, from the South African Council for Higher Education, and the President of AZAPO. Tutu called for maximum unity among Blacks and asked them to forget ideological differences. This unity was to be around the notion that racial capitalism was the main enemy. This allows the NFC to emphasize class and worker issues while still retaining a concentration on race. It is from this that the exclusion of Whites follows. Not surprisingly, AZAPO is the driving force behind the NFC and its themes dominate the policy and approach of the forum.

It has been claimed that the UDF is within the ANC tradition while the NFC is within that of Black Consciousness.[137] This is very simplistic and shows no regard for the internal conflicts and schisms within Black Consciousness organizations. The UDF is clearly identifying itself with the ANC and yet it also receives support from many Black Consciousness groups and supporters. These include ex-SASO figures, Curtis Nkondo, ex-president of AZAPO, Motlana and the Committee of 10, CUSA, MWASA, SCA, COSAS, and AZASO. It has of course, many organizations who fall outside the Black Consciousness tradition. For example, at the 1983 annual conference of AZASO, at which it committed itself to the UDF, addresses were delivered by Nkondo and Boesak, as well as by a former member of the Soweto Students' Representative Council and former SASO members. The position of MWASA is ambiguous. Some of its branches are affiliates to the UDF, and Zwelakhe Sisulu, President of the union, has spoken at UDF meetings; but formally MWASA has taken a stance where it refuses to affiliate to either the UDF or the NFC. This reflects its inability to side officially with either of the factions within Black Consciousness. Other Black Consciousness organizations have resolved this dilemma by affiliating to both, e.g. CUSA and the Committee of 10. Bishop Tutu has also taken this position. Conversely, the NFC has the support of the more orthodox faction within Black Consciousness, which includes AZAPO and AZACTU. Thus it too has supporters who are ex-SASO, the most notable of whom is Saths Cooper.

There are some organizations who are not affiliated to either, and not just because they do not wish to choose between two factions within a divided Black Consciousness tradition. The major non-racial trade union grouping in South Africa, FOSATU, rejected overtures to join the UDF although it expressed its support for the organization. A number of other independent unions did likewise. FOSATU pointed out that its members supported a variety of political organizations and identifying with one could cause divisions within the unions.[138] COSATU took this position on its formation in 1985. The General Workers' Union, which also refused affiliation but none the less expressed support for the UDF, did so on the grounds that it wished at present to place emphasis on strong worker organization. The formation of the UDF highlighted divisions within the trade union movement: the publicity secretary of the UDF, who is also a former organizer for the GWU, argued that the UDF was important because it recognized the workers' struggle and that this struggle did not end at the factory gates.[139] Many unions are affiliates and must also recognize this about the UDF. Indeed, the *South African Labour Bulletin*, in one of its briefings on the trade union movement and the UDF claimed that the unions were the most important organizations to join the UDF.[140] Unfortunately the NFC has not published a list of organizations which attended its launch or are affiliated.

The political affiliations of the UDF and the NEC ought more accurately to be described in the following manner. The NFC subscribes to the more orthodox position in Black Consciousness, while the UDF is associated with the ANC and the radicalized faction within Black Consciousness. The formation of the UDF therefore symbolizes the increasing importance of the ANC to political mobilization inside South Africa and the increasing association between the ANC and the radicalized faction within Black Consciousness. Thereby it also symbolizes the continuing divisions within contemporary Black Consciousness.

The UDF's connection with the ANC is becoming more openly and daringly expressed. Many of its affiliate organizations have identified themselves with the ANC ideologically and now, of course, also organizationally. Many individual members and office bearers are former ANC activists. Some affiliate organizations were also connected with the ANC in the 1950s, such as the Transvaal and Natal Indian congresses. It is significant that many of the organizations grouped within the UDF subscribe to the ANC's Freedom Charter. The front as a whole has clearly identified itself with the charter. This has led to criticism from many quarters. It is the Freedom Charter which the UDF has adopted, not the later 'Strategy and Tactics' statement where the themes of working-class struggle and armed conflict are more prominent. Some critics have claimed that the Freedom Charter is *petit bourgeois*,[141] and this has allowed some opponents to describe the UDF as 'radical *petit bourgeois*'.[142] The UDF is not ambiguous in its support for a worker-led struggle and it does see the problem as a class problem. It has gone even further in this than the NFC because it recognizes that class is more important than race and not merely a disguise for it.[143] Yet the UDF is ambiguous in its position on violence: this is a tactical posture designed to avoid further state repression. It may also reflect the influence of Black Consciousness groups within the UDF. The UDF describes itself as non-violent and opposed to armed struggle, but it follows this declaration by stating that violence is caused by the government. It warns that the patience of Blacks is fast wearing out and that violence may well be the outcome. Motlana expressed this same belief many times during 1980. So while it does not openly support armed struggle, the UDF does not dismiss it either. UDF figures have condemned action against ANC bases and often lead the oration at the funerals of ANC guerrillas. Motlana has also done this in the past. This earns the UDF the contempt of the liberal press in South Africa.[144]

Despite this ambivalence, the ANC welcomes the attention and support of the UDF. The external mission of the ANC has stated that it supports the UDF. Referring to this expression of support from the ANC, the publicity secretary of the UDF said that the two organizations could never be affiliated because the one was illegal and had a strategy encompassing violence while the other was committed to non-violence. However, the support of the ANC was welcome.[145] This is as much as could be expected when identification with the ANC and armed struggle is considered a serious crime. At the level of practical action the two organizations are associated. In May 1984, 6,000 people wearing UDF shirts and ANC colours attended a funeral. The service was addressed by Archie Gumede, president of the UDF, who read the message from 'Uncle Oliver' in Lusaka, believed to be Oliver Tambo, the ANC President.[146] In June 1984, 5,000 people attended the funerals of two ANC guerrillas in Port Elizabeth. The coffins were draped in the black, green and gold colours of the ANC and banners of the UDF were displayed before the coffins in the procession.

The NFC also criticizes the UDF for its expressions of support for the Freedom Charter and supports the ANC's emphasis on class, while rejecting the racial inclusivity associated with the ANC and the charter. The NFC advances the claims of its own 'Manifesto of the People of Azania'. This was adopted at the conference in 1983 and includes a set of fundamental principles, among them anti-racism and anti-imperialism, non-collaboration with the oppressor and his political instruments, an independent working class organization, opposition to all alliances with ruling class parties, and the paramountcy of workers' interests. Saths Cooper said that the manifesto was a natural development of the 1955 Freedom Charter and the 1976 Black People's Convention. He criticized the Freedom Charter's emphasis on racial inclusivity and, more importantly, its recognition of minority group rights. This attack on the charter drew a strong response from its supporters. Curtis Nkondo, a former AZAPO president, said that the charter could not be regarded as outdated since none of its demands had been met, and because it expressed support for the idea of guarantees for Whites.[147] This recognition that Whites require some guarantee of their rights in a future multiracial South Africa, although it is consistent with independence in Zimbabwe, has been criticized by the NFC as racism and the perpetuation of ethnicity. This is symptomatic of the conflict between the two broad fronts. Indeed, it seems that the conflicts between the radicalized and orthodox factions within Black Consciousness have resurfaced as a conflict between the UDF and the NFC. What it represents is a fundamental disagreement over the strategy by which liberation is to be achieved. It is agreed that it is to be achieved through mobilization of workers on class terms, but it cannot be agreed what role Whites are to play in liberation. This division is a long-standing one in Black politics and goes beyond the internal schisms within Black Consciousness; indeed, it gives these schisms their meaning. The NFC's base in orthodox Black Consciousness places it in the tradition of the PAC, and the NFC successfully brings together people from the old PAC and the newer Black Consciousness groups. The UDF's advocation of the Freedom Charter reopens the conflicts between the ANC and PAC but on this occasion aligns with the ANC a new generation of trade unionists, community activists, women's groups, student organizations, religious groups, and political activists, some of whom are from the radicalized Black Consciousness tradition. This latter group includes such organizations as COSAS, AZASO, MWASA, PEBCO, CUSA, SCA, and the Committee of 10, and such personnel as Nkondo, Boesak, Motlana, and Zwelakhe Sisulu, all former stalwarts of more orthodox Black Consciousness.

The conflicts between the two broad fronts have been acrimonious. AZAPO attacked the UDF as ethnic and in line with Pretoria's apartheid policy. This criticism is made despite the fact that the UDF, and many of its affiliates like the Transvaal Indian Congress, are open to membership from all races including Whites (as was COSAS before it was banned), and the fact NFC and its affiliates, like AZAPO, exclude Whites. Nelson Mandela's daughter Zinzi attacked the 'ideologically lost political bandits' who rejected the Freedom Charter and diverted the struggle.[148] However, there is a form of communication between them through those Black Consciousness organizations which are affiliated to both. The UDF has said that it is prepared to discuss with AZAPO the possibility of joint action. This occurred after the deaths of five people at the University of Zululand in November 1983 for which the UDF and AZAPO agreed that Buthelezi and Inkatha were to blame. In 1983 AZASO announced that it was prepared to work with AZAPO to rid South Africa of apartheid. While there are differences between the UDF and NFC over the participation of Whites and their role in the liberation struggle, there is some overlap in support and common ground in the total rejection of government-created political structures. This extends to unity in opposition to the new constitution, to the apartheid society which the constitution governs, and to those Black politicians who participate in it. They are also unified in being equally subject to state harassment.[149] Although the UDF was at first unimpeded by state action, after it had consolidated itself several key figures were detained for varying periods. In addition a series of bans on UDF meetings was served. Other organizations whose meetings were banned included the Release Mandela Committee, the Transvaal Indian Congress, and AZAPO. AZAPO estimated that at least twenty-three meetings by Black Consciousness organizations were banned in 1983. Especially during the second half of 1983 in the period before the White referendum, the government attempted to stifle opposition by using its legal power to ban meetings. This followed the lifting of a number of detention orders on individuals and constituted an alternative means of control. Almost all the bans were directed at the UDF, AZAPO, and the Release Mandela Committee. The UDF successfully challenged one of the bans in court. Even where meetings were not banned, the government responded with harassment of organizers or participants and the seizure of literature. After the court ruled that the police should release confiscated literature, much of it was classified as undesirable and prohibited. Some organizers came under harassment from the narcotics squad, while motorcades were classed as illegal meetings and banned. In June 1984, fourteen people were arrested for allegedly breaking a by-law by sticking UDF posters on municipal property. Prior to the elections to the new Black Parliaments thirty-five leading figures of the UDF were detained. Some detainees who were released by the courts were immediately redetained. Six took refuge in the British Consulate in Durban. After a protracted period of refuge all but one of the individuals were arrested on leaving the consulate. In an unprecedented move to quell protests in the townships over the elections, the government planned a joint manoeuvre between the police and the military to cordon off townships and arrest leading activists. The UDF was threatened with banning in November 1984. To be banned would be counter-productive to the ANC's interest, since it would be denied the opportunity to reassert itself politically inside the country. Yet to become cautious might risk disappointing the high expectations which the UDF's political activity has aroused. The government is also under some pressure not to prohibit the organization for fear of the international and domestic repercussions; thus it is likely to continue to harass the organization without formally banning it. In 1984 the Transkei government banned within its borders the UDF, AZASO, and COSAS, although during the state of emergency in 1985–6 the South Africa government banned only one of these organizations, COSAS. Boesak, however, was detained for a short period and legal action has been taken against many UDF leaders and regional officials.

The UDF has started to shift in focus away from the highly public acts of open opposition to the constitution towards the more grass-roots issues affecting the daily life of township residents. This is less a response to government harassment than an admission that the constitution will not remain the highly intense emotional issue it was in 1983–4. If the front is to survive this deflation of interest and fervour it has to move into other areas. This is also true of the NFC, but the UDF particularly has begun to articulate other issues. To some extent it realized that this needed to be done from the very beginning, for its conference resolutions covered a wide range of issues. The UDF was active in campaigning against the local authority elections in the African townships and it attacked the new legislation governing influx control. It has pledged to consult with people regularly to represent their views on their day-to-day problems. While the strongest support for the UDF is in the urban areas, reflecting the greater politicization in those parts, the UDF has begun a programme of organization in the rural areas to challenge the dominance of Inkatha among this constituency. Locally in the townships the UDF has become involved in campaigns against higher rents and increases in general sales tax. Through its connection with the trade unions it is active in industrial matters. Clearly the UDF is trying to link 'insider' and 'outsider' interests in a way which emulates Inkatha, and the ANC in an earlier period, and which was never true of orthodox Black Consciousness, cut off as it was from migrants and rural dwellers.

Far-reaching consequences follow from the degree of unity which presently exists around the two broad groupings of the UDF and the NFC. History shows that the issue of racial inclusivity has been an unresolvable source of division and it is difficult to see the UDF and the NFC coming to agreement. None the less, the unity of the various organizations within each umbrella structure is itself significant. It parallels the move towards unity within the trade union movement and between the trade union movement and political organizations. Through the UDF particularly, there is a closer involvement of the ANC in internal politics and a closer association between the ANC and the radicalized faction of Black Consciousness. If this particular association continues, or even strengthens, important developments will follow. This will be discussed further in the Conclusion. It is worth noting, however, that, among other things, it would link the professional middle-class support of Black Consciousness with the working-class support of the ANC. It would create a strategy of opposition based on revolutionary terrorism and open mass political mobilization. It would make labour and class issues more important to internal Black politics, thereby aligning the trade union movement with Black political movements and opening up the trade unions as a powerful constituency pushing for political liberation. It would isolate still further the moderate forces in African opposition, like Inkatha and the community councils. The final chapter demonstrates how Inkatha's position in the liberation struggle is increasingly isolating it from the radical opposition forces, and how these moderate forces are also uniting. However, before this, the role of literature in opposition will be discussed, for protest literature is inspired by the philosophy of Black Consciousness.

Notes

1. This notion has been elaborated in the author's paper, 'Apartheid, Change and Civil Liberties for the Black Communities in South Africa', for the European Consortium for Political Research, Workshop on Civil Liberties in Advanced Industrial Societies, Aarhus, Denmark, 29 March–3 April 1982.
2. A distinction has been made between the collaboration of Inkatha and the community councillors. Adam refers to the former as 'collaborative opposition', while the latter is merely 'opportunistic collaboration'. See H. Adam, 'Minority Monopoly in Transition: Recent Policy Shifts of the South African State', *Journal of Modern African Studies*, 18.4, 1980. However, the increasing co-operation between Inkatha and the Soweto Council suggests that Inkatha is similarly 'opportunistic'. This is the thrust of Chapter 6.
3. In the long term it is not 'conservative', for the development of class consciousness among workers by mobilization on plant-based issues has revolutionary consequences. In the short term, however, there is some justification for the view that some sections of the trade union movement are conservative (with a small 'c') because they refuse to

mobilize on extra-workplace issues. This can be a result of a number of factors which do not indicate a Conservatism with a large 'C', such as the fear of state reprisal, ideological unwillingness to blur the nature of plant-based issues, and controls of trade union activity, especially after the post-Wiehahn legislation.

4. J. Kane-Berman, *The Method in the Madness*, London, Pluto, 1978, p. 105.

5. T. Hanf, *South Africa: The Prospects of Peaceful Change*, London, Rex Collings, 1981, p. 316.

6. The beating up of Indian supporters by Zulu supporters is quite frequent after Sunday games in Durban.

7. This fact, unfortunately, is exploited by the pro-government *Citizen* newspaper. For example, see the issue of 19 August 1977.

8. The 1949 Zulu–Indian riots still remain a potent symbol of ethnic violence in Natal, which Chief Buthelezi sometimes alludes to for political effect.

9. F. Wilson, 'Current Labour Issues in South Africa', in R. Price and G. Rosberg, *The Apartheid Regime*, Berkeley, Institute of International Studies, 1980, p. 153.

10. The position of the Indian community is fascinating. Allegations of exploitation by Indian businessmen exploded into racial strife in 1949. The Indian community is aware of what liberation has meant in Black Africa. They are quick to react to any suggestion that they are turning their backs on Africans. In Natal alone the Indian community has given over R500,000 towards building African schools. But the fact remains that the state has offered a number of inducements in its liberalizations. This has intensified Indian feelings of marginality, which may push them further towards identification with Africans in order to avoid isolation from them.

11. A useful discussion of these concepts is found in A. D. Smith, 'Ethnocentricism, Nationalism and Social Change', *International Journal of Comparative Sociology*, 13, 1972.

12. Op. cit., p. 336.

13. See, for example, A. Phizacklea and R. Miles, *Labour and Racism*, London, Routledge and Kegan Paul, 1980.

14. T. Hanf, op. cit., p. 338.

15. Ibid., p. 266.

16. Ibid., p. 340.

17. Ibid., p. 342. See also L. Schlemmer, 'Black Consciousness: Pride and Dignity or Militancy and Racism', *South African Journal of Sociology*, 20, 1979, p. 2.

18. It has been noted many times before that a variety of Black politicians have claimed allegiance to Black Consciousness—Buthelezi and other homeland leaders are obvious examples. What they

tend to mean is their support for one or other of the main beliefs; but what distinguishes them is the quite different policy implications they draw from them.

19. G. Gerhart's book provides an excellent narrative account of Black Consciousness as does D. A. Kotzé's from another political standpoint. See G. Gerhart, *Black Power in South Africa*, Berkeley, University of California Press, 1978, and D. A. Kotzé, *African Politics in South Africa*, Pretoria, J. L. van Schaik, 1975. Unfortunately, both end their narrative in 1974–5. Gerhart points to the linkage between Black Consciousness and the PAC, but fails to appreciate the extent to which it was a new strategy after the hiatus following Sharpeville rather than a completely novel set of ideas.

20. On the formation of SASO see H. van der Merwe, *African Perspectives on South Africa*, Cape Town, David Philip, 1978. This is a reprint of a 1972 pamphlet by SASO called 'Understanding SASO', in which SASO makes a point of identifying its debt to a variety of precursors.

21. This is a view shared by many people; see particularly P. van den Berghe, *The Liberal Dilemma in South Africa*, London, Croom Helm, 1979.

22. *Frontline*, December 1979, carried an interesting article by a middle-class Black, entitled 'They Envy Me, The Fools . . .', which contained the following passage: 'I sometimes envy people who dig ditches. They know who they are. Me, I put on a good face but the feeling inside isn't good . . . I've become alienated without having succeeded.'

23. For example, see H. van der Merwe, *African Perspectives on South Africa*, 97, 105, 273–6, 279, 284.

24. Ibid., p. 102.

25. This view is criticized further in the author's article, 'Racial Politics and Nationalism: The Case of South Africa', *Sociology*, 16.3, 1982.

26. H. Blumer, 'Race Prejudice as a Sense of Group Position', *Pacific Sociological Review*, 1.1, 1958.

27. See, for example, P. Mtimkulu, 'Government-Nurtured Black Consciousness', *Weekend World*, 24 June 1977; S. Biko, *Reality*, March 1972; *Sunday Post*, 10 June 1979.

28. For example see SASO Newsletter, September 1971, p. 12. S. Variava, 'Black Consciousness', People's Experimental Theatre, Newsletter, September 1971, p. 4.

29. See H. van der Merwe, *African Pespectives on South Africa*, p. 71; BPC Information Brochure No. 1, 1973, p. 5; L. Schlemmer, 'Black Consciousness: Pride and Dignity or Militancy and Racism'; S. Biko, SASO Newsletter, August, 1970, pp. 19–20.

30. 'Azania' is derived from the Greek and means the land of Zan. The

name was first used in Ptolemy's second-century geography atlas to describe the east coast of Africa and was later adopted by Arab traders.

31. See L. Schlemmer, 'Black Consciousness: Pride and Dignity or Militancy and Racism', for the view of supporters who echo this belief. Motlana's views were expressed in the *Sunday Times*, June 1978; *The Cape Times*, 2 June 1978.

32. T. Hanf, *South Africa: The Prospects of Peaceful Change*, pp. 351, 439. Reporting in March 1982, the Buthelezi Commission rejected the idea of a unitary state with universal franchise, and advocated a federal solution for Natal initially, and for South Africa as a whole. This view was rejected by the government but supported in the Afrikaans press, as well as in the liberal English-speaking press. See the *South African Digest*, 12 March 1982, pp. 11, 21, 23.

33. B. Hirson, *Year of Fire, Year of Ash*, London, Zed Press, 1979, p. 7.

34. Ibid., pp. 4, 298.

35. See H. van der Merwe, op. cit., p. 93; SASO Newsletter, May 1971, p. 8; *Inkululeko yeSizwe*, August 1974.

36. *Inkululeko yeSizwe*, August 1974.

37. Ibid.

38. T. Hanf, op. cit., p.257; S. Variava, op. cit., p. 5.

39. For example, see BPC Information Brochure No. 1, 1973; *Inkululeko yeSizwe*, August 1974.

40. H. van der Merwe, op. cit., p. 119.

41. Ibid., p. 82.

42. On Black theology see H. van der Merwe, op. cit., pp. 293, 311, 315, 319, 324; Basil Moore (ed.), *Black Theology*, London, Hurst, 1973; Allan Boesak, *Farewell to Inocence*, Johannesburg, Ravan Press, 1977.

43. H. van der Merwe, op. cit., pp. 341–6.

44. Ibid., pp. 334–40.

45. Quoted by *Natal Mercury*, 8 December 1977.

46. B. Hirson, *Year of Fire, Year of Ash*, p. 284.

47. Ibid., pp. 84, 296, 299. Buthelezi makes this criticism and see also H. van der Merwe, op. cit., p. 77.

48. G. Gerhart, op. cit., p. 291.

49. SASO Newsletter, January 1972, p. 3.

50. Ibid.

51. B. Hirson, op. cit., p. 292.

52. Black Students' Society, Newsletter, March 1980, p. 9.

53. *Inkululeko yeSizwe*, August 1974.

54. Ibid.

55. SASO Newsletter, August 1970, pp. 19–20.

56. T. Hanf provides figures on the frequency of visits by urban dwellers

to homelands, and on the degree of social contact and identification, illustrating the urban-oriented nature of urban Blacks. See T. Hanf, op. cit., pp. 339, 440.

57. J. Kane-Berman, op. cit., p. 206.
58. Quoted in the *Nation*, vol. 3, No. 2, 1978.
59. Ibid., vol. 3, No. 1, 1978.
60. Reported in SAIRR, *Survey of Race Relations 1980*, Johannesburg, SAIRR, 1981, p. 325.
61. Quoted in the *Citizen*, 10 June, 1978.
62. See J. Kane-Berman, op. cit., p. 211, and SAIRR, op. cit., p. 312.
63. *Post Transvaal*, 25 March 1979.
64. Thebehali is a volatile political character. He was dismissed from the Johannesburg Chamber of Commerce, but went on to become Chairman of Soweto UBC. In 1975 he stood in the parliamentary elections for Qwa Qwa and lost. He joined Inkatha, then resigned, and has since rejoined. In the Soweto Community Council elections in 1978 he led the Sofasonke Party which was the largest single party represented.
65. *Post Transvaal*, 16 July 1979.
66. For an outline of the legislation see SAIRR, *Survey of Race Relations 1982*, Johannesburg, SAIRR, 1983, pp. 298–302, and SAIRR, *Survey of Race Relations 1983*, Johannesburg, SAIRR, 1984, pp. 253–5.
67. See SAIRR, *Survey of Race Relations 1983*, p. 253.
68. Quoted in the *South African Digest*, 9 March 1984, p. 7.
69. Quoted in SAIRR, *Survey of Race Relations 1983*, p. 93.
70. Quoted in the *South African Digest*, 6 July 1984, p. 3.
71. See SAIRR, *Survey of Race Relations 1983*, pp. 257–61.
72. Ibid., pp. 258–9.
73. *Post Transvaal*, 17 September 1979.
74. R. Stanbridge, 'Contemporary African Political Organizations and Movements', in R. Price and G. Rosberg, op. cit., p. 97, was mistaken in stating that the Committee had been banned.
75. Quoted by the *Weekend World*, 2 October 1977.
76. Noted by L. Nel, Nationalist MP for Pretoria Central, in the *Sunday Times*, 31 July 1977.
77. *Post Transvaal* documents an instance where the Dobsonville Chairman was able to intervene and grant a homeless couple a house. Headlines like these cause severe problems for critics of the councils. See the issue of 21 March 1979.
78. *Post Transvaal*, 16 April 1978 and 8 February 1979.
79. See, for example, the *Sunday Times*, 16 October 1977.
80. SAIRR, *Survey of Race Relations 1980*, p. 58.
81. 22 March 1979.

82. *Post Transvaal*, 10 June 1979.
83. See L. Schlemmer, 'Conflict in South Africa: Build Up to Revolution or Impasse?', European Consortium for Political Research, Freiburg, 20–5 March 1983.
84. 25 April 1979.
85. 4 September 1979.
86. T. Lodge, *Black Politics in South Africa Since 1945*, London, Longman, 1982, p. 355.
87. T. Hanf, op. cit., pp. 433, 435.
88. Op. cit., p. 113.
89. Noted by R. First, 'After Soweto: A Response', *Review of African Political Economy*, 11, 1978, p. 94.
90. T. Lodge, op. cit., p. 341.
91. E. Harsch, *South Africa: White Rule, Black Revolt*, New York, 1980; S. Nolutshungu, *Changing South Africa*, Manchester, Manchester University Press, 1982; J. Saul and S. Gelb, *The Crisis in South Africa*, New York, Monthly Review Press, 1981. Some Marxists dispute such a view: see particularly B. Hirson's *Year of Fire, Year of Ash*, London, Zed Press, 1979, and his 'Books on the 1976 Revolt', *Review of African Political Economy*, 11, 1978, p. 105. Other Marxists disagree with Hirson; see especially J. Saul and S. Gelb, op. cit., and R. First, op. cit., p. 97. Marxists in South Africa also agree with First. See F. Molteno, 'The Uprising of 16th June', *Social Dynamics*, 5.1, 1979 and 'South Africa 1976: A View from within the Liberation Movement', ibid., 5.2, 1979.
92. J. Saul and S. Gelb, *The Crisis in South Africa*, p. 132.
93. Quoted by L. Schlemmer, 'Black Consciousness: Pride and Dignity or Militancy and Racism', p. 2. However, there is evidence which suggests that the ANC was helpful to the Soweto Students' Representative Council in the protests of 1976. See J. Saul and S. Gelb, op. cit., p.109; Lodge, op. cit., p. 341. For a historical account of the contact between the ANC and Black Consciousness grouping see S. Nolutshungu, op. cit., pp. 141, 149, 150, 159–61, 179, 183.
94. F. Meer Papers, p. 70, n.d.
95. F. Meer Papers, p. 76, n.d.
96. SASO Newsletter, January 1972, p. 3, also noted by G. Gerhart, op. cit., p. 248.
97. 'Inkatha: The Paradox of South African Politics', *Optima*, 30, 1982, pp. 152, 158.
98. SAIRR, *Survey of Race Relations 1980*, p. 53.
99. *The South African Digest*, 2 April 1982, carries a report of the state's attempt at smearing any Black Consciousness–ANC link by getting a detainee to allege torture and violence supposedly committed by the ANC on Black Consciousness exiles.

100. *Post Transvaal*, 4 November 1979; *Sunday Post*, 25 November 1979.
101. 5 October 1979.
102. *Sunday Post*, 5 October 1979.
103. SAIRR, *Survey of Race Relations 1980*, p. 64.
104. *Post Transvaal*, 2 January 1980.
105. Ibid., 30 December 1979.
106. See SAIRR, *Survey of Race Relations 1980*, pp. 62–3.
107. May–June, 1980, p. 11.
108. Quoted in H. van der Merwe, op. cit., p. 326.
109. See the *Daily News*, 3 November 1979.
110. Ibid., 8 February 1982.
111. *Post Transvaal*, 30 April 1979.
112. Ibid., 18 November 1979, 9 December 1979, 11 December 1979.
113. *World*, 18 August 1977.
114. Quoted by the *Citizen*, 8 June 1980.
115. For example, see *Sunday Post*, 5 October 1979, *Post Transvaal*, 3 October 1979, 2 January 1980.
116. *Post Transvaal*, 6 July 1979.
117. Ibid., 23 December 1979.
118. Ibid., 7 October 1979.
119. SAIRR, *Survey of Race Relations 1980*, p. 57.
120. Ibid., p. 60.
121. Ibid., p. 56.
122. Ibid.; *Post Transvaal*, 15 January 1980.
123. See *Post Transvaal*, 16 and 21 January 1980.
124. All this is taken from SAIRR, *Survey of Race Relations 1981*, p. 28.
125. See, for example, C. Charney, 'Unrest Grows at "Mixed Race" University', *Times Higher Education Supplement*, 30 July 1981.
126. See SAIRR, *Survey of Race Relations 1983*, pp. 62–3.
127. For a discussion of the proposals see: D. Welsh, 'Constitutional Change in South Africa', *African Affairs*, 83, 1984; F. van Zyl Slabbert, 'Sham Reform and Conflict Regulation in a Divided Society: South Africa—A Case Study', European Consortium for Political Research, Freiburg, 20–25 March 1983.
128. *South African Digest*, 11 June 1982, p. 2.
129. 7 June 1982.
130. D. Welsh, 'Constitutional Developments', *Indicator: Political Monitor*, 1.1, 1983, p. 14; *Cape Times*, 5 January 1983.
131. For example: 'The constitutional developments create an atmosphere in which negotiations between all groups in South Africa can begin, and this course is more propitious at this crucial time in South African history than the strategy of boycott. Let us not despise small starts. The constitution offers to those communities which seek to

promote peaceful change a chance to put behind them the animosity that separates them because of the policy of apartheid. It is time for responsible leadership to look ahead rather than continually look back in self-destruction and bitterness. And it is significant that the proposals reflect an increasing awareness within South Africa of the need to move towards a broader sharing of power and the division of responsibilities. Once the process of change has been initiated it is irreversible and Solidarity believes that the momentum must be maintained. Solidarity accepts the procedure to achieve peaceful change by working within the constitutional framework.' *Sunday Times*, 20 May 1984, *South African Digest*, 15 June 1984, pp. 9–10.

132. *South African Digest*, 20 July 1984, p. 5.
133. See N. Charton, 'The Institutionalization of a Homeland Legislature', Association for Sociology in Southern Africa, Conference paper, Maseru, Lesotho, 26–8 June 1979, p. 1.
134. For example see his address on the opening of the Labour Party Congress at Eshowe, January 1983, and quoted in the *Irish Times*, 6 January 1983.
135. Quoted in SAIRR, *Survey of Race Relations 1983*, pp. 57–8.
136. Those who adopt a strict worker line abuse the UDF as being undemocratic because decisions are not taken by the members themselves with policy being formulated from above. It is also accused of blurring the working-class struggle because it does not mobilize solely on worker and plant-based issues. In this way the UDF is categorized along with many political unions as being radical *petit bourgeois*. See I. Silver and A. Sfarnas, 'Debates: The UDF', *South African Labour Bulletin*, 8.8, 1983.
137. For example, see D. Welsh, 'Constitutional Change in South Africa', *African Affairs*, p. 160.
138. See 'Trade Unions and the UDF', *South African Labour Bulletin*, 'Briefing', in the issue 8.8, 1983, p. 5.
139. Ibid., pp. 3–4.
140. Ibid., p. 3.
141. A. Mafeje, 'Soweto and its Aftermath', *Review of African Political Economy*, 11, 1978, p. 27. This view is disputed by L. Mqotsi, 'After Soweto: Another Response', 14, 1979, p. 104.
142. I. Silver and A. Sfarnas, 'Debates: The UDF', p. 104.
143. For an analysis of the views of the UDF and the NFC on racial capitalism see H. Adam, 'Racist Capitalism versus Capitalist Non-Racialism in South Africa', *Ethnic and Racial Studies*, 7.2, 1984.
144. For example, see *Rapport*, 7 July 1984.
145. Quoted in SAIRR, *Survey of Race Relations 1983*, p. 60.
146. See International Defence Aid Fund, Focus no. 54, September–October 1984, p. 10.

147. See SAIRR, *Survey of Race Relations 1983*, pp. 54–5.

148. Quoted in the *Irish Times*, 22 June 1983.

149. They are also criticized by Buthelezi. In the *South African Digest*, 3 August 1984, p. 4, Buthelezi is quoted as saying: 'the UDF direct all their energies at my political character assassination and vilification. They set the clock back as far as the Black liberation struggle in South Africa is concerned.' Elsewhere he has described them as Johnny-come-lately heroes (see Chapter 6). The UDF is also criticized by the Soweto Council. When he was mayor Tshabalala accused the UDF of causing township protests. However, he did call for a meeting with the UDF, AZAPO, AZASO, COSAS, and the Committee of 10 to discuss 'the misunderstandings which have caused the unrest'. He was referring to the service charge increases which the council were introducing. All the organizations refused to meet with Tshabalala, who was subsequently ousted from his position as mayor.

5

Black Literature and the Black Press

INTRODUCTION: ART AND POLITICS

Isaiah Berlin once said that ideas do not beget ideas as butterflies beget butterflies: meaning that they are social constructs. Ideas are made socially significant only if social actors consider them to be appropriate ways of seeing the world for the goals and purposes of their action. Whitehead referred to this when he argued that ideas emerge from a consciousness of shared feelings and action.[1] That is, they gain their currency and influence from their power to represent a view of social reality to the people who use or believe them. John Blacking put this point well when he argued that although a particular way of seeing the world may possess its detractors, this will not diminish the power of the idea to attract people if it springs from, and represents, the social reality these people experience and within which they act.[2] In other words, the most cogent ideas are those which symbolize or express real experiences and shared action patterns.

Two particular implications follow on from this. Language has an equally important role in social life because it conveys the ideas which symbolize shared experiences and common action patterns.[3] What it also means is that prose, poetry, and news stories, as particular constructs of language use, have their own dynamic in social life because they are special mechanisms through which this is communicated. In short, writing springs from an experience, with the author feeling an inner compulsion to explore the meaning of the experience. An empathy of feeling and interpretation produces resonances in the reader which are responded to. These resonances are the product of a shared experience of social reality with the writer. This is what sociologists mean when they refer to the 'social context' of writing—the shared events which the construct of language use tries to interpret and the common problems it labours to represent. Immediately this imparts to ideas, and the constructs of language use through which ideas are communicated, a role in politics by translating that shared conscious or physical experience of social reality which is the first ingredient for common political action. However, if thought, experience, and action are in symbiosis, it follows that social groups with different experiences within the structures of power can use the various constructs of language use to convey different ideas, which often communicate counterpoised visions of the world.

Mafika Gwala, writing in 1976 about the state of Black writing in South Africa, said of it: 'it means to us the structuring of an alternative context to the apartheid context . . . Apartheid is there. We revoke it. Black writers do have a Black experience.'[4] Aimé Cesaire once said that the function of art is to state a problem. There is only one problem which manifests itself in Black South African writing: the thesis advanced here is that Black literary and journalistic writing is an expression of the shared Black experience of degradation, humiliation, and oppression under apartheid, and that due to this experience Black writing has been politicized so that it communicates the shared Black rejection of apartheid and the common vision of a free multiracial world. There is a corollary to the thesis. Because Black writing conveys an idea at odds with how the dominant racial group see the world, two results follow. First, it has been politically suppressed to prevent it communicating its idea, which is reflected in the severe harassment suffered by Black authors and journalists and the injudicious use of banning orders on newspapers and literary works. Secondly, various forms of language use will be employed by the dominant racial group to convey their opposition to this idea and to forward their own way of seeing the world, which is reflected in the rejection of certain kinds of Black writing by the White 'liberal' literary establishment. None the less, despite the suppression of their way of seeing the world, this has not diminished the power of the idea to attract Blacks or reduced the appearance and popularity of literary and journalistic writing which communicates this idea, because they spring from and represent the shared physical experience of social reality for Blacks under apartheid.

A BRIEF HISTORY OF BLACK LITERATURE IN SOUTH AFRICA TO 1976

The development of Black literature parallels an international phenomenon, where a rich, colourful, working-class literature evolved from working-class dissatisfaction either with writing as a leisure-class activity for a privileged audience, or with young well-spoken men disguising themselves in dirty worsted trousers and trying to write a proletarian novel at second hand. As one author put it, the impetus to Black writing was to present 'true Black writings by Blacks, for Blacks and about Blacks'.[5] The 'Black way of life' had been represented by Whites since their first contact, reducing the Black experience almost to an anthropological museum showpiece for White consumption. Chief Lennox Sebe once complained that most translations of Black literature were collections of myths, legends, and fables, creating the impression that it consisted of nothing but tales about the tortoise and the spider.[6] Any brief survey of Black literature shows this impression to be false.[7] Thomas Mofolo was one of the first accredited Black authors in South Africa. His first novel, written in Sotho, was published in English in 1920, but he is primarily remembered for the classic *Chaka the Zulu*, recounting the Zulu Chief's tireless battles with the British. The notion of conquest and the absorption of one society by another through colonialism reappears in Solomon Plaatje's work. As a Tswana, he wrote a booklet, *The Mote and the Bean*, defending the right of Blacks against the Boer. His novel *Mhudi*, published in 1930, is a tale of a people whose inherited land was ravaged by the Zulu, the British, and finally the Boer; and he who is bitter writes about bitterness. R. Dhlomo's Zulu novel, *An African Tragedy*, and Yosia Ntava's, *Headman's Enterprise*, were written in the 1930s and both wrestle with the mysteries of power, greed, and wrong done to a proud people. H. E. Dhlomo's poem, 'The Valley of the Thousand Hills', written in 1941, tells of this 'wrong-torn land': 'Midst these sweet hills and dales, under these stars / To live and to be free, my fathers fought / Must I still fight and bear anew the scars . . .'[8]

Despite this long tradition, it was the decade after the war which witnessed the greatest development in literary work. From the beginning of the 1950s African nationalist movements linked literature with liberation. Conferences of Black writers sprang up as offshoots of the Pan African congresses. A *Pan African Cultural Manisfesto* was formulated in 1956. A young generation writing for *Drum*, a Black literary magazine which politically supported the ANC, commercialized Black literature for the first time. It was only in this period that Black literature conveying the idea of Black liberation was widely read by Blacks themselves. Among the contributors to *Drum* were Themba, Rive, Sentso, Motsisi, La Guma, Modisane, Matshikiza, Maimane, and Nkosi. Commercialization was at the cost of artistic merit and critics have since bemoaned the modern, journalistic, urbane style of *Drum*.[9] The contributors were acutely aware of the magazine's readership and of its primary aim, which was to reach the Black masses, and reserved their literary ambitions for other works—Ezekiel Mphahlele wrote *Down Second Avenue* in 1957, portraying life in a crowded Black ghetto near Pretoria; Bloke Modisane wrote the now famous *Blame Me On History*; La Guma published *A Walk in the Night* and *And a Threefold Card*; Nkosi wrote a play called *The Rhythm of Violence*; and Matshikiza composed a musical *King Kong*.

Bitterness turned to invective as the 1950s ended. The beginning of the decade had been marked, above all, by an optimism. The full vagaries of Afrikaner domination had yet to be witnessed. Chief Luthuli expressed this: 'the world seemed to be opening up for the Africans, it seemed mainly a matter of proving our ability and worth as citizens.'[10] The political activity by which Blacks articulated their demands was still possible. The end of the decade saw the Sharpeville massacre, the outlawing of peaceful protest, and the banning of the nationalist liberation movements. The relative powerlessness of Blacks dawned and most ·Black writers left the country. They did so either to escape arrest, harassment, and oppression, or because they were expelled after release from prison. Nearly all well-known writers went into exile abroad— Abrahams, Mphahlele, Modisane, La Guma, Brutus, Nkosi, Hutchinson, Ngubane, and Maimane. Themba and Matshikiza died in exile, Ngubane and Mphahlele have since returned to South Africa and undergone a political metamorphosis, professing support for Chief Buthelezi's Inkatha movement. For the rest, they can only find their inspiration in the increasingly distant memories of their home. As Wauthier noted, the very titles of their recent books identify their dilemma: *Home and Exile* by

Nkosi, *Poems from Algiers* by Brutus; before he returned, Mphahlele wrote *The Wanderers*.[11]

On reflection, not only did the new decade of the 1960s witness a political hiatus, there was also a literary lacuna. *Drum* suffered from political censorship and effectively folded as a serious literary journal in 1965. A line in one of Plomer's poems serves as an epitaph to this literary generation: 'hope dying of wounds'. Hence Wauthier could complain that the generation after Sharpeville produced no outstanding novelists among those remaining in South Africa.[12] This remained the case until Mtutuzeli Matshoba's *Call Me Not a Man* appeared in 1978, after the Soweto uprising. Literary quiescence paralleled very closely the state of Black political opposition, so that the re-emergence of vociferous Black protest in the form of Black Consciousness in 1969–70 caused a reinvigoration of literature. Black Consciousness is imbued with an appreciation of art and a recognition of the role of literature in Black life. In short, it is an appreciation of everything Black. This has consequences for the relationship between literature and politics. Inasmuch as this self-appreciation is linked initially to self-awareness, and eventually to 'Black' awareness, everything 'Black' becomes political, including art and literature, because it aids conscientization and Black unity. Thus, a Black Consciousness newsletter said, 'the sixties witnessed the death of relevant Black movements. However the seventies placed us on a threshold of renaissance in the form of Black Consciousness. The time is ripe for the practical implementation of Black Consciousness through the creativity and development of all the arts, music, poetry . . .'[13] This editorial is saying something significant about literature and politics. The Black arts are not separated from the rest of Black life, but are linked with it and take their content from it, because both are manifestations of a shared experience called 'Black Consciousness' which embraces everything Black. Encouraging this conscientization by literature, among other things, is the key strategy in political change.

The same sense of humiliation and degradation as in previous generations is there, but the new generation is characterized by its evocation of struggle, pain, and blood. It falls short of the explicit advocation of violence, yet its poetry is full of violent images. Oswald Mtshali's volume of collected poems, *Sounds of a Cowhide Drum*, alludes to the poverty and impoverishment of townships.

Serote has published *Yakhal' Inkomo*, an evocative title referring to the cry of agony of cattle being slaughtered. James Matthews' poem 'Cry Rage' is a better example, with lines running: 'Rage sharp as a blade to cut and slash', 'only blood can appease the blood spilled over three hundred years'. Sol Variava's poem 'Rape of the Land', itself a forceful title, includes the lines: 'They clench their fists / Pick up their spears / For the spear lives on / And must be well fed and nourished.' It refers to Whites as 'Mother fuckers from the gutters of the West'. 'Mother fuckers' is meant in a historically literal sense and in the metaphorical sense of 'Mother Africa'.

In 1973, a number of Black theatre movements, including Shiquomo in Soweto and Black Theatre in Lenasia, formed a group called the People's Experimental Theatre, whose motto was 'the spear lives on'. An editorial from the group explained their motto: 'shiquomo means spear, and this we use as a symbol of fighting'.[14] Other theatre groups already existed, such as the Shah Theatre Academy, Oceanview Group Theatre, Luyolo Players, Serpent Players, and Theatre Council of Natal. The South Africa Black Theatre Union was formed in Durban during July 1972 to co-ordinate these local theatre movements. The impetus behind Black theatre was the same as that at the root of Black literature. The South African Black Theatre Union expressed this in its publicity preamble: 'SABTU recognizes the fact that we, as the underprivileged, dispossessed, disqualified people in this land of our birth, have a need for art that is essential to the ultimate realisation of our self-respect and dignity. SABTU works on the basis that Black theatre is a people's theatre which will encourage activity that encompasses the experiences of Black people in this land of ours.'[15] This point is emphasized in the name of People's Experimental Theatre. Nomsisi Kraai, in PET's newsletter, explained PET's views of Black theatre: 'Black theatre is a dialogue of confrontation, confrontation with the Black situation.'[16] Its philosophy of bringing art to the people was reminiscent of 'negro theatres' initiated by the civil rights movement in America. Both were 'a revolutionary theatre' attempting to portray the reality of Black experience through drama. The link between them was cemented by the popularity in South Africa of Mackay's play *Requiem for Brother X* about Malcolm X.

The allusions to blood and fighting brought down the full

powers of the state in censorship.[17] In 1974 PET was banned, as was Variava's poem 'Rape of the Land', along with the main stalwarts of the Black theatre movement like Mosokoane, Kraai, Ismail, Molewa, Moosa, Modise, Mkize, Khumalo, Gamede, and Mokoctla: their offence was participation in 'terroristic activities' in contravention of Sections 2, 4, 5, and 8 of the Terrorism Act. The state realized the power of words. What it did not consider was that whereas a particular way of seeing the world may be suppressed, this will not diminish the power of the idea to attract devotees if it springs from, and represents, the social reality which these people experience: no amount of suppression has diminished revolutionary Black literature or the role this plays in conveying the vision of a free, multiracial world. Nowhere is this failure more apparent than in the upsurge in Black literature after the Soweto uprising in 1976.

POST-1976 BLACK LITERATURE

Black writing since the uprising has remained within the Black Consciousness tradition, where an appreciation of Black art is linked to a general Black self-awareness. As previous chapters have demonstrated, the uprising witnessed an increase in African revolutionary consciousness. One of its consequences has been an intensification of Black self-awareness because of both participation in the revolutionary struggle and the experience of its aftermath. As Black self-awareness has increased, so has an awareness of Black art. Theatre groups and associations of playwrights, poets, artists, and authors have sprung up in townships throughout the country. The first was probably the Azanian Poets' and Writers' Association (later Medupe), which used to hold fortnightly meetings in Orlando, Soweto. It was banned in 1977. Since then there has been formed the Zamani Arts Association in Dobsonville, Soweto; the Soweto Art Association; Khauleza in Alexandra; Morpa Arts Association, Randfontein; Madi at Katlehong; Bayajula Artists in Kwa Thema; Kwanza Creative Society, Mabopane East; the Mbakasima Group at Sebokeng; Mpumalanga Arts, Hammersdale, Natal; Gujo Book Club, Sibasa; Ga-Rankuwa Arts Association; Maokeng League of Painters and Artists; and the Creative Youth Association. The latter first began at Diepkloof, Soweto, in early 1977, as a group of young students at Madibane High School. Under the leadership of Manaka and Makhetha, groups sprang up in other schools. As the name indicates, the association encourages creativity among the young in all the arts. It receives the help of Kay Hassan (painter), Oupa Mojatau (musician), Mitchell Paledi (musician), and John Ledwaba (actor). Its philosophy is to align art with politics: 'nothing will separate the truth, and nothing will justify injustice. Our main aim—to bring political self-awareness to our people through art.'[18]

It is wrong to suggest that all literature and art intends to have this function. The increase in state expenditure of African education to prevent a recurrence of the 1976–7 incidents, and the increasing reliance, in the rural schools especially, on indigenous languages, have meant that official South African publishing houses bring out more and more short novels, stories, and collections of poetry in Zulu, Xhosa, Sotho, and Tswana in order to provide literature for those teaching these languages. This is inherent in separate development where art is seen as one of the main mechanisms by which ethnic self-identity is fostered. The intended market for these works, plus their government sponsorship, colours their content. Since the content is of a type which most of the best of South Africa's Black writers disagree with, much of the work is abysmally mediocre. None of the winners of prizes for books in the vernacular periodically awarded by the government has so far been translated into English.[19] The most notorious of these authors is perhaps Credo Mutwa, a witch-doctor resident in Soweto—what Mayer would call a traditional urban dweller who fails to adapt to urbanization and who escapes in reversion to the past.[20] His most famous book is *Africa is My Witness*, which glorifies his Xhosa upbringing. His house in Soweto is frequently attacked by radical Black forces; to the Cillié Commission on the Soweto uprising he gave evidence that supporters of Black Power started the flare-up and recommended the intervention of the army to break the influence of such modernizing urban tendencies as Black Consciousness.

These exceptions apart, most Black literature since the uprising, as before it, is a gesture of protest. There is a preoccupation with the evils of repression, police brutality, arbitrary imprisonment, degradation, and defiance. It is the kind of protest literature which has earned the contempt of what are called the more 'serious' Black artists, like Ezekiel Mphahlele.[21] Most of those who make this complaint are in exile (Mphahlele has returned) and are not suffering the experience which those Black writers are conveying in their work. If thought, experience, and action are related, those lacking a particular experience, or feeling it at second-hand, lack an essential ingredient to their thought. This is the explanation of why the White literary establishment rejects the new Black literature. Some White liberals like Paton and Sampson take recourse in romantic notions of love and human brotherhood and fail to appreciate the inadequacy of these themes after the Soweto uprising. Thus, Sampson wrote in a preface to *South Africa Writing Today*: 'the theme of racial conflict can become an obsessive one: the humiliations and revenges of oppression can drown everything else, like sex in pornography, losing all characters and compassion in the whirlpool . . . It makes for bad writing.'[22] To impose conventional literary standards is to lose the essential 'Blackness' which forms the experience the literature is translating. That is why Gordimer's anthology included few modern Black writers, despite its title, while the anthologies of Butler and Parker contained none.[23]

It is valid to contend that there is an inverted racism at the root of this, disguised by being presented in terms of 'standards', when these standards are knowingly artificial and unjustifiable, given the experience which Black literature is translating. The art-for-art's-sake movement in South Africa, represented by many in the White literary establishment, takes recourse in the outdated nineteenth-century notion that art is distinct from social reality. In this view art is for the artist, being a translation into another form of inner artistic compulsions. While it can be enjoyed and interpreted by others, the privacy of the artist's passion is reified. However, if we see the primary objective of art as communication, it is difficult to ignore the response it evokes in the audience.

What is reified in Black art is the process of communication between the artist and audience. It is *designed* to elicit a response —its point is to foster self-awareness. Because of the political implications of this awareness in South Africa today, Black art *is* politics. While it does involve the translation into artistic forms of inner compulsions, these drives are primarily political. To attack Black writing because of this is not only to misunderstand it completely, it is also to be oblivious to any relationship between art and politics. As Parker suggests, the critic who falls back on the view that art and politics do not mix really means that a particular kind of politics should not be brought into literature.[24] In the conditions of South Africa the very statement that politics and literature are separate itself brings politics into art: it involves a political judgement—that politics is too irrational to become involved with; it involves a political misconception—the failure to see that, however irrational, politics affects every decision of the daily lives of Black artists; and it has political consequences—it supports apartheid *de facto* by failing to condemn it. In other words, in situations as explosive as South Africa there can be no refuge in a private world of art.[25]

With the White literary establishment, politics is implicit in their art. Black writing in South Africa differs only because it is explicitly political. There are two different ways in which politics permeates Black literature. The first adopts a deep, quiet, often cryptic, but none the less incisive, approach that is calculated to enervate apartheid, stripping it of any moral validity. The writer either tends to address the oppressor or calls the attention of the concerned throughout humanity. The analogy in the title of Essop Patel's poem 'Black Analogy' is clear: 'The night is Black / She is Black / So is coal / When kindled / Black glows bright and beautiful.'[26] The pivotal emotional and economic role of the mother in African tradition, even in patrilineal kinship systems, makes for the frequent theme in Black poetry which draws an analogy with 'Mother Africa'. The vision of this beautiful, bountiful, fecund land parallels the vision of women in African tradition. Sikhalo kaMthembu's poem 'Cry Not Little One' is a good illustration of this: 'Cry not little one / Moan not little one / Mamma will live to love and raise / Cry not my love / Mamma rests / She is not dead.'[27] Mother Africa is the mother who will return to love and raise South Africa to its rightful place. Compare the quiescence of this with Glen Masokoane's poem 'Black Nana' which presents the imagery of a Black liberator born of a Black mother who is raped and then murdered by the White father unable to face his Black son. 'Black Nana' is used to describe the mother, the liberator, and the object of liberation, but it is put in language which is brutally sensuous. 'Rape them, fuck them, spoil them, arise Black Nana.'[28] The significance of making the father White is to present in this imagery a statement of the Black–White relationship in Africa as one of rape and pillage. Mabuse Letlhage's poem 'Crossroads', addresses the same theme but in a different manner. 'Jesus' cross / Reminds me of roads',[29] referring to the pillage of the Crossroads squatter camp.

This poem contains another theme which is characteristic of this type of protest literature, namely its recourse to the moral justness of Black rights, undermining on either humanitarian or Christian grounds any moral justification for racialism. Mabuse Letlhage's poem 'Need I' appeals on humanitarian grounds: 'Need I convince anybody / That underneath this Black skin of mine / There flows human blood.'[30] The idea of Jesus as a Black, which was common in the American civil rights movement, is cleverly rephrased in Abia Diutloileng's 'Black Jesus Christ': 'Jesus is in South Africa / As a Black man at Crossroads / He is suffering more than / He suffered on the cross.'[31] A common link across the colour divide in South Africa is the sharing of the same religion, and Duitloileng uses this to appeal to the oppressors to consider the similarity between Jesus' suffering and that of Blacks in South Africa.

The characteristics of this kind of protest literature are the powerful analogies and metaphors it makes in an almost diffident manner. In contrast, the second type of protest literature is much more openly aggressive, preferring a truculent, angry attitude meant to inspire a direct and physical confrontation with oppression. Here the audience tends to be fellow Blacks, who are summoned to assess their situation and act in a direct manner. The imagery of violence, confrontation, and hate runs through this like a thread.

The collection of essays by Mtutuzeli Matshoba, *Call Me Not a Man*, is autobiographical; he considers the Soweto uprising to be the moment when 'my country became my enemy'. He was born in the early Soweto, and the sprawling city forms the context against which he documents 'the contemporary Black experience in South Africa', from the townships of the Reef, the arid Transkei homeland, to the tiny prison island of Makana. The collection was published in 1978 and was quickly banned by the government. The period since 1976 has seen the publication of Mothobi Mutloatse's *Forced Landing* and Maria Tholo's *The Diary of Maria Tholo*, which records the coming of the revolt to Guguletu in the Cape and the mood of resistance it fostered. N. C. Manganyi has published *Looking Through the Keyhole*. At least three collections of photographs have been published by Black photographers, and a new journal *Staffrider* has emerged to cater for Black literati, although it also publishes the work of a few White authors. Its publisher is Ravan Press, who also bring out *New Classic*, which caters less exclusively for Black authors. Ravan Press in Johannesburg has begun a 'Books for Africa' series and a series on 'Books for the Children of Africa'. Bateleur Press in South Africa is doing likewise. These exist alongside the Heinemann African Writers Series. Ravan Press are also beginning to publish Black playscripts. The magazine *Frontline* publishes a great deal of Black poetry.

The publishing forum of *Staffrider* is very much the focal point. Both Matshoba's book and Miriam Tlali's *Muriel at Metropolitan* are collections of short stories first published in *Staffrider*. It describes itself as a magazine featuring 'committed writing and graphic art in the context of post-Soweto South Africa'—which is an apt description of Ravan Press as well. So one has to see the growth in this kind of protest literature after the uprising as partly a function of the availability of publishing channels which have transformed it from its confinement within secretive literary groups meeting privately into something visible to the public gaze. In the post-1976 period there has developed a definite market for this type of protest literature, to which its growth must be related. The causal factor, however, is not its generous patrons but rather the desire to convey, in language use, an idea, a way of seeing the world, now appropriate to the social reality which Blacks experience. That literature conveying this idea sells and has a definite market is evidence that it is expressing the experience of post-1976 Black life well enough for them to feel the resonances and want to buy it. So Black writing in South Africa has returned to its position in the *Drum* period: it is openly flaunted rather than restricted either to the circumscribed readership of party political organs or to private consumption at select group meetings. What the uprising has done, therefore, is not only to foster the growth of Black literature but also to make it more visible.

A survey of *Staffrider* from its inception in March 1978 until the July–August edition of 1979 shows a fair balance between short stories, poems, graphic art, and photographs. It is a forum for the best of the new generation of Black authors, as well as for the 'apprentices', as Chief Lennox Sebe described them, throughout the literary groups in the Republic. Some of the work has all the crudity of first beginnings, but, it could be said, it lacks the literary pretensions of 'serious' writing. It is none the less of value because it is expressing, in language use, a real experience, however crudely that experience is translated.

The majority of the work is of the angry, confrontationist type of protest literature. Seven themes seem to crystallize in poems of this kind:

1. The influence of the Soweto uprising on their work and the new era that has dawned since. In this category one could include Gottschalk's 'Anniversary', Patel's 'Black Recollections', Maake's 'June Sixteenth' and Mthimkulu's 'Nineteen Seventy-Six'. Maake expresses this quite simply: 'their tears flooded our hopes.'[32]

2. The continuation of oppression and the timelessness of apartheid. Examples here would be Asvat's 'Possibilities for a Man Hunted by SB's' (Special Branch), kaDitshego's 'Ghetto', Rachilo's 'The Shebeen', Bafana Buthelezi's 'Black Mother', Motaung's 'Garden Boy', Mphulo's 'Destitutes in the City', and Rabothata's 'Soweto is . . . . .'. Bafana Buthelezi is an exiled Black radical in Botswana and his poem is a poignant one to his aging mother, full of sorrow at their separation and of anger that it must be so. It is also full of hope, containing this reassurance for her: 'Your plight is my plight / Your freedom is my career.' Through him she will 'Regain the whipend / Of what is yours by right'.[33] 'The Ghettoes', by kaDitshego, is likewise prophetic, comparing Black life to life in the womb, thus bringing into the poem the symbolism that eventually Blacks will depart from their predicament as embryos depart their womb.

3. Defiance. Icaboth Maubane's poem 'Nostalgia' is worth quoting at length on this. Lamenting in the first verse for 'the beloved faces of home', recalling 'childhood friends', he uses the term 'home sickness' in the third verse in a dual sense—as nostalgia and as literally the sickness of his native land. At this point the defiance emerges: 'Home sickness / You bring sorrows to miners, prisoners, boarders and exiles / You torture, you haunt me / You frustrate and assault me / Yet I've one thing to thank / Nature gave us power.'[34] Since Blacks are in all other senses powerless, this 'power' can only refer to the power of his skin that comes from an awareness of its colour.

4. References to grief, sorrow, sadness, and the evocation of tears, not just in a self-pitying way, but expressing a sorrow that now they have to hate and take recourse to physical confrontation. A powerful graphic example of this is Ntsu kaDitshego's untitled drawing in *Staffrider*, March 1979, showing, within the image of Africa, a small South African child crying. The sun is dawning over the hills and perhaps the tears are not only for the deprivations which that particular day brings, but for what must be done for true enlightment to dawn in South Africa. In poetry, this theme is found in Molahlehi waMmutle's two poems recounting his suffering on Robben Island, 'My Sanctuary' and 'Dedicated to My Only Sister', also in Maupa Kadiaka's 'Love', Maoka's 'An African Woman', Makungo's 'Peace', waLedwaba's 'It Hurts to be Lonely' and 'All That I Live', and kaMthembu's 'Cry Not Little One'. A verse from Kadiake epitomizes the sadness of South Africa: 'And my love turns to hate / How I who used to hate hate before / Love hate now.'[35] Hate in itself is sad, but the sadness is deepened because hate rebounds on hate, which is something most Black writers are aware of. Mtutuzeli Matshoba's short story *A Pilgrimage to the Isle of Makana* expresses this dilemma: 'When I start hating I do not expect the reaction to be love. I expect a reaction equal to my action, a relationship of hate for hate. So if I hate, the same hatred boomerangs on me with the same intensity.'[36] It is precisely this realization which causes the sadness when faced with a situation where they see hate becoming inevitable.

5. Relief from oppression through direct action, physical confrontation, and the allusion to violence. Examples are Letlhage's 'Untitled', Sefakwe's 'My Thoughts', Kadiaka's 'The Fighter', waLedwaba's 'Freedom', and Manaka's 'Don't Delay'. Letlhage expresses the principle behind this theme succinctly: 'Let's die now and live later.'

6. In memory of dead comrades, the imprisoned, or the banned. Because of the many to whom homage is due, this is a prominent theme, found in such poems as Skeef's 'Prayer for Steve Biko', Diphoto's 'Lament for a Former Detainee', Marema's 'The Island', Pillay's 'Letter to Bandi' and 'On Friends', Banfana Buthelezi's 'Tribute to Mapetha', Gottschalk's 'Letter to a Widow' and 'The Assassination of Richard Turner', Them Sanqa's 'Song for Steve', Banoobhai's 'For Fatima Meer', and Mthimkulu's 'Tribute'. As Banoobhai subtitled his poem for the formerly

banned Black sociologist Fatima Meer, these are people for whom there is 'so much love'.

7. The theme of 'Africa' and the close identification of South Africa's problems with those of Africa generally. This is not meant in the narrow sense of Pan Africanism, although orthodox Black Consciousness is within this tradition. It is meant primarily as a message to South African Blacks that their victory over colonialism and externally imposed oppression will triumph as it did in the rest of Africa. Exemplifying this are Lebethe's 'Afrika', Diutloileng's 'The Black Newspapers', kaMnyayiza's 'When Will It End', Skeff's 'Afrika' and 'My Peace With Life', and Thusini's 'Afrika, Afrika'. One of the essential points in this theme is a belief that Africa can bring peace, emphasized by Skeef's poem particularly. In 'Afrika' he makes the plea for Africa to help her 'children in South Africa to be free'. Diutloileng's poem is explicit on this: 'Oh Mother Africa / Help to free your children / From the claws of the hawk.'[37] In certain instances practicalities intervene in poetic metaphor, and some poems contain a bitterness arising from the realization that so far Africa has done little. Lebethe writes: 'I stretch out my hand / But where is your touch / Cold air strikes me instead.'[38]

THE ROLE OF PROTEST LITERATURE

South Africa presents a paradox, for there is an abundance of conflicts that give rise to protest literature but an absence of those minimum conditions of freedom which permit the full expression of it. Contained within this paradox is the kernel of apartheid. Black art is concerned with struggle—a struggle for Blacks to be free, to be able to express themselves as they wish. The denial of this freedom in art is only one manifestation of its denial throughout Black life. One of the problems in institutionalizing Black protest literature in a number of publishing channels, like Ravan Press or *Staffrider*, is that it becomes more identifiable and readily amenable to control through political censorship. Without specifying complaints against constituent pieces, the whole publication can be prohibited, such as happened very rapidly to *Donga*, a similar journal to *Staffrider*. Business considerations may well then enforce an added voluntary censorship by the publishers. The very first issue of *Staffrider* was found 'undesirable' by the Publications

Directorate. Among the 'undesirable elements' the Director of Publications listed those passages in which the authority and image of the police were undermined, material which was prejudicial to 'peace and good order', the use of 'offensive language', and material calculated to harm 'Black–White relations.'[39] The next four issues came before the Publications Directorate. The fifth issue in March 1979 was banned, with the Directorate explaining that it contained 'undesirable material of unfair, one-sided and offensive portrayals of police actions and methods calculated to evoke hatred and contempt for them'. An aggravating factor was a poem by Bafana Buthelezi, an exiled radical, from which the Directorate inferred that the journal was 'offering a medium of expression for virulent attacks on South Africa's institutions by hostile persons living abroad'.[40] This is only one reflection of the government's insistence that South African exiles are not to be included in any internal debate. With Ravan Press now having to abide by that restriction their journal loses some credibility. The publishers have tried to defend the journal by arguing that it expresses only what Blacks are feeling, presumably taking recourse in the belief that art communicates experience and is therefore subjective, and without the same experience the government cannot objectively evaluate Black art. True as it is, the government is likely to be unmoved by that defence and further harassment will continue.

There will be two reasons for this. First, the government does not believe that these are the feelings and experiences of most of the Black community, and therefore, as it has admitted often, they consider Black literati to be agitators trying to convince people of something they are normally unaware of. Secondly, the government misunderstands the mode of expression which the Black literati use in representing their view of the Black experience. The former claim does not bear serious consideration. The government's misunderstanding of the nature of literary expression is more fundamental in this regard. It has permeated everyday common sense understanding that there is a phenomenon called 'poetic licence', but very little academic attention has been directed to it. It describes the fact that language can be used in some contexts in a qualitively different form from that of ordinary discourse. In ordinary discourse language is used according to common rules or conventions which enable the inference of meaning. Language which does not employ these shared rules is a defiance of ordinary discourse and cannot be understood by it. J. P. Ward has made the claim that certain characteristics place this kind of non-conventional language use in a separate category—characteristics which have traditionally been regarded as features of poetry, such as explicit imagery, metaphor, inversion, and indirect allusion.[41] Certain recurrent terms in Black poetry, such as 'hate', 'violence', 'revenge', 'rape', 'death', 'blood', and so on, are being translated by rules of ordinary discourse which define a particular meaning but should be understood in terms of the special features of poetry. It is the incongruence of these two realms of meaning which leads to the curtailing of freedom of expression in Black literature. In this instance, the harassment is more understandable, for the government is merely employing rules to infer meaning which are shared throughout ordinary discourse. Where it can be criticized is in its failure to make allowances for 'poetic licence'. The Director of Publications wrote of this on banning the March 1979 issue of *Staffrider*, explaining that he was fully aware that 'poetic licence generally applies to publications of this nature' but this does not 'outweigh the undesirable material'.[42] Yet many of these terms have to be understood figuratively.

The constant use of the word 'White', for example, is meant not in the personal sense of referring to a race of people, but in a figurative sense as an attitude of mind. Blacking recounts a tale which verifies this interpretation: 'When I asked rural Africans how in a free Black South Africa, they would cope with the shortage of skilled persons, they invariably said they would hire people from France, Germany, Scandinavia, the United Kingdom. They did not consider such people as "White" in the same way as South African Whites.'[43] 'White' stands for an attitude of mind predicated on racism, oppression, and domination, just as 'Black' is an attitude of mind predicated on self-awareness and pride in the ending of oppression. Neither are references to colour but to the structure of social relations which colour represents. The 'White man' ceases to be 'White' once relations of oppression and discrimination have been replaced. That is precisely why Black Consciousness argues for a multiracial and harmonious future despite the racial exclusivity of its struggle. Once racism as a system of social relations, if not as a set of attitudes, is abandoned, 'White-ness' ceases to exist and the function of 'Black-ness' falls away, to be replaced by 'South Africans' in a non-racial society. Literature of this genre, therefore, is not anti-White but anti-racist.

This is the meaning within which the imagery of violence and emnity should be understood. There are poems which still cannot overthrow the Black pacifist traditions: Essop Patel's poem 'To My Son' asks us not to 'forget the White hand'. However, most make reference to 'hate' as a strong emotion caused by recent political history. Neelan Pillay's poem 'Barefeet' is a good example, containing the lines: 'Like my heart bleeds White hate / My feet wish for shoes / My heart wishes for freedom / Many died fighting for my shoes.'[44] This summarizes what the conflict in South Africa is about. It centres on the niggardly deprivation of basic needs and amenities under racism. Only from the hate of racism can the heart fight for the end to these deprivations. Maupa Kadiaka's poem 'The Fighter' expresses this very well: 'I'm a soldier / I'll keep on fighting / For justice instead of injustice / For love instead of hatred / Building friendship instead of emnity / For in Azania we hate no man / But man's deeds.'[45] The hatred is for racism, and the references to 'kill', 'death', 'fight against', 'spoil', 'break' all refer to racism, not people. The imagery of violence must be understood as being directed against a set of social relations rather than against the occupants of those structures. Such imagery does serve as a warning of what may come should the occupants not want to change the racist structure of social relations, but it is significant that even here the violence is not explicit. Nor could one expect it to be, given the nature of Black Consciousness, which has naively failed to confront the problem of how liberation will be achieved once Blacks reach self-awareness.

In banning the performance of the play *Shanti* because of its imagery of violence, the government was in fact preventing the transmission of an essentially peaceful message. *Shanti* was a gentle play about two young people consumed by the yearning for liberation. Thabo, the hero, is a reformer who rejects violence and armed struggle, whereas Mobu becomes a guerrilla. The search is for peace and the hero believes in peace through dialogue. He is cheated out of this when he is wrongfully and unjustly convicted of murder and imprisoned. The play comments, in one sense, on the hopelessness of dialogue—not because it fails, but because it never occurs: Thabo is snatched away and imprisoned before he is even allowed to take his place at the negotiating table. Yet the play comments powerfully on the hopelessness of armed struggle. Mobu's guerrilla group is presented as leading an unhappy, wandering, and lonesome life. In Act III Mobu sadly admits that he hates his 'life of terrorism' and regrets 'taking to arms'. This comment is made more vividly powerful by Thabo, who, despite his disillusionment with negotiation, upon his death does not endorse Mobu. The warning for the future comes from the fact that it is Thabo, representing disillusioned moderates, who is killed, not those symbolizing armed struggle. Even so, it is difficult to see the play as a eulogy of terrorism, although those associated with it were charged under the 1967 Terrorism Act. In fact the play is a warning against harbouring terrorists; one of the characters is given the line 'the terrorists don't know you, don't trust you . . . the government imprisons you and the terrorists kill you.' The play goes further by implying that the guerrillas do not know themselves. Mobu is essentially a pacifist, even though he is a general, and his instructions are defied by Mangaya, who kills him. The implication is clear that there is no honour among guerrillas: Mobu does not honour himself and Mangaya does not respect leadership.

There is one last testimony against the government's interpretation of Black protest writing. The mere fact that Black writers chose this medium to express the idea of liberation is premissed on their belief in the power of the written word above violence. This is fundamental to Black Consciousness and the literary tradition within it. Liberation, it argues, comes from raising consciousness —not raising it through participation in an armed revolutionary struggle, as Lenin and Luxemburg thought, but by increasing the conscious awareness of being Black. As conceived by Biko, and as represented today, armed struggle is not necessary for that Black self-consciousness. The mechanisms for achieving it are through such things as Black community projects, self-help groups, and an appreciation of Black art. The power of the pen in representing social reality for Blacks was instrumental in raising them to self-awareness and eventual liberation. This view of revolution is analogous to that of Marx, who likewise underplayed the role of violence, seeing social change as an automatic corollary of shared consciousness among the oppressed. Violence was unneccesary because the motivation behind change was the conscious awareness of societal contradictions. In other words, change is the inevit-

able outcome of shared realization for its need. Subsequent Marxists realized that something else had to be done, and armed
struggle may well be the outcome of the realization in Black
Consciousness that Black self-awareness is not the solution, that
something more has to be done for the dominant racial group to
accept those who are their equals on equal terms. That position
has probably been reached with the radicalization of Black Consciousness, discussed in an earlier chapter.[46]

However, the growth of Black self-awareness through the written word, among other things, still plays a major role in liberation.
There is an old African proverb to which Black writers adhere:
wisdom is better than force. A similar theme is apparent in an
epigram by George Bulwer-Lytton, later Baron Lytton, who
quipped that 'the pen is mightier than the sword'.[47] The proverb
forms the symbol of the cover of Matshoba's book *Call Me Not a
Man*, showing the clenched fist of liberation but clutching, instead of
a sword or spear, a pen and paintbrush. The proverb is explictly
alluded to in Mafika Gwala's poem 'In Defence of Poetry', and
Meshack Mabogoane's poem of support to *Staffrider* called by the
same name. It also constitutes a major principle of the Black press
in South Africa. The newspaper in Xhosa, *Imvo Zabantsundi*,
created by missionaries, was one of the first recognized newspapers to be especially designed for Africans. Its editor John Tengo
Jabavu, who used it to fight political campaigns, believed that
'words and votes are stronger than *assegais*'. An *assegai* is a
traditional Zulu weapon of war; Jabavu was giving primacy to
the power of the pen. He could well have added that words also
make better peace than *assegais*, since reconciliation after
bloodshed is always traumatic. These twin beliefs characterize the
position taken by the Black press today.

THE BLACK PRESS

The complex nature of the Black press mirrors the complexity of
the ethnic divisions maintained and enhanced under apartheid. It
is long established in studies of the press that newspapers cater for,
and are designed to satisfy, a specific market as perceived by the
editorial staff and/or confirmed in its sales. This market tends to be
defined on economic, political, status, or religious grounds, as in
some cases where religious cleavages persist. In South Africa the

market is defined ethnically. This is especially true for editorial perceptions. Hence, the minority of newspapers which do want to appeal across ethnic divisions produce a separate edition catering for this different ethnic market, implying that its normal edition is somehow unsatisfactory. In terms of sales this ethnic division is not rigid because many Blacks read the English-speaking press catering for the White English-speaking community. But, not surprisingly in view of their support for the government, this is not true of the White Afrikaans-speaking press. Nor is the reverse true, for newspapers catering for the Black community have a very low White readership. A Black market exists for some newspapers, therefore, which the newspapers are not specifically designed to meet. This category will not be discussed here.

There are four types of newspaper catering specially for Blacks. The following typology is based on intended and, to a lesser extent, actual market, not on ownership and control. There have been a few African-owned and -controlled newspapers,[48] and most of these have appeared in indigenous languages circulating in the tribal areas. The more widely read English-speaking Black press circulating in urban areas is controlled and financed by White interests, though staffed and edited by Blacks. In 1931 Bantu Press was established by two White entrepreneurs searching for advertising revenue from a market catering for a growing urban African population. Their first venture was *Bantu World*, which, as the *World* and *Weekend World*, became the largest Black daily newspaper. Bantu Press assumed control over most of the surviving African newspapers and was itself taken over by the large Argus Press Group which publishes most of the English-speaking opposition newspapers and their Black editions. Very few independent newspapers survived the competitive power of the Argus Group. The only major exception has been the *Voice*, an ecumenical newspaper published by the Ecumenical Trust Fund in Braamfontein. It strongly supports Black Consciousness and the stand Bishop Tutu and the South African Council of Churches have taken against apartheid. It describes itself as the only Black-owned and -edited newspaper in South Africa, but is published weekly and in 1980 had a small circulation of 20,000. The only effective rival to the Argus Group in publishing for Blacks is the Afrikaanse Pers Group, which publishes most of the Afrikaans-speaking newspapers which support the government. The group publishes

Bona and it purchased *Imvo Zabantsundu* and *Zonk* from Bantu Press. Voortrekker Press publishes *Our Own Mirror*, first published independently in Natal under the name *Eletha*.[49]

The various kinds of newspapers catering specially for a Black market are:

1. 'White'[50] English-speaking newspapers publishing separate editions for the Black communities, such as the Post Group, including *Transvaal Post* and *Golden City Post, City Press, Sunday Tribune, Sunday Times*, and many more. In recent years there has been a significant increase in the number of ethnic editions of established English-language newspapers. A minority are published in the vernacular or several vernaculars. This has meant an increase in the number of Black journalists and editorial staff on 'White' newspapers. Leading Black journalists like Qoboza and Sisulu reject this kind of press because they claim that it reinforces the tradition of White paternalism.

2. The Black English-speaking press catering exclusively for one or other of the different ethnic Black communities, such as the *Indian Opinion*, *Muslim News*, and the African *Our Own Mirror*.[51]

3. Black English-speaking newspapers catering for the Black community generally. Examples here are *Voice* and, before they were banned, the *World* and the *Post Transvaal*, plus their respective Sunday editions. The *Sowetan* and its sister paper the *Sunday Mirror* replaced the banned newspapers in this category, although the *Sunday Mirror* was closed down for economic reasons in August 1985.

4. Independent of the vernacular editions of English-speaking newspapers there are indigenous language newspapers catering exclusively for one of the indigenous language groups. They are mostly African, such as *Imvo*, *Ilanga*, and *Bono*, although there are some Asian vernacular newspapers.

The intention here is to concentrate on the third category only. Newspapers in this category have four special characteristics. They have an independence from other markets and offer the full range of newspaper content. They are also published in English. A wealth of research shows English as the favoured language of non-traditional urban Blacks, especially in what Bernstein calls the 'public' rather than 'private' language code use, because for most non-traditional urban Blacks indigenous language in an urban environment smacks of tribalism.[52] The language of politics, if not of the home, is English. A common tongue is essential for unity across ethnic–language divisions. English has been the unifying language chosen by the ANC and Black Consciousness. One has only to recall the demand in 1976 by students, which was supported by their parents, to be educated in English. The language of the Black literati is English. Finally, newspapers in this category refuse to cater for the separate ethnic markets within the Black community, unlike the ethnic editions, sometimes published in the vernacular, of the English-speaking 'White' press. These last two qualities have political consequences. In terms of current Black politics, these newspapers are attempting to satisfy the all-important market of the politically aware, English-speaking, urban Black. As one might expect, therefore, Black newspapers catering for this market strongly support Black Consciousness and, latterly, the ANC. Also unsurprising is that these newspapers are subject to the greatest state inteference. As a daily newspaper the *World* was banned in 1977 and the *Post Transvaal*, which replaced it, was banned in 1980. The *Sowetan* quickly replaced the *Post Transvaal* in 1981. There are no precise figures for their circulations, but before its banning the *World* had a circulation of 200,000 and an actual readership of around a million. No figures exist for the *Post Transvaal*, although it is likely to have matched this. Within a year of its launch, official figures released by the government showed the *Sowetan* to have a circulation of 72,846, making it the fifth-largest daily in South Africa. Actual readership is likely to well exceed this figure. Even so it was the fastest-growing paper in South Africa, with an 11 per cent increase in sales over six months. The *Voice* is quite small in comparison and is only published weekly, but it has also been subject to temporary banning. The harassment serves as an index of the government's sensitivity to the information being presented to this crucial market: in recent years it has not exercised its full repressive powers against any newspapers catering for other markets. These are the reasons why this limited category within the Black press is the focus of attention.

THE URBAN BLACK DAILY PRESS

The *Bantu World* was conceived originally from commercial, not political, motives. In terms of its political content, the ANC was critical. Jordan Ngubane, a member of the ANC Youth League and a former journalist on the paper, left to establish his own paper *Inkundla ya Bantu*. With the ANC failing to finance and manage a paper of its own, the communist press filled the void, particularly through *New Age*, *Liberation*, and *Fighting Talk*. The *New Age* was the successor to the *Guardian*, *Clarion*, *People's World*, and *Advance*, all banned in succession under the Suppression of Communism Act. The government even introduced a special measure to compensate for this plethora for an amendment to the Act permitted any journal or periodical to be banned if, in the opinion of the state, it continued or replaced, whether or not under the same title, a periodical which was formerly banned. There was no reliance by the ANC on the *Bantu World*. For most of its fifty years it was a politically innocuous mixture of sex, sport, and parochial Sowetan news. It was only in 1974 that Elaine Potter's study of the role of the press as opposition in South Africa totally overlooked the newspaper and the Black press generally.[53]

Such an omission is impossible today. A transition towards an aggressive political stance in the *World*, as the *Bantu World* became, began in 1974 with Frelimo's accession to power in Mozambique. The African community especially took an interest in the Mozambique situation, and sales rose. Attention was turned to political matters in South Africa and circulation figures justified this transition. In the three years from this transition to its banning circulation increased to a point where it was the second-largest of all the daily newspapers in South Africa, exceeded only by the *Johannesburg Star*. In taking up the editorship, Percy Qoboza pushed the newspaper into politics. After a Fellowship at Harvard University, Qoboza returned to South Africa and began to enunciate more frequently the hopes and aspirations of urban Blacks. His views on the role of the Black press in Black politics have been subsequently stated: 'I want to say to the critics of Black journalists that we do not live in a vacuum . . . we share, most intimately, our people's fears and aspirations . . . we view what is happening in our country as a moral crisis. We do not intend to remain neutral in that crisis.'[54]

It is no irony that Qoboza is a peaceful man, for these are not extreme views. He has campaigned against the more radical elements in the liberation struggle and particularly against men of violence. He is opposed to terrorism (but not to the ANC), and he was critical of certain activities of the Soweto Student Representative Council in the uprising of 1976–7. For its editor at least, the *World* was a bridge across the racial divide providing a channel of communication to allow Whites to learn, should they so wish, what Blacks were thinking and doing. The paper was by no means radical, however, upon reading it the average White person would have been shocked. It gave prominence to the intrusion of political activity in the life of urban Blacks, demanded inquiries into allegations of police brutality, and told of people being evicted from their homes, exposing the haughty unconcern of White officials. It encouraged the political aspirations of its readers and catalogued the attempts by the authorities to thwart them. The paper defended the right of Blacks to create the world in which they lived. It strongly supported the student uprising in 1976–7 and maintained a commitment to the philosophy of Black Consciousness within which the uprising occurred.

The death of Steve Biko troubled the paper greatly, for Biko was a man similar to Qoboza—visualized by the government as an extremist but in truth a man of patience and moderation. The seeming death of tolerance with Biko's murder did not cause Qoboza to change his position. An editorial in the *Weekend World* is worth quoting at length to verify this:

Will those embittered by his death become racist? The temptation is there and the longer the present heartless system rules the greater the pressure for a reverse racism will grow. But let us always remember Steve's example. Let us stand fully and firmly against the injustice of racism but let us never turn to a new racism in retaliation. Let us, like Steve, fight the fight for freedom with integrity and humanity and with methods we will never later become ashamed of. Let us like Steve fight wrong with right. Let us not fall into the trap of fighting one form of evil with another.[55]

Within exactly a month and a day of this editorial statement, the *World* and *Weekend World* were permanently banned and Percy Qoboza was imprisoned for five months. A series of meetings between Qoboza and Jimmy Kruger, the Minister of Justice, had been occurring since 29 July 1977, when Qoboza had been warned to moderate criticism of the government. At a meeting of all newspaper editors the previous June, they had been told to take cognizance of the implications of 'inflammatory material'. In singling out the urban Black daily press for banning in October 1977, the government accused it of 'creating unrest' and 'fanning unrest', and Connie Mulder, Minister of the Interior, accused it of 'instigating the unrest'.[56] While the government talked of law and order and dark conspiracies, no complaint had been brought before the Press Council and no comment had caused the papers to be brought before the court. A simple inference was drawn by Qoboza: the urban Black daily press did not have to break the law to be punished, but had simply to be outspoken in its opposition to government policy.[57]

No story is that simple. There were special reasons why the urban Black press, the Union of Black Journalists, and certain Black Consciousness organizations were singled out when outspoken White newspapers were untouched. The editor of the *Daily Despatch* was placed under house arrest, but the paper continued to function and no other act was carried out against White newspapers or White journalists at that time. There were three sorts of reasons behind the bannings. The most simple was panic. In the growing chaos produced by student unrest, Biko's death and the revelations after it, the government, unable to find fault in itself, hoped to correct matters by silencing critics. The powerlessness of the Black majority is demonstrated here, for it was a Black newspaper that was chosen as the sacrificial lamb to warn the equally outspoken English-speaking opposition press. The second reason was electoral expediency. The banning occurred at a time when Prime Minister Vorster was seeking a mandate at the polls and the government was using the bannings to rally Nationalist support in a massive *kragdadigheid* campaign against Africans. This was reinforced by the fact that fundamental ideological concessions to apartheid were being made in Namibia, with the abolition of many racist laws there in preparation for a possible negotiated settlement on South West Africa. The third reason had to do with internal political control. The bannings came two days before the announcement that community councils were to be introduced in Soweto, one week before the initial Coroner's report on Biko's death was expected and just prior to rent, electricity, and service charge increases in Soweto. Through anticipated reactions, the government was preparing the conditions for effective political policy—either to initiate the policy experiment of community councils or to remove hostility caused by the implementation of its policy towards political prisoners or the management of urban townships.

Repression of this extremity came from a Prime Minister who was himself interned by the British at Koffiefontein for his political beliefs. At the time of the bannings another ex-internee headed the Republic's Bureau for State Security and another ran the powerful communications network of the South African Broadcasting Company. The moral of this is that you cannot ban ideas and ways of seeing the world which spring from a shared experience of social reality. The truth of this moral was lost to them, for thirty-eight years later the *Post Transvaal* quickly replaced the banned newspaper and new Black Consciousness organizations sprang up. Taking over the personnel of the *World* and its editor, *Post Transvaal* emerged more openly politicized by the episode. It strongly identified itself with Black Consciousness and then the ANC, and supported Motlana's Committee of 10 against the government-sponsored community council in the power struggle over the leadership of Soweto. It engaged in a vituperative campaign against Chief Buthelezi and Inkatha, and reported in detail on Black Consciousness meetings and its organizational and policy developments. Although ignored in the White English-speaking press, it carried extensive reports on the formation of COSAS and AZAPO in October 1979. Because of these close links with Black Consciousness, newspaper copy reflected the ideological shifts in it. For the first time since its inception in 1978, the months of November and December 1979 saw a focus on trade union and worker issues. The paper announced during November that it was to monitor the EEC Code of Conduct on working conditions and pay among European firms in South Africa, and it gave wide coverage to PEBCO's role in the Ford strikes in Port Elizabeth during the Christmas season 1979–80. The paper initiated a 'Workers' Watch' in November 1979, focusing on the indignity of Black workers, paralleling its 'Dignity Watch' which identified the indignity to Blacks generally, and from that period its support for the ANC was openly acknowledged. This may well have been the reason for its banning. Like its predecessor, it was silenced at a time when a Prime Minister, now P. W. Botha, was going to the polls on an occasion when ideological concessions to apartheid were having to be justified in South Africa. The silencing was not permanent, for the *Sowetan* quickly replaced the *Post Transvaal*. The *Sowetan* has continued the *Post Transvaal's* political stance, as reflected both in its copy and its close support of MWASA. While the *Sowetan* itself has not been banned, its editor Thami Mazwai, also National Secretary of MWASA, has been detained and one of its reporters, Joe Thloloe, a former president of MWASA, was banned and eventually imprisoned for possessing banned material. In fact all the newspapers satisfying this crucial market have been subject to harassment.

Banning is only the more extreme manifestation of government pressure. Harassment of journalists and even of newspaper vendors on street corners is a much more frequently applied repressive measure. The Black journalists' union, the Writers' Association of South Africa, which was established in 1978 to replace the banned Union of Black Journalists, was the main focus of the government's attention. Its Secretary was Joe Thloloe, once Secretary to the Union of Black Journalists, who was detained without trial, and without even charges laid against him, for 547 days. In May 1979 six members of its executive were in prison. WASA was interesting because it was one of the main Black Consciousness organizations. Frequently meetings were addressed by members of AZAPO and there was a great deal of common membership between the two organizations. The union was one of those leading the Free Mandela Campaign, and some of its members were ex-ANC. It placed great emphasis on the role of literature in Black politics, seeing no separation between the press and art. At every meeting poems were read and occasionally plays were performed. Because of its strong political identification with Black Consciousness and the ANC, WASA members were frequently detained. Between 1977 and 1979, twenty-two journalists were known to have been detained, some more than once; of these half were known to be members of WASA.[58] It is interesting to note that the detainees were more or less evenly split between journalists on Black newspapers and those on Black editions of White English-speaking newspapers. The government saw a threat, therefore, in the newly formed ethnic editions of White newspapers. The banning of journalists working on separate ethnic editions serves as a warning and intimidation to those White journalists working on the main copy. This could be one of the reasons why very little direct harassment of White journalists takes place: it is not needed in view of the lessons to be learned from their Black colleagues.

Before the banning of the *Post Transvaal*, WASA changed its name to the Media Workers' Association of South Africa. This was in line with WASA's intention to open itself up to press workers as well as professional journalists. This itself was part of the developments taking place in Black Consciousness that were noted in the last chapter. MWASA has since been subject to considerable repression. Although the number of Black journalists who have been detained is low compared with the total number of detentions, all were in leadership positions within MWASA. In 1982 only 2.7 per cent of detainees whose occupation was known were journalists, rising to 3 per cent in 1983. In both years, all known detainees who were journalists were MWASA members. They included Tsedu, the President, Thloloe, a former president, Mazwai, National Secretary, and Zwelakhe Sisulu, a former National Secretary. Copies of MWASA's newsletter *Kwasa* have been banned. This reflects the government's attempt to strip the organization of its effective leadership, which is itself a product of the government's attempt to control the Black press and restrict MWASA's involvement in community politics, where it has taken a radicalized Black Consciousness and ANC position.

The asymmetry of power between journalists and the state is enormous. The state is aware of the journalists' powerlessness and prepared to abuse the situation. To a Black reporter from the *Weekend World* who was obviously annoying him by asking questions, Jimmy Kruger, Minister of Justice at the time, said 'Do you want to get arrested?'[59] The source from which this powerlessness emanates is the battery of press laws at the disposal of the state. Controls on the information which is fed Africans pre-date the National Party's victory in 1948 by twenty-one years.[60] After the 1948 election there was a considerable reinforcement of these controls, the enactment of others, and an extension of them more generally to the Black community. Immediately upon forming a government, the National Party sought to encroach upon the freedom of the press, initially to control the English-speaking opposition press. In the years since, the source of the threat to the government has changed, and now controls are applied to the

Black and communist press alone. A Press Commission was established to examine methods by which control and freedom could be equated. A Press Board and a Press Code of Conduct were formulated as guidelines.[61]

The 1,400-page report of the Steyn Commission of Inquiry into the mass media was tabled in February 1982. It was the result of eighteen months of enquiry into the functioning of South Africa's media. The report complained that the media did not adequately serve the interests and needs of South Africa. Indeed, it argued that the media accentuated and perpetuated divisions within the country. In short, the media were being blamed for partly creating the unfavourable conditions and incidents which they saw themselves as reporting neutrally. While it is the case that no news is ever neutrally reported, and that reporters do have a role in framing the news, the commission decided that the unfavourable incidents which the press had reported in recent years would not have been so unfavourable were it not for the nature of the reporting. Thus, while the commission's recommendations rejected what it called 'state control, censorship legislation or a draconian "media law" ', it sought to introduce other controls over journalists. It suggested that a register of journalists be formed, from which they could be struck off for unprofessional conduct. It also suggested a new central council for journalists to replace the present press council. It would be empowered to hear cases against journalists involving matters not brought before civil or criminal courts, and to fine them up to R3,000 and remove them from the register, or report them to the government or Parliament. Obviously a new set of offences was envisaged here which fall short of those offences which could be pursued before the civil and criminal courts, but their nature went unspecified. For its first twelve months of operation, the report recommended that the council be staffed by twelve members appointed by the Minister of Internal Affairs. Thereafter it was to have three government appointees, three members appointed by the SABC, and the remainder from business. The English-speaking press would have up to two nominees. In both forms, then, the general council for journalists was a body weighted in favour of nationalist opinion. Journalists who do not meet the standards of behaviour of this politically weighted body can be fined and refused the right to work.

Critics saw this report as an attack on press freedom. The attack does not take the form of draconian press laws, but is rather directed against the independence of journalists. To this end the report also suggested that shareholdings in the media be restricted to 1 per cent for private companies and 10 per cent for public companies. While this might seem to protect the editorial independence of the press, it also ensures that ownership becomes so diluted as to make common purpose or policy difficult to achieve. This affects the Afrikaans press as much as the English-speaking press, and the conservative Afrikaans press may well have been in mind here. This aspect of the report has even been criticized by the conservative South African Society of Journalists. They have been joined by *verligte* Afrikaans journalists like W. de Klerk, a former editor of *Rapport*. The government has yet to publish the white paper on the report, although during a debate in Parliament P. W. Botha described the report as a comprehensive document which demanded thorough study and consideration. Its findings, he said, had to be set against the background of a full-scale communist-inspired onslaught on South Africa, suggesting that the draconian controls envisaged by the commission were justified when set against the supposed attack. In the process of rationalizing the controls, Botha reassured MPs that the country had a high degree of press freedom, notwithstanding the communist onslaught.[62] This statement may well be believed by the new State President. The rationality of such a view lies in the fact that there are few direct press laws as such. Control takes the form of applying to the media statutes pertaining to other matters. One of the problems which the English-speaking opposition press faced, and which now confronts the Black press, is that many of the restrictions do not flow from a direct assault on press freedom and are not defined within the code of conduct. Rather, they are by-products of legislation aimed primarily at someone else.

The Suppression of Communism Act and its amendments, which have eventually culminated in the 1982 Internal Security Act, enable the government to suppress any 'publication'[63] which is found 'undesirable'[64] in terms of the Act; *inter alia*, it became an offence to convey any information which furthered these 'undesirable' ends. Any organization proscribed under the Act could not have its views printed. The Criminal Law Amendment Act made it an offence to infringe by way of protest, to campaign against, or to call for the repeal or modification of, the country's laws, or to use language calculated to cause the commission of such an offence. This makes it difficult for journalists to criticize laws, for there is no way of knowing whether criticism might result in the law being broken in protest. The Public Safety Act empowers the government to declare a state of emergency which enables it to prohibit the printing, publication, and dissemination of information considered subversive. It became an offence to publish the name of anyone detained under the emergency regulations. The Riotous Assembly Act allows the government to ban publications which it considers calculated to engender hostility between the races. The onus of proof that the publication is not of this nature lies with the editor—a complete reversal of conventional legal practice. Under the terms of the Internal Security Act, the state has the right to ban any publication (or journalist) without judicial safeguard. The Supreme Court ruled that the Act does not allow the publisher (or the journalist) the right to a court hearing before the banning. Nor can the courts set aside bannings; they cannot even extract from the Minister of Justice the reason for it. The Criminal Procedure Act provides machinery by which witnesses must appear and answer questions before magistrates, which has the implication of removing the confidentiality of a journalist's sources.

The role of the press in overseeing military, security, and police excesses has been explicitly removed by the state. The Official Secrets Act, in conjunction with the Defence Amendment Act, imposes a virtual blanket prohibition on all matters concerned with defence, and their publication needs the permission of the Minister of Defence. The consequence of this is that the country can be taken into war without the citizens' knowledge, let alone support, as happened with South Africa's intervention on the side of UNITA in the Angolan War. In 1983 proceedings were brought against several editors for publishing information on the government's involvement in the attempted coup in the Seychelles. Several prosecutions followed from reporting the government's involvement in international oil frauds. The Minister of Mineral and Energy Affairs said that the Powers and Privileges of Parliament Act might be reviewed to prevent the publication of information contained in MPs' speeches. This threat followed publication of revelations concerning the government's role in the Salem oil affair in which a PFP MP alleged that tax-payers had been defrauded of R30m. Section 10 of the 1969 General Law

Amendment Act supplemented the Official Secrets Act and extended restrictions on publishing military information to security issues. 'Security' was defined as any issue related to the security of the Republic including any issue dealing with or relating to the Bureau of State Security, as it was then, or to the relationship between any person and the Bureau. Revelations occurring in Britain from time to time about MI5 or MI6, and in America about the conduct of the CIA, are illegal in South Africa. These restrictions even apply to the civil police force. The Prisons Act affects the right of newspapers to publish pictures or sketches of prisoners, or reports on conditions in prisons or the experiences of prisoners at the hands of the police. The onus of proof of the validity of any information lies with the press. This inhibits the role of the newspaper in exposing public abuse, and newspapers publish only reports which present the Prisons Department in a favourable light or which emanate from the authorities. To publish adverse information is dangerous unless the editor is prepared to produce his information before the courts. Even here the paper runs the risk that the judicial officer will take a different view and find that the witness in whose veracity the editor believes is untruthful, and that what the editor takes as corroboration will be considered improbable by the court. Following the violent murder of twelve prisoners in a farm prison by warders, the government announced its willingness to relax the clause in the Prisons Act which prevented investigatory reporting. It has not done so for the similar clause in the Police Act.

Statutes such as these greatly intimidate newspapers and journalists. Any power the press has derives from the fact that people read it. There is an added dimension to this truism in South Africa. The Black press acquires a unique role because three-quarters of the population cannot engage directly in dissemination of information through participation in the political process, nor do most of them have access to televised news. They can read newspapers, but only those made available to them. There are added dimensions to this truism as well. Societies have to balance the need for a free press and the interests of government. Blackwell and Bamford showed in 1963 how the South African government disrupted this balance.[65] Three methods were used by it to further the interests of government, and these apply equally decades later. The first was direct intervention through censorship; the second was the encouragement of internal self-control through intimidation; finally, there was a reliance on the courts to impose sanctions. The third is almost non-existent now, since the government rely on the first two methods. But while the balance between the means has changed, the end result is the same: freedom of the press is curtailed and Blacks are denied the newspapers they want to read.[66] Freedom of the press has a dual aspect—the freedom to inform and the freedom to be informed. So press freedom has to be considered in conjunction with the right of Blacks to discuss opinions and participate in certain types of activity by which information is assimilated. Libertarians recognize that freedom is not indivisible; neither, as a corollary, is repression. Encroachments on press freedom are only one example of a general encroachment on civil liberties in South Africa.

On press freedom the government has admitted its position. The Minister of Public Works at the time, L. le Grange, confessed to the Newspaper Press Union in 1978 that in South Africa 'the freedom of the press is not a civil liberty and the public do not have the right to be informed. Privilege cannot be allowed to be abused and create a state of unrest and chaos in the name of press freedom. The position of South Africa's integrity is a supreme obligation.'[67] The two interesting points in this statement are its view of the origins of unrest and, more important, the reasons for its frankness (the government has yet to be so frank on other freedoms). With regard to the more important point, the reason for this frankness lies in how the government sees civil liberties under apartheid. A familiar theme in élitist attacks on representative democracy is that civil liberties do not accrue by right but have to be earned by an exhibition of enough responsibility to possess the 'privilege'. This is an oft-quoted statement by South African government ministers. The government is prepared to admit encroachment on press freedom as a way of chastising the press for being irresponsible. Thereby it shifts blame for unrest on to irresponsible newspapers. This too is a familiar theme of government ministers. The example of the Afrikaans-speaking press is usually employed to illustrate how a responsible press operates.

The same argument cannot be applied to other civil liberties for Blacks, because the implication would then be that Blacks, by definition, do not have the same rights as Whites but first have to earn them. At one time the government was prepared to admit such a thing—that was the point behind apartheid. But they can afford to admit that no longer—that is the point behind the 'liberalizations' introduced since the Soweto uprising. In other words, what the uprising has done (and Black literature and the Black press have contributed to it) is to undermine the government's resolve to stick to the traditional style of apartheid. The government recognizes the need for change, even if it has yet to implement genuine reforms. How this affects those opposition forces working within state-sponsored platforms, like the homelands, is the subject of Chapter 6.

Notes

1. A.N. Whitehead, *Adventures of Ideas*, New York, Free Press, 1933.
2. John Blacking, 'The Power of Ideas in Social Change: The Growth of the Africanist Idea in South Africa', *Queen's University Papers in Social Anthropology*, 3, ed. D. Riches, Queen's University, Belfast, 1980. See pp. 111–13.
3. This is a point essential to conversation analysis in sociology. This point is expanded in J. Brewer, 'Literature and Liberation in South Africa', *Ethnic and Racial Studies*, 9. 2, 1986, pp. 250–7.
4. *Staffrider*, 1. 3, 1978, p. 54.
5. Editorial in People's Experimental Theatre Newsletter, no. 1, 1971.
6. 'Some Aspects of African Literature', in H. van der Merwe *et al.*, *African Perspectives on South African*, Cape Town, David Phillip, 1978, p. 81.
7. Details of the early Black writers are taken from A. Tibble, *African English Literature*, London, Peter Owen, 1965.
8. Ibid., p. 50.
9. On *Drum*, see A. Sampson, *Drum*, London, Collings, 1956. On its critics see G. Gerhart, *Black Power in South Africa*, Berkeley, University of California Press, 1978, p. 129; A. Tibble, op. cit., p. 51; C. Wauthier, *The Literature and Thought of Modern Africa*, London, Heinemann, 1978, 2nd edn, pp. 335–7.
10. Quoted by J. Olney, *Tell Me Africa*, Princeton, Princeton University Press, 1973, p. 255.
11. C. Wauthier, op. cit., p. 337.
12. Ibid., p. 335.
13. People's Experimental Theatre Newsletter, no. 1, 1971.
14. Ibid.
15. Taken from the Supreme Court, Transvaal Provincial Division, Indictment and Annexures, in the trial of Sadecque Variava in 1973–4.

16. People's Experimental Theatre Newsletter, no. 1, 1971.
17. This use of violent metaphors is discussed further below, as is the state's misunderstanding of their meaning.
18. Quoted in *Staffrider*, 1. 1, March 1978, p. 32.
19. Noted by C. Wauthier, op. cit., p. 348.
20. P. Mayer, *Townsmen and Tribesmen*, London, Oxford University Press, 1961. See also his 'Migrancy and the Study of Africans in Towns', *American Anthropologist*, 64, 1962.
21. See Gakwadi, op. cit., p. 11.
22. N. Gordimer and L. Abrahamson, *South African Writing Today*, London, Penguin, 1967, p. 12.
23. See G. Butler, *A Book of South African Verse*, London, Oxford University Press, 1959; K. Parker, *The South African Novel in English*, London, Macmillan, 1978.
24. K. Parker, *The South African Novel in English*, p. 16.
25. R. N. Egudu, op. cit., pp. 1–2, dismisses the 'arts-for-art's-sake' tradition in African literature as a whole.
26. *Staffrider*, 2. 3, 1979, p. 22.
27. Ibid., 2. 2, 1979, p. 58.
28. Taken from the Supreme Court Indictment of Sadecque Variava (above, n. 15).
29. *Staffrider*, 2. 1, 1979, p. 38.
30. Ibid., 2. 2, 1979, p. 33.
31. Ibid., p. 29.
32. Ibid., 1. 4, 1978, p. 56.
33. Ibid., 2. 3, 1979, p. 49.
34. Ibid., p. 6.
35. Ibid., 2. 1, 1979, p. 5.
36. Ibid., 2. 2, 1979, p. 15.
37. Ibid., 2. 3, 1979, p. 53.
38. Ibid., p. 6.
39. Correspondence can be found ibid., 1. 2, 1978, pp. 2–3.
40. Correspondence can be found ibid., 2. 2, 1979, pp. 2–3.
41. 'The Poem's Defiance of Sociology', *Sociology*, 13, 1979.
42. *Staffrider*, 2. 2, 1979, p. 2.
43. J. Blacking, op. cit., p. 125.
44. Taken from the Supreme Court Indictment of Sadecque Variava (above, n. 15).
45. *Staffrider*, 2. 3, 1979, p. 52.
46. See Chapter 4.
47. In his poem 'Richlieu', line 11. This forms the central point of those sociological studies of power which emphasize the need for legitimation of power, and is thus inherent in the distinction between power and authority.

48. See A. Friedgut, 'Non-European Press', in Ellen Hellman (ed.), *Handbook on Race Relations in South African*, Cape Town, Oxford University Press, 1949.

49. Noted by E. Potter, *The Press as Opposition*, London, Chatto and Windus, 1975, p. 48.

50. 'White' is meant in the general sense of that population group which forms the main readership of the newspaper and that market for which the newspaper is designed. There is some Black readership of these newspapers, but they see their main contact with the Black community as coming through separate ethnic editions.

51. One can use the term 'exclusive' here with confidence because there is very little inter-ethnic readership of vernacular newspapers on account of the language difficulty and very little readership of Black English-speaking newspapers by Whites. This justifies use of the term 'Black'. To cater for White interest in the Black press, most White English-speaking newspapers carry an occasional brief survey of the Black press.

52. See B. Hirson, 'Language in Control and Resistance', in S. Marks (ed.), *The Societies of Southern Africa in the Nineteenth and Twentieth Centuries*, London, Institute of Commonwealth Studies, 1981, pp. 53–68.

53. E. Potter, p. 7, where she states that there are only two types of newspaper in South Africa, the White English-speaking press and the White Afrikaans-speaking press.

54. *Post Transvaal*, 19 September 1979.

55. *Weekend World*, 18 September 1977.

56. Quoted by the *Citizen*, 20 October 1977.

57. Reported in the *Daily News*, 20 October 1977.

58. This number is by no means definitive because of the difficulty of obtaining information on detainees and, under some Acts, of even knowing of their detention.

59. *Weekend World*, 16 October 1977 (the last issue before its banning).

60. See K. Stuart, *Newspapermen's Guide to the Law*, Durban, Butterworth, 1968, 1978. D. Welsh has argued that the roots of apartheid generally lie in British segregation policy in the nineteenth century. See *The Roots of Segregation*, Cape Town, Oxford University Press, 1971.

61. See E. Potter, op. cit., p. 102, for a historical account of this development.

62. Quoted in the *South African Digest*, 5 February 1982, p. 3.

63. The definition of 'publication' includes all newspapers, books, periodicals, pamphlets, writings, typescripts, photographs, prints, records, and manuscripts available to the public. This definition comes from the Publications and Entertainment Act no. 25, 1963.

64. The definition of undesirable includes indecent, obscene, or offensive acts, acts harmful to public morals, acts which are blasphemous or offensive to religious convictions, acts which bring any section of the inhabitants of the Republic into ridicule or contempt, acts harmful to the relations between the population groups in South Africa, and acts prejudicial to the safety of the state, the general welfare, or peace and good order. This definition is taken from the 1963 Publications and Entertainments Act.

65. L. Blackwell and B. Bamford, *Newspaper Law in South Africa*, Cape Town, Juta Press, 1963.

66. The International Press Institute, in *Government Pressures on the Press*, Zurich, IPI, 1955, p. 108, formally pronounced South Africa to be a country where press freedom did not exist. So has the New York-based Committee to Protect Journalists, and many others. For a wider discussion see W. Hocking, *Freedom of the Press*, Chicago, University of Chicago Press, 1957; F. Williams, *The Right to Know*, London, Longman Green, 1969; F. Castberg, *Freedom of Speech in the West*, London, George Allen and Unwin, 1960.

67. Reported in the *Daily News*, 7 October 1978.

6

Inkatha and Political Opposition in the Homelands

INTRODUCTION: HOMELAND POLITICS

Inkatha and its leader Chief Buthelezi elicit a variety of emotions, but it cannot be denied that they play a prominent role in South African politics. Irrespective of what opinion is held on the nature of that role, Inkatha's paid-up membership of 700,000[1] alone ensures its significance. This confirms Inkatha as the largest single political organization in South Africa's political history. Political interest in Inkatha has grown with its importance,[2] although academic analyses of the organization lag some way behind.[3] So important has it become as a model of rapid political growth and effective organization that other homeland leaders have formed their own equivalents to Inkatha. Ximoko Xa Rixaka was established in 1983 as the 'national cultural and liberation movement' in Gazankulu. To recount political opposition in the homelands is to anatomize Chief Buthelezi and Inkatha. Within the context of homeland politics Inkatha is an important, even unique, organization. Inkatha presents a paradox precisely because it is the least obedient of the homeland organizations. Without it one could assume that homeland political opposition was transparent puppetry, but Inkatha gives it some credibility. It confounds all the accepted truths about politics in South Africa's homelands.[4]

Until recently, African politics were a peculiarly urban affair. The ANC and Black Consciousness were urban in their concern and support. There was only a small involvement by chiefs in the ANC, and tribalism is anathema to Black Consciousness. With the development of homeland political structures in 1970, an urban–rural dichotomy occurred in African politics.[5] For most homeland politicians these have remained separate spheres, with little cross-fertilization of personnel, organizations, and, to a lesser extent, issues.[6] Inkatha is an exception because it traverses this dichotomy. It intends its constituency to be the Black cause generally and sees no distinction between the interests of urban and rural Africans.[7]

In maintaining this dichotomy, homeland political parties have little influence in urban areas, despite the larger proportion of their population residing there. Since 1979 there has been an increase in the population of the homeland's own ethnic group which is resident in the homeland.[8] The increase reflects the consolidation of the territories, the high birth rate in the homelands, and the government's policy of relocating Africans from 'White' areas. The decreases tend to reflect the under-enumeration of population size in the past and readjustments of the boundaries between the homelands. KwaNdebele became a self-governing homeland in 1979 and was due to take 'independence' in December 1986. This territory was formerly part of Bophuthatswana.

Tables 23, 24 and 25 show that the territories are not homelands in a demographic sense. Ever since they were secured for African occupancy, the homelands have encompassed only a proportion of their 'ethnic group'; they are not homelands in any meaningful historical sense. The territories contain places of traditional significance but are considered to be only a part of more extensive historical patrimonies. No homeland leader regards present borders as adequate or legitimate. In comparison with conditions facing Africans in the towns, these territories are seen as marginal. Urban participation in homeland politics is minimal. It has been estimated that only 30 per cent of those who participated in homeland elections were urban dwellers.[9] Many illegal urban residents cannot participate without revealing their illegality. As a consequence, homeland parties have a poor organizational apparatus in urban areas. Inkatha is a striking exception, having a degree of support and a strong organizational framework in these areas, especially in townships with a high Zulu population.

Usually homeland political parties are conservative forces, and their expressions of opposition are not vociferous. Political parties developed in the homelands only after these 'separate development' structures were established a few decades ago. Many are only parties in name and lack a formal structure. Good examples are the Ciskei National Party, the Zulu National Party, and the Tswana National Party. The term 'national' is common, having an obvious attraction to these newly constituted 'nations'. This serves

Table 23. *Total Numbers of Homeland Population**

Territory	Population of Own Group in Homeland		Population in White Areas		De Jure Population	
	1973	1979	1973	1979	1973	1979
Bophuthatswana	600,241	1,246,700	1,108,838	946,606	1,719,367	2,219,660
Ciskei	509,707	553,700	—	469,200	—	1,025,200
Gazankulu	239,331	353,200	106,684	505,900	737,109	858,900
KaNgwane	—	219,000	—	402,600	—	622,300
Kwa Zulu	2,057,471	2,894,300	1,891,107	2,466,400	4,026,058	5,364,500
Lebowa	946,137	1,469,100	714,406	650,406	1,785,602	2,121,200
Qwa Qwa	24,189	94,900	1,307,785	1,696,600	1,451,796	179,700
Transkei	1,650,825	1,783,700	1,723,905	1,659,100	3,930,087	4,142,800
Venda	239,331	357,400	106,684	115,600	357,919	473,200

* The 1973 statistics are from M. Horrel, *The African Homelands in South Africa*, Johannesburg, SAIRR, 1973, pp. 37–9. The 1979 figures are from *Survey of Race Relations 1979*, Johannesburg, SAIRR, 1980, p. 70. The figure in the third column is not the sum of the other two columns because of the small number of those living in a homeland defined for another ethnic group.

Table 24. *Homeland Population (%)**

Territory	Population of Own Group in Homeland		Population in White Areas (%)	
	1973	1979	1973	1979
Bophuthatswana	34.91	56.16	64.49	42.66
Ciskei	—	54.11	—	45.85
Gazankulu	31.78	41.04	46.70	58.90
KaNgwane	—	35.19	—	64.70
Kwa Zulu	51.10	53.95	46.97	45.95
Lebowa	53.00	69.25	46.01	30.67
Qwa Qwa	1.60	5.35	90.08	94.64
Transkei	54.97	43.05	43.80	40.06
Venda	66.87	75.52	29.81	24.44

* Some change has occurred due to the consolidation of Bophuthatswana, Venda and Transkei and the incorporation of townships formerly in 'White areas' into the homelands. This is also occurring in Kwa Zulu. Note that the figures will not add up to 100% because they exclude those living in a homeland other than that defined for their ethnic group.

Table 25. *Percentage Increase in Population of Own Group in Homeland (1979–1983)*

Territory	Increase (%)
Bophuthatswana	+14.30
Ciskei	+30.18
Gazankulu	+57.02
KaNgwane	−20.56
Kwa Zulu	+27.55
Lebowa	+28.25
Qwa Qwa	+78.60
Transkei	+40.28
Venda	−5.17

to emphasize the ethnocentricism on which they mobilize support. Anthony Smith calls this 'ethnic-based nationalism',[10] and it can have revolutionary implications, especially in the retreat of colonialism and the urge for national liberation. In South Africa it acts as a conservative force serving the interests of the dominant racial group by obstructing Black conscientization. This underlying conservatism is enhanced by the fact that homeland political structures have deliberate in-built conservative tendencies. A permanent role for chiefs has been institutionalized, with tribal representatives outnumbering elected members by up to a half. The Bantu Homelands Constitution Act entrenches the power of chiefs by making the proportion of nominated to elected members of a legislative assembly subject to central government authority. One of the consistent themes of apartheid has been the preservation and strengthening of the role of traditional rule in African politics. The dominant racial group is intensely aware of the necessity of preserving its own cultural identity.

Tribalism itself tends to be conservative, but chiefs have an added economic and political dependence on the homeland government which acts as a brake to opposition.[11] They rely totally on the homeland government for their remuneration as minor government functionaries and, especially, for the recognition of their status as chiefs, by which they are eligible to participate in local governing boards and act as the community's spokesmen. Threats of withdrawal of scarce resources or proud status dampen the likelihood of opposition to a redistribution of power and status. The Kwa Zulu House of Assembly has 77 chiefs to 55 elected members. The development of Inkatha as an organization with a role independent of the Assembly is a way of breaking from the circumscribed conservatism of the homeland political framework, should it so wish. At first it did so, and Inkatha was more vociferous in its opposition to apartheid than all other homeland organizations. However, recently, in Inkatha's shift towards a more moderate position, it has taken to creating new chieftainships in an attempt to manipulate this conservatism and strengthen its position in rural areas.

Entrenching the power of chiefs is a deliberate policy to constrain opposition. The work of Southall, Stultz, and Charton[12] has provided an accurate description of the development in the homelands of a petty bourgeoisie of chiefs, politicians, civil

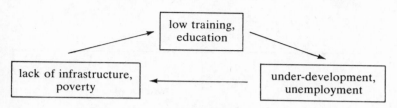

FIGURE 3. Homeland development

servants, and businessmen. Particularly important from the view of economic development is the role of the chiefs who have the power to allocate land and dominate the local and regional administration. In its political development of the homelands the South African government has greatly propped up the position of the chiefs. For the same purpose of political stability, the home-lands have been structured to be economically, politically, territor-ially, and strategically dependent on the central government. The homelands are subject to a vicious circle which hampers their development.[13] Not only does a large proportion of a homeland's population live outside its boundaries, but many of its remaining labour force work temporarily as migrant workers. There is an absence of any economic infrastructure and the land is inhospit-able. Of Qwa Qwa's 48,224 hectares, only 7,400 are fertile agricul-tural land. Mountainous areas comprise 30 per cent. Kwa Zulu has 58 per cent mountainous land and a full 70 per cent unsuitable for crop production.[14] It is the most fragmented of all homelands, with 70 enclaves of varying sizes scattered over Natal. Its density of population per square mile (173) is the highest of all the home-lands. The density of the arable land rises to 3,000.[15] A develop-ment plan for Kwa Zulu estimated that R4,000m. was needed to create a viable economy based on agriculture.[16] This is a heavy price to pay for National Party ideology.

As Rex and others have pointed out, the homelands are vital to the system of labour supply in South Africa and are therefore essential to apartheid. They are not areas reserved for native agriculture but places where a reserve army of labour is kept.[17] The impoverishment of the homelands has proceeded to such an extent that virtually all able men must attempt to enter wage labour in order to have any hope of surviving on a rural plot with their families. This impoverishment is enhanced by the exclusion of the homelands' population from the liberalization measures

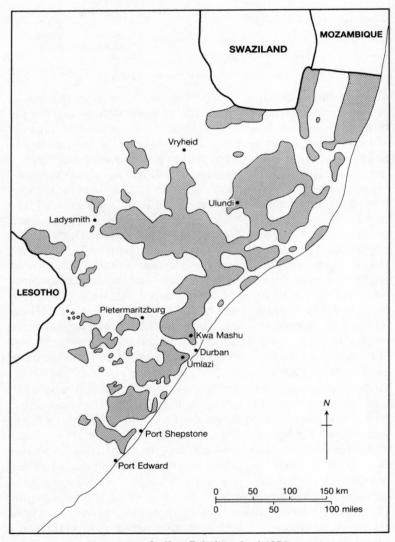

MAP 2. Kwa Zulu homeland 1975

which the state has introduced. As Saul and Gelb note, the stabilization of the urban African labour force seems to be dependent on stepping up control over the disqualified sections of rural Africans.[18]

Economic development of the homelands occurs within the policy of 'regional development', which encourages decentralization of economic activity to various places in and around the homelands. The Decentralization Board reported that since the announcement of new incentives in April 1982 the value of approved private applications for industrial settlement at decentralization points has increased from R904m. in 1981–2 to R2,500m. in 1982–3. What lies at the root of this are projections such as those which the Minister of Finance noted in 1983. Owen Horwood predicted that urbanization of Africans would increase from the present 35 per cent to 70 per cent by the year 2000. Whether urbanization would occur was not a choice, he said, but where urbanization occurred was within the ambit of the government to determine. The regional development policy is an attempt to encourage urbanization in the homelands and rural areas, keeping Africans out of the 'White' cities. In June 1983 the Department of Co-operation and Development announced the allocation of R142m. for the development of towns in the homelands. A key feature of this is the decentralization of economic resources to provide employment in the new homeland cities.[19]

In the 1982–3 financial year the government spent R1,700m. on decentralization to the homelands. This figure is more than the sum which the government intended to spend on the homelands as a whole in the financial year 1984–5. The incentive package to firms is impressive. In the Transkei and Ciskei, for example, firms were being offered in 1983 a 120 per cent relocation allowance, 125 per cent transport grant, 60 per cent housing interest rate subsidy, and between 80 per cent and 90 per cent of workers' wages.[20] Yet the considerable publicity which surrounds the development of the homelands obscures a subtle yet important change. The pattern in the 'White' metropolitan areas is one of continuing concentration of high-order business functions alongside a progressively capital-intensive form of manufacturing production. In the homeland and border growth-points are being located the low-wage and labour-intensive industries. Thus, as Rogerson emphasizes, a new spatial division of labour in manufacturing is taking place in South Africa.[21] This division is again one in which Africans are the subordinate partner, because no matter how large the expenditure it is woefully inadequate to meet the needs and aspirations of Africans in the rural areas. In the fifteen years up to 1983, a total of 150,000 decentralized jobs were created in the rural areas: just over half of one year's requirements if Africans are to stay in rural areas. If separate development is to be only partially successful, jobs, social services, and infrastructures will have to double to maintain the grossly inadequate developmental levels which exist at present. The rural areas are unlikely to be able to sustain their level of population, which, with a birth rate of 45–50 per 1,000, is among the highest in the world.[22] South Africa is simply unable to grow fast enough to provide jobs for its rapidly increasing African population. Despite decentralization, there are increasingly scarce employment opportunities in the homelands, so that a growing gap is emerging between those who can find work as migrants and those who cannot. In a recent survey, it was found that even in good years agricultural yields are inadequate. About two-thirds of the migrants interviewed had to buy maize for their family at home to eat. Those interviewed were people who currently had land, but the same survey showed that almost a third of migrant workers have no land or any expectation of it.[23]

Venda is in one of the most advantageous positions, with deposits of coal and asbestos. It has one of the highest per capita incomes of the homelands and surpasses the per capita income of twenty-six Black African states. Yet the reference group by which the Venda judge themselves is the more proximate Whites in South Africa, and there the imbalance is great. Eighty-two per cent of Venda's gross national income in 1976 came from migrant workers or commuters in employment outside its boundaries. That such a large proportion of gross national income comes from labour reveals a great deal about the infrastructure of Venda's economy, but it says more about the production and income opportunities of those who remain there.

With a poor economy, the education and training levels in homelands are lower than in urban areas and the per capita income is fractional compared to Whites. Table 26 shows some economic indicators of the homeland economies for 1980.[24] In 1980 35.7 per cent of the population of the Republic of South

Table 26. *Homeland Economic Indicators (1980)*

Homeland	Non-economically Active Population (%)	Real GDP per capita in Rands	GDP as % of GNP	Migrant income as % of GNP	GNI per capita (R)
Bophuthatswana	75	159	44	33	314
Ciskei	80	70	39	39	168
Gazankuku	90	44	33	58	120
KaNgwane	84	54	20	48	229
KwaNdebele	88	—	—	—	—
Kwa Zulu	82	45	21	30	196
Lebowa	87	46	30	54	137
Qwa Qwa	89	68	21	70	249
Transkei	76	85	43	56	174
Venda	81	69	41	53	154

Africa was resident in the homelands. However, the homelands produced only 3.4 per cent of South Africa's total gross domestic product. The magnitude of this imbalance is amplified because upward social mobility is linked to a centripetal geographical force pulling to the urban areas, where the opportunities are greater. South Africa therefore drains the homelands of their best human material. The outflow of labour and skills is matched by the outflow of capital. African retail patterns favour the White economy, where most wages are spent.[25] The return on natural resources is slight. Venda, for example, receives only 3 per cent royalties on its coal reserves.

For the central government this dependence has three dimensions. Economic functions are manifest, providing cheap labour and raw materials. Strategically it compels a homeland, which is unable to maintain a large police force of its own, to utilize the South African Police and Defence Force to patrol borders against the external liberation forces. A buffer is therefore provided between the White industrial and residential areas and the point of infiltration by revolutionary terrorists. Politically, it allows the central government to control homeland governments through manipulation of their budget, the major source of homeland finance. This acts as a powerful conservative force against any obstreperous homeland government.[26] It is not merely that 80 per cent of homeland revenues come from the central government, but that they come by annual parliamentary appropriation, not by right.[27] Moreover, the major part of the monies comes in the form of grants for specific forms of expenditure and therefore remains under the direction of the central government. For example, in 1983–4 the Kwa Zulu government's budget was R464.5m., yet its statutory grant was only 28.5 per cent of this. That is, just over a quarter of the government's revenue is directly under its control. Devolution of function without devolution of control over finances to support these functions strangles homeland governments.

Legislative assemblies of the non-independent homelands are even more impotent because of the large number of subjects reserved for the central government and because their legislation has to be ratified in the Republic. Homeland legislatures spend a great deal of their time ratifying decisions made elsewhere. The central importance of Inkatha as a social movement is that it constitutes a mechanism to circumvent this legislative impotence and widen Chief Buthelezi's role in politics. As one reflection of Inkatha's role in circumventing the legislature, Buthelezi has asked all Inkatha branch members to monitor activities of each member of the assembly, to judge whether they were performing the role they were elected for. In this way, the movement is a form of control over the legislature.

Homeland politicians are in a neatly woven web of constraints, and this has led to what Kotzé calls a 'deflation of demands'[28]— by which is meant a reduction of political activity in the home-lands. This is reflected in many indices — the decline of opposition parties in the legislature, the increase in uncontested seats, and the decline of participation in elections. The Transkei, as one of the first to receive self-government and thus possessing a longer political life, is a good example.[29]

In the last Transkeian election before 'independence' in 1976 the number of unopposed seats increased to sixteen. The position on electoral participation is shown in Table 28.[30] However, elec-toral polls in African politics need to be treated with caution.

Table 27. *Political Activity in the Transkei*

Activity	1963	1968	1973
Registered Voters	880,425	907,778	952,369
Votes Cast	601,204	451,916	323,092
Candidates	180	146	96
Unopposed Seats	0	3	5

Table 28. *Homeland Electoral Polls*

Homeland	Year	Total Population (1970)	Votes Cast	Poll (%)
Bophuthatswana	1972	1,680,000	213,843	12.72
Ciskei	1973	915,000	343,292	37.50
Lebowa	1973	2,097,000	189,344	9.00
Venda	1973	360,000	69,325	19.20
Gazankulu	1973	650,000	39,259	6.00
Qwa Qwa	1975	1,400,000	220,000	15.00

Voting analysis in social science tends to be based on four assumptions: the typical voter votes; typical voters have a more or less equal opportunity to vote; the typical voter's failure to vote is in itself a reflection of opinion on the merit of the parties; and the typical voter at least knows the manifest reason why he votes. All assumptions but the last are untenable in African politics. None the less, the polls are extremely low. Kotzé concludes from them that African participation in homeland elections can be regarded as a symptom of stability and an expression of loyalty to the homelands.[31] In contrast, Nancy Charton quite correctly documents what she terms the 'decline of legislatures' in the homelands.[32] This is attributed to the identity crisis which homelands have in being ill-defined geographic expressions of ethnicity which have too little power, are economically dependent, and suffer from a shortage of land. Precisely because Inkatha is not typical of other homeland political organizations, Kwa Zulu has not seen this 'deflation of demands'. Political activity there is on a higher level than the norm. Its first election in 1978 compares favourably with the first elections held elsewhere (see Table 29). Inkatha won all the seats. The poll varied from 25 per cent at its lowest to 52.6 per cent at its peak. Within the urban centres in Kwa Zulu the poll was 55 per cent at Kwa Mushu and 33 per cent at Umlazi. Note, however, the very low percentage of Kwa Zulu's population who registered to vote. Apart from factors such as fear or ignorance about the procedure, clearly a great many Zulu did not think enough of the homeland principle to register to participate in it, and of those registered to vote only 38.18 per cent actually did so. While this is high compared with other homelands, it is much lower than the central government would hope.[33]

Mechanisms within South Africa have promoted the appearance of certain types of opposition rather than others. It is a society where even reformist sentiment is not permitted among most subordinate racial groups, and little open expression and association is permitted. In this instance, shared dissent has either failed to emerge as collective action or it has been forced into secret and illegal activity, militarized or made revolutionary. Some elements of African opposition were forced to become clandestine. Because of this, they were not able openly to pursue their goals free from state harassment, although their goals may have been no less revolutionary had they not been banned. This is even true of the

Table 29. *Kwa Zulu Election (1978)*

Category	No./%
De Jure Population (1979)	5,364,500
Registered Voters	630,000
Population Registered (%)	11.74
Candidates	45
Opposition Candidates	21
Votes Cast for Inkatha (%)	90.99
Votes Cast for Opposition (%)	9.01
Spoilt Papers (%)	0.73
Unopposed Seats	12
Average Poll (%)	37

UDF and those Black Consciousness groups which have yet to be banned, and which are only slowly and partially returning to the normal political process of barter politics and negotiation. Finally, Inkatha is unique because it alone has the luxury of being able to operate in an openly political manner, free from state harassment. The extent to which Black Consciousness groups have been harassed in pursuing this open political style has engendered in some of them only a small, grudging willingness to consult with the perpetrators of the harassment. Inkatha's willingness far exceeds that of Black Consciousness.

The irony is that this platform of criticism against the government is one which the government allows by leaving Inkatha unbanned. Inkatha therefore utilizes two government-sponsored platforms, not one, as is usually argued. It has the apartheid platform of Kwa Zulu, but in leaving it free to operate by conventional means the government is providing it with an exclusive platform of opposition, whereby Inkatha can engage openly in national politics free from state harassment. And the government controls both. This is the basic reason why Inkatha remains legal. Admittedly it is difficult to ban a homeland leader without throwing apartheid in disgrace.[34] Yet the government has discovered that the best form of control is simply to leave it be. This is why, after making a number of threats, successive Ministers of Police have not translated words into deeds. By leaving it free they allow Inkatha to pursue its ends by other than revolutionary means, and thus it becomes isolated from other radical Black forces and so has a negligible influence upon them.

Chief Buthelezi feels this ambiguity very much. It was reflected in Sobukwe's funeral. Buthelezi's reaction to his reception was more significant than the violent reception itself. The almost hysterical attempt to disprove that any serious violence occurred, or that there were any threats, reveal three things. It reveals his personality and especially the charisma he is trying to cultivate. No person with such great charisma could be seen to be frightened by secular forces—hence his urge to prove that he never flinched in the face of death. More important, under pressure from the government-sponsored platforms which he realizes that Inkatha uses, Buthelezi's presence at the funeral was necessary in order to identify links with the older radicals like Sobukwe. Equally, he did not want to be seen to be rejected by the newer, younger radicals. Pressure from radical Black forces led to violence and his response was an attempt to show that he had a right to be at this great PAC event and that the instigators of violence were a minority among the young whose numbers had been greatly exaggerated by the press. Inkatha is caught in a cleft stick between the government and more radical Black forces. On the one hand these dual platforms provide numerous subtle controls for the government; conversely, they enforce isolation from the left. Inkatha's dilemma is simple: the longer it is trapped between these two pressures— of government sponsorship and control, and isolation from radical Black forces—the more moderate it is forced to become.[35] This warrants further explanation.

INKATHA'S ROLE IN RACIAL LIBERATION

Beyond whatever constraints the government can use to stifle opposition, Inkatha's role is subject to self-imposed limitations. Its dual platforms give it a dual role — as a political party in the sponsored platform of Kwa Zulu and as a social movement in wider South African politics, where it utilizes the second platform. So, while using apartheid-sponsored platforms, it claims a constituency among the victims of apartheid generally. This gives

Inkatha two contradictory aims. On the one hand it functions as a political party to govern an ethnic base, while as a social movement it calls for solidarity across ethnic divisions among those who are the victims of ethnic discrimination. This results in two sets of constraints on the organization: the tension between being a social movement and a political party, and the tension of using ethnicity to destroy ethnicity. These constraints propel Inkatha towards a progressively more moderate position.

Gordon Smith has alluded to the great similarity existing between social movements and political parties.[36] Both rely on securing broad popular support and have relationships with mass publics, but their particular versions of support and mass public differ. A movement demands commitment and active participation, while a party treats the electorate as a largely passive reservoir of voting support. There can be overlap. Some political parties require active participation and some movements take on the features of electoral machines. For example, a social movement may first articulate social demands and a party may develop from it to fulfil the more specialized role of implementing them within the political framework. Sinn Féin became the political wing of the Irish Republican Army, and the Labour Party became the party of the British trade union movement. This party dimension adds features which cause tension. Electoral and other strategies have to be adopted and a greater emphasis placed on permanent organization. The party is geared to obtaining a share of political power in the popular assembly or at the level of government. Numerous compromises are forced upon it in order to reach that position. The survival of the party in the assembly and the maintenance of its share of power may become prime considerations. Extending the electoral support beyond the bounds set by the movement may lead to a playing down of the movement. Renewed signs of activism within the movement may not be welcome if they jeopardize the party's electoral standing. The conflict in Zimbabwe between Mugabe and some of his former ZANLA men in the assembly points was an example of this tension.

Inkatha's dual role raises the same kind of problems. The goals of each differ, as do the mechanisms for realizing them. Its political party role in Kwa Zulu integrates it into the established social and political order. It may desire the overthrow of that order, but it obeys the existing rules to do it. It needs to utilize and manipulate the system before it can change it. Throughout, this has been Buthelezi's justification for his position.[37] History provides many precedents. Hitler was forced to do the same to gain his electoral victory in 1933, and Muzorewa claimed this as his role in Zimbabwe. The dilemma for Inkatha is that its role as a social movement does not have this need. The course of revolutionary confrontation is the best guarantee that its aim of Black unity for Black rule will not be diluted. It does not require of its members a passive participation through the ballot box and then subservience to elected representatives who will agitate for goals via parliamentary means. Its imperative for change is a heightening of experience and consciousness through participation in the struggle, with the collectivity as a whole being the vehicle for change.

Some political parties may adopt in an assembly a quasi-revolutionary strategy by using tactics which disrupt its operations.[38] But Inkatha's responsibility of governing Kwa Zulu prevents the emergence, for example, of the 'wrecking tactics' employed by the Labour Party in the Coloured People's Representative Council. In sum, this dual role forces on Inkatha an acceptance of strategies and goals in one role which are at odds with the other. Its role of a political party in Kwa Zulu requires compromise, barter politics and negotiation with the central government, and an alliance with traditional forces like the chiefs. In contrast, its role as a social movement forces it to reject the very government it negotiates with, to reject the ethnic base it governs, and to reject the traditionalism it is in alliance with. There is no easy marriage between the two roles. In wider South African politics it seeks to achieve radical change through peaceful means by an organized, disciplined political force that can be marshalled,[39] arguing that the South African government must recognize the power of this political force which must be reckoned with. Simultaneously, it is consolidating its governance of Kwa Zulu and participating in the apartheid structure, developing strategies and goals which do not further its overthrow.

From the simple fact of this duality flow all Inkatha's contradictions and internal conflicts. Central to the task Inkatha has set itself is a disciplined, organized force. A movement advocating liberation and attenuation of oppression thus offers its own kind of dictatorship. An organization committed to pacifism shows itself quite prepared to use violence against its detractors. A rational commitment to Black unity is united with an emotional manipulation of Zulu ethnicity. An organization once strongly against negotiation and participation in the central government has now become thoroughly immersed in White politics. Inkatha's ambiguity on all these matters reflects its inability to resolve the demands of this dual role. Also central to this task is the emergence of internal conflicts with those who are more idealist and who fail to recognize the hierarchical, authoritarian pattern on which most social movements are based. Conflicts likewise develop with those who are disillusioned with the gradual, evolutionary, pluralist tactics of political parties or the changes in Inkatha's policy.

INKATHA'S AMBIGUITY

Black unity—ethnicity

The greatest contradiction Inkatha contains is the place of Zulu ethnicity within it. Its role of political party manipulates a Zulu ethnic social base, while its role of social movement needs to rid itself of ethnicity. Zulu ethnicity is built into the very name of the organization. Zulu women carrying water pails and other burdens on their heads use a soft pad or grass coil to ease the discomfort. The pad is called an *inkatha* and it symbolized the purpose of *Inkatha yakwa Zulu* when King Solomon founded it in 1928— literally, the grass coil of the Zulu nation.[40] Solomon's nephew, Chief Buthelezi, renamed it in 1975 *Inkatha Yenkululeko yeSizwe* —no longer 'of the Zulu' but 'for the freedom of the nation'. The deliberate manipulation of tradition is manifest in another way. Buthelezi had earlier tried to revive Inkatha in 1959 but King Cyprian withdrew his support. The fact that Buthelezi thereupon abandoned the idea indicates that the support of the traditional Zulu figure was essential to the purpose of the organization—that it was necessary to be seen as part of the Zulu heritage.

Extracts from the 1975 Constitution and 'Aims and Objectives' make this clear.[41] The preamble to the constitution reads: 'our national unity and models for development should be based on values extrapolated from our culture.' It defined a number of aims: 'To foster the spirit of unity among the people of Kwa Zulu throughout South Africa . . . and to keep alive and foster the tradition of the people. To help promote and encourage the development of the people of Kwa Zulu. To promote and support, worthy indigenous custom and culture.' This is an unambiguous manipulation of Zulu ethnicity. The ambiguity comes in the very clear statements that Inkatha would abolish all forms of discrimination based on tribe, clan, sex, colour, and creed, and ensure the acceptance of the principles of equal opportunity, justice, liberty, solidarity, and peace. It also listed other aims: 'To establish contact and liaise with other cultural groups in South Africa. To co-operate with all progressive African movements which work for the complete eradication of all forms of colonialism, racialism, neo-colonialism, injustice and discrimination, and to strive for the attainment of African unity.'

In a more recent 'Statement of Inkatha Principles',[42] Buthelezi lists seventeen commandments which have significant differences and emphases. The references to Kwa Zulu are deleted. Explicit references are made to the 'poor' and 'under privileged', implying not so much a Zulu liberation as a liberation of all the oppressed. There is an increasingly political shift, reflected in the listing of specific demands of the South African government. It reads less like a statement of ethical principles and more like a political manifesto. In this way, Inkatha shows the same long-term shift from a cultural liberation movement to a political liberation movement evident in Ossewabrandwag, the Afrikaner organization four decades earlier which came to offer a peculiarly Boer type of German National Socialism. In July 1979 Inkatha scrapped nineteen of the twenty references in its constitution to Kwa Zulu, its peoples, institutions, and King. Both 'Zulu' and 'African' were replaced by 'Black'. No longer are only Zulu eligible for membership of the Central Committee and the King is not automatically Patron-in-Chief. There is no racial restriction of any sort on membership.[43]

There has obviously been intense debate within Inkatha on this issue, but the ambiguity has not been resolved. As with Ossewabrandwag, ethnicity has not been successfully purged. In Soweto's Jabulani Amphitheatre, amidst a surge of urban Zulu on the Witwatersrand, Buthelezi committed Inkatha to paying homage to great African warriors — not just Zulu, but Xhosa, Tswana, Sotho, and Shangaan as well. In 1978 he said that Kwa Zulu meant no more to Inkatha than 'just a local regional administration'.[44] Ten months later, at King Shaka Day celebrations in Kwa Zulu, he answered those who criticized him for advocating a Zulu empire by rhetorically asking whether the Whites had abandoned their cultural heritage? To masses of Zulu celebrating this historic Zulu figure, Buthelezi warned, 'the amaZulu must not abandon their cultural heritage simply because their ethnicity was being exploited by their political enemies.'[45] To a crowd at Kwa Zulu's Umlazi township in March 1980, Buthelezi said he would apologize to no one for being Zulu—history had decreed that he serve the Zulu.[46] Certainly in these instances Inkatha was reserving one image for Kwa Zulu audiences and quite another for urban Zulu, and even after the constitutional changes in 1979 the ambiguity had not been resolved.

There is evidence of this in many acts. The flag of Inkatha is Kwa Zulu's flag. Its newspaper, the *Nation*, after being published partly in Zulu and partly in English, then all in English, has now reverted to Zulu alone, restricting its propaganda to Zulu speakers. It was printed in Johannesburg and Natal, but the employees on the Rand were made redundant when they refused to move nearer to Kwa Zulu after the closing of the printing works in Johannesburg. Were sales in this urban area too few to justify the cost? Inkatha was once very critical of the Makgotla—tribal movements like community guards to prevent crime in the townships by imposing tribal punishment and discipline codes. It referred to them as 'outmodish tribal courts'.[47] It has co-operated with the Makgotla in fighting the Soweto Community Council elections.[48] It expressed its opposition to tribal dancing, which it described as a homeland circus, containing 'everything that smatters of apartheid' and the 'promotion of ethnicity'.[49] Yet at all Inkatha meetings bands of Zulu impis, in full tribal dress, chant in the speakers. Buthelezi has often danced a Zulu Royal Salute to guests sharing his platform; and within two months of printing this description of tribal dancing the *Nation* eulogized it on King Shaka Day, when it also described this Zulu king as the greatest South African statesman.[50] Symbolic aspects of a social movement are important in developing loyalty to it. A movement needs values, standards, and symbols. Despite what it says about tribalism, the cathectic symbols which Inkatha utilizes are predominantly Zulu—its flag, tribal dancing, impis, and so on. Yet, as if to emphasize its ambiguity, its uniform is in the old colours of the ANC, an organization which epitomizes modernity in African politics. This ethnic ambiguity has a symbiotic relationship with Inkatha's membership base and Buthelezi's style of leadership—they both reflect this ambiguity and in some part determine it.

In effect Inkatha is calling for non-Zulu support for an expression of political opposition which utilizes Zulu ethnic symbols in its mobilization. On Inkatha's estimate this has resulted in 'less than' 20 per cent of its membership coming from other ethnic groups.[51] Just how much 'less' is difficult to judge. We shall return to this. A more important question is to what extent this predominantly Zulu collectivity persuades the individual Zulu to accept its ideological belief system. There are two types of reply. Marxists argue that consciousness is broadly determined by social position and the common interests that arise from a shared social position. Consensus theorists, drawing on Parsons, see ideology functioning to integrate actors into the collectivity. The emphasis here is on values and support for a collectivity expressing a value system. In reality both interests and values play their part. Borrowing heavily on Weber, Heberle has defined three kinds of socio-psychological motivations: the value-rational, being a feeling of spiritual community and fellowship; the emotional-affectual, being the following of a charismatic leader; and the purposive-rational, being the pursuit of interests.[52] These motivations are likely to vary with commitment. Some people are drawn more deeply into a pattern of activities of an organization than others, despite a common belief in its programme. There are various levels of membership commitment, ranging from the professional full-time officer for whom the organization is a livelihood, to the activists who devote their leisure time to the organization, to rank-and-file members for whom the organization has greater or lesser significance, and finally to the 'fellow travellers', who share nothing more than a vague consensus about the programme.

The consequence of this variety is that as in any such organization there will be multiple sources of membership commitment and motivations, which has two consequences. First, different social bases may be involved in the movement, and they have to be coalesced: Nazism, for example, was able to link agrarian populism, the petty bourgeoisie, and unstable conservative élites. Secondly, individual motivations may be present independent of group position. The question which this raises in connection with Inkatha is the nature of its social bases, membership motivations, and commitment. Until a membership sample is obtained, one can only infer the answers from what is known about Inkatha generally. Inkatha did win 90.99 per cent of the votes cast in the 1978 election, but this was only 34.7 per cent of those who registered to vote, and 4.08 per cent of the *de jure* population. In 1979 it claimed a membership of 300,000, which was 5.59 per cent of the *de jure* population of Kwa Zulu in 1979. Its support is highest in the rural areas of Kwa Zulu and this says a lot about its base in Zulu ethnicity and tradition—what Heberle called the value-rational and emotional-affectual motivations. However, Inkatha does put great pressure on people to join. This is especially the case where the Kwa Zulu government has a hold over citizens and can enforce membership. Tales are common of students having to join the Youth Brigade before they can enrol in school, of teachers being forced to take out membership before they are employed, of pensioners being refused benefits unless they are members, of public servants having to join before they can continue their careers, and of the homeless needing membership before a house is allocated. There is no way of judging the true extent of this practice, but what Inkatha needs to learn is that total numbers mean little. What counts is the level of commitment and the number of 'activists'. In fact, there is a rough guide available. In 1979 Inkatha claimed a membership of 300,000 whereas only 218,902 votes were cast for it in the Kwa Zulu election, leaving 27.03 per cent not voting for it. Admittedly younger members are ineligible to vote, but equally it is an error to assume that all who voted for it were members. These numbers could cancel out one another. The missing 81,098 members may be non-Zulu and thus unable to vote. This number would be in accord with Inkatha's estimate of non-Zulu support. Maybe, also, they represent those who were unwilling to vote because they were compelled to join. It is perhaps some combination of the two, and until the veil is lifted on Inkatha no one will know the size of this category.

In the urban centres Inkatha has no benefits to redistribute and few controls, except on the families of migrant workers. It would say much for Inkatha's social base and for the place of ethnicity in it, if the organization had support from urban Blacks who possessed motivations other than ethnic in character. Are these elements of Heberle's purposive-rational motivations, with Inkatha fulfilling their economic, political, and social interests? In Soweto's Jabulani Amphitheatre Buthelezi draws crowds of up to 30,000. The longitudinal study by the Arnold Bergstraesser Institute found that 43.8 per cent of urban Blacks rated Buthelezi as the leader they most admired.[53] There is an obverse of these figures: 56.2 per cent admired other leaders, and 21.7 per cent of Zulu in Durban voted for other leaders, which increased to 45.8 per cent for Zulu in Soweto; nationally, 40 per cent of urban Blacks had not heard of Inkatha. If support for Buthelezi weakens even among Zulu when they reside in more metropolitan townships, support from non-Zulu urban Blacks is probably much weaker, and this would impel the organization towards an ethnic character, even more so if its urban social base came from what Brotz[54] and Mayer[55] call 'traditional' rather than 'modern' urban Africans. Anthropologists have documented the bifurcation which exists in townships. At the one pole are the 'traditional' Africans who resist change, especially the inner change necessary for adjustment to life in towns. In their language, customs, and behaviour they are reluctant to forgo their traditional values. At the other pole are the 'townsmen' who have made this profound inner change. Inkatha's social base would be much less ethnic if its urban support came from those who had undergone the process of acculturation. It is difficult to judge this,[56] although, as an earlier chapter demonstrated, Schlemmer does show Buthelezi's support to be variable over time.

Empirical analysis of Inkatha's membership is beginning to emerge now and suggests that its major support-base lies in rural Kwa Zulu. Despite Inkatha's dual role where it attempts to mobilize support outside the Zulu ethnic group and territory, Schlemmer has estimated that in mid-1978 95 per cent of its membership was Zulu and that of nearly 1,000 branches only 36 existed outside Natal, with 203 in urban areas. In 1982 Kane-Berman updated Schlemmer's figures, pointing out that there were 1,200 branches by this time. Although 30 branches were in Soweto alone, the majority were still in rural Kwa Zulu.[57]

The fact that membership is structurally located in the rural areas of Kwa Zulu explains many other observations which Schlemmer made about membership. It accounts for the disproportionate number of females who are members, for a vast number of the economically active males are absent as migrant workers. This also explains the high number of members drawn from particular economic groups and occupations. Support is especially evident among the economically inactive sectors of Kwa Zulu, particularly from schoolchildren, among those economically active sectors which either administer or work within the Kwa Zulu bureaucracy, such as teachers and civil servants, and among members of the professions and business who service their own community in Kwa Zulu. It is the migrant workers who are seen as providing Inkatha's tenuous link with the urban areas.[58] By 1982 Kane-Berman had revised this view, arguing that Inkatha was now very broadly based in class terms, including a large number of members from the stable urban proletariat. Unfortunately he provided no empirical support for this claim.[59] Southall thinks that Inkatha has little support among either the stable African working class or among trade unionists.[60]

Migrant workers constitute approximately 60 per cent of the urban male work-force and their ratio has been growing. Since migrants legally remain outsiders from the urban labour market and are liable to be sent back periodically, their political militancy is tempered by severe material insecurity. Many migrants resort to political escapism in religious cults, drugs, and alcohol. Since they depend on the chiefs for land allocation and old-age security, they cannot afford to show their frustration in the homeland. The small amount of empirical analysis of the attitudes of migrants and illegal squatters which is available shows them to be politically moderate. Schlemmer and Möller found that 80 per cent of migrants adapted to stress through acquiescence. They resigned themselves to their bleak and impoverished circumstances through one of three responses: conformists rationalized their situation by either lowering their expectations or inflating actual progress; retreatists coped by engaging in rural fantasies; and the alienated overcame initial intense dissatisfaction by escaping into a sense of despair and passivity.[61] Inkatha's political moderacy can be seen as both cause and effect of the fact that its main constituency lies among these groups. Indeed, Buthelezi's supporters often under-emphasize the degree of radicalism which other groups possess and amongst whom Inkatha has little support.[62]

It is wrong to suggest that Inkatha has no support among the stable urban proletariat. In a sample of members from the urban township of Kwa Mashu, I found that the movement was successful to some degree in mobilizing support among the African

Table 30. *Occupation of Respondents from Kwa Mashu*

Occupation	Inkatha Members		Non-members	
	No.	%	No.	%
Retired	2	1.9	4	2.7
Student	25	23.8	7	4.7
Farming/Agriculture	—	—	1	0.6
Construction/Building	10	9.5	20	13.3
Factory, unskilled	31	29.5	48	32.0
Factory, skilled	15	14.3	21	14.0
Clerical/Office	9	8.6	18	12.0
Professional	13	12.4	31	20.7
Total	105	100	150	100

working-class and highly educated groups.[63] Given the socio-demographic structure of African townships, urban workers and the young will naturally predominate in any sample. The sample of Inkatha members from Kwa Mashu reflects this age and class structure, irrespective of whether socio-economic class position was determined by occupation, level of education, or income. But while in absolute frequencies urban workers and the young do dominate the sample, it is clear from the socio-demographic breakdown of the Inkatha respondents that the organization does have some limited appeal to all socio-economic classes and age-groups. In this sense it is very broadly based: there is no strong statistical over-representation of any one group. In the Kwa Mashu study it was also possible to establish the socio-demographic character of a wider sample of non-members, which acted as a control against which to measure the Inkatha respondents. In this regard, by comparing the two samples, a tendency was discernible for the Inkatha respondents to be younger and more working class. Table 30 shows the occupations of the two samples. Significantly fewer Inkatha respondents came from the higher occupational grades than in the larger group of non-members. This reflects Inkatha's tendency in Kwa Mashu to appeal more to the urban proletariat. Nor was there any tendency for the Inkatha members in the sample to be more upwardly mobile occupationally than their counterparts who were not Inkatha members. If anything, there was a slight tendency for the reverse to be the case.

This support amongst the urban proletariat needs to be kept in proportion. While the sample of Inkatha members did reveal this tendency, the respondents were still a minority of all those who worked in the urban proletariat. The only occupational grade in which there was a majority who were members of Inkatha was students. Elsewhere the proportion of Inkatha respondents was around one-third. It reached 39.2 per cent for all unskilled factory workers, and 41.6 per cent for all skilled factory workers. This reconfirms Inkatha's appeal to the urban proletariat. As a consequence, there was a marked tendency for Inkatha respondents to be unemployed or to have experienced unemployment within the last year: 33.3 per cent of non-members were currently unemployed and 58.7 per cent had been unemployed in the last year, whereas the figures for Inkatha respondents were 44.2 per cent and 70.5 per cent respectively. This is certainly a high level of unemployment for both sets of respondents (not brought about by the biasing effect of the fieldwork because the interviewing was carried out at times when employed workers were at home). Inkatha's support among those subject to bouts of unemployment is a very significant factor in reducing the extremism of such workers.

As observed above, for some categories of people Inkatha membership is a prerequisite for their employment and for the receipt of services and facilities. Of the 105 respondents who were members of Inkatha, 82.3 per cent said that they wanted to join: perhaps many of those who were obliged to join did not identify themselves as members of Inkatha. Having said this, 81 per cent said Inkatha had helped them in either their employment or career, and 75.2 per cent indicated that Inkatha membership was necessary in obtaining it. However, all of them unanimously rated Inkatha as the most important organization to them of all those they belonged to. The majority feeling was obviously that while Inkatha membership may have been obligatory, they nevertheless *wanted* to join. In the light of this, the motivations for joining Inkatha are interesting. Members were asked which came nearest to their main reason for joining. Table 31 compares the result with the migrant workers who were members, studied by Meer and Mlaba. With absolute frequencies being so small for migrant

Table 31. *Reasons for Joining Inkatha*

Reason	Kwa Mashu Sample		Migrant worker Sample	
	%	No.	%	No.
Improve standard of living	6.7	7	8.0	6
Safeguard career/job	9.5	10	3.5	3
Improve wise decision-making	31.4	33	2.6	2
Obtain one-man one-vote	8.6	9	—	—
End discrimination against Blacks generally	43.8	46	7.5	5
Other	—	—	—	—
No response	—	—	78.4	54
Total	100	105	100	70

workers, the role of chance factors influencing the results is high, although there was a tendency for those who replied to mention personal economic considerations relating to their employment and standard of living. This may well reflect the precarious economic position of migrant workers. In complete contrast, the members from the urban township considerably under-emphasized personal economic considerations, mentioning community-oriented or political reasons. There was a marked degree of hope among members from the urban sample that joining Inkatha would help abolish discrimination in all its facets, not just its material ramifications.

This tendency to mention political rather than economic motivations holds true when cross-tabulated with age, occupation, income and level of education. What is surprising is the degree of political motivation among the economically underprivileged members. This under-emphasis shows itself in the respondents' views on what is the major issue facing Inkatha. Table 32 presents the results obtained. Just over one-fifth mentioned directly economic issues, while a very clear majority saw Black unity as the key issue. But unity to what end ? Clearly, the political motivations of the respondents suggest that Black unity was primarily a political strategy, although no doubt with economic implications. Again this tendency transcended all socio-demographic variables.

Table 32. *The Major Issue Facing Inkatha*

Issue	%	No.
Reducing unemployment	18.1	19
Raising the standard of living	4.8	5
Universal franchise	5.7	6
Abolishing discrimination	11.4	12
Forging Black unity	60.0	63
	100	105

These results suggest that the Inkatha respondents were politically sophisticated and highly motivated by questions of pragmatic policy. The suggestion that their support lay in a charismatic, traditional, or tribal devotion to Chief Buthelezi was not supported in this particular sample. When the Inkatha respondents were specifically asked whether they joined the movement because Chief Buthelezi was its leader or because its policies were what they believed in, only three respondents refused to answer and 86.7 per cent of the rest mentioned policy. The age, occupation, income, and education of respondents did not affect this overwhelming choice of policy over the appeal of Buthelezi. Respondents were also asked to assess Buthelezi's leadership, and although there was a non-response rate of 10.5 per cent, 87.6 per cent of the remainder said he was a good leader. When those who replied in the affirmative were asked why they thought so, only 3.8 per cent felt so because he was a Zulu prince, 3.8 per cent thought he was a good man, while 89.5 per cent said the reason was that he aimed to secure a better life for them. There was a non-response rate of 2.9 per cent. Clearly, then, the policies of Inkatha constitute its appeal, not its leader. Following upon Max Weber, these are what Heberle has called 'purposive-rational' motivations, where members are drawn to a movement by the pursuit of individual or community goals and by a rational evaluation of the movement's policy. Contrary to what might have been expected, there was no evidence in the data to suggest that members had 'emotional-affectual' motivations, which are generated in the personal following of a traditional or charismatic leader. It was policy which influenced the sample of urban supporters, and the policies tended to be seen primarily in political terms.

The ambiguity concerning ethnicity was not reflected in the attitudes of Inkatha members in the sample. They are less conservative than Buthelezi in this regard, for they are ahead of their leadership in rejecting a political role for Zulu ethnicity. It has already been established that the overwhelming majority of Inkatha respondents saw the encouragement and forging of Black unity as the main issue facing the organization. Their motivations to join reflected an interest in wider political goals and showed no traditional, tribal, or charismatic following for Buthelezi. In response to the question of which group they saw it as Inkatha's role to help, nearly three-quarters of the Inkatha respondents said 'all races', rather than 'all Blacks' or 'only Zulu'. This support for an ethnically neutral role for Inkatha among its supporters in the sample held true across all social variables, although it was even more pronounced among the young and better-educated.

This degree of ethnic neutrality may be over-representative of Inkatha membership as a whole due to the urban nature of the sample and the bias in Inkatha membership towards the rural dwellers. Meer and Mlaba's study of women in Nqutu showed them to be more ethnocentric than the Kwa Mushu respondents, with only 1 per cent supporting the view that it was Inkatha's role to help 'all races', 1.5 per cent feeling it should be 'only Zulu', and 14 per cent 'all Blacks'. There was a non-response rate of 85.5 per cent, so it is impossible to know what significance this finding has, although this tendency toward ethnocentricism among rural Africans is to be found in other research on the ethnic attitudes of rural Africans in South Africa. In this sense, the ambiguity in Inkatha policy may well reflect the different constituencies within it and represent Buthelezi's attempt to reconcile the different interests of these constituencies. This suggests, as Kane-Berman has argued previously, that Inkatha is a coalition of radical and moderate elements. If the sample reflects the radical element, it further suggests that there is a rural–urban split within the movement which it is necessary to contain. Conflicts in the past between Buthelezi and the Soweto branches of Inkatha over strategy in Soweto are evidence that this tension has proved difficult to withstand. If this dichotomy between the rural and urban members does exist, it forces upon us the necessity to distinguish between the different kinds of Inkatha membership. Inkatha membership can no longer be portrayed as a monolithic and homogeneous entity to be accounted for in sweeping generalizations. If anything emerges from this empirical data it is that it now becomes necessary, when referring to Inkatha membership, to distinguish between its different types—urban, rural, moderate, radical, young, old, petty bourgeois, proletarian, highly educated, poorly educated, and so on.

Inkatha is a coalition of members with different social backgrounds, attitudes, interests, and aspirations. This exposes the organization to a range of internal policy conflicts. The leadership of Inkatha have not only to create a strategy which gives the organization a role in wider South African politics, they have simultaneously to tend to the bureaucratic task of forging a united membership. There is already evidence of internal conflicts over policy and strategy, which will be discussed below.

In an attempt to extend its social base, Inkatha has formed an alliance with other Black forces—the South African Black Alliance. This widens its ethnic character, containing as it does Inkatha from Kwa Zulu, the Dikwankwentha Party from Qwa Qwa, the Inyandze Party from KaNgwane, the Indian Reform Party and the Coloured Labour Party before it left the Alliance. There is less formal association with the Chief Ministers of Gazankulu, Ciskei, and Lebowa. In effect this is an alliance of those already working within central government-sponsored institutions —the homelands, Natal Indian Congress, and Coloured People's Representative Council. There is no alliance with those outside ethnically defined platforms and it has no White participation. The Afrikaans press treated the formation of the Alliance as an ethnic consolidation under the design of the Zulu against its own ethnic base. Much reference was made to the other ethnic groups being 'duped' by the Zulu, who are numerically and positionally dominant in the partnership.[64] There is no mass support in any ethnic group other than the Zulu. At Alliance meetings in Natal, even in Indian townships, few Indians attend. It represents no more than an alliance among leaders, not a choice by masses, and the audiences are generally small. This confirms Inkatha's ethnic social base. Most Zulu who support Inkatha, especially rural Zulu, seem to have a strong ethnic self-identity, and contact with other ethnic groups does not meet with their full support.

In fact, the different interests of the ethnic platforms make the Alliance very fragile. The Chief Ministers of Gazankulu, Lebowa, and Ciskei have been reprimanded by Buthelezi for their discourtesy in irregularly attending meetings. The Coloured Labour Party disagreed over the issue of disinvestment and participation in constitutional dispensations. This was only resolved by the retirement of its leader Sonny Leon. Eventually the Labour Party was thrown out of the Alliance when it decided to support and participate in the new constitutional dispensations. After this Buthelezi sought new partners, and, in 1983, he repaired his relationship with President Matanzima of the Transkei. He has also met other homeland leaders, most notably Phatudi of Lebowa, to forge a united front amongst African leaders. At their meeting in June 1984 Buthelezi and Phatudi announced that they were to forge a 'new spirit of unity' against apartheid: but it was a unity of those already working within apartheid institutions. This call followed the unification of the non-collaborative opposition forces around the two organizations of the UDF and NFC. During 1985 Buthelezi sought allies elsewhere, for Inkatha formalized its links with the PFP to form the Convention Alliance, which provides a forum for both organizations to meet regularly and plan joint political action. The announcement of the Convention Alliance generated little interest or excitement amongst the media or radical Black politicians.

To reiterate the point, Inkatha's ambiguity on the issue of ethnicity is a reflection of its dual role. Its support in Kwa Zulu is mobilized via Zulu ethnic symbols. Yet, to widen its appeal and its role in the liberation struggle, Inkatha also tries to underplay its ethnic character. Accordingly, Buthelezi's leadership style evidences all three of Weber's ideal types of authority. Traditional authority is strong in Buthelezi's leadership—he is a Zulu prince with very close connections with the royal family. This traditional position is manipulated in mobilization of support; it features as a significant point in his biography.[65] In his speeches he often explains that he has no need to apologize for holding his position as Chief Minister since the Buthelezi clan by tradition always provide the King's Prime Minister.[66]

It cannot be denied that Buthelezi also presents a charismatic figure, if by charisma is meant Spencer's notion of 'secular charisma'[67] (rather than Weber's sense). African politics is conducive to claims of charisma. The leaders of Black Africa dominate the affairs of their peoples, overshadowing elected legislatures. The wresting of independence from colonial powers provided the legitimacy that persists in the form of strong, undivided leadership. The Chief Ministers, like the earlier anti-colonial nationalists, dominate their cabinets and legislatures. This is in part a product of the institutional weakness of assemblies, the personalities of the leaders, and their desire to legitimate their position against opponents by deliberately cultivating a personal following. Buthelezi tries hard in this respect, and he has met with some response. His biography is full of such references,[68] and because of his moderacy the liberal press in South Africa are a considerable help in cultivating this image.

There are concomitants to 'secular charisma', and this is where Spencer's use of the term is misleading, for these concomitants are not so pejorative in the original Weberian, religious sense. Buthelezi does have a sense of mission—a reluctant hero whose role is pre-ordained.[69] This has been another of his justifications in taking the Chief Ministership of Kwa Zulu. As his biographer reports, 'as one Zulu after another approached him to give his leadership, he began to see that the choice was not his at all ... it was pre-ordained.'[70] Buthelezi shares other characteristics of 'secular charisma'. He tends to play up the importance of his role, personalizing events to give himself rank and significance. His early role in politics, including his stay at Fort Hare, is a little like Stalin's role in the Russian Revolution—subject to considerable *ex post facto* embellishment. Trotsky called Stalin a 'grey shadow' at the time; Buthelezi's critics echo this. Also, Buthelezi is an exceedingly arrogant, egocentric man; without this personality trait, none of the other facets of his 'secular charisma' would be possible.

The feud with Bishop Tutu provides an index of Buthelezi's character. Tutu was subject to a diatribe of abuse, continued for months in speeches, in the press, and on the pages of *Nation*, for admitting there was violence against Buthelezi at the Sobukwe funeral. Tutu was singled out with excessive vehemence.[71] Precisely because he personalizes politics, Buthelezi personalizes criticism of Inkatha and tends to personalize his counter-attack. Conflict between Inkatha's role in the liberation struggle and that of its opponents is portrayed as Buthelezi versus Motlana, or Buthelezi versus Tutu. Buthelezi's abusive name-calling helps no one except for salving his own offended ego: nearly every criticism is met with this kind of response. Arrogant to a fault, his lengthy letters in reply generally end with Buthelezi's full title—President of Inkatha, Chief Minister of Kwa Zulu, and Chairman of the South African Black Alliance. Depending on the readership of the newspaper, the order of the titles is sometimes altered, and the Chief Ministership excluded. The Sobukwe funeral also provoked attack on 'double dealing White liberals', merely because a journalist surmised that Buthelezi may suffer international embarrassment as a result of the incident.[72] In response to an article by a Black journalist which omitted Buthelezi from a list of Black leaders, he felt the need to say that many regarded him as a leader.[73] He responded once more when it was claimed that Tutu had a bigger following than himself.[74] The South African Broadcasting Company was told to withdraw its representative from Ulundi for making comments which Buthelezi disagreed with; a Natal Parks Board official was forced to make a public apology for making a private joke about Buthelezi to a friend which was overheard by a Zulu worker; a man was forced to rename his pet dog because he called it Buthelezi; and a New Republic Party MP was attacked as politically incompetent, a 'greenhorn and pipsqueak', because he dared to say that Mandela would win an election in South Africa. Delicate negotiations with the party faltered while Buthelezi's bruised ego healed.

It is this kind of arrogance and egoism which allowed Buthelezi without compunction, and in the midst of an impoverished Zulu people, to build himself, in 1980, a house valued at R250,000, to accept a pay increase to R18,864, and to spend time at health farms at R200 per week to counter the effects of corpulence and over-consumption. By 1982 his salary had risen to R35,000: the poverty of his supporters provides a stark contrast. In an attempt to prevent criticism of this kind Buthelezi cut the salaries of Kwa Zulu officials by 35.83 per cent in March 1985. It is not known who was affected by the cut. There are also a number of as yet uninvestigated allegations, made by an administrative employee of the Kwa Zulu Development Corporation, about wide-scale corruption to the benefit of Buthelezi. One example is said to be the granting of lucrative liquor licences to him and his mother. The Kwa Zulu Development Corporation is also supposed to have granted him large personal loans without the necessary collateral and deposit. This is also supposed to have happened in the case of

Cabinet Ministers. Huge financial sums in the form of subscriptions, and income from the sale of uniforms, badges, films, and so on, are generated by Inkatha. One wonders where this money goes.

The paradox of the man is that in conjunction with manipulating Zulu tradition and cultivating 'secular charisma', Buthelezi offers Weber's rational-legal authority. This leadership style makes use of rational, pragmatic programmes, detailing future political and social organization. The Buthelezi Commission is a good illustration, as we shall see, but this leads to Buthelezi's biggest irony: he appeals to the head, whilst simultaneously appealing to the heart through his supposedly extraordinary personal traits and traditional ethnic symbols.

Policy metamorphosis

The function of Inkatha's role as a political party is to govern Kwa Zulu, but its role as a wider social movement seeks the liberation of Blacks from White minority rule. In reality this second role is much more than that: it is to realize the accession to power of Inkatha. That in itself is no criticism (Machiavellians would have us believe that all politicians need an element of selfishness), if Blacks were liberated *en route*. The metamorphosis in policy which Inkatha has undergone suggests that Black liberation is secondary to Buthelezi's accession. It is prepared to negotiate itself into power at the sacrifice of moderating its demands. This has been admitted by one of Buthelezi's lieutenants, Jordan Ngubane, a political exile and supporter of the ANC in the 1950s, who, with Buthelezi's help, spent three years trying to return to South Africa. On his return he explained why they had both tried so hard: 'one of the reasons why I came home is that I am fully convinced Inkatha now has enough power to force a negotiated settlement. We will get everything we want if we succeed in negotiating an alliance with the Afrikaner.'[75] If this mirrors the leadership's thinking, Inkatha has no rivals in the liberation struggle. Some Black Consciousness groups are slowly coming to the position where they are negotiating with Whites—although sullying themselves by contact with the perpetrators of past harassment causes internal disputes which may threaten such a movement towards negotiation. Two things differentiate Black Consciousness and give Inkatha an open field—the extent of negotiation and the policy being negotiated. Inkatha's policy metamorphosis suggests that it is not negotiating an end to apartheid—Inkatha's programme is not that—but is seeking an alliance with the Afrikaner. It is negotiating itself into power. This metamorphosis can be dated to the rise of Muzorewa early in 1978, and Buthelezi is supremely confident that he can avoid Muzorewa's fate. Inkatha's general secretary, who is also the Education Minister, said in November 1983 that one day Inkatha would rule South Africa and that the ANC would form a 'minority opposition group'.

In order to negotiate itself into power Inkatha began formal and regular contact with political representatives of the dominant racial group, independent of the contact between the South African and Kwa Zulu governments. It met the Broederbond for the first time in November 1978. Referring to this custodian of the Afrikaner *Volk* Buthelezi said, 'your people and my people are South Africans . . . we will fail in our leadership if we cannot bring our people together'.[76] One wonders which 'people' Buthelezi was speaking for. Jordan Ngubane put his own interpretation of the negotiation in less ambiguous language: 'If Botha wants to solve the race problem of this country, he has to start with the Zulu.'[77] Inkatha met nine members of the National Party for the first time in September 1979. Within four months it was negotiating with the arch-conservative Andries Treurnicht on 'real decisions affecting all South Africans'.[78] As Southall makes clear in claiming that Inkatha has moved to the right, these formal and informal links with the government should be considered as an important measure of Inkatha's political moderacy.[79] In this regard, Inkatha has come to be seen by some people as a potential channel of communication between the National Party and the ANC.[80] This is unrealistic, for, as we shall see, Inkatha's relationship with the government is not matched in intimacy and affection with that of the ANC.

Contact is no bad thing if it does not compromise what Blacks are fighting for. Inkatha's policy metamorphosis suggests that it is prepared to sacrifice a great deal. One aspect of this metamorphosis is Inkatha's attitude toward Black Consciousness. The once close links have faded. In 1974, in a speech at Curries Fountain, Buthelezi expressed his affinity with leaders of Black Consciousness, and he often attended SASO conferences and wrote in SASO newsletters. A year later he reiterated this.[81] Since then his attitudes toward more radical Black forces have changed drastically, especially toward the banned organizations SASO and the Black People's Convention.[82] This deterioration is reflected most acrimoniously in Inkatha's relationship with Dr Motlana and the Committee of 10. In the *Nation* survey of 'people who count', Motlana was praised in 1978 as someone 'warm and genuine, a man concerned with the welfare of the people, a very shrewd and agile mind, one of the country's most vital resources'. The Committee he headed was 'celebrated, encompassing the broader spectrum of Black organizations'. Inkatha refused to participate in the 1978 Soweto Community Council by-election because of Motlana's detention and the *Nation* pledged support for the Committee of 10.[83] By 1979 Motlana was being derided as a baboon.[84]

In August 1979, the Revd Jesse Jackson, who was visiting from the USA, organized a unity meeting between Buthelezi, Tutu, and Motlana. Opposition from other members of the Committee of 10 forced Motlana to withdraw and he subsequently announced that there was no hope of establishing common ground with Buthelezi. Buthelezi's response was typically full of pique, accusing Motlana of working to establish himself as the sole authentic leader in the country at Buthelezi's expense.[85] In Soweto this seems to have happened. A survey conducted in 1980 revealed that 69 per cent of the sample expressed support for the Committee of 10, compared with only 9 per cent for Inkatha. A further poll found that Motlana had a higher level of support among Soweto Zulus than Buthelezi.[86]

These acrimonious relations have continued with the formation of the UDF, which Buthelezi has described as 'Johnny-come-lately heroes'. History was not created, he said, by 'forming committees and getting the audience to clap'. The politics of rhetoric was supposed to shine through the UDF's declarations, for the organization was 'two or three steps away from the daily lives of ordinary people'.[87] In 1984 he accused the UDF of not directing their anger at apartheid but at Buthelezi himself, focusing 'all their energies at my political character assassination and vilification'.[88] This antipathy often forces Buthelezi to criticize the acts of protest and opposition which the UDF and its supporters engage in. Buthelezi had earlier attacked the Anti-Republican Day protests in 1981 and he was also critical of the October 1984 stay-aways.

The opposition between Buthelezi and the UDF has been vituperative. One of the most immediate issues which divides them is contact with the ANC. This issue is important because the ANC is still held in awe in South Africa twenty-five years after its banning. Both organizations want to be seen as taking up the mantle of the ANC. Inkatha has stressed its links with older radical forces.[89] This is reflected in the publicity which surrounded its 1979 meeting with the ANC in London. It stresses the number of former ANC supporters in its ranks, and Inkatha's colours are the same as the ANC's. The politics of exile do tend to be remote and, by nature, terrorist organizations demand an internal wing because force of arms is insufficient on its own. A number of organizations wanted to be in the position to benefit from the status of the ANC and the remnants of its support. Motlana was no different: to forestall a close link between Inkatha and the ANC he called Buthelezi a traitor. This was the signal for a long and venomous conflict. In many ways the ANC was responsible for this since it did not see the use which Inkatha would make of whatever contact the ANC did have — 'formal', 'informal', 'social', or 'political', as various interpreters saw it. Many of its former supporters saw their opposition to Inkatha as contradictory. This is very much the case with Motlana, an ex-ANC supporter, who first refused to believe that it had ever met Buthelezi. The ANC realized this, and subsequently tried to play the meeting down; the flirtation is now over. This explains Buthelezi's revelation in May 1980 of a plot by the ANC to assassinate him five years previously. On 8 June 1980, in Kwa Mushu, Buthelezi attacked the ANC in stronger tones than ever before. They were criticized for not bringing liberation after twenty years and were now described as a fringe movement. Liberation could never come through them, he said. In attacking the ANC in this manner, Inkatha is either very sure of the social base of its support, or very hurt by the ANC playing down the significance of its meeting with them and working now with Black Consciousness. In 1983 Buthelezi defiantly said that the ANC were frightened because Inkatha was the largest liberation movement in South Africa. He abused the ANC as 'a bedfellow' of the National Party.

Important as it is, the issue of contact with the ANC is only a symptom of a deeper conflict between Inkatha and organizations like the Committee of 10 and the UDF; this centres around participation with dominant racial-group political dispensations and initiatives. The ANC, of course, have taken one stand on this with their revolutionary underground tactics. This makes their contact with Inkatha all the more surprising, for Inkatha is now fully in support of using most of the government-sponsored platforms which are provided. This is contrary to the UDF's and the NFC's stance, as the leading unbanned radical political organizations. Inkatha's position has undergone a major shift, inevitable given its new willingness to negotiate. To the allegation that Inkatha works 'within the system' it counters that all Blacks work within the system—they live their entire lives according to the dictates of apartheid. This position had little impact, for there is a qualitative difference between obeying the law under compulsion and voluntarily accepting it.

Although Inkatha has long used government-sponsored platforms and participated in its political framework by representing a homeland, it was strictly against any further participation. For example, it was very critical of community councils.[90] The *Nation* quoted one assessment of them: 'nobody of significance in Soweto cares a hoot for the so-called council. It is seen as yet another treacherous institution imposed on the residents against their will.'[91] The last such critical reference was in December 1978. In 1980 Inkatha decided to participate in the Soweto Community Council elections before they were postponed. The corollary of this metamorphosis is a change in its opinion of Thebehali, the former leader of the Soweto Council. In October 1978 relations were so bad that Thebehali was threatening to take the *Nation* and its editor to court. Within exactly one year, he was sitting on a platform with Buthelezi as a member of Inkatha, announcing that 'Soweto belongs to Inkatha'.[92] To coincide with this, Buthelezi wrote in a leading liberal newspaper: 'at all costs we must work with any White and we must negotiate. We as Blacks dare not prejudice any White initiative . . . only political cowards refuse seats at negotiating tables.'[93] Accordingly, Inkatha is prepared now to utilize platforms it once derided, and to sit with those it once ridiculed. Holding the political power of Soweto's masses would put Inkatha in a stronger bargaining position in any negotiation. To this end also it has sat on Dr Koornhoof's Liaison Committees on the position of urban Africans, and participated with the central government's commission on constitutional changes.

Inkatha is eager to portray community councils as legitimate. In a speech in Sebokeng in 1981, Buthelezi praised the 'leaders' who sat on the council. 'As far as I am concerned,' he said, 'you have a clear indication of a mandate from the people.'[94] He repeated this in 1982. Yet the cleft stick which Inkatha is caught in, between state control and ostracism by the left, means that Buthelezi has an uneasy relationship with both. He has rejected the new constitution because it excludes Africans, and this has persuaded him to review Inkatha's position on other forms of contact. He announced in 1983, after some vacillation, that Inkatha would not participate in the November community council elections. This was just as well, for the swell of opposition to the constitution led to a massive boycott of them. To have participated would have invited considerable humiliation. As it was, Buthelezi was astute enough to see the way opinion was going over the constitution. In this respect, for all his co-operation with the state, Buthelezi did not have enough influence when it mattered, for he was unable to persuade the government of the folly of excluding Africans from the new constitutional proposals. This temporary discomfiture of Buthelezi is seen by his radical critics as justification for their stand against consultation and co-operation with the state.[95]

The Soweto Civic Association, the Committee of 10, and the UDF eschew the same degree of contact as Buthelezi, fearing it would compromise their radical position. The compromises which Inkatha has made are many. It has compromised its former stand and affinity to all the other Black opposition forces, internally and externally, who work for a more radical solution, and it has compromised the position of all Blacks expecting such a solution. Inkatha's greatest compromise is on the question of majority rule. Its position has caused a division within African politics between those working for universal franchise within a unitary state and those prepared to concede a federalist solution. Both sides of this divide now face a dilemma. Those who refuse negotiation and participation reduce their immediate influence; those who do participate in order to negotiate lose their credibility among most of the Black élite, let alone many of the masses. They bring to their dilemmas different assumptions about the transference of power. Inkatha is visualizing a relatively ordered transfer, with the dominant racial group granting power and legitimacy to its chosen Black heir; the other liberation forces visualize the transference as disorderly enough for this procedure to be bypassed and for their lack of influence among the dominant racial group to be of no consequence. In other words, the decision on participation presupposes not only different strategies to achieve Black liberation, but also fundamentally different views on the transference of power and the independence of a Black government from White domination. It is not only the strategy which Inkatha has adopted that has changed, therefore, but also the assumptions behind it.

So Inkatha has reneged on its November 1977 demand for majority rule[96] through the adoption of a confederal solution. In 1978 Buthelezi defined Inkatha's stance. There would be three kinds of state in South Africa—White, African, and multiracial.[97] One of the issues Inkatha negotiated with the National Party was the consolidation of Kwa Zulu as a state within P. W. Botha's proposal of a constellation of states. Buthelezi repeated this view in the Buthelezi Commission.[98] Its main thrusts were calls for the merging of the province of Natal with Kwa Zulu in a regional federation; a multiracial system of power-sharing, based on universal franchise with proportional representation guaranteed for all groups in all branches of government, a minority veto, and a bill of individual and group rights; and large-scale devolution of power from central government to the regional federation. None the less, its primary intention was to define the economic, political, and territorial boundary between Kwa Zulu and Natal, as if to pre-empt the central government's plan on consolidation of Kwa Zulu. Buthelezi has made it quite clear, that he wants the major part of Natal. Would achieving this in P. W. Botha's constellation be enough to placate Inkatha? No one can do more than guess although Jordan Ngubane views Inkatha's role in these terms, seeing the future as a union of eleven states in South Africa. It was believed by journalists from the liberal English-language *Sunday Times* that the merger of Natal and Kwa Zulu was discussed at a meeting between Buthelezi and P. W. Botha in May 1985. After initially rejecting the Buthelezi Commission report, Botha had said that there were items in it which could be positively explored in negotiation and consultation with the Kwa Zulu government. Further discussions took place when Botha visited the homeland late in 1985. Significantly *Die Vaderland* warned Botha after the May 1985 meeting about Botha's own power base and about the splits which a political accommodation with Coloureds and Indians had caused in the National Party. In August 1985 members of the Inkatha Youth Brigade met students from the University of Stellenbosch to discuss 'political matters'. A communiqué issued afterwards said there was agreement between them that South Africa should have 'regional power-sharing'. But whether in P. W. Botha's constellation or in Buthelezi's confederal solution as demanded by the Buthelezi Commission, any confederal solution sells out both urban Africans and the ANC: the first because they can never become states, the second because of its overriding goal of a unitary state. It does not need acceptance of the constellation idea for Inkatha to compromise these two Black forces—its own policies have already done so.

Inkatha has two potentially contradictory aims. It wants to end apartheid while maintaining the stability and prosperity of South Africa so as not to threaten the leadership of a Black government (or governments) whether in a unitary state or confederal union. It is for this reason that Inkatha uses whatever platform the government provides. To go underground would be to force Inkatha to become revolutionary and destroy the second aim. It is also for this reason that Inkatha advocates investment in South Africa, despite disinvestment being a means of securing the first aim. A corollary of Inkatha's recent moves to negotiate itself into power —either in a unitary state or a redrawn confederation—is a metamorphosis in its policy concerning disinvestment. In 1977 Buthelezi announced that sanctions were the only mechanism to achieve peaceful change and withdrew his support for foreign investment in South Africa.[99] Inkatha has reversed this position. It is now not prepared to destroy the foundation of the economy. In part this is because it would constrain Inkatha's future action, and in part because it is by inclination a supporter of the free enterprise system.

Inkatha's economic policy is unclear. In its July 1979 'Statement of Beliefs', it proposed the greatest possible redistribution of wealth but only consistent with maximizing productivity.[100] Buthelezi has often spoken up for capitalism modified with 'African communalism'. The implications of that qualification for the free enterprise system are unknown (although when Inkatha's urban representative, Gibson Thula, told a businessmen's conference that Inkatha would nationalize the mines, Buthelezi explicitly denied this). Maré has shown how Buthelezi supported the interests of capital in granting White chain stores access to Kwa Zulu.[101] For Marxists, this espousal of free enterprise explains Inkatha's political moderacy. Thus Southall, for example, sees it as a consequence of its character as a petty bourgeois organization utilizing a populist disguise in order to strengthen the position of the petty bourgeoisie in the political centre.[102] For others Inkatha's unwillingness to engage in economic reorganization is only one more reflection of the compromises it is prepared to make. Either way, the interests of capital provide another social base for Inkatha. It is the nature of capital, however, for this base not to belong exclusively to Inkatha.

Democracy-dictatorship

Inherent in Inkatha's task of building a strong, disciplined force as a demonstration to the government that it cannot be bypassed in any negotiation is the development of a rigid code of discipline, a hierarchical structure, and an authoritarian character. Within both its roles—Inkatha as a social movement and as a governor of Kwa Zulu—there has been an emergence of dictatorial methods. It needs to maintain support among Zulu or it loses its potential bargaining power. To this end Inkatha has taken to enforcing compulsory membership and become more disciplinarian. Its notion of 'constituency politics', where local branches are consulted for suggestions and opinion, fails to work for two reasons: many local branches are not organized enough to elicit opinion from ordinary Zulu, and there is no requirement that suggestions will be listened to by Buthelezi. The idea of 'constituency politics' satisfies more the image Inkatha wants to present of a democratic movement fighting a democratic and just cause. In practice, as an organization Inkatha has authority flowing downwards, while discipline and obedience flow upwards. This puts the organization at odds with the more idealist demands of the younger radicals and former ANC members. A group of University of Zululand students attacked Buthelezi in the press, stating their disillusionment with Inkatha's dictatorial methods. He was a benevolent dictator operating under the guise of traditional African democracy. Reference was made to 'closed door meetings' and decisions being made without discussion. Inkatha 'should allow the democratic principle of freedom of thought to flourish in a people's movement'.[103] This is a good statement of the classic contradiction facing social movements representing the poor and oppressed. They are people's movements claiming their legitimacy from the masses, seeking to realize freedom and equality, while this very task itself demands the negation of freedom and the enforcing of rigid discipline. This has been true, for example, of all the great revolutions in the name of the people, causing the contrast of Louis XVI's autocracy and Robespierre's terror, or the Tsar's oppression and Lenin's 'dictatorship of the proletariat'. The contrast is thus not unique to Inkatha.

None the less, like all social movements, Inkatha needs to keep the pretence of democracy. The word 'democratic' is often used in the name of even the most totalitarian of social movements. To counter criticism like this, Buthelezi has often said that the final authority is not the Inkatha President but the Central Committee of fifty members. The power of the single man is subservient to the representative body. In a letter to the author, Buthelezi wrote that he had no authority 'without the sanction of the general conference'. In a formal sense this may be true. A prime minister in Britain has no authority except that which the House of Commons grants. *De facto*, Buthelezi's power, like that of a prime minister, is entrenched. For Buthelezi this is true because the President of Inkatha must be Chief Minister of Kwa Zulu, and both positions give Buthelezi powers of patronage. The Central Committee outnumbers Buthelezi 49–1. It comprises all chairmen of Inkatha sub-committees, all members of the Kwa Zulu Cabinet, a representative of the Women's Brigade and the Youth Brigade, those elected from the general conference, and those nominated by the President of Inkatha.[104] As well as being able to nominate members personally, it is Buthelezi who appoints the Kwa Zulu Cabinet and heads of sub-committees. The majority of its members hold their position at his behest, and this gives him wide power should he wish to use it: the personality of the man suggests he would.

It could well be significant that the formation of Inkatha as a social movement independent of the Kwa Zulu Assembly came one year after the Assembly rejected Buthelezi's decision on deferring Kwa Zulu self-government.[105] Not only is Inkatha more directly under the control of its President than the Assembly was under the Chief Minister, it also provides a new system of patronage under the direct control of Buthelezi. Now that Inkatha has all the elected seats in the Assembly, Buthelezi's control has widened still further. The patronage comes in the form of full-time posts within Inkatha, within the Kwa Zulu government or its public service, or in the creation of new chieftainships—it dispenses wealth, power, and status under the direct control of Buthelezi as President of Inkatha, Chief Minister of Kwa Zulu, or Chairman of the Black Alliance. This is where Inkatha's role as the governing party in Kwa Zulu is an advantage.

Kwa Zulu is the product of central government policy rather than successful national liberation. Its government evolved out of a territorial authority that is an instrument of administrative, not political, decentralization of power. Neither is it subject to the normal constraints that come from having what Almond and Verba call a 'civic culture',[106] nor to the restraints on autonomy that come from the need to maintain legitimacy. In 1975 the South African government was officially asked to co-operate in prohibiting other forms of political opposition in Kwa Zulu. This has seen the decline in opposition to Inkatha's role as the governing party in Kwa Zulu, despite Inkatha's support of virulent opposition to the central government. In order for Inkatha to oppose apartheid in its role as social movement, opposition to its role as a political party is systematically denied. This is essential for Inkatha's bargaining position. Hence Buthelezi has said that opposition forces in Kwa Zulu are a luxury and would lead to needless bickering.[107] The opposition in Kwa Zulu has been derided as the agent of White oppression and state security.[108] So Inkatha's commitment to barter politics and the pluralist political game is less than total. It is prepared to use that as a strategy in its opposition but denies the strategy to its opponents in Kwa Zulu. Despite what the liberal press in South Africa say about Inkatha sharing their view of politics, Inkatha is no different from Black Consciousness or the ANC. There is no value commitment in Inkatha to barter politics. It is merely a mechanism to realize an overriding end. To achieve this, Inkatha has chosen negotiation and participation precisely because by the norms of the dominant racial group (if not their political practice) it singles Inkatha out from other opposition forces. Paradoxically, this is the reason why Inkatha can allow no challenge to its role in Kwa Zulu, for this would threaten its ability to play according to the rules of the dominant racial group: in order to be pluralist it has to deny this right to its opposition, or else Inkatha would no longer be that large, organized, strong, disciplined force which cannot be bypassed. This fundamentally distinguishes Inkatha from, say, the UDF, SCA, or Motlana, who are moving towards a position of consulting with Whites.

This formula is behind Buthelezi's attempt to circumvent the power of traditional authority in Kwa Zulu by making new chieftainships and by displacing the political role of the King. Buthelezi is reserving the manipulation of tradition for his own authority. The oddity is that King Goodwill, as the most traditional legitimate figure in Zulu culture, can only be removed by rational-legal or charismatic means, as Weber would say. The rational-legal manner is shown in portraying the King as unconstitutional on account of his involvement in politics. It is significant that King Goodwill has taken a different political stance from Buthelezi, advocating armed struggle to overthrow apartheid, and he is against participation in central government initiatives. On a visit to Los Angeles, the King was firm in his rejection of the homeland principle, and thus by implication, of the territorial and administrative unit of Kwa Zulu.[109] To begin the procedure for impeachment, he was called before the House of Assembly to answer these allegations. Calling upon his traditionally validated authority, the King refused to remain and listen, like Catherine of Aragon when judged by Cranmer. The issue has not been resolved since. This is perhaps because, independent of this process, the authority of the King is being superseded by Buthelezi's attempt to portray himself as the greater charismatic figure. The King's authority is undermined by allegations that he is in the pay of Iscor, the state-funded steel corporation.[110] In attempting to diminish the King's claim as a charismatic figure, Buthelezi is portraying his claims as more valid. The *Nation* saw the Zulu as Buthelezi's 'people', while he was their 'leader'. For example, 'as the sun rose higher, the valleys of Kwa Zulu reverberated with the echo of song, ululating and chanting. The first cheers had erupted—King Goodwill had arrived. But the cheers grew louder, almost hysterical—Chief Buthelezi had arrived among his people.'[111]

Pacifism—violence

In public statements Inkatha is pacifist. In part this is an attempt to define itself *vis-à-vis* the external liberation forces, and in part a reflection of mass Black opinion, which is strongly in favour of a peaceful solution to South Africa's problems.[112] Yet it is intrinsic to the dual role which Inkatha plays that violence will be threatened or used against its detractors, opponents, or internal dissidents—it is inherent in its wish to become a strong disciplined force, in its tactics of compulsory membership, in its authoritarian methods, and in its opposition to those who threaten its claim to negotiate with the central government.

Violence is of many types. Symbolic violence is evident in Inkatha's threat to use the power that lies in Zulu numbers and by allusions to Zulu military history. It is an ethnic symbolism which calls upon the Zulu as a proud fighting nation full of warriors steeped in military tradition. This kind of violence thus involves both the threat of force and an appeal to Zulu ethnicity. Responding to those who are engaging in a 'calculated campaign of vilification against the Zulu people', Buthelezi warned that the 'Zulu will respond in kind . . . the campaign will not go unanswered.'[113] The symbolism of the Zulu spear in its folklore is frequently used by Inkatha. At a seminar on the Anglo-Zulu Wars, Buthelezi admitted that the Zulu spear was a precious symbol: 'It remains the powerful symbol which inspires us towards the liberation of our land.'[114] The symbolism of Zulu ethnicity is as important here as the threat of violence.

Much less symbolic and more dangerous are the threats and use of actual physical violence. Many such threats have been made against those whom Buthelezi labels as extremists. It could be no more than coincidence that a few days after Buthelezi appeared in Soweto during the 1976 uprising to investigate, among other things, alleged intimidation against Zulu migrant workers, the hostel-dwellers erupted in violence against students. The physical violence against Committee of 10 supporters is less coincidental. To Motlana's criticism of Inkatha Buthelezi responded by saying 'it may ultimately cost him lives.'[115] Inkatha's General Secretary warned that Motlana would be 'dealt with harshly indeed'. Following these threats, a mob of fifty Inkatha members physically attacked Alex Mbatha in Durban, under the illusion that he was Motlana coming to speak at an Indian political rally. Mbatha was tarred and feathered and badly injured. Perhaps even more destructive of Inkatha's claims of pacifism were the statements made by the attackers—'Why does he speak to Indians first? You are not Blacks'—which nullifies Inkatha's claim to be advancing Black unity.[116] It is no justification to excuse this as impromptu action by peripheral elements when Buthelezi spent the best part of a five-hour speech personally attacking his opponent prior to the assault. No disciplinary measures were taken against the perpetrators. Normally even the smallest criticism of Buthelezi ends in expulsion. In the past he has even called in the Security Police to deal with those critics whom he alleges to have had contact with the banned SASO and Black People's Convention. The South African police were called in against boycotting students in Amanzimtoti in March 1979, leaving one schoolchild dead and another injured. This was repeated in the May 1980 boycott in Kwa Mashu. To protect Buthelezi against his critics at the 1980 University of Zululand Graduation Ceremony, shots were fired by the South African police and tear-gas was used. Threats against Buthelezi are met with a tough response from Inkatha or the police, but no action is taken against Inkatha members who actually attack Buthelezi's critics.

Physical violence has been used against Kwa Mashu residents and pupils by Inkatha officials. Six Durban attorneys pursued these assaults before the courts for civil damages. For example a force of several Inkatha officials attacked a Kwa Mashu pupil at his home before taking him to Ulundi, where he was paraded before the House of Assembly and verbally abused.[117] This incident came after Buthelezi had told students that any provocation in whatever form would be met with force.

Considerable violence was used by Inkatha against its opponents in 1983–4. For example, early in the year, Inkatha Youth Brigade members attacked Indian students at the University of Durban Westville who objected to Buthelezi speaking on the campus. Four students died and one hundred were injured at the University of Zululand when members of Inkatha attacked students who had tried to stop Buthelezi speaking. A member of Inkatha Youth Brigade was killed the following day in a revenge attack. The UDF, AZASO, and AZAPO called for a day of mourning, while Buthelezi blamed the students for allegedly 'saying things which offended' the Inkatha Youth Brigade members. [118] When the University reopened in 1984 students who received bursaries from the Kwa Zulu government were told that their grants would be withdrawn unless they signed a declaration not to criticize Buthelezi, Inkatha, or the Kwa Zulu government. This also applied to Zulu students at the University of Natal's medical school. In a second attack, Inkatha Youth Brigade members attacked a prayer meeting in November 1983, which had been called by Mpumalanga Youth Organization, an affiliate of the UDF. The police had to be called to protect the UDF supporters, whereupon Inkatha members burnt a bus, slashed tyres, and smashed car windows. Chief Mapumulo was assaulted by Inkatha youth outside the legislative assembly for refusing to join the organization. In a violent clash with youths at Lamontville four youths were killed by Inkatha supporters.[119] Buthelezi condemned both attacks, but said that whoever challenged him challenged the people and the people would deal with them. He warned that Inkatha youth would demonstrate their strength and prowess if he was subject to further vilification.[120] In all there were twelve deaths in Durban in clashes between UDF affiliates and Inkatha during 1984. Within weeks of the formation of COSATU in December 1985 its meetings were attacked by Inkatha youths. During 1985 Inkatha youths were also thought to be responsible for attacks on the homes of prominent UDF supporters in Natal, such as Fatima Meer.

The intention of physical violence is to inflict injury. There are other forms of violence which create fear without the infliction of injury. This can be called psychological violence. Its intention is to intimidate, like terrorism, which is an extreme form of psychological violence. The instrumental target of terrorism may be strategic oil depots, police stations, or whatever, but the primary target is to create terror amongst the populace as a lever against the political élite. The instrumental targets differ in Inkatha, but the creation of psychological fear is a common feature. Thus, to students on the Indian university campus at Durban Westville who taunted Buthelezi, he made threats of a repeat of the bloody Indian–Zulu riots of 1949. Similar threats were made to Indians during the 1976 uprising. To the Coloured and Indian political forces opposing contact with Inkatha in the South African Black Alliance, Buthelezi gave a warning of a civil war of Black against Black. To the editor of the *Sunday Tribune* who documented Inkatha's violence against boycotting students in May 1980, Buthelezi retorted that he was laying the foundation for anti-White violence. This fear is not only created by the clever propaganda use of the potential power that lies in Zulu numbers or past incidents of violence. It comes also with the realization that Inkatha has the resources through the

Youth Brigade or the Kwa Zulu government to carry out these threats. Inkatha has formed local vigilante groups and is now pressing for its own police and defence forces.

In 1982 Buthelezi announced the establishment of a Youth Services Corps, which he saw as necessary to carry out development work and educational programmes among the poor. It has a paramilitary character because, as Buthelezi said, 'nothing short of large-scale paramilitary developments' is necessary to give Blacks a 'disciplined and organized approach';[121] but the corps is also to have a policing function.[122] This is the political danger. In May 1984 Buthelezi announced in the Kwa Zulu assembly that the Kwa Zulu police force were to have an operational paramilitary wing. This was in order to 'defend property and life but also to hit back with force at those who destroy and kill'.[123] Buthelezi has both the ANC and those who engage in mass protests in mind here. His opposition to the October 1984 stayaway organized by the UDF and FOSATU was based on the fact that stay-aways were supposed to be merely opportunities for destruction to life and property. This clearly suggests that Buthelezi intends his paramilitary force to be directed at both external and internal threats.

There is a clear historical parallel. Fascism was unique for its conjunction of a disciplined, armed, and violent stratum with a parent political organization. This dichotomy is coming to be represented in Inkatha. Its stand on Kwa Zulu unrest is a good illustration. Unrest in educational centres is frequent in Kwa Zulu; teachers at Nqutu were actually murdered by students in August 1978. Buthelezi has taken a tough stand. He seems to feel that his leadership is on trial among Whites and takes all unrest as a personal challenge to him and his movement. The 1980 schools' boycott throughout South Africa was, he exclaimed to the Kwa Zulu House of Assembly, 'a carefully orchestrated international campaign against Inkatha, my leadership and this Assembly'.[124] Quite disturbing delusions of grandeur are evidenced if he believes that; disturbing because if unrest is seen as a personal attack it elicits a personal response which can be violent and emotive. To the students who boycotted in Kwa Zulu, Buthelezi said that they would have their skulls cracked and that they were playing with fire. Members of Inkatha have been taken to court for attempting to carry this out. All this happens while Inkatha is praised in the South African press for its willingness to negotiate and participate in the democratic political process.

The nature of Inkatha's response to the unrest reveal something of the organization. It could redirect the students to the real cause of their protest—the apartheid society within which Black education functions. That it does not do so and strongly suppresses unrest validates the point that its audience is now the dominant racial group. Their response decides whether Buthelezi fails the test, and the tough repressive measures against students are a response designed to impress Whites. Besides the nature of the response, this point is confirmed in Inkatha's apportioning of the blame for the unrest. The cause did not lie with the dominant racial group or its policy of apartheid. In 1977 the Kwa Zulu education unrest was the result of Black agitators from Soweto and King William's Town.[125] The following year the unrest was Transvaal-inspired.[126] The 1980 incidents lay with Xhosa lawyers, 'foreign representatives', radical Blacks, and Dr Bengu, a former Inkatha general secretary. The central government also takes this view of unrest in urban areas; it serves an important function since it clouds the realization that their own politics are at the root of the unrest. Unrest, therefore, is not structurally determined and inherent in the society they uphold. It is *ad hoc* and arbitary, depending on the ability of agitators to convince the masses of something they are unaware of normally. Oscar Dhlomo interpreted the 1979 unrest as only lawlessness and vandalism.[127] Buthelezi saw the 1980 boycott as psychotic. Clearly singling him out for attack, Buthelezi said that the Student Representative Council President at the University of Zululand was the type of person who would assassinate him.

Inkatha shares more than this with the dominant racial group. They are both of the opinion that force can quell opposition: to reverse Rousseau's dictum, they believe that might is superior to right. Rather than directing student anger towards the apartheid structure over which Inkatha has no control, it expels students, refuses to register them, calls them before the Kwa Zulu Cabinet, subjects them to various types of violence, imposes a 'riot deposit' for good behaviour, or simply hands them over to the South African Security Police. Inkatha has learnt well from its oppressor how to carry out its own oppression.

Inkatha's relationship with the young is interesting. There is a strong and active Youth Brigade, but its support tends to be ambiguous. Buthelezi tries strenuously to cultivate their allegiance. His response to the Sobukwe funeral incident is an example. To stress these links, he enjoys being pictured with young Africans giving the Black Power salute, and he heaps eulogies on Steve Biko. While publicly against terrorism, Inkatha expresses sympathy with the young Africans who turn in despair to this tactic. It emphasizes its harassment by the Security Police and is thus seen to share the same fear and insecurity as politically aware students. Inkatha is proud to note that policemen have tried to infiltrate it, that members have been detained or approached to become informers, that newspaper vendors of the *Nation* have been harassed, the paper banned, and its reporters questioned. Buthelezi's biography is full of similar references. Yet his support among the young is variable; among UDF and Black Consciousness supporters it is nil. Meetings at universities are invariably disrupted: neither Inkatha nor its leader is popular at the University of Zululand, where UDF and Black Consciousness support is high. In 1980 there were thousands of Kwa Mashu high school children boycotting classes against Inkatha's call for them to return. They threatened to assassinate Buthelezi should he appear in Kwa Mashu.

The organization is trying to remedy this ambiguity. It has initiated a more subtle repressive measure to forestall Kwa Zulu unrest and win the support of the young. Not only are the young more in favour of UDF and Black Consciousness, and critical of the homeland principle, but they also have minds which politicians want to mould for future stability and support. It is significant that totalitarian leaders uniformly gave a high priority to the political potential of youth. If the new system is to endure and the ideology carried forward, the leaders must look to the generation from which the next élite will be draw.1 and from which the next followers will come. This is the reason why such regimes have a vested interest in institutionalizing and controlling the education of the young. Inkatha has its Youth Brigade and has taken a hand in the curriculum of Kwa Zulu schools. This is also something they have learnt from the Afrikaners, who have their Voortrekkers and their Christian National Education system. The Kwa Zulu syllabus employs the same methods of youth preparedness and cultural aggrandizement untilized by the Afrikaners for four decades. This is achieved through the teaching of Inkatha in Kwa Zulu schools.

The general aim of this addition to the curriculum emerged from a conference of 1,500 Zulu educationalists in 1978. They were to acquaint pupils with the role and significance of Inkatha, and make them realize that a successful nation must be well organized; to equip youth with the knowledge and skills to enable them to develop a sense of nationhood; to develop behaviour patterns that will make the young worthy citizens; and to make pupils understand the contribution that education, work and a strong national culture can make to the building of a nation. The ethnocentricism of the syllabus is its chief mark. It lays great emphasis on Zulu history, tradition, and national development. The pupils study the lives of Shaka, Dingane and Buthelezi. Stress is also placed on the unifying role of Inkatha for all South Africans, with, of all things, 'the constitution (of Inkatha) being respected as the arbiter of all differences'.[128]

The latent intentions behind this are to control not only the minds of the young but also their actions. In June 1978 the organizing secretary of Inkatha, D. M. Msane, noted the decline of discipline in Kwa Zulu schools. This realization came after two years of repeated unrest in the wake of the 1976 Soweto uprising. Removal of the missionary influence in African schools was identified as the cause, with the vacuum being filled by various 'political ideologies'.[129] In November of that year the Inkatha curriculum was devised. With this step, Oscar Dhlomo, Kwa Zulu Minister of Education and now General Secretary of Inkatha (emphasizing Inkatha's interest in education), announced that unrest in Kwa Zulu schools must stop. To achieve this end, teachers were urged to become members of Inkatha and to impose the discipline of the movement on the schools, and if they refused to join they were still to carry out official instructions and assist with Inkatha Youth Brigade meetings. A circular issued by the Kwa Zulu government instructed teachers to give schools the opportunity to form youth brigades and to take part in Inkatha activities. It added that this was a departmental instruction, and failure to comply constituted insubordination.[130] This situation poses a contradiction for Inkatha. Its role as a social movement advocates pacifism, peace and freedom, while its role as a political party in Kwa Zulu enforces a vacuum, keeping out argument and information which challenge the official ideology, by violence if necessary.

INTERNAL CONFLICTS

From an analysis of Inkatha's role in racial liberation, it is clear that the organization sees a predominantly political solution to

African demands, as do its members (as the empirical research showed). Economic policy is subservient to geopolitical solutions and the granting of territorial and political rights. It does recognize the need for material advancement and economic development, but visualizes them as following on from a geopolitical solution. The emphasis is on redefinition of territorial boundaries and political liberation within them, and while it accepts that there are corollaries to this, they remain unspecified. This is clearly demonstrated in Inkatha's Buthelezi Commission, whose primary intention was to redraw the geopolitical boundaries between Natal and Kwa Zulu. The details of economic reorganization are submerged in a basically confederal solution, aimed at altering territorial boundaries and political functions. Without the necessary devolution of economic function, the geopolitical unit will not become a viable state. In contrast to this political solution, there are a number of studies suggesting that mass African opinion is primarily concerned with an economic solution, calling for economic and social reorganization to aid material advancement of the oppressed to the level of Whites.[131] Insufficient money, low wages, poverty, the high cost of living, and job reservation are problems often listed as the priority.[132] In practice, economic oppression is a direct consequence of apartheid, and in attacking the racially unequal distribution of income, wealth, and welfare, Africans are still attacking apartheid. But many Africans see the dynamics of change as economic.[133] Inkatha sees them as political.[134] This is where Inkatha shows the influence of its social base in capitalism.

This disparity has two consequences. First, Inkatha as a social movement will become disunited as members come to realize that its view of the future, its aims, strategies, and tactics, are not theirs. Social movements need their membership to internalize the cognitive categories they offer; without this, the movements lack cohesion, splits could follow, and the likelihood of achieving power diminishes. Secondly, if Inkatha does achieve its geopolitical solution and these economic aspirations and changes are frustrated, as the African masses see it, the struggle will continue. The unrest in Kwa Zulu could well be due to this phenomenon. Inkatha has a distinct disadvantage in playing two simultaneous roles in the liberation struggle. Most social movements are not in a position to redistribute economic resources prior to achieving power. Inkatha's role as the governing party in Kwa Zulu provides it with just this opportunity, and so the organization can be judged by its ability to meet economic aspirations. This can affect the judgement of its role as a social movement. It is for this reason that Inkatha is very sensitive to allegations of corruption, laziness, drunkenness, theft and mismanagement in the Kwa Zulu government.[135]

The economic strangulation which the central government is applying to homeland economies restricts Inkatha's ability to satisfy economic solutions. They are circumscribed by Kwa Zulu's dependence on South Africa. Inkatha's dilemma, therefore, is that the longer it governs Kwa Zulu in its present territorial, political and economic form, the stronger the likelihood that anger in the homeland over shortage of land,[136] rent increases,[137] poor wages, migrant labour, and so on will be shifted away from the central government on to the Kwa Zulu government and Inkatha, as its governing party. This could well explain the urgency within Inkatha for a geopolitical solution and its willingness to accept a reconsolidated Kwa Zulu. Yet without the development of an economic infrastructure it presents no solution. That is why the question of the inclusion of the Durban-Pinetown industrial centre in a reconsolidated Kwa Zulu assumes so much importance. Without this, the only industrial belt in Natal, Kwa Zulu will be no better for its geopolitical solution.

Many of the internal conflicts within the organization are over issues like these: some members realize the disparity between their economic dynamic and Inkatha's political one, others become disillusioned with Inkatha's inability to satisfy economic aspirations, both in Kwa Zulu and potentially in a liberated South Africa. This is a conflict essentially about policy and ideology, and while it is common to most social movements it is more sensitive in Inkatha because of its dual role. The conflict, however, is a manifestation of a deeper phenomenon—the transformation of a movement that occurs as it becomes more successful and established. As a theme this is paralleled in Weber's notion of the routinization of charisma. Rush and Denisoff have argued that once a social movement emerges its demise is inevitable, either through 'failure' or through 'success' (merging with the status quo).[138] To rephrase Inkatha's dilemma: while its role as a social movement has not failed, as a political party in Kwa Zulu it has merged with the status quo and became tainted by it. This inevitably causes conflicts over the adaption of policy and ideology to this merger. Inkatha's metamorphosis in policy is an example, and conflicts have followed. Kolinsky and Paterson have shown how it is relatively difficult to change policy and ideology without admitting that the movement's goals have been transformed or diluted.[139] Clashes may develop between 'revisionists' who do not want to change their emotional or rational investment in the ideology and the 'pragmatists' who seek to adapt the ideology to new conditions. The National Party in South Africa was torn apart by these conflicts, centred on Treurnicht and P. W. Botha. Such conflicts in Inkatha have been precipitated by its coalescence with the status quo. There is a reluctance to threaten the stability it has now achieved, and any opposition to this new policy is branded as deviant, opportunist, or renegade. Such conflicts nullify the assumption of common interest within the movement and the renegade faction are often dealt with by repression before splits can solidify. Hitler's annihilation of Roehm and Stalin's repression of Trotsky and the 1927 Left Opposition are examples. These conflicts can cross-cut, however, so that cohesion is reinforced through the overlapping division of opinion. The changing transitory alliances of opinion lead to compromise in much the same fashion as British or American political parties operate.

In Inkatha there is evidence of the first kind of conflict, and one can assume that the second normally takes place. The evidence for the first, more dramatic, type is plentiful. The Youth Brigade members were expelled in October 1978 on conflicts over the issue of Inkatha's new stand on disinvestment. They wanted to challenge the capitalist system and called for a more radical distribution of wealth and resources than Inkatha proposed. The organization, they alleged, had become a part of the capitalist structure which they wanted to attack.[140] Inkatha's new policy towards participation in central government-sponsored platforms has also caused internal conflicts. An Inkatha official in the Transvaal was expelled because he refused to make a public apology to Gibson Thula, Inkatha's urban representative, after attacking him for participating in Koornhof's Liaison Committees.[141] A similar conflict occurred over Inkatha's participation in the Soweto by-elections of 1978, when the Soweto branch was disciplined for criticizing the initial decision to participate. They felt that Inkatha's radical image was compromised. The conflict was resolved by Inkatha candidates sitting as Independents. This reserve has since been cast off and Inkatha is openly participating. It is significant that these conflicts occurred in urban centres where Black Consciousness is active. If they continue, these policy and ideological conflicts could well cause an urban–rural split in Inkatha, pushing it even further into an ethnic social base.

Merging with the status quo is not the only kind of transformation that can occur in a social movement. Zald and Ash identify what they call the Weber–Michels model of transformation, of over-bureaucratization and oligarchy.[142] It implies the replacement of political and ideological goals by organizational goals, causing a split between what Roche and Sachs term 'bureaucrats' and 'enthusiasts'.[143] The general impression which social movements present is of a spontaneous, passionate, iconoclastic break with the old regime. These elements are undoubtedly present. But the success of a movement's political goals depends on how the 'colder aspects of movements' are managed[144]—organization, recruitment, administration, discipline, and so on. There must develop some regularized method for carrying on the ordinary activities of the movement. This necessitates a division of labour and the emergence of specialized administrative and political roles. Lenin's is the classic discussion of this problem.[145] In argument with his fellow revolutionaries he developed a strategy for organizational tactics. Contrary to Luxemburg, Trotsky, and Bakunin, he argued against committing the Social Democratic Party to positive action, urging instead the development of a sound organizational base. This culminated in the formation of the Bolshevik faction within the party.

However, with organization comes a paradox. A number of political analysts of working-class movements in the early twentieth century stressed the ways in which the development of specialized organizational roles and structures led to that structure, its enhancement, maintenance, and continuity, becoming a major goal of the movement, often displacing political and ideological goals. In this way, they explained the failure of the proletarian revolution despite the existence of working-class parties, especially in the two most advanced capitalist societies, Britain and Germany. In isolation from other variables, this explanation tends to be inadequate. Barrington Moore's work *Injustice: The Social Base of Obedience and Revolt* returns to this theme. The two Germans, Weber and Michels, called this 'over-bureaucratization' and the 'iron law of oligarchy' respectively; it is also called the process of institutionalization.[146] This demands of Inkatha an efficient organizational structure. Its members must be prepared to believe in its commitment to political and ideological goals, while respecting the movement's organizational operating norms, which may seem a departure from these goals. Important questions therefore arise concerning Inkatha: has it developed organizational goals? have they displaced political goals? is there conflict because of this? how is this conflict expressed? If there are these conflicts, Inkatha's ability to withstand competition from rival opposition forces which support the same political goals will be correspondingly weakened. For Inkatha there are redeeming features: its rivals are themselves racked with division, and Inkatha has changed its political goals in order to be distinct from its former rivals.

Beyond the first question in fact, no one knows the answers to these questions, given Buthelezi's reluctance to accept the anatomization of the organization. It has developed an organizational structure and goals which enable it to carry out the mundane chores which any movement creates. As far as one can tell, this structure is as shown in Figure 4. To qualify as a branch, thirty members are needed. Usually members are galvanized by an official from Ulundi before a local member is appointed branch leader. Each branch is given a name. A branch 'area' is an administrative unit comprising fewer than eight branches, whereas a 'region' is a larger unit of eight or more branches. The General Secretary is the leading administrative officer, responsible to the Central Committee, on which he sits, and to the President. The Kwa Zulu Cabinet sits en bloc on the Central Committee, and its President is also Chief Minister of Kwa Zulu.

Answers to other questions can only be inferred. One suspects many organizational conflicts in the lower echelons, most having to do with a clash of personalities. One major schism emerged when the General Secretary, Dr Bengu, was expelled in January 1978.[147] It is significant that Buthelezi took the opportunity to reshuffle the Central Committee—perhaps to purge 'disloyal' and 'dissident' factions, although he only admitted to severely reprimanding 'disloyal and unruly elements'.[148] Three members of the Youth Brigade were expelled and, in addition, four Inkatha

Social movement   Political party

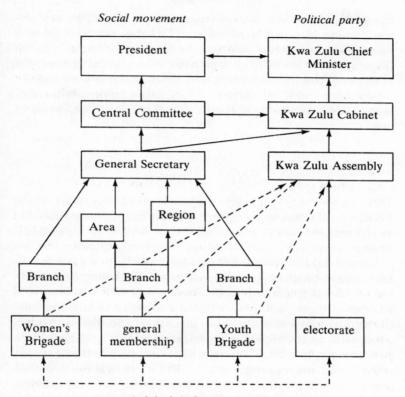

FIGURE 4. Inkatha's Organizational Structure

members were reprimanded and suspended from holding office indefinitely. These decisions took place during a Central Committee meeting which had previously heard Buthelezi condemn 'anyone who seeks to do their own thing outside the limits of the Constitution' and insist that Inkatha was 'committed to peaceful change'.[149] Bengu refused to take on a full-time organizational role as General Secretary, and this coupled with Buthelezi's intimations, may indicate a conflict between organizational and political goals. It may be significant also that in a letter to the press one of the expelled Youth Brigade members stated that Inkatha had become a large and oppressive machine.[150] Was he searching to express Weber's notion of over-bureaucratization or Michel's iron law of oligarchy? Bengu certainly had more support than Buthelezi among the radical, activist students at the University of Zululand, where he was Dean.[151] Oscar Dhlomo, the new General Secretary, subsequently said that Bengu was inciting the Youth Brigade against Buthelezi.[152] The point to be made is that because of the dual role Inkatha plays, and the need for organization to satisfy both roles, the nature of the organization itself blunts Inkatha's activism further. The Bengu affair is a good example of this.

CONCLUSION

This analysis has probably provoked more questions about Inkatha than it has answered: the chapter can justly be described as preliminary. This must always be so while the organization remains secret and closed. What has been demonstrated is that it is an error to take Inkatha at its face value; like Janus it presents two faces, one of which can be extremely ugly. This chapter has attempted to show the depth of the contrast between the two images. It has traced these contrasts—Inkatha's so-called contradictions—to the dual role which it plays in liberation. This duality involves constraints which propel the organization to a progressively more moderate position. This feature is what endears it to the dominant racial group and ostracizes it from Black political opinion. The social base of Inkatha's support was seen to be quite narrow, founded in Zulu ethnicity and capitalism. The latter is likewise two-faced, and Inkatha shares this aspect of its social base with most, if not all, political forces in South African politics—even corners of the National Party. The constraints identified were of many types—organizational conflicts, the manipulation of ethnicity, the use of oppression and violence, the possession of a political dynamic to change—all of which were related to its dual role. The purpose of the chapter will have been served if it has identified the uglier face of Inkatha, and shown it to be inherent in the roles it has set itself. The negative image is often ignored by liberals in South Africa and in the West,[153] whereas its role in the liberation struggle ought to be judged precisely by this almost hidden image. The dynamics of its role show Inkatha to be a moderate force in African opposition, increasingly isolated from radical opposition forces and dependent on state-sponsored platforms. This has significant consequences for the future of African opposition.

Notes

1. Quoted by J. Kane-Berman in the *Irish Times*, 21 June 1983.
2. For a range of viewpoints see: 'Inkatha: Centrepoint of the Gathering Storm', *Frontline*, December 1979; 'Will Zulu Party Change the Shape of Apartheid Politics?', *New African*, March 1978; South African Communist Party, 'The Compromising Role of Inkatha', *African Communist*, 74, 1978; Counter Information Service, *Buying Time in South Africa*, London, 1979.
3. For example see: J. Brewer, 'The Modern Janus: Inkatha's Role in Black Liberation', Institute of Commonwealth Studies, *The Societies of Southern Africa in the Nineteenth and Twentieth Centuries*, 12, 1981; id., 'The Membership of Inkatha in Kwa Mashu', *African Affairs*, 84, 1985; J. Kane-Berman, 'Inkatha: The Pardox of South African Politics', *Optima*, 30, 1982; L. Schlemmer, 'The Stirring Giant: Observations on the Inkatha and other Black Political Movements in South Africa', in R. Price and G. Rosberg, *The Apartheid Regime*, Berkeley, Institute of International Studies, 1980; R. Southall, 'Buthelezi, Inkatha and the Politics of Compromise', *African Affairs*, 80, 1981; id., 'Consociationalism in South Africa: The Buthelezi Commission and Beyond', *Journal of Modern African Studies*, 21, 1983.
4. The difference between Buthelezi and Inkatha on the one hand and the other homeland leaders and organizations on the other, is noted even by Buthelezi's most radical critics. See, for example, J. Saul and S. Gelb, *The Crisis in South Africa*, New York, Monthly Review Press, 1981, p. 128, and R. Southall, 'Buthelezi, Inkatha and the Politics of Compromise', p. 467.
5. South Africa creates terminological confusion. The term 'urban Black' is an example. There are many kinds of urban dwellers—illegal dwellers, temporary migrant workers, and permanent urban residents with rights granted under Section 10 of the Urban Consolidation Act. I refer to this category only.
6. The issue of the migrant labour system has ramifications for urban–rural politics, despite the migrant workers being considered as temporary urban dwellers.
7. See Buthelezi's biography: B. Temkin, *Gatsha Buthelezi: Zulu Statesman*, Cape Town, Purnell, 1976, pp. 157, 196–7, 206, 215, 300.
8. Compiled from figures contained in SAIRR, *Survey of Race Relations 1983*, Johannesburg, SAIRR, 1984, p. 102.

9. D. A. Kotzé, 'African Politics', in A. de Crespigny and R. Schrire, *The Government and Politics of South Africa*, Cape Town, Juta, 1978, p. 125. Also see his *African Politics in South Africa*, Pretoria, van Schaik, 1975.

10. A. Smith, 'Ethnocentricism, Nationalism and Social Change', *International Journal of Comparative Sociology*, 13, 1972.

11. The exceptions to this are many, but the issues on which they challenge the homeland government have been quite parochial, in view of the wider issues at stake. For the role of chiefs see: H. Tooke, 'Chieftainship in Transkeian Political Development', *Journal of Modern African Studies*, 2, 1964.

12. See: N. Charton, 'Political Élites in the Transkei', *Politikon*, 3. 2, 1976; id., *Ciskei*, London, Croom Helm, 1980; R. Southall, 'The Beneficiaries of Transkeian Independence', *Journal of Modern African Studies*, 15, 1977; id., 'African Capitalism in Contemporary South Africa', *Journal of Southern African Studies*, 7. 1, 1980; N. Stultz, *Half a Loaf*, Cape Town, David Philip, 1979.

13. Taken from T. Lamont, 'The Developmental Relationship Between South Africa and the Black Homelands', Association for Sociology in Southern Africa, Conference paper, Maseru, Lesotho, June 26–8 1979, p. 6.

14. See L. Thompson and J. Butler, *Change in Contemporary South Africa*, Berkeley, University of California Press, 1975, p. 107.

15. Taken from J. Butler *et al.*, *The Black Homelands of South Africa*, Berkeley, University of California Press, 1977, p. 19.

16. E. Thorrington-Smith, B. Rosenberg, and L. McCrystal, *Towards a Plan for Kwa Zulu: A Preliminary Development Plan,* 3 vols., Durban, 1979. Also see J. Nattrass, *Migrant Labour and Under-Development: The Case of Kwa Zulu*, University of Natal, Department of Economics, Black–White Incomes Research Report No. 3, 1977.

17. See J. Rex, *Apartheid and Social Research*, Paris, UNESCO, 1981, pp. 14, 92. This is a common view shared by those from the Marxist and liberal-pluralist schools of South African historiography.

18. J. Saul and S. Gelb, op. cit., p. 84. See also S. Duncan, 'The Effects of the Riekert Report on the African Population', *South African Labour Bulletin*, 5. 4, 1979; id., 'Reform: Quo Vadis?', *South Africa International*, 13. 2, 1982.

19. For a study of urbanization in the homelands see P. Smit, J. Olivier and J. Booysen, 'Urbanization in the Homelands', in D. Smith, *Living Under Apartheid*, London, Allen and Unwin, 1982.

20. *Rand Daily Mail*, 10 February 1984.

21. 'Apartheid, Decentralization and Spatial Industrial Change', in D. Smith, op. cit., p. 63.

22. S. Cilliers and C. Groenewald, *Urban Growth in South Africa 1936–2000*, Stellenbosch, University of Stellenbosch, 1982.
23. L. Schlemmer and V. Möller, 'Emergent Stress in the Migrant Labour System', unpublished paper commissioned by the Urban/ Rural Project, Unit for Futures Research, Stellenbosch, 1982.
24. Compiled from figures contained in SAIRR, *Survey of Race Relations 1983*, pp. 363–6.
25. See G. Maasdorp, *Economic Development Strategy in the African Homelands*, Johannesburg, South African Institute of Race Relations, 1974.
26. These dimensions operate even for the 'independent' homelands. One wonders what kind of independence they have if the central government can decide to remove the embarrassment of the Crossroads squatters by shipping them to camps in the Transkei. In 1979 Bophuthatswana had one telephone for every 1,000 of its population, one doctor for every 15,000, one post office for every 78,000 and a GDP which was 0.28% of South Africa's. Seventy per cent of its gross domestic income came from South Africa, making it one of the most dependent independent states.
27. The Kwa Zulu Chief Minister reported in the *Daily News*, 15 April 1978, the following statement made by a central government Minister: 'As it is not within the competence of the governments of self-governing territories to advise the Government of the Republic of its budget, the Honourable Minister will not comment.'
28. D. A. Kotzé, 'African Politics', p. 130.
29. Ibid.
30. Ibid., p. 131.
31. Ibid.
32. N. Charton, 'The Institutionalization of a Homeland Legislature', Association for Sociology in Southern Africa, Conference paper, Maseru, Lesotho, June 26–8 1979, p. 1.
33. In the second election in Kwa Zulu there was a similar 'deflation of demands', only four constituencies were contested after Inkatha candidates had been returned unopposed in all other seats. Inkatha cadidates won all four.
34. They could perhaps ban Inkatha, but not Buthelezi, and, like the *Führerprinzip* of the fascist movements in the 1930s, the two are inseparable.
35. This ostracism by the left is noted by R. Southall, 'Buthelezi, Inkatha and the Politics of Compromise', pp. 468 ff. In his study of the working class in England, Bendix has shown how by granting them political representation as a means of regulating and channelling their protest, the ruling class turned it into less disruptive and more peaceful forms. Dissent was legitimated, accepted, and regu-

lated under prescribed forms. See R. Bendix, 'The Lower Class and the Democratic Revolution', in *Industrial Revolution*, Berkeley, University of California Press, pp. 91–116. On a similar theme, S. M. Lipset has argued how elections have become the democratic translation of the class struggle: see *Political Man*, London, Heinemann, 1959, Chapters 3 and 7.

36. G. Smith, 'Social Movements and Party Systems in Western Europe', in M. Kolinsky and W. Paterson, *Social and Political Movements in Western Europe*, London, Croom Helm, 1976, pp. 331–54.

37. See B. Temkin, op. cit., pp. 48, 74, 129, 131, 137, 147, 193.

38. For a discussion of this see A. Carter, *Direct Action and Liberal Democracy*, London, Routledge and Kegan Paul, 1973.

39. Hence the 'Broederbond' tag which Inkatha has: Both P. W. Botha and Buthelezi have likened it to the Broederbond. In the *Sunday Times*, 25 September 1977, Buthelezi is quoted as saying: 'If anyone asks you what you will gain by following Inkatha, ask him where the Broederbond got the White man.' This could mean many things— that they are both secret, both cultural and political organizations, and both solid, authoritarian movements based on a hierarchical pattern of strict obedience and discipline. P. W. Botha tends to imply the first, Buthelezi the second, and myself the third.

40. For a discussion of the earlier organization see S. Marks, 'Natal, the Zulu Royal Family and the Ideology of Segregation', *Journal of Southern African Studies*, 4, 1978. She discusses the significance of the earlier name on p. 188.

41. See B. Temkin, op. cit., pp. 395 ff.

42. Printed in *Race Relations News*, January–February 1978, p. 5.

43. With this change Inkatha's President is no longer required to be Chief Minister of Kwa Zulu and hence a Zulu chief. To qualify, the President has to be Head of Government in any government which Inkatha is entitled to form—which means, for the foreseeable future, the Chief Minister of Kwa Zulu. So the wording has changed, not the effect. If Buthelezi resigns as Chief Minister he must forfeit his presidency of Inkatha.

44. *Daily News*, 30 January 1978.

45. *Voice*, 9 October 1978.

46. *Daily News*, 24 March 1980.

47. *Nation*, 2, no. 19, July 1978.

48. *Sunday Tribune*, 2 April 1978.

49. *Nation*, 2, no. 19, July 1978.

50. Ibid., 2, no. 21, September 1978.

51. Taken from 'Inkatha: Centrepoint of the Gathering Storm', *Frontline*, December 1979, p. 22.

52. R. Heberle, 'Social Movements', *International Encyclopedia of Social Science*, vol. 8, p. 440.

53. Reported in T. Hanf *et al.*, *Südafrika: Friedlicher Wandel*, Munich, 1978. An English edition was published in 1981 by Rex Collings under the title *South Africa: The Prospects of Peaceful Change*. In a Postscript to the English edition, Schlemmer considers changes in Buthelezi's support and shows its decline in comparison to the rise of Dr Motlana. See Chapter 4.

54. H. Brotz, *The Politics of South Africa*, London, Oxford University Press, 1977, pp. 123–4.

55. P. Mayer, *Townsmen or Tribesmen*, London, Oxford University Press, 1961. See also his 'Migrancy and the Study of Africans in Towns', *American Anthropologist*, 64, 1962.

56. King Solomon's Inkatha had a more identifiable appeal to the 'traditional' urban Black. See S. Marks, op cit., p. 185.

57. L. Schlemmer, 'The Stirring Giant', p. 115; J. Kane-Berman 'Inkatha', p. 155.

58. L. Schlemmer, 'The Stirring Giant', p. 115.

59. J. Kane-Berman, 'Inkatha', p. 154.

60. R. Southall, 'Buthelezi, Inkatha and the Politics of Compromise', pp. 455, 457; 'Consociationalism in South Africa', pp. 110, 111–12.

61. See L. Schlemmer and V. Möller, 'Migrant Labour in South Africa', Centre for Applied Social Science, University of Natal, 1982. See also H. Adam, 'Ethnic Politics, Violence and Conflict Management: A Comparative Exploration', European Consortium for Political Research, Freiburg, 20–5 March 1983, pp. 14–16.

62. For example see J. Kane-Berman, op. cit., p. 159.

63. The following analysis is based on J. Brewer's 'The Membership of Inkatha in Kwa Mashu'. This analysis also makes reference to research conducted by Y. Meer and M. Mlaba, which used questions from the Kwa Mashu questionnaire and applied them to migrant workers and rural women. Occasionally this research will be referred to in this analysis, although the very low response rate obtained by Meer and Mlaba seriously prejudices the findings. For Y. Meer and M. Mlaba's work see *Apartheid—Our Picture*, Durban, IBR, 1982.

64. For example see *Die Burger*, 13 January 1978.

65. B. Temkin, op. cit., pp. 27, 73.

66. For example see the *Daily News*, 24 March 1980. See also Buthelezi's 'The Early History of the Buthelezi Clan', in J. Argyle and E. Preston-Whyte, *Social System and Tradition in South Africa*, Cape Town, Oxford University Press, 1979.

67. M. E. Spencer, 'What is Charisma?' *British Journal of Sociology*, 24, 1973. 'Secular charisma' refers to the personal qualities of a leader:

a leader is a secularly charismatic figure if he 'attracts a following on the basis of his personal attributes' (p. 341). It therefore loses its reference to divine gifts or supernatural powers, and relates rather to 'magnetic personalities' (p. 342) or 'extraordinary talents' (ibid.).

68. B. Temkin, op. cit., pp. 5, 7, 8, 23, 34, 37, 50.

69. Ibid., p. 124.

70. Ibid. See also J. Butler, *et al.*, op. cit., p. 35.

71. For example see: *Daily News*, 5 April 1978; *Nation*, 2, no. 17, 1978, 3, no. 9, 1979.

72. Reported in *Daily News*, 10 May 1978.

73. Quoted in *Post Transvaal*, 3 May 1979.

74. Ibid., 18 May 1979. See also *Sunday Post*, 10 May 1979.

75. Quoted in *Daily News*, 11 April 1980.

76. Ibid., 10 November 1978.

77. Ibid., 11 April 1980.

78. Quoted by O. Dhlomo, General Secretary of Inkatha, ibid., 12 January 1980.

79. R. Southall, op. cit., p. 474.

80. D. Welsh, quoted in the *Rand Daily Mail*, 7 November 1979.

81. See the foreword to D.A. Kotzé, *African Politics in South Africa*, Pretoria, van Schaik, 1975.

82. For example: *Daily News*, 27 April 1978; *Sunday Tribune*, 17 March 1978; *Weekend World*, 2 October 1977.

83. 3, no. 1, December 1978, p. 7.

84. Quoted in *Post Transvaal*, 22 October 1979.

85. *Sunday Post*, 2 November 1980.

86. *Johannesburg Star*, 17 November 1980.

87. Quoted in SAIRR, *Survey of Race Relations 1983*, p. 53.

88. Quoted in the *South African Digest*, 3 August 1984.

89. For example see B. Temkin, op. cit., pp. 26, 31, 79, 116–7; G. Thula, 'The Process of Power Sharing', paper at the forty-eighth Annual Council Meeting of the South African Institute of Race Relations, Cape Town, 17–20 January 1978, p. 6. For an analysis of Buthelezi's early attempts to link up with the ANC see R. Southall, op. cit., pp. 422–3.

90. See *Nation*, 2, nos. 17, 18, and 19, 1978; and 3. no. 1, 1978.

91. Ibid., 2, no. 19, July 1978.

92. Reported in *Post Transvaal*, 25 October 1979.

93. *Sunday Tribune*, 28 October 1979.

94. Quoted by J. Kane-Berman, op. cit., p. 160. For statements in 1982 see SAIRR, *Survey of Race Relations 1982*, p. 36.

95. In an article in the *Pretoria News*, 31 October 1984, a day when the UDF and FOSATU were organizing a stay-away, Buthelezi appeared extremely conciliatory in an attempt to get the government to

change their minds over the constitution. The response of many Black politicians has been to intensify their opposition, whereas Buthelezi's response has been to become even more conciliatory. He directed his comments to Dr Viljoen, the new Minister of Co-operation and Development. 'I have been looking forward to meeting you and I received your invitation to do so with gratitude. I am, I think, in a position to understand just how difficult your job is. I would like to give you an undertaking from my side that I will co-operate with you wherever it is positive. It is patently clear to me that the whole country would benefit from a rapprochement.'

96. On this support for majority rule, see the *Daily News*, 3 November 1977, in which he said, 'certainly I believe' [in majority rule], Blacks 'will accept nothing less'.

97. Quoted by N. Rhoodie, 'Key Socio-Political Determinants of Inter-communial Power Deployment in a South African Plural Democracy', Paper at the forty-eighth Annual Council Meeting of the South African Institute of Race Relations, 17–20 January, 1978.

98. For information on this see the *South African Digest*, 12 March 1982.

99. *Daily News*, 3 November 1977.

100. Noted by *Frontline*, p. 24.

101. G. Maré, 'Class, Conflict and Ideology among the Petite Bourgeoisie in the Homelands: Inkatha—A Case Study', in the Student Development Studies Group, *Conference on the History of Opposition in South Africa*, Johannesburg, University of Witwatersrand, 1978.

102. For example see R. Southall, 'Buthelezi, Inkatha and the Politics of Compromise', p. 457, and 'Consociationalism in South Africa', p. 112.

103. *Sunday Tribune*, 1 October 1978.

104. Revealed by the General Secretary of Inkatha in the *Sunday Times*, 22 October 1978.

105. Noted by J. Butler *et al.*, op. cit., pp. 55–6.

106. G. Almond and S. Verba, *The Civic Culture*, Boston, Little Brown, 1965. 'Civic culture' is what Montesquieu calls the 'animating principle' of democratic governments as a 'governmental form'—civic values, moral responsibility, legitimacy, restrictions on mass pressure and on élite encroachment, and so on.

107. B. Temkin, op. cit., p. 151, 219.

108. For example, ibid., pp. 219, 224–39.

109. *Daily News*, 7 November 1977. See also ibid., 8 August 1979.

110. Ibid., 6 June 1979.

111. 2, no. 17, May 1978.

112. For example see: T. Hanf *et al.*, op. cit.; IBR, *Soweto: A People's*

Response, Durban, IBR, 1976; H. Lever, 'Attitudes and Opinions of Africans', in H. Lever, *South African Society*, Johannesburg, Jonathan Ball, 1978. This point is demonstrated in the early history of African opposition, which drew for support on Gandhi's pacifism. The UDF, Black Consciousness and Inkatha take this position in current opposition politics.

113. *Daily News*, 28 April 1978.
114. Ibid., 8 February 1979.
115. *Post Transvaal*, 22 October 1979.
116. Ibid., 17 October 1979.
117. For example see the *Daily News*, 9 June 1980.
118. *Guardian*, 3 November 1984.
119. See SAIRR, *Survey of Race Relations 1983*, p. 53.
120. Ibid., pp. 347, 476.
121. Quoted in J. Kane-Berman, op. cit., p. 164.
122. Ibid., p. 165.
123. Quoted in the *South African Digest*, 22 June 1984.
124. *Daily News*, 13 May 1980.
125. *Citizen*, 20 October 1977. This is common to all homeland leaders. See, for the Transkei, the *Citizen*, 17 October 1977 and 18 October 1977, and, for the Ciskei, the *Daily News*, 12 October 1977, *Weekend World*, 10 October 1977. It is in the nature of leadership under these conditions that the leaders are marginal and feel threatened by anyone who claims to subscribe to more radical Black opposition forces. They tend to react to any incident that publicizes their marginality.
126. *Daily News*, 26 April 1978.
127. Ibid., 3 March 1979.
128. T. Muil, 'Inkatha Learns from the Afrikaner', *Natal Mercury*, 9 November 1978.
129. *Daily News*, 5 June 1978.
130. Ibid., 10 May 1979.
131. This is emphasized in: T. Hanf *et al.*, op. cit.; H. Lever, op. cit.; H. Lever, 'Public Opinion and Voting' in A. de Crespigny and R. Schrire, op. cit.; M. L. Edelstein, *What Do Young South Africans Think?*, Johannesburg, SAIRR, 1972.
132. H. Lever, 'Public Opinion and Voting', in A. de Crespigny and R. Schrire, op. cit..
133. This is true even for both sides of the Marxist/liberal-pluralist divide. This is obviously true for a Marxist interpretation. The liberal-pluralists usually perceive the situation in South Africa in terms of race and racial prejudice. The dynamics of change, therefore, are attitudinal. The exception is O'Dowd, who sees a liberal-ization in race attitudes coming from the demands of advanced

industrial capitalism. For a discussion of this topic, including O'Dowd's approach, see: A. Leftwich, *South Africa: Economic Growth and Political Change*, London, 1974; L. Schlemmer and E. Webster, *Change, Reform and Economic Growth*, Johannesburg, Ravan Press, 1978.

134. This point is emphasized more strongly in the author's article, 'The Concept of Political Change and the Language of Change in South Africa', *Africa Quarterly*, 21. 1, 1981.

135. For example see the *Daily News*, 27 April 1978.

136. Ibid., 25 May 1978.

137. Ibid.

138. Rush and Denisoff, *Social and Political Movements*, New York, Harper and Row, 1971.

139. Introduction, M. Kolinsky and W. Paterson, *Social and Political Movements in Western Europe*.

140. *Sunday Tribune*, 1 October 1978.

141. *Post Transvaal*, 24 October 1979.

142. 'Social Movement Organizations: Growth, Decay and Change', *Social Forces*, 44, 1966.

143. 'The Bureaucrat and the Enthusiast: An Exploration of the Leadership of Social Movements', *Western Political Quarterly*, 8, 1965.

144. M. Kolinsky and W. Paterson's term (op. cit.).

145. See: 'Where to Begin', vol. 4, Book 1, in V.I. Lenin, *Collected Works*, New York, 1929, especially pp. 109–12, and 'What Is To Be Done', vol. 4, Book 2, especially pp. 194–201. In 'Where to Begin' Lenin wrote: 'It is not a matter of choosing the path we are to travel but of the practical measures and methods we must adopt on a certain path' (p. 109). Lenin put organization above political commitment and activism.

146. Institutionalization has two meanings: the movement itself becomes regularized and routinized in organized ways—this makes it similar to the Weber–Michels model of oligarchy and over-bureaucratization; or the movement achieves some of its goals and merges with the status quo—this makes it similar to Rush and Denisoff in note 138. Some additional examples of work done on institutionalization in either of its two senses are: R. Hooper, 'The Revolutionary Process', *Social Forces*, 78, 1949–50; S. L. Messinger, 'Organization Transformation: A Case Study of a Declining Social Movement', *American Sociological Review*, 20, 1955.

147. See the *Daily News*, 30 October 1978.

148. *Natal Mercury*, 16 October 1978.

149. *Daily News*, 16 October 1978.

150. *Sunday Tribune*, 1 October 1978.

151. For example, see the *Daily News*, 18 December 1977.

152. *Sunday Times*, 22 October 1978.
153. Buthelezi's international position is strong. In 1983 he opened an external mission in Europe. As a reflection of his international support, he frequently visits the West on speaking tours and has been awarded several distinctions and honorary awards.

Conclusion: Whither African Opposition?

In the view of John Kane-Berman, the Soweto uprising achieved nothing:[1] like Sharpeville sixteen years earlier, the uprising was another turning-point where South Africa did not turn. Kane-Berman might have borne in mind that living histories tempt judgements which hindsight often reveals as hasty. The changes of direction which the uprising helped to initiate have encouraged other commentators to make more pessimistic prognoses about South Africa's survival.[2] These depend for their reliability on the evidence used. Few of them have considered the nature and extent of internal Black pressure as a symptom.[3] This is understandable. It is extremely difficult to do justice to the complexity of the forces contributing to this pressure. Apartheid is one of the last moral issues to be regarded as simple in a world otherwise determined to find complexity. Yet apartheid is complicated and will not be understood unless this is realized. Misunderstanding of the nature of South African society is even more pronounced when prognoses rely, as most do, on those secondary sources which are filtered through to the comfortable vantage-points outside South Africa from where analyses are usually made.[4] This tends to limit assessment of internal Black pressure to those data which are automatically reported, such as the outbreaks of collective protest which periodically erupt on South Africa's streets, or the present position of the main political organizations and movements. This led in the past to the unfortunate tendency to equate internal opposition with the ANC. A similar tendency exists today with the trade union movement.

The preceding chapters have not put forward a prognosis and have attempted to do justice to only one of the factors which influence South Africa's future. They have emphasized two elements which suggest that Kane-Berman's assessment was injudicious. First, the uprising helped initiate a series of liberalizations which have implications far beyond those which the government intended. Secondly, the uprising has helped to bring about a vociferous period of protest and resistance. The implication of this opposition is that African protest and resistance have themselves been changed in such a way as to strengthen it. The language of change dominates discussion in South Africa, but the uprising has not only influenced government policy towards the reformation of apartheid, but also the African response to it.

The liberalizations are unparalleled in Afrikaner political history since 1948. They have produced a new environment for Black South Africans. In an economic sense, limited *embourgeoisement* has changed the African occupational structure and increased opportunities for job mobility. The growth of free collective bargaining has enormous potential for workers. There has been an extension of civil liberties in some areas, a relaxation of petty apartheid restrictions in social life, and the provision of new, more effective, political platforms. Changes in the bureaucratic structure of the state illustrate this point. In 1982 the government founded the Centre for Black Advancement and created the new Ministry of Constitutional Development. Also in that year, three commissions reported on security legislation, press censorship, and the constitution. In 1984 the long-awaited constitutional structures were introduced, with Coloureds and Indians having some limited parliamentary representation. Simultaneously, more effective local councils were provided for Africans in the urban areas. In this period, the government lost the certainty it once had. Formerly, it was convinced that it should consider only Afrikaner interests in decision-making, that it could take decisions for other racial groups without consultation, that it knew how best to govern other racial groups, and that it had a sure moral and ideological foundation on which to base this rule. The state now recognizes the need for change. So do the majority of Whites. Schlemmer and Welsh quote a study in 1980 which showed that two-thirds of National Party voters supported the idea of some power-sharing with Africans.[5] A poll among Whites which was published in *Rapport*, 19 May 1985, showed that 75 per cent supported constitutional possibilities which moved away from traditional apartheid, and 31 per cent favoured changes in the Group Areas Act to include 'grey areas' of multiracial residence. It is easy to make a long catalogue of changes that are taking place—multiracial sport, rising wages, free collective bargaining, constitutional changes, trade union reform, local government autonomy for Africans, land tenure reform, the ending of job reservation, the relaxation of influx control, and so on. The government feels aggrieved that international opinion has not taken account of these changes. However it operates under the illusion that because its attitudes towards change have altered practical changes must already have taken place. After returning from a visit to South Africa, David Watt wrote in *The Times* that a visit to that country is a fascinating but dispiriting experience: 'Things are changing, yes, but the more they change the more they stay the same. And the more they stay the same, the more they seem to go backwards.'[6] Thus it was that, in spite of all the constitutional changes occurring in 1984, six Africans were still thrown out of a Dutch Reform Church and not allowed to attend the funeral of their employer because a permit had not been obtained to allow them to attend a White service. Even in death apartheid is alive.

There is no simple relationship between government recognition of the need for change and Black expectations. There are three complicating factors in the equation: the interests of the right wing in South Africa which seeks to reserve a major power bloc for Whites; the demands of radical opposition forces against which attempts to satisfy these interests must be set; and lastly the involvement of external forces, like the world powers, who can apply international economic and diplomatic pressures. The outcome of this equation so far has been the victory of change as an idea but not yet as a genuine practice. The major alteration has been in the government's recognition of the need for change. Practical policy changes following on from this have mostly been cosmetic. The marginal relaxations must be weighed against retrogressive changes that are occurring—the tightening up of security, continued harassment of trade unionists and political opponents, censorship, and stricter implementation of influx control for the unprivileged outsiders in the homelands and resettlement camps. The changes have not affected the basic asymmetry of power between the dominant and subordinate groups in South Africa. While apartheid may be crumbling at the periphery, towards the centre it is very much alive. Further, the minor relaxations have constituted refinements of control over the Black population, not its abandonment. The examples of trade union reform and local autonomy for Africans illustrate the point. Free collective bargaining was implemented in such a way as to restrict demands emerging from the trade unions to economic ones only. This attempt to depoliticize the trade unions paralleled the redirection of political demands through the new sponsored platform of the community councils, and was coupled with severe harassment of non-sponsored organizations and personnel. Lack of real power is also the major problem affecting the Coloured and Indian Parliaments in the new constitutional structure.

This process of introducing changes which both refine control and devolve greater function to Africans is inherently contradictory and unstable. Change can develop a momentum of its own: the community councils are a case in point. The government was forced to devolve greater powers, in a series of *ad hoc* stages, which were much more extensive than originally intended in order to make the community council system work and win over African opinion to them. The replacement of the 1979 Industrial Conciliation Act by the 1981 Act, which opened up access to trade union membership, is another example. Once change develops dynamics of its own, it only excites African expectations for more. Thus, the repeal in 1985 of the much hated Mixed Marriages Act and the Immorality Act has increased pressure for the repeal of the Group Areas Act—the kernel of apartheid. Allowing people to marry across the colour-line is meaningless if they cannot live together. This problem will cause the government to think seriously about some limited form of residential integration (perhaps so-called 'multinational areas' to parallel the 'multinational hotels'). Referring to this problem on BBC radio in May 1985, Pik Botha, Minister for Foreign Affairs, was evasive and vague but the evasion was full of suggestion. Mixed race couples will live, and their children will go to school, where they currently live and attend school, which is itself based 'largely on what I would wish to call a process of natural selection of the community'. That is, mixed race couples can live in either of the communities which they come from that will accept them. Contraventions of the Group Areas Act seem to be being countenanced, which was also the case, for example, with job reservation and the sex law for a long time before they were eventually scrapped. It is within this general atmosphere of reform that the National Party published a booklet in May 1985 called *What About the Black People* in which it admits past mistakes over policy, and *Rapport* published an opinion poll in which 31 per cent of Whites favoured residential integration in 'grey areas' of multiracial contact. The retention of residential segregation was supported by 37.8 per cent, while 23 per cent thought that group areas would be phased out anyway.

Announcements hinting at the possibility of future reforms are common in South Africa. They have a twofold effect, exciting expectations and causing dissatisfaction when these are unfulfilled. Those theories in the sociology of revolutions often labelled the 'rising expectations' or 'relative deprivation' theories suggest that revolutionary change is more likely to erupt when liberalization begins.[7] The theories have their critics, but one can see the logic of the argument in South Africa. Liberalization will almost certainly generate new and higher demands. One of the leading experts on Afrikaner politics, Heribert Adam, noted this process working:

The South African state is now championing deracialization [but] has not found an acceptable framework for the political incorporation of the excluded majority. Increased economic integration continues to contrast with enforced political segregation. The longer the South African state delays political deracialization the more it politicizes the excluded to search for alternatives. Faced with the hostility of politicized masses, collaborators only represent themselves. They become useless as agents guaranteeing stability.[8]

This passage comments on the inherent contradiction in the new conditions existing in South Africa after the Soweto uprising: political co-option for Africans has not paralleled either economic *embourgeoisement* or the relaxation of restrictions in social life. Adam suggests that this will only politicize the African majority into generating new demands, which will isolate the new sponsored platforms and make them ineffective. This point is worth emphasizing. There are a number of dimensions to the contradiction in the new social conditions existing in South Africa of which two in particular can be mentioned. Education for the African majority is being extended rapidly, but education for what? The extension of education is far out-stripping the granting of those economic, social, and political privileges normally associated with an educated society. Again, employment opportunities are being widened but this has not been matched with either the granting of citizenship or political rights. The creation of an African professional and managerial class has been effected without taking into account the role which the bourgeoisie have historically played in developing societies. They have not been a conservative force, but have often spearheaded change. In decolonizing societies, the support for a native nationalism has been shown to be strongest among the bourgeoisie.[9]

Things in South Africa may be changing, but they sometimes do so in ways which the government did not intend. All the policy changes it has made have been forced on it by the need to lessen the strains of the country's internal contradictions. It is interested in reform but only within limits which it sets. These are unacceptable to the African majority: African antagonism and resistance to apartheid continues despite the liberalizations. This fundamental contradiction between current White willingness to reform and Black expectations of change gives the process of change dynamics of its own which may make these government-imposed limits irrelevant. At a time when Whites are easing discrimination, there is a movement among Africans to become more militant and refuse to take up sponsored platforms. This works counter to the state's intentions in introducing the platforms, because it tends to isolate the collaborators from the public opinion they were supposed to represent or placate. The desire to win over radical public opinion to the platforms has, in the case of trade union reform and local autonomy, caused further changes to be introduced. The same may subsequently apply to the constitution.

The ultimate object of this momentum may or may not be the revolutionary change that the 'rising expectations' theory predicts, but certainly the liberalizations are creating a state of flux in South Africa. In the short term this can lead in a variety of directions. The interests which the right wing represent in South Africa have been successful in signalling to the government that they remain a focus of opposition to the liberalizations. The Conservative Party's showing in the Germiston by-election in August 1982, where their candidate would have been elected had the vote not been split by the HNP, came in an urban constituency where it was not expected to do well. This tended to contrast with a *Sunday Times* opinion poll which showed lower support for the Conservative Party in the urban areas. Other by-elections in urban areas during 1984 and 1985 have seen the Conservative Party come near to defeating the National Party, although the Conservative Party does better electorally in rural areas, that is, it receives its greater support in the National Party's traditional power base of the *platteland*.

Moreover, its overall support expressed in opinion polls shows the Conservative Party to have rallied against the National Party, although the latter has gained support against all other parties (see Table 33).[10] The furrow which the government is ploughing with its liberalizations could in the short term deviate to the right. Even so, it is an error to suggest, as Kane-Berman does, that the Soweto uprising was an instance where the government of South Africa remained fixed in its direction.

The reforms introduced by the government since 1976 constitute the nature of African opposition which the uprising helped to initiate. This suggests that the furrow could turn to the left. It would be a simple error to over-represent the degree to which the uprising initiated opposition. The preceding chapters have demonstrated how the various forms of resistance go back to earlier generations and organizations. What the uprising did was to create new conditions in which this opposition was undertaken and give it new characteristics.

The reforms introduced by the government since 1976 constitute a major part of this new environment for African opposition. They have influenced it in two ways. New and more powerful platforms have been defined which can be used to pursue opposition and a new and more effective brand of state-sponsored politician has emerged. Secondly, the liberalizations have generated new demands and rising expectations, which have politicized the excluded African majority and sustain a variety of unsponsored organizations and personnel. In other words, the liberalizations have given substance to, and provided mechanisms for, African opposition. These two effects differentiate the post-1976 period from the earlier phase. The uprising itself has had a more direct effect. The result of the uprising was a new-found determination not to accept South African society as unchanging or unchangeable and a psychological readiness to act in this cause. Studies conducted since 1976 show this marked shift in the political thinking of rank-and-file Africans. Schlemmer and Welsh note that in 1972, for example, apathy was the dominant characteristic. The White power structure was seen as massive and impenetrable and Africans were far less concerned with politics than other racial groups. Since 1976 they show how attitudes have been politicized and how political and economic equality with Whites has become the major demand.[11] The post-1976 generation are indeed the

Table 33. *Party Support 1982–1985 (per cent)*

Party	Oct. '82	Mar. '83	May '83	July '83	Feb. '84	July '84	Oct. '84	Feb. '85
NP	44.3	48.9	50.0	50.8	54.4	55.8	51.4	51.7
CP	15.6	12.9	12.2	12.1	11.1	9.8	10.9	12.5
HNP	2.5	2.1	2.9	2.5	2.0	1.9	2.3	1.5
PFP	18.4	20.1	18.1	19.3	16.6	17.0	18.9	17.8
NRP	5.5	5.8	5.8	4.5	6.1	4.9	4.1	3.2
No vote	13.7	10.2	10.9	10.7	9.8	10.7	12.4	13.3

heirs to a political tradition going back to Lembede, but, as other commentators have noticed, they do represent a new urban generation psychologically prepared to confront apartheid and willing to resist it irrespective of the heavy price to be paid.[12] It is unfair, however, to suggest that the generation active in the 1950s and early 1960s lacked this commitment. None the less, other characteristics differentiate African opposition after the uprising.

An independence war is being fought in South Africa, but no longer with passive resistance and occasional mass action. It is now fought with bombs and bullets. Yet if that were all, African opposition would not have the intensity it does. The preceding chapters have shown how the war is fought with industrial strikes, poetry, religion, political organization, examination boycotts, classroom disruption, newspaper copy, street riots, the theatre and mobilization in the factories. It involves detailed party manifestos, pavement daubings, patient organization, and spontaneous collective action, calculated negotiations and strategic boycotts, stones, bricks, and pens. Opposition has become dispersed and is expressed in many ordinary aspects of the daily lives of Africans under apartheid, in a way that was only briefly true before in the defiance campaign of the 1950s. More formal channels of opposition are either met with harassment or are denied to the African community, so opposition has taken over their education, work, religious observance, leisure, sport, literary writings, media, and community welfare. When organizations are proscribed, others come to the fore or are created anew. On those occasions when the trade unions are reluctant to push extra-workplace demands, workers involve extra-workplace organizations. A readiness to suffer personally is shown when African students threaten their future livelihood by boycotting examinations and disrupting classrooms, or when workers go on strike. Africans persist in confronting police guns with placards, in resorting to armed attacks and in publicizing their aspirations through prose, poetry, or theatre.

A review of resistance in 1983–5 is instructive. Popular opposition to apartheid was more widespread and assertive in these years than ever before. Though localized, the township protests over housing, transport, education, and removals created a climate of heightened resistance. A significant development was the establishment of new organizations co-ordinating struggles in different localities or over different issues. The formation of the UDF as a vehicle for the national co-ordination of popular resistance represented a further stage in the process which saw first the growth of community-based organizations concerned with specific grievances. The policy of forcing Black workers to live in segregated residential townships far from their places of work makes the cost of transport a frequent cause of conflict in South Africa. In this period there were successful bus boycotts. Rent campaigns to resist increases took place in several areas, most notable around Durban. The Joint Rent Action Committee was formed to co-ordinate resistance. Unrest in African schools led police and community workers to compare the situation with the uprising of June 1976. The immediate issues included: falling educational standards reflected in a very poor pass rate in African matriculation examinations; age restriction regulations barring many older students from education; and the representation of students in schools. As before, these immediate educational concerns were broadened to become an attack on the whole apartheid system within which education exists in South Africa. Although the trade unions made increasing use of official negotiating procedures, the level of militancy in 1983–5, as measured in the number of strikes, was higher than in previous years. The level of strike activity was prompted by grievances related to plant-based issues and more long term political goals. Elections to the new African local authorities took place shortly after the White referendum on the constitution. The boycott campaign against the elections was supported by a wide range of organizations and the low poll confirmed the rejection of the councils. Polls were lower than they were in 1978, when the wounds of the Soweto uprising were still raw. Subseqently, the boycott campaign was extended to cover elections to the new Black parliamentary institutions, and was equally successful. A rising level of armed struggle inside South Africa was also discernible. More people were killed and injured in political violence during the first five months of 1983 than in the previous six years. Incidents of political violence and sabotage increased sixfold between 1980 and 1983.

Tension in the township disturbances in the second half of 1984 continued during 1985 and led to a more violent response by Africans than in 1976. Violence is directed towards representatives of the state and towards fellow Blacks. In October 1985 the Minister of Law and Order announced that fourteen policemen and one member of the SADF had been killed in the previous eighteen months of unrest, and 500 homes of policemen had been burnt and gutted. Two young children of a policeman were burnt to death in an attack on their father's home. He also estimated that since 1983 232 Black people had been killed by other Blacks in the unrest. Many liberal Whites in South Africa fear this explosive mixture of political discontent among Blacks and a greater willingness to have recourse to violence. John Kane-Berman explained the violence by Africans as the product of two factors: overwhelming White approval of the new constitution, and the signing of the Nkomati accord between South Africa and Mozambique.[13] The referendum success for the government was universally seen by Africans as a final rejection of their claim to a voice in Parliament. This has provoked protest on a scale not seen for many years. The Nkomati accord deprives the ANC of one of its major strategies—guerrilla incursion. It has removed ANC bases from Mozambique, which in turn has prevented an exodus of students fleeing to the protection of the ANC. Students in 1984 and 1985 remained in South Africa and are working at the grass-roots level to organize and mobilize around issues like rent and bus increases, detentions, and the constitution. It is also necessary to take into account the state's role in escalating violence, for the state's repressive terrorism has contributed to an atmosphere in which violence of all sorts is a daily occurrence. But above all, township protests have become more vociferous because Black wages are not keeping pace with inflation, and the service charge increases imposed in the townships in this period have reduced the standard of living and economic expectations of Blacks. What is more, responsibility for these decisions about rent and service charges has been shifted by the government on to the African local authorities themselves, which compounds the lack of legitimacy of the councils. The problem of the councils is that they have responsibility without power to discharge it. In 1983–4 at least four councillors were murdered by protesting and angry crowds, and there has been a score of petrol bomb attacks on the homes of councillors. Between September 1984 and May 1985 there were 243 cases of attacks on the homes of community councillors. The stay-aways organized in the autumn of 1984 were successful but saw scenes of unprecedented violence directed against those who wished to go to work. The November stay-away in the Transvaal saw a death toll of twenty. This led even the radical *Sowetan* to complain about political protests degenerating into masochistic violence. Eight people were killed by protesters in the nine months between September 1984 and May 1985. Yet in the same period there were 373 recorded deaths of protesters and 1,497 were wounded. Damage to property was estimated to be R43m. This degree of violence and counter-violence has to be seen in the context of the political struggles which give it meaning and purpose. In April 1985 alone there were 1,549 reported incidents of unrest and collective protest; an average of 51 every day. Meanwhile, the government remains intransigent on the fundamentals of political apartheid: no Africans will be allowed in Parliament. This remains the underlying cause of African anger, which, more frequently than before, spills over into violence.

Dispersed opposition such as this has its cumulative effect but suffers from the problem of being uncoordinated. The effect would be greater if these forms of resistance were linked into a national strategy. This would require co-operation between the trade unions, political movements, journalists, schoolchildren, literati, parents, workers, and the Church. Such co-operation itself requires organization, leadership, and solidarity. In the past African opposition has been extremely fissile, perhaps with the exception of a brief period during the defiance campaign, but there are signs since 1976 of a more concerted national strategy among the various tendencies in African opposition. One of the major divisions to emerge in this period is the contrast between the strategies of collaboration and non-collaboration. Opposition forces have coalesced around these two.

New and more effective platforms have been defined as part of the government's liberalizations, which devolve greater functions to Africans than ever before. Theoretically it is possible for these platforms to be used as constituencies pushing for change. Independence for a homeland, the local government system of councils, and Inkatha's protective umbrella of the territorial and political unit of Kwa Zulu are examples of such platforms. They carry the protection of the state and relative freedom from harassment. Short-term advantages are provided in that the platforms are used to make decisions which affect the immediate lives of Africans and are used to distribute some scarce resources and satisfy some socio-economic needs. In order to perform this role in Soweto,

Black South Africa's unofficial capital, Inkatha is eager to co-operate with the Soweto Council. But the web of constraints which the state has wound around the platforms makes it difficult to step outside government-imposed limits. This study has shown how there is very little opposition in the local councils and Inkatha, and this costs them their credibility and in turn creates the dilemma of whether to strike away from state sponsorship or identify further with the state. Two different sources of legitimacy are being sought here. Public opinion can grant affection and legitimacy, and legitimate authorities can transfer their legitimacy to a chosen heir. The nature of legitimacy in South Africa is a particularly vexed one, however. The state's legitimacy is recognized by only a small numerical minority of Whites. The collaborators, therefore, are isolated from the vast majority of the Black population, who do not recognize a racist society. Collaborators also suffer under a racist society whose problems become their responsibility, since they are the sponsored politicians charged with the administration, although they are helpless to do anything about the root causes. The difficulties which this creates for Inkatha are particularly acute, and Southall has commented on what he describes as Inkatha's lurch to the right.[14] The position assumed by the collaborators is one which increasingly tends to push them into a more moderate position as they come to rely more and more on the state's legitimacy. In this way Inkatha, like the local councillors, is visualizing a relatively ordered transference of power, with the White government granting what authority it has to its chosen Black heir. Paradoxically, sponsored platforms are beginning to attract a more sophisticated, calculating type of African politician. The UBCs were discredited institutions and a set of dubious political characters were attracted to them. At first the community councils attracted the same sort—in some cases the membership of the two bodies remained almost identical. With the devolution of greater function to the local councils and because of the particular nature of legitimacy in South Africa, these councils are beginning to attract less peripheral politicians. Inkatha's support for the system is an example. A similar process has benefited Inkatha, for a number of radical exiles from the 1950s have returned to South Africa and are now members of the organization.

Non-collaboration is the most popular strategy in African opposition. It carries with it the certainty of state repression.

Therefore some non-collaboration has taken the form of clandestine activity, and this separates non-collaborators from political mass mobilization. The ANC was originally a movement based on mass mobilization. Its transformation into a revolutionary terrorist organization was hampered because of the incompatibility between terrorism and mass mobilization, and its reluctance to give up its hope of politically mobilizing the African masses. Leaflet bombs acted as an occasional compromise between these conflicting demands. The dilemma for the ANC was therefore simple. It was cut off from mass mobilization by being an underground clandestine organization but could not relinquish its aspiration to mobilize the masses, which in turn weakened the ruthlessness of its revolutionary terror. In the end it did neither effectively, although its support in the African community has remained high. For these reasons the strategy of non-collaboration pursued by Black Consciousness organizations was unique for a long while. They refused to participate in government-sponsored platforms but retained a commitment to pursue opposition through peaceful mass political mobilization. Potentially this strategy could have widespread legitimacy among the African community, given its hope for a peaceful solution and its rejection of sponsored platforms. The state perceives this strategy as illegitimate and the cost of it for Black Consciousness organizations has been high. Since 1983 the UDF has joined with Black Consciousness organizations in utilizing the strategy of non-collaboration. In the long term the non-collaborators see the eventual transference of power as disorderly enough for their lack of immediate influence with the state to be of no consequence. In the short term they run the risk of state harassment, which adds to the political credentials and legitimacy of the oppressed among the African community. This is why Inkatha claims so vehemently that it is subject to state harassment, despite its use of state-sponsored platforms. But Black Consciousness organizations have particularly encountered problems in reaping the benefits of this legitimacy. They engaged in mass mobilization while enunciating a philosophy which hampered their effectiveness, and the philosophy cut them off from a constituency in the African working class and from White liberals working in the trade unions or opposition parties who were pushing for change. It also denied them any form of consultation with Whites, which would enable them either to recoup the effects of the mobilization in state policy changes or to participate in resource distribution and affect the immediate lives of Africans in the townships.

There is pressure on non-collaborators to moderate their position. It is not just that non-collaboration is popular. Leaders employing the strategy of non-collaboration exceed in popularity those who collaborate. In 1981, for example, 69 per cent of a sample of respondents in Soweto expressed support for Motlana, with 9 per cent for Buthelezi. Motlana even won a higher level of support among Soweto Zulu than Buthelezi.[15] Six thousand people attended the funeral of Sebina Letlalo, a founder member of the ANC and several thousands also attended a memorial service for the twelve ANC fighters killed by the SADF in Mozambique. Dr Motlana described the SADF's actions as first-degree murder. Schlemmer and Welsh provide figures showing that 40 per cent of respondents on the Witwatersrand were prepared to openly admit their support for the ANC, and in another study by Schlemmer in May 1984, among 551 semi-skilled and skilled African industrial workers in the Witwatersrand and Port Elizabeth areas, 39 per cent expressed support for the ANC, the UDF, and its affiliates, with 5 per cent supporting AZAPO and 14 per cent supporting Inkatha. Only in the Durban area did Inkatha's support exceed that of the ANC, the UDF, and its affiliates; but the latter's support there only dropped by 4 per cent.[16] Oddly enough, however, support for the strategy of non-collaboration is more qualified. Kane-Berman quotes an opinion survey which revealed that two-thirds of a sample of Soweto residents would support the community council if those elected to it were to change the body into one which 'really represented Africans' and 'gained improvements'.[17] This confirms a point which Schlemmer and Welsh make: an 'exceedingly high' proportion of Africans said they were prepared to accept a second-best *political* solution if it meant improvement in the provision of basic services.[18] Quite clearly, Africans want material advancement and non-collaborators are presented with a problem when they shun involvement with those platforms which could be reformed into ones which did genuinely provide material gain. The moves within some Black Consciousness organizations and the UDF towards some form of consultation with Whites come from their awareness of this problem. The converse of this is that African public opinion does not see the councils as able at present to provide this advancement. A by-election for the Soweto Council in 1982 achieved a poll of 6.84 per cent. The 1983 elections saw a poll of around 10 per cent.

Notwithstanding, opposition to the councils has been left in a state of disarray. These research findings imply that African public opinion could legitimate a strategy where the non-collaborators participate in the local government system in order to make the councils more effective bodies. This would blur the distinction between collaboration and non-collaboration and work against the unity that has emerged around these strategies. The end result of the moves towards limited consultation with Whites in the UDF and certain Black Consciousness organizations might be participation in a reformed local government system. If they rejected inducements to do this, these groups would then have to set out the grounds on which they did so. This could threaten what legitimacy they have among the African community. If they did participate it would open up the non-collaborators to all the economic, political, and bureaucratic pressures which have deflected Inkatha from its attempt to institute change while using the sponsored platform of Kwa Zulu. This shows that the strategy of non-collaboration is in a state of flux and this serves the interests of those using collaboration: Inkatha makes a great deal of political capital out of the practical powerlessness of the UDF and Black Consciousness. Yet this 'second-best political solution' does not extend to support for separate development institutions. What precisely the term 'second best' means is difficult to judge, and it is extremely unlikely that all respondents meant the same thing by it. There is some evidence of what it is not: Schlemmer and Welsh make it clear that economic advancement should not be at the expense of political equality with Whites. The respondents were envisaging a second-best political solution which still involved equality. Africans do want material gain, but when presented with the choice between higher material gain coupled with continued inequality and lower material gain coupled with equality with Whites, 8 out of 10 respondents chose lower material gain.[19] Africans clearly want material advancement but not at the expense of full political liberation. This is a trend in African public opinion which, for example, the African trade union movement has begun to take account of and to incorporate in its demands. There are implications for other opposition forces. Some form of negotiation seems to be legitimated so long as the policy being negotiated does not compromise long-standing hopes for an end to apartheid, which includes universal franchise in a unitary state and the redistribution of wealth. This is the position which the ANC adopted in a letter from Oliver Tambo which circulated underground during 1979, and which stated that some form of consultation was legitimate so long as it was done for the right reasons. These are the ideals which the UDF and the radicalized Black Consciousness organizations formally set out as the conditions to win them over to participation on sponsored platforms. The fact that Inkatha has compromised them and is prepared to accept something considerably less differentiates its stand on consultation from that of the UDF and the radicalized Black Consciousness organizations, who are slowly being convinced of the need to become involved in some kind of limited contact with Whites of all political persuasions.

This is an aspect which is often ignored in discussions of change in South Africa: it is assumed to be something which only the dominant racial group has to do. What is most significant about the period after 1976 is the new circumstances it presented to African opposition. New problems were created requiring different solutions. Change has taken place in African protest and resistance in order to accommodate these changed circumstances. Inkatha has moderated its former position so as to take up additional sponsored platforms, and Buthelezi's compromise with the state has concentrated protest and resistance around the strategy of non-collaboration, although it is non-collaboration of a particular kind. This trend in African public opinion towards supporting some limited negotiation, but only over certain fundamental issues, has forced most Black Consciousness organizations to move away from their original stand against negotiation on any terms. The dynamics of their struggle for leadership in the urban areas suggested this change. With it came other changes. The most profound of these has been the formation of the UDF and the co-operation within the UDF between radicalized Black Consciousness organizations and the ANC. A situation is occurring in which the various trends in African opposition employing non-collaboration are uniting into two broad factions centred on the larger and more popular UDF and the smaller and less popular NFC. What is important about the UDF is that it has given the ANC a political role inside South Africa and encouraged co-operation with the radicalized elements within Black Consciousness. This is another demonstration that change in South Africa is clearly developing dynamics of its own and that this is not only change in apartheid but also in the African response to it.

The politics of exile and the use of infrequent and ineffective terror tactics cut the ANC off from the mass political mobilization it aspired to. The fast-developing struggle for leadership in the urban areas seems to have convinced the ANC that it needs to be a part of it and to help to directly determine its outcome. It first courted Inkatha: this was understandable. Inkatha seemed to be more effective in mass mobilization, as its membership figures suggest. Black Consciousness groups only had a stable constituency among the young professional Black middle class, and its support-base was restricted to the Witwatersrand: Black Consciousness groups were not mass movements in that sense. The Committee of 10 was only a committee of notable Soweto residents opposed to the community council. Conversely, Inkatha only effectively mobilized support among the Zulu; and its policy after 1978 obviously involved a compromise which the ANC was not prepared to make, even for the sake of having an internal political surrogate. The first signal that Black Consciousness organizations were prepared to act in this fashion came with the opening up of the Committee of 10 to mass membership and its reorganization into the SCA. The formation of AZAPO quickly followed to act as the new Black Consciousness organization responsible for mass mobilization at the national political level. With AZAPO also came a new emphasis on class and labour issues, which had been championed by the ANC since its banning. AZAPO made the greatest movement to accommodate the ANC's emphasis on class. Yet AZAPO has not thought through the logic of its class approach, for it still rejects racial inclusiveness. Hence it has rejected contact with Whites, even those sharing a class approach. It also rejects consultation with the state. So on the one hand AZAPO finds itself in ideological agreement with the ANC but fails to act in a manner which is appropriate to the ANC's need for an internal wing. The SCA has made the greatest movement in this direction, although Motlana is more reticent on the issue of class as the key to South Africa's liberation from racism. Thus, the changes which African opposition is undergoing are neither simple nor uniform, and they often create as many problems as they solve.

Black Consciousness, for example, has been left in a state of confusion by the closer association of some of its organizations with the ANC. Motlana's supporters include COSAS and AZASO, who agree with AZAPO in emphasizing the role of class in social and political change. During 1981 COSAS and AZASO changed their position on negotiation with Whites. They now support the idea of racial inclusiveness and of consultation with Whites of all political persuasion. This theme seems to be more central to them than that of class, for they have sided with Motlana against AZAPO, despite Motlana's support for free enterprise and AZAPO's commitment to a socialist Azania. This suggests that either the desire to fulfil the role of the ANC's political surrogate comes before any ideological differences, or that Motlana's position on class is not that hesitant. Motlana did share in the view of the 1981 conference which defined race as a class determinant, although his vision of Azania is very much a capitalist one.

This association is taking place within the wider structure of the UDF and is evidenced in its policy statements, support-base, and political activities. Its affiliated organizations cover such former ANC supporters as the Transvaal and Natal Indian congresses, and this links them with radicalized Black Consciousness groups like PEBCO, COSAS, AZASO, the SCA, Committee of 10 and MWASA, and a variety of registered and unregistered trade unions. None the less, coalitions like these bring their own internal problems and conflicts which pose a threat to any future co-operation between the opposition forces. The state also constitutes a threat, for the link exposes the UDF and the radicalized Black Consciousness groups to the same repression reserved for the ANC. The squabbles within Black Consciousness have been vituperative. The faction centring around Motlana and the student organizations is willing to consult with Whites of all political persuasion in order to act as a political surrogate of the ANC. But Motlana's reticence on the theme of class (although his supporters do support a class approach) could be used by the combatants in the power struggles within the ANC between the Marxist and Black Nationalist factions in such a way as to threaten the co-operation which exists at present. This provides another demonstration of how African opposition, as well as state policy, has been left in a state of flux by the new environment of post-1976 South Africa.

At the moment, however, co-operation is emerging within the UDF between the ANC and radicalized Black Consciousness organizations. This has enabled some Black Consciousness figures to weave the threat of revolutionary terror into their open political mobilization. For example, Dr Motlana said in 1980: 'in South Africa we hope violence will come to stop. But often it is a response to violence. External training of terrorists is a response to government unwillingness and inability to negotiate. We do not want violence but the one way to make sure it does not continue is to create a system in which all people can come together in a democratic, all-embracing power structure.'[20] This passage alludes to Motlana's willingness to negotiate over certain fundamental issues which will produce a democratic power structure, and ties this to the ANC's armed struggle. It also enables the ANC's revolutionary terror to have greater political effect. In May 1982 a bomb exploded at the Foreshore Building which housed the President's Council, then discussing new proposals on the constitution.[21] This occurred at the same time as the SCA was declaring the proposals to be inadequate becase they excluded Africans and would do nothing to forestall the violent apocalypse which would surely come if the government did not negotiate over fundamental issues. This is a clear example of how a strategy based on revolutionary terror tactics and open mass political mobilization is being forged. During the referendum and later election campaigns the ANC's sabotage was timed to fit in with the opposition protests. This acts as another demonstration of the marriage between armed struggle and political mobilization that is contained within the support-bases and constituencies represented by the UDF.

This coalescence has other consequences. It has enabled the radicalized Black Consciousness organizations to identify themselves with the ANC and to reap the benefits of its legitimacy. More important, it has opened up most Black Consciousness groups to mobilization on a mass scale, and particuarly to mobilization amongst the ANC's constituency in the Black working class. This is a constituency which Black Consciousness has always lacked in the past. This will now make class and labour issues more important to internal political movements. Until recently these were peripheral to open political mobilization because the only groups engaging in political mobilization were Black Consciousness groups, whose philosophy underplayed class and labour issues, and Inkatha, whose ethnic character led to effective mobilization only among Zulu migrant workers. This bifurcation between organization in the trade unions and mass political organization is now ending because of the ideological changes taking place in the trade union movement, which has become more politicized, and within Black Consciousness groups, who have become more interested in labour issues. Black Consciousness organizations like AZAPO, COSAS, PEBCO, and AZASO intend to link their political mobilization with organization in the factories. They have made the ideological commitments necessary for this to occur and are beginning to translate it into action. Their identification with the themes of the ANC will legitimize their efforts among workers, which was a problem which Black Consciousness organizations encountered in earlier attempts to mobilize among workers. The corollary of this development is to increase the likelihood of a link between the trade union movement and internal political movements, opening up the trade unions as a powerful constituency pressing extra-workplace demands, something they have been reluctant to do in the past. This will enable political movements to use the leverage of the African working class, and workers will become central to the liberation struggle outside the workplace. This is precisely what the UDF and all Black Consciousness organizations mean when they say that workers are the hub of the South African struggle.

The peculiar position of the trade union movement is worth elaborating. One must distinguish between African trade unions as organizations and the African workers whom they organize. Industrial action in the period after 1976 showed that workers wanted extra-workplace issues to be incorporated in trade union demands. Where trade unions were reluctant to do this, extra-workplace organizations were drawn in to fill the void. Most strikes, however, did combine plant-based issues with extra-workplace demands. This is consistent with the trend in African public opinion, which demands equality with Whites in all its dimensions. The fact that no political rights have accompanied the extension of collective bargaining will make it almost certain that industrial action will continue to be used for economic and political purposes, however much the government may try to stop it. This will allow African political organizations to take advantage of the strategic place of

African labour in South African society, which results from the sheer number of African workers. By the year 2000 it has been estimated that 80 per cent of the work-force and two out of every three managers will be African.[22] Other changes are attendant on this. Three-quarters of all Africans will then be urban, a proportion which will outstrip all other population groups by two to one.[23] Their strategic position comes also from their location in the economy. The shortfall in skilled labour and managerial expertise is now being filled by Blacks.

The government is aware of projections like these and fears workers more than guerrillas. It is presently attempting to depoliticize the unions by restricting demands from them to economic ones only. When the 1979 Amendment to the Industrial Conciliation Act failed miserably to do this, it was replaced by the tougher 1981 Act. This effectively abolishes the distinction between state-registered and unregistered unions by applying all the controls on registered unions to their unregistered counterparts. At the same time, harassment of trade union officials continues. At the beginning of 1984, 42 trade unionists were in detention. Earlier Neil Aggett had died in police custody. This tends to pull the trade unions in opposite directions. There is a great urge to politicize, but the constraints imposed by the state could be effective. By 1982 trade union members belonging to registered unions had risen by 359 per cent to a total of 260,000, surpassing the numbers belonging to unregistered unions. Parts of the trade union movement have decided to make use of the provisions which the 1981 legislation defined. This has left a small section of independent unions which, although unregistered, are subject to the same controls as registered unions. These include radical unions like MWASA, SAAWU, and GWU. But the unregistered unions have been placed in a difficult position. In order to carry out their role in collective bargaining effectively they need official recognition as trade unions, and this usually comes with registration (although some multinational companies are prepared to deal with unrecognized unions). Thus, there are pressures pulling towards politicization and conformity. This will be a difficult dilemma to resolve for the independent unions. In 1982 FOSATU decided to register, but it announced that it would deregister in order to bring about greater unity with the political unions who are unregistered. The unity talks culminated in the formation of

COSATU in December 1985, and FOSATU disbanded on joining the new federation, but COSATU's position on registration is not clear.

Once again African opposition remains in a state of flux, having to respond to the new environment. This may make trade unions reluctant to agitate on extra-workplace issues. Some may become reluctant collaborators, although there is a large difference between collaborating under duress and voluntarily accepting sponsorship. None the less, given the pressure to politicize, which is a direct reflection of the interests and aspirations of African workers, where the trade unions do not articulate these issues extra-workplace organizations will be drawn in to take their place. The alignment of African workers with extra-workplace organizations, like the UDF and the Black Consciousness groups AZAPO and PEBCO, is one which arises not only from the new policy direction of Black Consciousness, but also from the interests and aspirations of African workers. This will strengthen the alliance between internal political movements and African labour irrespective of whatever controls the state has over trade unions as organizations. The alliance is the outcome of the demand in African labour, and the African community generally, for equality with Whites in its political as well as economic sense. There is an irony in this for the government. Imposing stricter controls on the trade unions to depoliticize them actually increases the chances of political organizations becoming involved in industrial action. Another example is thus provided of how change in South Africa is developing dynamics of its own and often moves in directions which the government does not intend.

In sum, African opposition since the uprising has intensified, become dispersed away from the main political and economic organizations, and solidified around the strategy of non-collaboration. It is non-collaboration of a particular kind. The new environment existing after 1976 has created a period of transition for African opposition in which the African community expects its opposition forces to negotiate with the state when this is beneficial and when it is over fundamental issues. The formation of the UDF, and the co-operation within it between the ANC and the radicalized Black Consciousness organizations is the outcome of this transitional period, but the alliance is a fragile one. If it continues, this would suggest that the transitional period after the 1976 uprising has played itself through and that African opposition lies at the dawn of a new era, demarcated by four consequences or conditions which follow from the formation of the UDF and its internal alliance. If the UDF remains unbanned and this co-operation continues, it links the Black professional middle-class support of Black Consciousness with the working-class support of the ANC. It provides the ANC with an internal wing so that a strategy based on revolutionary terror and mass political mobilization can be forged. It isolates still further the collaborative opposition forces, pushing them into an even more moderate position. Finally, it makes class and labour issues more important to internal Black politics, opening up the trade union movement as a force pushing for political liberation.

There are, of course, divisions within the non-collaboration forces between the UDF and the NFC, although the NFC is small when compared with the UDF. Indeed, what is characteristic of Black politics in the period covered by this study is how the philosophy of Black Consciousness, espoused by the NFC, has declined in popularity and has been overtaken by a variety of organizations pursuing the traditional ANC theme of non-racialism. Black Consciousness as a philosophy and strategy dominated African student and community politics in the 1970s, but in the 1980s it has been displaced as the dominant element in Black politics by the non-racialism of the UDF and its affiliates, some of whom were connected with the ANC and Congress Alliance in the 1950s. These organizations have successfully reintroduced the ANC into internal politics, where it is becoming as prominent as it was before it was banned. During 1985 officials of the ANC in exile met with church leaders from South Africa, South African businessmen, and representatives of the PFP. In resigning from the leadership of the Official Opposition, van Zyl Slabbert indicated that he had done so partly in order to be able to negotiate with those working outside parliamentary politics. The South African press took this to mean the ANC. The release of Nelson Mandela became a strong domestic and international demand in this period, which the South African government seems prepared to accede to under certain conditions. The recognition of the symbolic importance of Mandela, and the contact with the ANC in exile, illustrates how important the ANC has become to internal politics. It has been so successfully reinstated inside the country that other organizations active in the 1950s have been revived in the hope of being swept along on this tide. In 1984 the African People's Democractic Union of Southern Africa was revived, declaring its support for the programme of the Unity Movement, to which it was affiliated in the 1950s.

There are many reasons to explain why the ANC and its policy of non-racialism have become so popular in internal politics. There has always been a residue of support for the organization and the prominence of the ANC's military activities gave it a prestige which legitimated, in internal politics, the non-racialist stance of the UDF and its affiliates, some of whom, like AZASO and COSAS, are from the radicalized section of Black Consciousness. But there are additional reasons which explain why the UDF, and the organizations within the radicalized faction of Black Consciousness, were prepared to advance non-racialism in order to identify themselves with the ANC rather than orthodox Black Consciousness. As this study has emphasized, some Black Consciousness students came under the protection of the ANC when they fled into exile and have since returned to South Africa as ANC activists. Most of the Black Consciousness organizations active in the late 1970s were led by ex-ANC figures, and their ineffectiveness in contesting the leadership struggle in the townships made Black Consciousness leaders and supporters realize that a closer relationship was needed with workers. The adoption of a class analysis was also facilitated by the structural changes in the economy which increased Black economic power. The emphasis on class culminated in the theme of non-racialism, for many Black Consciousness organizations thought through the logic of a class analysis and linked themselves with Whites working for change in the trade unions and in extra-parliamentary politics. Non-racialism is a necessary corollary of the emphasis on class, which gives AZAPO's ideology an inherent contradiction. In their conflict with the community councillors for the leadership of the townships, it also became obvious to Black Consciousness spokesmen that they were prolific articulators of grievances but that they had not constructed the viable grass roots structure and organization around their high reputation. The ANC has a viable structure and organizational base which other groups have sought to utilize, and is itself using co-operation with the UDF, radicalized Black Consciousness groups, and other UDF affiliates to reinstate itself in the country.

The growing intensity of the political struggle inside South Africa since 1976 convinced the ANC of the need to become involved in internal politics again, which was an aspirátion it never relinquished despite its use of terror tactics. Some activists within the ANC also argued that revolutionary terror on its own would not bring an end to apartheid, and the idea of non-racialism became a unifying theme which allowed the ANC to co-operate with organizations who were playing an active role in internal politics, many of whom were led by ex-ANC figures anyway. A survey conducted by Schlemmer in May 1984 showed how beneficial for their popularity this strategy of co-operation, within the umbrella of the UDF, had been for both the ANC and the radicalized Black Consciousness groups (see Table 34).[24] The table clearly demonstrates how the organizations espousing non-racialism, like the ANC, the UDF, and its affiliates, have superseded in popularity the organizations, like AZAPO, who support the themes of orthodox Black Consciousness. Indeed, the collaborationist parties of Inkatha and Sofasonke polled better than AZAPO in both areas where the survey was conducted. One other interesting point is that it illustrates how geographically widespread that support for the ANC, the UDF, and its affiliates is compared to the narrow geographical base of Inkatha.

This support for political organizations who adopt non-racialism is also not surprising given that many attitude surveys over a number of years have consistently shown that Blacks want, as a preferred first choice, a peaceful, non-racial future. As chapter 2 emphasized, there is considerable sympathy for political comprom-

Table 34. *African Support for Political Organizations 1984*

Organization	Witwatersrand and Port Elizabeth, 1st choice (%)	Durban 1st choice (%)
ANC/UDF and affiliates	39	35
AZAPO	5	1
Inkatha	14	54
Sofasonke	15	6
Other	5	4
None	22	—

ise and negotiation, and the minimum demands of a wide cross-section of Black South Africans are moderate, despite their high levels of dissatisfaction and discontent. In particular, majorities of Blacks in various surveys are willing to accept consociational arrangements which amount to a substantial compromise with White interests. This is a factor which the military wing of the ANC and Black Consciousness groups have been forced to take into consideration. The ANC's growing involvement in internal politics, mobilizing on the theme of non-racialism, is in part a reflection of the attitudinal sympathy that exists for this idea. Black Consciousness leaders also had this sympathy in mind when they drew a distinction, as explained in chapter 4, between South Africa's peaceful and non-racial future and the racially exclusive nature of the struggle to achieve this. The inherent contradiction of these beliefs made it easy for some supporters of Black Consciousness to change towards believing that non-racialism could be a strategy to achieve a future non-racial Azania, and to legitimate this change by arguing that they were responding to the majority opinion of Black South Africans. As chapter 4 makes clear, this is what the radicalized Black Consciousness groups did in the light of the problems which orthodox Black Consciousness presented them in challenging for the political leadership of the townships.

This shift in popularity between the themes of orthodox Black Consciousness and the idea of non-racialism prompts a further issue. Whereas the pattern in earlier periods was that of a rather one-dimensional conflict betwen White and Black over apartheid, the future seems to point to growing cleavages among both Whites and Blacks. In Black politics there is the cleavage between the strategy of collaboration and non-collaboration, and within the non-collaborative strategy the theme of non-racialism constitutes a major division between the UDF and NFC. The conflicts between Inkatha, the UDF, and AZAPO have been affected by the growing violence and counter-violence inside South Africa. Members of each organization have attacked supporters of the others. The violence with which the political struggle is pursued in South Africa by Blacks themselves is another of the distinguishing features of protest in the post-1976 period. It proved difficult for leaders of these organizations to contain the violence of some of their more youthful supporters. Special religious services instigated by Bishop Tutu were held throughout South Africa in May

1985 in an attempt to reconcile differences between AZAPO and the UDF. While the leaders undertook to heal their differences and concentrate on the struggle against apartheid, violence broke out among some rival supporters after the services. A leader comment in the *Sowetan* called for unity and peace. Unity may eventually arise among leaders, but peace is unlikely. But one unintended consequence of the violence against fellow Blacks may be to increase pressure on them to form a united front. Several youth organizations from Pretoria's African townships released a joint statement in February 1986 which noted their concern with 'escalating Black-on-Black violence' and appealed to Soweto residents to come together and find unity. The ANC's call in December 1985 for a grand alliance of anti-government groups met with considerable support among trade unionists and political leaders, with the exception of AZAPO.

None the less, Nolutshungu correctly ended his account of modern South Africa by saying that there was now a sound basis for a united front of Black organizations.[25] He is right, for even if the conflicts between the UDF and the NFC remain, the unity which the much larger and more popular UDF already represents is itself very significant. The four conditions which follow from its formation, identified above, define the beginnings of a new period in South Africa. They produce a situation which the South African government has never faced before, and create for African opposition forces a solidarity they have lacked in the past. In this way, even if there is still a considerable distance to travel, the journey's end may have been signposted.

Notes

1. *Method in the Madness*, London, Pluto, 1978, p. 232.
2. The debate was first initiated by R. W. Johnson, *How Long Will South Africa Survive?*, London, Macmillan, 1977. A response came from L. Gann and P. Duignan, *Why South Africa Will Survive*, London, Croom Helm, 1981. Along the way there have been others who have made their case, including: R. Bissel and C. Crocker, *South Africa into the 1980s*, Boulder, Westminister Press, 1975; R. Rotberg, *Suffer the Future*, London, Harvard University Press 1980; G. Carter, *Which Way is South Africa Going?*, Indiana University Press, 1980.
3. This is a point emphasized by R. Hodder-Williams, 'Well, Will South Africa Survive?', *African Affairs*, 80, 1981, p. 410.

4. From the vantage-point of South Africa quite a number of prognoses emerge which are less pessimistic. See, among others, P. R. Botha, *South Africa: Plan for the Future*, Johannesburg, Perskor, 1978; D. Worrall, *South Africa: Government and Politics*, Pretoria, van Schaik, 1975; W. Thomas, *Plural Democracy: Political Change and the Strategy of Evolution in South Africa*, Johannesburg, SAIRR, 1977; SAIRR, *South Africa and Sanctions*, Johannesburg, SAIRR, 1979; F. Clifford-Vaughan, *International Pressure and Political Change in South Africa*, Cape Town, Oxford University Press, 1978; V. Razis, *South Africa and Political Change*, Johannesburg, Ravan, 1980; P. Laurence and F. van Zyl Slabbert, *Towards an Open Plural Society*, Johannesburg, Ravan, 1980; Spro-Cas (Special Programme for Christian Action in Society Commission), *South Africa's Political Alternatives*, Johannesburg, Ravan, 1980.

5. L. Schlemmer and D. Welsh, 'South Africa's Constitutional and Poltical Prospects', *Optima*, 30.4, 1982, p. 215. 'Power-sharing' is a nebulous term and it is unlikely that all respondents interpreted it the same way. The figure, therefore, must be treated with caution.

6. *The Times*, 7 December 1985.

7. For example see: J. Davies, 'Toward a Theory of Revolution', *American Sociological Review*, 27, 1962; J. Geschwender, 'Explorations in the Theory of Social Movements and Revolutions', *Social Forces*, 47, 1968; T. R. Gurr, *Why Men Rebel*, Princeton, Princeton University Press, 1970.

8. H. Adam, 'Minority Monopoly in Transition: Recent Policy Shifts of the South African State', *Journal of Modern African Studies*, 18.4, 1980, p. 625.

9. A. D. Smith, 'The Diffusion of Nationalism', *British Journal of Sociology*, 29.2, 1978.

10. A *Sunday Times* poll, published on 22 August 1982, showed support for the Conservative Party to be 5.8 per cent in the urban areas. In the Germiston by-election on 25 August, the Conservative Party polled 39.2 per cent of the vote. Figures in Table 33 are taken from Mark-en Meningsopnames' nation-wide opinion poll published in *Rapport* 10 March 1985.

11. L. Schlemmer and D. Welsh, op. cit, p. 225.

12. Noted by G. Gerhart, *Black Power in South Africa*, Berkeley, University of California Press, 1978, p. 315; F. Molteno, 'The Uprising of 16 June', *Social Dynamics*, 5.1, 1979, p. 69.

13. *Guardian*, 7 December 1984.

14. R. Southall, 'Buthelezi, Inkatha and the Politics of Compromise', *African Affairs*, 80, 1981. This article contrasts with the view of J. Kane-Berman, 'Inkatha: The Paradox of South African Politics', *Optima*, 30.2, 1982. The differences of interpretation between the

two authors are explained by the different faces of Inkatha which they focus on in formulating their judgements. The tension between Inkatha's two faces has been emphasized in Chapter 6. For an earlier statement by the author see 'The Modern Janus: Inkatha's Role in Black Liberation', Institute of Commonwealth Studies, University of London, Seminar Paper Series SSA/80/5, December 1980, reprinted in *The Societies of Southern Africa in the Nineteenth and Twentieth Centuries*, Institute of Commonwealth Studies, 1981. Inkatha has provoked very little academic interest. In addition to the above see: L. Schlemmer, 'The Stirring Giant: Reflections on Inkatha and Other Black Political Movements in South Africa', R. Price and G. Rosberg, *The Apartheid Regime*, Berkeley, Institute of International Studies, 1980. Schlemmer is a close personal friend and political ally of Buthelezi. He heads the Inkatha Research Institute and sat on the Buthelezi Commission. Schlemmer also provides an important link with the PFP as he has close contacts with F. van Zyl Slabbert, leader of the PFP.

15. R. Southall, 'Buthelezi, Inkatha and the Politics of Compromise', p. 477.

16. L. Schlemmer and D. Welsh, op. cit., p. 224; L. Schlemmer, 'Black Worker Attitudes', Indicator Project, September 1984.

17. J. Kane-Berman, op. cit., p. 160.

18. L. Schlemmer and D. Welsh, op. cit., p. 226.

19. Ibid., p. 225. It must be remembered that public opinion surveys such as this are notoriously unreliable. Respondents' interpretation of questions can vary, and can be at odds with the intention of the questioner. Political attitude surveys are also influenced by the social, economic and political circumstances prevailing at the time. They can tap quite transitory feelings. However, Schlemmer and Welsh's findings confirm the results of the survey conducted by *Post Transvaal* in 1979, commented upon in Chapter 4. The community councils were rejected as ineffective institutions, yet the non-collaborators were urged to become involved in consultation.

20. Quoted by the *Citizen*, 8 June 1980.

21. As we saw in Chapter 4, the constitution created three separate institutions at the legislative level, with an Executive Cabinet being elected from an electoral college. This is a reversion back to earlier proposals in 1977, which were rejected by Indian and Coloured politicians and eventually withdrawn by the government. It is interesting to speculate on why the 1977 proposals were resurrected. Either the government had not learnt from its previous mistakes, or it was confident of winning the support of Asian and Coloured politicians. Clearly in the intervening years these politicians were subjected to considerable government persuasion and pressure. On this point see

D. Welsh, 'Constitutional Change in South Africa', *African Affairs*, 83, 1984.

22. J. Kane-Berman, op. cit., p. 229.
23. Ibid., p. 229.
24. L. Schlemmer, 'Black Worker Attitudes', op. cit.
25. *Changing South Africa*, Manchester, Manchester University Press, 1982, pp. 206–7.

BIBLIOGRAPHY

ANNUAL REVIEWS

Africa South of the Sahara, Europa Publishers.
Annual Conference Papers, South African Institute of Race Relations.
Official Yearbook of the Republic, Department of Information, Pretoria.
South African Statistics, Department of Statistics, Pretoria.
Survey of Race Relations, South African Institute of Race Relations.

COLLECTIONS OF PAPERS

Fatima Meer (uncatalogued)

NEWSPAPERS, JOURNALS AND NEWSLETTERS

Beeld
Black Sash
Black Students' Society Newsletter
Citizen
Daily News
Die Burger
Die Transvaler
Die Vaderland
Financial Times
Frontline
Ilanga
Indicator
Inkululeko yeSizwe
International Defence Aid Fund Briefing Papers
Johannesburg Star
Natal Mercury
Nation
Observer (London)
Oggendblad
Oosterlig
People's Experimental Theatre Newsletter
Post Transvaal
Race Relations News
Rand Daily Mail

Rapport
Republic of South Africa, House of Assembly Debates
SASO Newsletter
Security Factors
South African Digest
South African Labour Bulletin
South African Security
Sowetan
Staffrider
Sunday Mirror
Sunday Post
Sunday Times
Sunday Tribune
Terrorism Research Centre Information Sheets
Transvaal Post
Voice
Weekend World
World

TRIAL MATERIALS

Moss, G. *Political Trials in South Africa 1976–79*, Development Studies Group, University of Witwatersrand, Information Publication, no. 2.

Supreme Court of South Africa, Transvaal Provincial Division, *S. Cooper and Eight Others* (BPC/SASO).

Supreme Court of South Africa, Transvaal Provincial Division, *Sadecque Variava* (PET).

SELECTED BOOKS AND ARTICLES

Adam, H., 'Ethnic Politics, Violence and Crisis Management: A Comparative Exploration', European Consortium for Political Research, Freiburg, W. Germany, 20–5 March 1983.

——, 'Minority Monopoly in Transition: Recent Policy Shifts of the South African State', *Journal of Modern African Studies*, 18.4, 1980.

——, *Modernizing Racial Domination*, Berkeley, University of California Press, 1971.

——, 'Racist Capitalism Versus Capitalist Non-Racialism in South Africa', *Ethnic and Racial Studies*, 7.2, 1984.

——, *South Africa: Sociological Perspectives*, London, Oxford University Press, 1971.

——, and Giliomee, H., *The Rise and Crisis of Afrikaner Power*, Cape Town,

David Philip, 1980 (as *Ethnic Power Mobilized*, New Haven, Yale University Press, 1979).

Barber, J., Bumenfeld, J., and Hill, C., *The West and South Africa*, London, Routledge and Kegan Paul, 1982.

Blacking, J., 'The Role of Ideas in Social Change: The Growth of the Africanist Idea in South Africa', *Queen's University of Belfast Publications in Social Anthropology*, 3, ed. D. Riches.

Blumer, H., 'Race Prejudice as a Sense of Group Position', *Pacific Sociological Review*, 1.1, 1958.

Bonner, P., *Strikes in South Africa*, Johannesburg, Ravan Press, 1980.

Brewer, J., 'Black Protest in South Africa's Crisis', *African Affairs*, 85, 1986.

——, 'Literature and Liberation in South Africa', *Ethnic and Racial Studies*, 9, 1986.

——, 'Modern Janus: Inkatha's Role in Black Liberation', *The Societies of Southern Africa in the Nineteenth and Twentieth Centuries*, London, Institute of Commonwealth Studies, 1981.

——, 'Racial Politics and Nationalism: The Case of South Africa', *Sociology*, 16.3, 1982.

——, 'The Concept of Political Change and the Language of Change in South Africa', *Africa Quarterly*, 21.1, 1980.

——, 'The Membership of Inkatha in Kwa Mashu', *African Affairs*, 84, 1985.

——, and Smyth, J. 'A Comparison of Political Violence and Conflict Management in Northern Ireland and South Africa', in T. Hanf, *Deeply Divided Societies*, Munich and Mainz, Kaiser and Grunewald, 1986.

Brotz, H., *The Politics of South Africa*, London, Oxford University Press, 1977.

Butler, J., *et al.*, *The Black Homelands of South Africa*, Berkeley, University of California Press, 1977.

Callinicos, A. and Rogers, J., *Southern Africa After Soweto*, London, Pluto, 1977.

Campbell, K., 'Prospects for Terrorism in South Africa', *South Africa International*, 14.2, 1983.

Charney, C., 'Class Conflict and the National Party Split', *Journal of Southern African Studies*, 10.2, 1984.

Charton, N., 'The Institutionalization of a Homeland Legislature', Association of Sociologists in Southern Africa, Conference paper, Maseru, Lesotho, 26–8 June, 1979.

Cilliers, S., and Groenewald, C., *Urban Growth in South Africa 1936–2000*, Stellenbosch, University of Stellenbosch, 1982.

Davenport, T., *South Africa: A Modern History*, London, Macmillan, 1977.

Davidson, B., *et al.*, *Southern Africa: The New Politics of Revolution*, Harmondsworth, Penguin, 1976.

Davies, R. C., 'Capital Restructuring and the Modification of the Racial

Division of Labour in South Africa', *Journal of Southern African Studies*, 5.2, 1979.

Davies, R. H., *Capital, State and White Labour in South Africa 1900–60*, London, Harvester, 1979.

De Crespigny, A., and Shrire, R., *The Government and Politics of South Africa*, Cape Town, Juta, 1978.

Duncan, S., 'Reform: Quo Vadis', *South Africa International*, 13.2, 1982.

Du Toit, B., *Ukubamba Amadolo*, London, Onyx, 1978.

Du Toit, D., *Capital and Labour in South Africa*, London, Routledge and Kegan Paul, 1981.

Gerhart, G. *Black Power in South Africa*, Berkeley, University of California Press, 1978.

Giliomee, H., 'Crisis and Co-option in South Africa', European Consortium for Political Research, Freiburg, 20–5 March 1983.

——, 'Structural Change and Political Options in the 1980s', lecture at the Centre of Applied Social Sciences, University of Natal, 13 May 1980.

——, *The Parting of the Ways*, Cape Town, David Philip, 1983.

Greenberg, S., *Race and State in Capitalist Development*, New Haven, Yale University Press, 1980.

Hanf, T., Weiland, H., and Vierdag, G., *South Africa: The Prospects of Peaceful Change*, London, Rex Collings, 1981.

Hill, C., *Change in South Africa: Blind Alleys or New Directions*, London, Rex Collings, 1981.

Hirson, B., *Year of Fire, Year of Ash*, London, Zed Press, 1979.

Institute of Black Research, *Soweto: A People's Response*, Durban, IBR, 1976.

Jackson, J., *Justice in South Africa*, Harmondsworth, Penguin, 1980.

Johnson, R. W., *How Long Will South Africa Survive?*, London, Macmillan, 1977.

Kane-Berman, J., 'Inkatha: The Paradox of South African Politics', *Optima*, 30.2, 1982.

——, *The Method in the Madness*, London, Pluto, 1978.

Karis, T., and Carter, G., *From Protest to Challenge*, 4 vols., Stanford, Hoover Institute Press, 1972, 1973, 1977.

Kotzé, D. A., *African Politics in South Africa*, Pretoria, van Schaik, 1973.

Lamont, T., 'The Developmental Relationship Between South Africa and the Black Homelands', Association of Sociologists in Southern Africa, Conference paper, Maseru, Lesotho, 26–8 June 1979.

Leggett, J. C., *Class, Race and Labour*, New York, Oxford University Press, 1968.

Lever, H., *South African Society*, Johannesburg, Ball, 1978.

Lipton, M., *Capitalism and Apartheid*, London, Temple Smith and Gower, 1985.

Lodge, T., *Black Politics in South Africa Since 1945*, London, Longman, 1983.

Malherbe, E. G., *Education in South Africa*, Cape Town, Juta, 1979.

Marks, S., 'Natal, the Zulu Royal Family and the Ideology of Segregation', *Journal of Southern African Studies*, 4, 1978.

Mason, D., 'Industrialization, Race and Class Consciousness in South Africa', *Ethnic and Racial Studies*, 3, 1980.

Mathews, A. S., 'Legislation and Civil Liberties in South Africa', *Optima*, 32.1, 1984.

Matshoba, M., *Call Me Not A Man*, Johannesburg, Ravan Press, 1978.

Maxwell, C., and Molteno, F., *Black South Africans on the Streets*, Johannesburg, Ravan Press, 1980.

Mayer, P., 'Class, Status and Ethnicity as Perceived by Johannesburg Africans', in Thompson, L., and Butler, J., (eds.) *Change in Contemporary Southern Africa*, Berkeley, University of California Press, 1975.

Meer, Y., and Mlaba, M., *Apartheid: Our Picture*, Durban, Institute of Black Research, 1983.

Molteno, F., 'The Uprising of 16 June', *Social Dynamics*, 5, 1979.

Moore, B., *Injustice: The Social Bases of Obedience and Revolt*, London, Macmillan, 1978.

Morris, M., *Armed Stuggle in Southern Africa*, Cape Town, Spence, 1975.

——, *Terrorism*, Cape Town, Timmins, 1971.

Nattrass, J., 'Migrant Labour and Underdevelopment: The Case of Kwa Zulu', University of Natal, Department of Economics, Black–White Incomes Research Report, no. 3. 1977.

——, *The South African Economy: Its Growth and Change*, Cape Town Oxford University Press, 1981.

Nolutshungu, S., *Changing South Africa*, Manchester, Manchester University Press, 1982.

——, 'Issues in the Afrikaner "Enlightenment"', *African Affairs*, 70, 1971.

O'Meara, D., 'Muldergate and the Politics of Afrikaner Nationalism', *Work in Progress*, Johannesburg, 1982.

——, *Volkscapitalisme*, Cambridge, Cambridge University Press, 1983.

——, 'White Trade Unionism, Political Power and Afrikaner Nationalism', *South African Labour Bulletin*, 1.10, 1975.

Potter, E., *The Press as Opposition*, London, Chatto and Windus, 1975.

Price, R., 'Pretoria's Southern African Strategy', *African Affairs*, 83, 1984.

—— and Rosberg, G., *The Apartheid Regime*, Berkeley, Institute of International Studies, University of California, 1980.

Rex, J., *Apartheid and Social Research*, Paris, UNESCO, 1981.

Robertson, I., and Whitten, P., *Race and Politics in South Africa*, New Brunswick, Transaction Books, 1978.

Saul, J., and Gleb, S., *The Crisis in South Africa*, London, Monthly Review Press, 1981.

Schlemmer, L., 'Black Consciousness: Pride and Dignity or Militancy and Racism', *South African Journal of Sociology*, 20, 1979.

——, 'Conflict in South Africa: Build Up to Revolution or Impasse', European Consortium for Political Research, Freiburg, 20–5 March, 1983.

——, 'The Stirring Giant: Observations on the Inkatha and other Black Political Movements in South Africa', in Price, R., and Rosberg, G., *The Apartheid Regime*.

——, Stopforth, P., and Möller, V., *Black Urban Communities*, Centre of Applied Social Science, Document and Memorandum Series, 1980.

——, and Webster, E., *Change, Reform and Economic Growth*, Johannesburg, Ravan Press, 1978.

——, and Welsh, D., 'South Africa's Constitutional and Political Prospects', *Optima*, 30.4, 1982.

Smith, A. D., 'Ethnocentricism, Nationalism and Social Change', *International Journal of Comparative Sociology*, 13, 1972.

——, 'The Diffusion of Nationalism', *British Journal of Sociology*, 29.2, 1978.

South African Institute of Race Relations, *Laws Affecting Race Relations in South Africa*, Johannesburg, SAIRR, 1978.

——, *PEBCO*, Johannesburg, SAIRR, 1982.

——, *South Africa in Travail*, Johannesburg, SAIRR, 1977.

Southall, R., 'Buthelezi, Inkatha and the Politics of Compromise', *African Affairs*, 80, 1981.

——, 'Consociationalism in South Africa: The Buthelezi Commission and Beyond', *Journal of Modern African Studies*, 21, 1983.

Stasiulis, D., 'Pluralist and Marxist Perspectives on Racial Discrimination in South Africa', *British Journal of Sociology*, 31.4, 1980.

Temkin, B., *Gatsha Buthelezi: Zulu Statesman*, Cape Town, Purnell, 1976.

Thompson, L., and Butler, J., *Change in Contemporary South Africa*, Berkeley, University of California Press, 1975.

Tibble, A., *African English Literature*, London, Peter Owen, 1965.

Thorrington-Smith E., Rosenberg B., and McCrystal L., *Towards a Plan for Kwa Zulu: A Preliminary Development Plan*, 3 vols. Durban, 1979.

Van der Horst, S., and Reid, J., *Race Discrimination in South Africa*, Cape Town, David Philip, 1981.

Van der Merwe, H., *et al.*, *African Perspectives on South Africa*, Cape Town, David Philip, 1978.

Wauthier, C., *The Literature and Thought of Modern Africa*, London, Heinemann, 1978.

Webster, E., 'Stay-Aways and the Black Working Class Since World War Two—The Evolution of a Strategy' (mimeo.), n.d.

Welsh, D., 'Constitutional Change in South Africa', *African Affairs*, 83, 1984.

——, 'The Nature of Racial Discrimination in South Africa', *Social Dynamics*, 4, 1975.

Wilkinson, P., *Political Terrorism*, London, Macmillan, 1973.

Wolpe, H., 'Apartheid's Deepening Crisis', *Marxism Today*, January 1983.

Index